CREATIVE EDITING

From the Wadsworth Series in Mass Communication and Journalism

General Mass Communication

Anokwa/Lin/Salwen, *International Communication: Issues and Controversies*

Biagi, *Media/Impact: An Introduction to Mass Media,* Eighth Edition

Bucy, *Living in the Information Age: A New Media Reader,* Second Edition

Craft/Leigh/Godfrey, *Electronic Media*

Day, *Ethics in Media Communications: Cases and Controversies,* Fifth Edition

Dennis/Merrill, *Media Debates: Great Issues for the Digital Age,* Fourth Edition

Gillmor/Barron/Simon, *Mass Communication Law: Cases and Comments,* Sixth Edition

Gillmor/Barron/Simon/Terry, *Fundamentals of Mass Communication Law*

Hilmes, *Connections: A Broadcast History Reader*

Hilmes, *Only Connect: A Cultural History of Broadcasting in the United States,* Second Edition

Jamieson/Campbell, *The Interplay of Influence: News, Advertising, Politics, and the Mass Media,* Sixth Edition

Karnalipour, *Global Communication,* Second Edition

Lester, *Visual Communication: Images with Messages,* Fourth Edition

Overbeck, *Major Principles of Media Law,* 2008 Edition

Straubhaar/LaRose, *Media Now: Understanding Media, Culture, and Technology,* Fifth Edition

Zelezny, *Cases in Communications Law,* Fifth Edition

Zelezny, *Communications Law: Liberties, Restraints, and the Modern Media,* Fifth Edition

Journalism

Bowles/Borden, *Creative Editing,* Fifth Edition

Craig, *Online Journalism*

Hilliard, *Writing for Television, Radio, and New Media,* Ninth Edition

Kessler/McDonald, *When Words Collide: A Media Writer's Guide to Grammar and Style,* Seventh Edition

Poulter/Tidwell, *News Scene 2.0: Interactive Writing Exercises*

Rich, *Writing and Reporting News: A Coaching Method,* Media Enhanced Fifth Edition

Rich, *Writing and Reporting News: A Coaching Method, Student Exercise Workbook,* Media Enhanced Fifth Edition

Stephens, *Broadcast News,* Fourth Edition

Wilber/Miller, *Modern Media Writing*

Photojournalism and Photography

Parish, *Photojournalism: An Introduction*

Public Relations and Advertising

Diggs-Brown/Glou, *The PR Styleguide: Formats for Public Relations Practice*

Drewniany/Jewler, *Creative Strategy in Advertising,* Ninth Edition

Hendrix, *Public Relations Cases,* Seventh Edition

Newsom/Haynes, *Public Relations Writing: Form and Style,* Eighth Edition

Newsom/Turk/Kruckeberg, *This Is PR: The Realities of Public Relations,* Ninth Edition

Research and Theory

Baran/Davis, *Mass Communication Theory: Foundations, Ferment, and Future,* Fourth Edition

Baxter/Babbie, *The Basics of Communication Research*

Littlejohn, *Theories of Human Communication,* Seventh Edition

Rubin/Rubin/Piele, *Communication Research: Strategies and Sources,* Sixth Edition

Sparks/*Media Effects Research: A Basic Overview,* Second Edition

Wimmer/Dominick, *Mass Media Research: An Introduction,* Eighth Edition

CREATIVE EDITING

DOROTHY A. BOWLES
University of Tennessee

DIANE L. BORDEN
San Diego State University

FIFTH EDITION

THOMSON ™

WADSWORTH

Australia ■ Brazil ■ Canada ■ Mexico ■ Singapore
Spain ■ United Kingdom ■ United States

Creative Editing
Fifth Edition
Bowles • Borden

Publisher: *Lyn Uhl*
Editorial Assistant: *Kim Apfelbaum*
Senior Marketing Manager: *Karin Sandberg*
Associate Technology Project Manager: *Lucinda Bingham*
Associate Content Project Manager: *Jessica Rasile*
Manufacturing Manager: *Barbara Britton*
Associate Print Buyer: *Linda Hsu*

Senior Rights Acquisition Account Manager, Images: *Sheri Blaney*
Photo Researcher: *Jill Engebretson*
Senior Rights Acquisition Account Manager, Text: *Bob Kauser*
Production Service/Compositor: *Graphic World Inc.*
Senior Art Director: *Maria Epes*
Cover Designer: *Gia Giasullo*
Cover/Text Printer: *Thomson West*

Printed in the United States of America
1   2   3   4   5   6   12   11   10   09   08   07

ISBN-13: 978-0-495-09571-2
ISBN-10: 0-495-09571-0

Library of Congress Catalog Card Number: 2007924037

Thomson Higher Education
25 Thomson Place
Boston, MA 02210-1202
USA

For more information about our products, contact us at:
Thomson Learning Academic Resource Center
1-800-423-0563
For permission to use material from this text or product, submit a request online at **http://www.thomsonrights.com** Any additional questions about permissions can be submitted by e-mail to **thomsonrights@thomson.com**

Contents

Chapter 3   Consistent Style and Correct Words   51

Chapter 4   Checking Facts   75

Chapter **5**   **Editing Stories**   93

Student Workbook

Preface

Copy editors of the 21st century will reside at the very heart of print and online media organizations, supplying the expertise that helps build credibility and serving as gatekeepers of news and entertainment for the public. More than at any time in history, media managers recognize and appreciate the value of good copy editors. This recognition makes even better an already excellent employment picture for copy editors, who are rewarded at many organizations with higher salaries than those of reporters or writers with comparable experience.

Journalists with the personal attributes and word and visual skills explained in this book will have no trouble finding stimulating and rewarding careers in the mass media and its ancillary industries. In addition, those who aspire to become managers will discover that the copy desk is a fertile training ground for learning the intricacies of the print or online production process and is a frequent path to management positions.

Revision highlights

The fifth edition of *Creative Editing* addresses the impact that technological and competitive changes have had on traditional media industries, particularly as they affect the roles of copy editors. The new edition continues to recognize the pedagogical need to incorporate information for public relations practitioners. At the same time, the book emphasizes traditional and still highly valued print-editing skills: using correct grammar, punctuation, style and vocabulary; fact checking; writing headlines; handling photographs and informational graphics; using typography; understanding legal and ethical matters; and designing and laying out pages.

A special feature of *Creative Editing* continues to be the extensive collection of in-book exercises, which allows students to test their understanding of the material in each chapter and to practice their editing skills. Exercises for this edition appear in a special workbook section at the end of the text instead of at the end of each chapter. New exercises have been added, and students may download exercises from a Web site to practice electronic editing and layout. Answers to all exercises are found online on the Book Companion Web site.

The authors believe that the Internet and online publishing offer great potential as an expanding job market for copy editors. The fifth edition underscores the growing importance of digital editing, with a strong emphasis on the Web. Practical material integrated throughout the book focuses on how to edit copy for Web sites, how to access Internet discussion groups of interest to communicators, how to use Internet search and fact-checking tools, how to write online headlines and how to design and lay out Web pages.

This edition also contains updated material on journalism ethics, including new discussions about media credibility, media convergence, online ethics and recent incidences of ethical lapses by journalists at large media organizations.

The popular feature called "Professional perspective," which spotlights a media professional to help students understand the work of copy editors, has been updated with new profiles. Examples include question-and-answer interviews with a Web designer based in London and a managing editor who helped her newspaper win a Pulitzer Prize for its coverage of the Columbine killings.

Throughout the book, the authors have attempted to adhere to Associated Press style and have sought to avoid sexism, racism, ageism, homophobia and other discriminatory language.

Organization of the Text

As in prior editions, the organization of *Creative Editing* remains logical and progressive. Chapter 1 explores how 21st century copy editors will be asked to hone their multitasking skills to perform in a variety of media forms—print, broadcast, and online.

Chapters 2 through 5 focus on the copy editor's tools: the proper use of grammar and punctuation; the importance of precision and consistent style when editing words, sentences and paragraphs; the importance of editing leads and making news judgments when editing stories, whether in print or online; and the need to check facts, including how to use electronic databases. An extensive list of frequently misused words appears in Chapter 3 of this fifth edition rather than in an appendix as in earlier editions.

Chapter 6 discusses legal concerns that affect editors, including libel, invasion of privacy and copyright infringement. Chapter 7 examines ethical situations of specific concern to editors, including online ethics, and suggests an analytical framework that should prove useful in ethical decision-making. This chapter includes the ethics codes that leading journalism and public relations professional organizations have adopted, as well as updated examples of ethics guidelines from individual publications across the country.

Chapter 8 discusses typography, particularly type sizes, widths, styles, weights and families, and includes an expanded section on Web typography. Chapter 9, which focuses on the art of writing headlines, discusses the function and characteristics of headlines, increasingly important in the online environment, and offers rules for writing, counting, placing and styling headlines in all print media, including magazines.

Chapters 10 and 11 examine visual journalism, focusing particularly on editing pictures and infographics, including digital photographs, and on designing and laying out pages, both for print publications and on the Web. Chapter 11 also discusses how to create public relations materials.

Teaching resources

We have provided additional teaching resources to assist you in teaching your copyediting courses:

- **Web Site for *Creative Editing*** This Web site will continue to provide online exercises for students as well as answers to exercises, a glossary, Web addresses, and other resources students can use to improve their skills:

    www.thomsonedu.com/masscomm/bowles

- **InfoTrac® College Edition** Access to this online database of reliable, full-length articles (not abstracts) from thousands of academic journals and popular sources may be packaged with the book. Students will receive a passcode, which will provide them with access to InfoTrac College Edition for four months. Contact your local representative for more information.

Acknowledgments

The authors would like to express their heartfelt gratitude to the professional journalists across the nation who helped supply materials and insights for this book. Special thanks go to those who agreed to provide "Professional perspectives": Sharon Bibb, Edgar Miller, Mary Kay Martire, Jeanette Chavez, Joe Gillespie, Peter Bhatia, Steve Dorsey, Lynne Perri, Michael Donnelly, Chris Barber, the Poynter Institute faculty and Matthew Lee.

Special appreciation goes to Professor Rebekah Bromley, University of Tennessee, Chattanooga, for newsletter layout materials and for her insights throughout the book regarding editing for public relations professionals.

Dorothy Bowles thanks her colleagues and students at the University of Tennessee who contributed ideas or assistance for this and previous editions of *Creative Editing*, including Bonnie Hufford, Ed Miller, Wynne Brown, Sally Guthrie, Jodi Lockaby Ware, Xiang (Julie) Zhou and Christa Carter.

The authors also thank San Diego State University photographer Tom Farrington and Knoxville photographers Rob Heller, Michael Anderson, Miles Cary and Heather McCoy. Others who deserve our utmost appreciation are: Wadsworth communication publisher Lyn Uhl, former assistant editor Nicole George, content project manager Jessica Rasile and permissions editor Bob Kauser.

We also offer our special thanks to the reviewers of this fifth edition, who gave us many valuable suggestions: Timothy Anderson, University of Nebraska-Lincoln; Dana Eversole, Northeastern State University; Diana Huffman, University of Maryland; Cees Kendall, California State University Fullerton; Barbara Luebke, University of Rhode Island; Tom Mullen, University of Richmond; and Bob Wyss, University of Connecticut.

Dorothy A. Bowles
University of Tennessee

Diane L. Borden
San Diego State University

Acknowledgments

[faded, illegible acknowledgments text]

CREATIVE EDITING

The Copy Editor's Role

"ALL human activities, from a Mozart opera to pornography, to war on Saddam Hussein, to a learned article in a scientific journal . . . are reducible to digital bits and bytes, evermore tightly compressed, evermore quickly flashed . . . around the globe in the blink of an eye," said noted journalist Robert MacNeil a decade ago. MacNeil was talking about a new age in media content, an age that generates technologies so quickly that information industries cannot keep up with the demand. We live in an age that on one day produces a science fiction movie showing a newspaper as a small, thin, wireless, foldable video screen and on the next day announces the manufacture of that same electronic paper, capable of displaying documents and playing MP3 files. For journalists, and particularly for copy editors, the production of content for such new technologies is, as it always has been, an essential ingredient in any media company's success.

Companies that supply content to those who control the technological means to transmit it will benefit most in this new age. Newspapers, magazines, broadcast stations, public relations firms, advertising agencies and World Wide Web sites will be competing for bright, energetic, talented people who understand this brave new world of content convergence.

The often-unspoken theme that underlies these discussions is the need for good editing and good editors. Today's copy editors are less likely than their predecessors to perform media-specific tasks or to think in narrowly defined media boxes. They perform all the tasks discussed in this book—copy editing, headline writing, layout and design, and so on—in a variety of media forms. Increasingly, editors will prepare a story for a print publication, then later in their workday, add video and audio for a broadcast version or an online version—or a version that will be "published" on a cell phone. At places like MSNBC (a media organization put together by Bill Gates' Microsoft Corp. and the National Broadcasting Co.), The New York Times and others, editors already perform this multitasking and find it's an exciting new world.

How we got here

It is now commonplace for reporters and editors to go online to retrieve information from government documents; to gather information from sources and online discussion groups; and to publish information in many formats, including electronically, for their readers. By 2007, virtually all daily newspapers in the United States had a presence on the Web. In addition, thousands of magazines, newsletters, wire services, broadcast stations, film companies, book publishers and content companies (such as MSNBC) had created online products.

The immediacy and the relatively easy access to electronic information have lured millions of people to the Internet, but for journalists and copy editors, in particular, the beauty of the relatively new resources may also be a beast. Nonmedia corporations gobble up media companies with dizzying speed, resulting in conglomerates that use their individual components to promote each other, part of a concept known as vertical integration (see Figure 1-1). At the same time, the media

Figure 1-1
Collage demonstrates the importance of content and the subtle but important similarities in appearance of Web sites from several different forms of news media—newspapers, magazines, broadcast networks and content companies such as Microsoft. Note the reference to MSNBC on the Newsweek home page (and in the Web address) as well as the corresponding reference to Newsweek on the MSNBC home page, an example of vertical integration of the mass media and the resulting convergence of content.

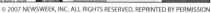

marketplace has become increasingly fragmented, and many forms of traditional mass media are struggling to maintain their market share. In a time of blogs and podcasts and citizen journalists, both newspapers and network news programs have shown declines. More than 250 daily newspapers have folded in the past 50 years, bringing the total to 1,452 in 2005. Viewership of television network news programs continued to decline in 2005, especially for evening newscasts, according to the 2006 "State of the News Media" report, issued annually by the Project for Excellence in Journalism. At the same time, the report said, viewership for the PBS evening newscast, "The NewsHour with Jim Lehrer," has remained stable for the past several years, but cable news, such as that found on CNN, Fox or MSNBC, may have trouble competing in the future with what viewers can find online. For all journalists and news media organizations, then, the challenge to relate to readers in new and exciting ways is stronger than ever (see Figure 1-2).

Figure 1-2
The New York Times Web site is an industry leader in reader interactivity. For example, the Multimedia/Photos page allows users to enter an interactive photograph review of 2006; listen to podcasts of Times editors and reporters as they discuss the day's news; watch and listen to an audio slide show in which a correspondent reports from Iraq, where he is traveling with a battalion of Marines; or engage in "China Rises," a four-part television series and interactive Web site co-produced by the Times and several international partners.

REPRINTED COURTESY OF THE NEW YORK TIMES

Traditional concerns about core journalism values such as accuracy and balance also have come under renewed scrutiny as more journalists use online technologies to gather and analyze news and information (see Chapter 7 on ethics).

With the headlong rush into the new technologies, most news publications appear to be better organized, concentrate more on their primary geographic communities, use more color and attempt to squeeze more information into less space than in the past.

Whatever form the publications take, their future is secure. Print news products are likely to be around for many years to come. However, they may look more like a medium that blends text, sounds, still pictures and video through technological advances in fiber optics and computers. This format will make the verbal and visual skills of good copy editors even more valuable in newsrooms of the future.

Another scenario, outlined in the May/June 2002 issue of The American Editor magazine by ASNE President Diane McFarlin, might require editors and reporters to become fluent in all media forms but maintain their own specialized skills as well. For example, McFarlin, publisher of the Sarasota (Fla.) Herald-Tribune, said that the Herald-Tribune's lead education reporter rarely appears on the newspaper's 24-hour cable news channel. But by feeding story tips and background information to the cable TV staff, he is providing the audience with an expertise that the TV station ordinarily might not be able to afford.

In the end, McFarlin suggests, "The convergence debate ought to focus on how we can improve our journalism and strengthen our communities, not whether photographers should carry two cameras or whether print reporters will have to start dressing for TV. The mechanics of convergence are best left to individual circumstances." Multimedia news products are available now, and the people who produce the newspaper or magazine or newsletter of the future—editors, reporters, designers,

Figure 1-3
TBO.com is a regional portal published in partnership with The Tampa (Fla.) Tribune and WFLA-TV. The three organizations are owned by the same parent company, Richmond, Va.–based Media General, and all three cooperate in their media efforts in the Tampa Bay region.

photographers and artists—are the ones likely to be affected most by technological changes. Copy editors are key bridges between information gatherers and information consumers and will be called on to perform all the traditional copy editing tasks plus some duties that are now the domain of other news personnel (see Figure 1-3).

The importance of good copy editing

Good newspapers, good magazines, good news broadcasts and good press releases all have one thing in common: strong teams of editors. Bylines give reporters name recognition copy editors do not have, but the strength of the copy editing staff is an important predictor of the strength of the news organization.

Perhaps more than at any previous time in print media history, senior editors, producers and marketing directors are recognizing the value of good copy editors, an appreciation that makes an already excellent employment picture even better for copy editors of the future. Linda Grist Cunningham, chair of an ASNE committee that conducted a survey of copy editors, said: "As the literacy skills of even our better writers decline and as the demands of technology complicate our production schedules, editors will be forced to pay attention to the needs of copy editors if we are to improve our newspapers." Copy editors are a rare breed, and they are scarce. Just ask any editor or publisher trying to hire one. And they are dedicated, intelligent individuals whose love of language and penchant for precision make many reporters look good. Copy editors are the very heart of the media organization, supplying the lifeblood for healthy existence and serving as gatekeepers of the news for the public. In this regard, their place in the future of the news and information industry is assured.

The importance of copy editors is recognized and rewarded at many publications with salaries higher than those of reporters with comparable experience. In particular, online editors (and writers) seem to be garnering good salaries (see Figure 1-4). According to salary.hotjobs.com, a Web site that allows users to conduct an

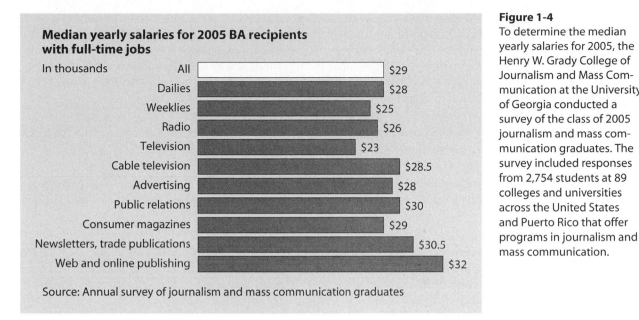

Median yearly salaries for 2005 BA recipients with full-time jobs

In thousands

All	$29
Dailies	$28
Weeklies	$25
Radio	$26
Television	$23
Cable television	$28.5
Advertising	$28
Public relations	$30
Consumer magazines	$29
Newsletters, trade publications	$30.5
Web and online publishing	$32

Source: Annual survey of journalism and mass communication graduates

Figure 1-4
To determine the median yearly salaries for 2005, the Henry W. Grady College of Journalism and Mass Communication at the University of Georgia conducted a survey of the class of 2005 journalism and mass communication graduates. The survey included responses from 2,754 students at 89 colleges and universities across the United States and Puerto Rico that offer programs in journalism and mass communication.

instant online salary comparison, in 2006 an associate Web editor earned an average of $51,116 a year. These editors and writers found jobs in a multitude of fields, from mass media to health care to corporate communications.

Journalists who possess the personal attributes and verbal and visual skills described in this book will have no trouble finding stimulating and rewarding work as copy editors. In an earlier era, few copy editors were without reporting experience; desk work was seen as a promotion from reporting. However, those in charge of hiring today no longer insist that reporting be a prerequisite to working on the copy desk. Also, journalists who aspire to management positions will learn that the copy desk is a good place to learn the intricacies of print and online production and is a frequent path to management jobs.

The duties of a copy editor

Editing in an online world may require placing more emphasis on certain editing skills than others. For example, some educators believe that the ability to write good headlines ranks near the top in Web-based editing skills, while others believe that, with the growth of Flash and other visual story forms, the ability to write cutlines and captions is important. In addition, copy editors are being asked to learn new skills, such as how to handle Web links, images, audio and TV-quality video. Still, the chief duties of the copy editor continue to include the following:

▶ **Improving stories by making dull or verbose copy interesting and concise.** Copy editors can transform halting stories into ones that sing. Creativity is essential. However, as long as the information has been expressed clearly, the aim of the copy editor is to preserve as much as possible the words of the reporter and to retain the tone of the story as it was written.

▶ **Correcting errors of grammar, spelling and style in all copy, including informational graphics.** Too many reporters, triumphantly bringing in stories that were difficult to pry loose from sources, refer to minor errors as "just typos." Yet, the smallest error or inconsistency can cause readers to wonder whether that carelessness also extends to the reporting.

▶ **Correcting errors of fact and emphasis.** An expert copy editor is invariably a walking compendium. Although reporters are better acquainted with their beats and their sources, the copy editor can supply a context—other stories, the city, the county, the nation, the world—that the reporters, whose single-minded focus is their story, almost inevitably fail to comprehend. Copy editors unfamiliar with the context must be adept at using many reference sources for quick research.

▶ **Judging news value.** Copy editors must be alert to the flow of current affairs and understand how a single item integrates with the stream of news.

▶ **Guarding against libel and other legal problems.** The copy desk is usually the last line of defense against legal concerns that could prove costly to a publication in money and in lost time.

▶ **Protecting and enhancing the publication's reputation and image.** Most news publications would like to have a reputation for accuracy and thoroughness in news coverage. It is up to copy editors to build and preserve that reputation. The personality or image of the publication—conservative or breezy, formal or informal, for example—is also largely in the hands of the copy desk.

▶ **Writing headlines that summarize stories and capture readers' attention.** Copy editors' skill with concise wording and the ability to work quickly are especially valuable in this aspect of the job.

▶ **Selecting, cropping and sizing photographs and other art.** Section editors, along with the photography and graphics staff, handle much of this work, but copy editors frequently are involved in the process.

▶ **Writing illustration captions.** The idea that "a picture is worth a thousand words" may become meaningless unless the picture is accompanied by a carefully crafted caption, also known as a cutline.

▶ **Using computer codes to designate the headline and body type style, size, width and leading.** As print media became computerized during the 1970s, copy editors assumed many production tasks previously performed by others. With expert knowledge of the publication's computer system, a copy editor can, with just a few keystrokes, do much of the work previously performed by teams of production specialists.

▶ **Laying out pages.** Many decisions about how the publication will look each day are in the hands of copy editors. Designers and other graphics experts determine the basic look of the paper, but copy editors work within the overall design pattern to lay out individual pages.

▶ **Exercising news judgment.** Expert news judgment is essential as copy editors, working with other editors, make decisions about which stories will go on the front page or an inside page and how much emphasis to give individual stories.

▶ **Keeping up with the newest technology.** Computer graphics, computer pagination and digital photography are rapidly changing. Editors knowledgeable about the most recent versions of software for graphics, layout and digital-image enhancement can produce better-quality work faster and more efficiently. Such technical expertise is especially valuable for editors working at online publications.

The characteristics of a good copy editor

In a report from the Associated Press Managing Editors Writing and Editing Committee, William G. Connolly Jr., an editor of The New York Times Week in Review section, offered this checklist of the qualities of an outstanding editor:

▶**Confidence.** Good editors have confidence in their own intelligence, knowledge and writing skills. They know the publication's style, production capabilities and politics. They know the system—and use it.

▶**Objectivity.** Editors have an extra obligation to be objective. They must be able to review the material in a broader context and disregard the personality of the reporter who wrote it. Every newsroom has problem people, but great editors have the ability to look beyond the person to the essence of the story.

▶**Awareness.** Editors must be aware of the readers and the personality of the publication. Layout, selection of stories, art, graphics and headlines should all come together to reinforce the publication's personality. Look at products that are in trouble, and you'll find a personality problem. Good taste and knowing what's important are the essential elements of personality.

▶**Intelligence.** Good editors must have a diverse background that enables them to bring to every story a sense of why it is important and what it means in a broader context. They must be instinctively aware of what is right or wrong with a story.

▶**Questioning nature.** Good editors know there is no such thing as a stupid question. They question everything. Editors know that if they have doubts, so will the reader.

▶**Diplomacy.** Editing is a confrontation. Writing is both an intellectual and emotional experience, and good editors try to minimize the inevitable tension that arises between an editor and a writer. They understand the reporter's problems. Nevertheless, although civility and diplomacy are important, neither behavior can be permitted to overwhelm the need to edit.

▶**Ability to write.** Editors should be better writers than reporters are, but they still must be able to retain a writer's style and ideas. A great editor's work is invisible to both the writer and the reader.

▶**Sense of humor.** Good editors are able to laugh at the absurdity of some aspects of the business—bad hours, bad tempers, bad deadlines, bad copy—and plunge ahead.

Another editor, speaking at a journalism educators' seminar at the American Press Institute, said the following attributes would produce an "almost-perfect" newspaper copy editor, but the same general attributes would apply to all copy editors:

- Has a college education
- Has newspaper experience, including reporting and editing
- Is well-read, in both fiction and nonfiction
- Is familiar with the news and its background
- Has hobbies, enjoys cultural events and is well traveled
- Is quick and thorough when editing copy

- Has a healthy skepticism that leads to the questioning of information in stories and a desire to release no story with unanswered questions

- Is familiar with the rules of grammar, with punctuation and spelling, and with style

- Appreciates good writing and knows what to do with it

- Is able to listen to the rhythm of a story

- Has a sense of wit and pathos and the ability to discern the difference

- Has an orderly and well-balanced mind, which implies judgment and a sense of perspective and proportion

- Knows the laws of libel, privacy and copyright

- Has a team spirit

The copy desk in a modern newsroom

Before the use of computers, the traditional copy desk physically resembled a horseshoe. The chief copy editor, called the "slot editor" or simply the "slot," sat at the center of the inside curve of a semicircular desk. Copy editors sat along the outside curve of the horseshoe, known as the "rim" and were thus known as "rim editors." Although the terms *slot editor* and *rim editor* persist, the computerization of editing has changed the physical arrangement of the copy desk. Modern copy desks are arranged in a rectangular shape and generally include separate stations with an electronic editing terminal for each editor.

To help speed the flow of copy, many small and medium-size newspapers have instituted a system of centralized editing called the universal copy desk. Universal desk copy editors handle copy for all sections of the newspaper.

Conversely, most large metropolitan newspapers have specialized copy desks that process stories for particular categories of news: local, state, national, international, business, sports, opinion, lifestyle or entertainment.

In the past several years, many newsrooms have been experimenting with teams or clusters of journalists who work together in small groups to conceive, report, edit and illustrate stories. Such clusters often comprise a team leader, usually someone from the city desk; a copy editor; a reporter or several reporters; and a photographer or graphic artist. Frequently, the stories each team produces are enterprise packages, in-depth articles about issues of significance in the local community.

Some metros also have separate reporting and editing staffs for "zoned" editions, those pages or sections that target news and advertising for a particular circulation area. In many newspaper markets, zoned editions have proved successful with both readers and advertisers. Subscribers receive the individual section containing news and advertising focusing on their neighborhood, along with the rest of the metropolitan newspaper. Some newspapers publish up to 24 different zoned editions a week; others publish several zoned sections each day. Zoning is becoming more common with other forms of media, too, such as magazines, radio and television.

The fast pace of editing often allows little time for reflection. In today's newsrooms, where editors are increasingly asked to perform production functions previously handled by a separate staff of production personnel, editors find that their time is at a premium.

An age of rapid technological advances in the publishing industry has introduced computer-generated copy and computer-activated layout and paste-up, or pagination. For print publications, therefore, the copy editor's job has become at once more complex, more exciting and more vital to the quality of the final product.

The technological revolution included pagination, a computerized layout program that continues to have a major impact on a newsroom's copy editing staff.

Pagination is the vital link to a grander scheme for automation. It calls for the end of the "composing room," the place where the publication is mechanically produced. Partial pagination, now used at many newspapers, magazines and public relations firms, allows editors to create pages on computer terminals with all the text in place, eliminating the need for pages to be pasted up. Devices that permit the digitization of photographs, a step necessary to achieve total pagination, allow editors to produce an entire page on computer terminals. When total pagination is in place, most work now done in the composing room, a department that accounts for perhaps 25 percent of the total news publication's payroll, will be unnecessary. (Pagination is discussed further in Chapter 11.)

Clearly, newsroom editors and managers of the future must be ready to meet the challenges of incorporating new technology into newsroom processes. As in many business settings, internal communication occurs more often via computers, particularly through e-mail.

The organizational structure of newsrooms of the future may look quite different.

Today most newsrooms are organized in a hierarchical structure like the one shown in Figure 1-5. That is, the organization looks like a pyramid, with the editor at the apex and the reporters, copy editors and photographers—the workers—forming the base.

Newsrooms of the future may require a more circular structure, in which job functions rather than titles determine the organization and in which jobs are interrelated rather than separated. Copy editors, many believe, will be at the center of this new newsroom because of the breadth of their job functions.

The editing process

Computers have improved the efficiency of the production process for the print media by adding functions to the copy desk that were formerly handled by production teams in the composing room.

Copy editors not only perform more functions but are now also the last people to process copy before the final paste-up stage. Typesetters and proofreaders no longer exist as a final check to prevent errors from being published. Electronic layout has all but eliminated the physical paste-up stage as well. To demonstrate the editing and production process, let's track two different publications: a newspaper story, from idea to publication, and a public relations brochure, from concept to distribution.

News story

Before a news story is assigned to a reporter or accepted from a beat or general assignment reporter, an editor must decide that the story is newsworthy. Knowledge of the newspaper's audience is the key to determining which news values to emphasize, and many news organizations today periodically conduct sophisticated surveys to help editors stay abreast of readers' interests.

In exercising news judgment, editors evaluate the extent to which each story contains one or more traditional news criteria, which include the following:

▶**Timeliness.** Something that happens today has more reader impact than something that happened yesterday. Timeliness means that up-to-the-minute information is valuable.

▶**Proximity.** Something that happens nearby physically or geographically is important to readers, but so is information about others who share a common interest, such as people who participate in the same online discussion groups.

Figure 1-5

Today's newsroom is organized hierarchically. This chart illustrates the organizational plan at a large metropolitan daily, which has separate copy desks for general-interest news, business, sports, features and the zoned editions. Many newspapers have a universal copy desk, which edits stories for all sections of the paper.

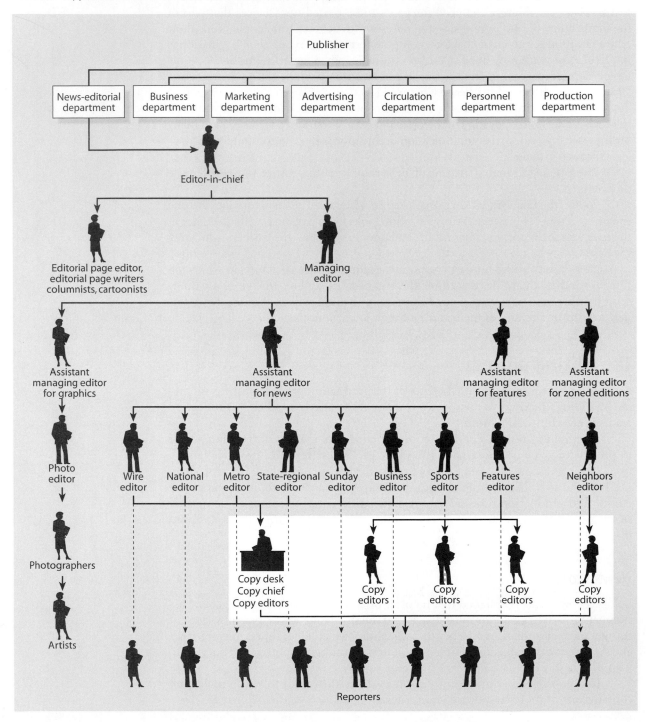

▶**Prominence.** People who are well-known or hold positions of authority, such as the President of the United States, often are newsmakers. But others in the community often have interesting stories, too.

▶**Relevance.** A story often has an impact on its audience, whether emotional or rational. The more people affected by the consequences of a story, the more significant the story will be.

▶**Unusualness.** It's not usually big news if it snows in Colorado in January. But snow in Colorado in July could be newsworthy because it would be out of the ordinary.

▶**Conflict.** Whether personal or institutional, we all deal with conflicts in our daily lives, from minor fender-bender accidents to labor strikes to courtroom trials, and conflicts often are newsworthy. But journalists should always remember that conflicts involve more than two extreme positions. Many different views can be represented.

▶**Human interest.** Stories that touch readers' lives and may help them improve their lives are newsworthy.

On any given day, the number of possible stories far outnumbers the actual stories that get covered or that make their way into print. Editors who decide which stories get published or broadcast and which ones don't are called gatekeepers. They use the news values outlined previously to make decisions about which stories to include, but they also have in mind their intended audience. For example, the editor of a small weekly newspaper in rural Colorado might be very interested in publishing stories about agriculture and the environment, whereas the editor of a monthly magazine for teens likely would be more interested in publishing stories about music and entertainment figures.

Editors also understand the commercial need to attract readers or viewers. Local television news bombards viewers with images of crime and disaster to attract their attention in the ratings race. Newspapers and magazines publish feature or human-interest stories or stories about weird or unusual events to attract readers for circulation gains. Editors weigh the relative importance of the story using a combination of all these factors.

Thus, the editing process begins before a story is ever written. Despite the idea of news teams discussed earlier, it is not usual that a copy editor is involved at this stage. Rather, it is an editor, sometimes called an *assigning editor,* in charge of a newspaper section or category of news. Typical examples of types of assigning editors are city, state, sports, lifestyle and entertainment editors, but they vary with the organization and size of the paper. Whether the assigning editor conceives the idea for a story or accepts a reporter's idea, he or she then helps direct the reporter's work by suggesting angles that the story might examine, sources to interview and questions to ask. The assigning editor, often in consultation with other editors or the reporter, also determines whether photographs or other artwork should accompany the story. If so, a photographer or graphic artist is assigned to begin working on the story.

Once the story is written, the assigning editor reads it, primarily for content rather than style or tone. If substantial content changes are needed—for example, if obvious questions remain unanswered—the editor generally sends the story back to the reporter for additional work. If the editor is satisfied with the overall content of the story, he or she decides where it will be placed in the newspaper, how long it will be, and what size and style of headline will accompany it. Sometimes a story is sent to the copy desk with an *HTK* ("headline to come") notation, meaning that the headline form has not yet been determined. Decisions about story placement and headline specifications are made by the person who lays out the page—the assigning editor, the copy desk chief, a copy editor, or perhaps a layout editor or graphics specialist.

The story is then sent to the copy desk chief, who may edit it loosely before passing it along to a copy editor sitting on the rim. In assigning copy, the copy desk chief often considers the special knowledge or ability of each rim editor.

Like reporters, some copy editors are experts in certain fields, and this expertise can be useful in editing particular stories. Other copy editors are especially talented at handling stories based on statistics, writing bright or clever headlines for feature stories, or editing stories of exceptionally difficult topics or length.

In modern newsrooms, all this shuffling of stories is done electronically from computer terminal to computer terminal. But as recently as the mid-1970s, the staff at many newspapers still edited paper copy with pencils, reorganized paragraphs using scissors and glue, and physically moved copy from person to person.

A rim editor edits the story carefully, perhaps cutting it to fit a specified length for the page layout. Copy editors, even experienced ones, should read each story at least three times. During the first reading, the copy editor analyzes the thoroughness of the content and the appropriateness and effectiveness of the lead and organization of the story. The copy editor should make few, if any, changes during this first reading.

Next the copy editor rereads the story to make changes where needed. For example, a buried or uninteresting lead may be rewritten; the overall organization of the story may be rearranged; facts are verified; and style, grammar, punctuation and spelling errors are corrected. In addition, the copy editor addresses questions of ethics, taste and sensitivity, as well as legal problems with the story.

Finally, the copy editor reads the story a third time to be sure all errors have been corrected and everything possible has been done to produce a clear, concise, accurate and well-organized story. During the copy editing process, the editor may need to talk to the reporter about unclear passages or to ask for details. Often the copy editor uses standard reference books or telephones sources to verify information or fill in gaps in the story.

When the copy editor is satisfied with the story, he or she writes the headline according to the specifications assigned by the editor. Computer codes are inserted so the body and headline type will be set (or *output,* as it is expressed in computer jargon) in the desired style, size, width and leading (space between the lines of body type). If an informational graphic or photograph is to accompany the story, the copy editor edits it and writes a caption for it (processes that are discussed in Chapter 10).

Then the copy editor sends the story back to the chief copy editor for approval.

If the copy chief finds fault with the editing or the headline, the story may be bounced back to the copy editor to make still more changes. If the copy and the headline meet with the copy chief's approval, the computer command is given to send the story to the composing room.

Before the advent of pagination, the story was printed on a long strip of photosensitive paper that emerged from a mainframe computer in the composing room. Following a sample layout prepared by an editor, composing room personnel trimmed excess paper and pasted the type onto a page. Most newspapers today use offset printing. In this process, after all elements for the page are pasted into position, the entire page is photographed, and a printing plate, made of plastic or metal, is made from the resulting negative. This plate is then placed on the printing press.

Brochures

The publication of public relations brochures also is based on a set of very distinct production considerations. Within a large, bureaucratic organization, developing a comprehensive brochure from concept to distribution of finished copies requires 60 to 85 working days, or three to four and one-half months. The schedule may be shorter if organizational approval is either quick or not required, if the brochure is simple, if brochure work continues through the approval processes, if art is readily available, and if printing and distribution are easily accomplished. Assuming that one week is five working days, the typical schedule would be as follows:

- 1 week—Preliminary research

- 1 week—Concept planning and development; preliminary budget and production schedule developed

- 1 week—Concept, schedule and budget approval

- 1 week—Subject and audience research

- 1 to 2 weeks—Writing and editing

- 1 week—First draft approval

- 1 to 3 weeks—Preliminary design and layout; art selection or production; revised draft for final approval

- 1 week—Final copy approval; preliminary design and layout approval

- 1 week—Development of camera-ready pages

- 1 week—Final approval of brochure

- 1 to 2 weeks—Camera-ready pages at printers (before press run, ask for a press proof and approve)

- 1 to 2 weeks—Distribution of final copies

Perfectly serviceable brochures can be photocopied from a laser printer master. However, after investing the time and effort required in the typical three- to four-month process of brochure development, most firms and organizations choose to spend a few extra dollars per page to reproduce camera-ready masters from a phototypesetter or page compositor. The master then can be used to develop plates for offset printing of the final copies. In offset printing, a press reproduces brochure pages from plate images that have been transferred, or offset, to a rubber blanket or cylinder that puts ink to paper. Offset printing will produce sharper images than photocopying and allow for four-color and oversize pages. What is common to the production of quality newspapers and quality brochures is a team of crackerjack copy editors.

Gene Foreman, former deputy editor and vice president of The Philadelphia Inquirer, is a strong supporter of copy editors in the newsroom. As part of an examination of the state of copy editing in U.S. newspapers a few years ago, he wrote that although the copy desk maintains a relatively low profile in most newsrooms, it is more important today than in years past.

Today's copy editors still perform the traditional tasks of refining grammar, punctuation and spelling; tightening and straightening prose; and crafting headlines and captions with reader appeal. With their computers, they also have absorbed the functions of yesterday's legions of blue-collared compositors. If the technological revolution had not drastically reduced production labor costs, many newspapers would not generate a profit.

Not satisfied with merely rearranging stories or rewriting headlines, a good news publication continually updates its editions to reflect the latest developments in the news. New page layouts may require that stories be edited and headlines be written as many as three or four times.

As the editions or online sites are updated, copy editors assume responsibility for rechecking material from earlier editions. The job of reading a story already in print differs markedly from the job of handling a story before it is set in type,

Looking to the future

Q: What is the most important resource for a copy editor, and how can it be used effectively in everyday copy editing?

A: Databases have become a key tool for reporters, and they're a key resource for copy editors as well. The only difference is that copy editors have been slower coming around to tapping their power—as well as the power of the Web—largely because of insufficient newsroom training. An in-house database expert who can pool public records and make it easy for reporters and copy editors to check facts and crunch data is a must for every news operation. The information is out there, but copy editors can use it as a tool only if it's efficient and expedient. Copy editors must become adept at tapping the Web and the databases that can be generated from what's available. More important, they should take a proactive role in advising the database expert about what information they need and in what form.

Q: How will the role and duties of copy editors change in the next decade?

A: Competition and the drive for profits (and survival) demand that copy editors be even more keenly aware of what they can contribute to a story—the details, the overview, relevance, context, impact, immediacy. That's traditional copy editing pushed to a higher standard. But the new generation of publishing systems tends toward two radically different tools for copy editors: a large database of information about their own publication, and Microsoft Word or a Word-like program as their text editor. Copy editors will be able to see not only the stories assigned to them but every story, image and graphic that will be used, and how they will be presented. Editors must be able to comfortably navigate far beyond the old familiar screen showing simply a list of stories they're assigned to edit. Mastering Word, managing multiple screen views and understanding how their computers work will be among the requirements. Editors will need to deftly handle new newsroom technologies while upholding the deadlines and the standards of their organizations.

Q: How will convergence change the copy editor's role?

A: It has never been more true than now that copy editors must embrace the big picture. New delivery

Sharon Bibb received a bachelor's degree in 1975 and a master's degree in 1977, both in communications, from the University of Washington in Seattle. She has served as a copy editor at several metropolitan newspapers and currently is the assistant to the editor of news technology at The New York Times.

systems are designed to customize news, so the editor's "customer" could be the longtime city resident, a foreigner living in the United States or overseas, the businessperson downloading the top stories to a handheld device. In some newsrooms, the job of taking a story and producing parallel copy for print, Web site, e-mail or mobile Web delivery, radio, and even television can fall to a single editor. Understanding these market demographics, while maintaining a cohesive corporate profile, will be critical as news operations expand their delivery systems.

Q: Will copy editors be in more demand as technology progresses, or in less demand? Why?

A: Solid copy editors will always be in demand, but those who master whatever new technology arrives in the newsroom will be at a premium. Computer systems of the past 15 years were geared toward reducing production costs—sometimes, unfortunately, transferring production work to the newsroom. Today's new systems promise to further automate noneditorial processes, such as text coding, so that story files can be sent along the chain and repurposed for multiple presentations. Properly utilized, new systems will free editors to focus their efforts on the very thing machines can't do—editing. Newsroom administrators will look to hire, keep and covet those copy editors who are the most flexible, interchangeable among departments and capable of using all the technologies available. The so-called superusers—good copy editors who have mastered newsroom systems—will be best equipped for future iterations of news production.

although practices vary from publication to publication. Between editions of a newspaper, for example, copy editors read to update old information and to correct errors of fact or omission rather than read for grammatical and stylistic errors. Updates are handled quickly by making the required changes on the computer screen and outputting the entire story again. In addition to saving time, this method reprocesses the new version of the story in one clean piece and reduces the chances of error.

The copy editor's work, day or night, is usually marked by roller-coaster fluctuations in activity. At newspapers, most action comes in the last few hours before press deadline, regardless of whether the newspaper is distributed to readers in the morning or in the afternoon. Editors often process breaking news on deadline or incorporate new developments into stories they have already worked. They weigh the news values of stories competing for space and make last-minute calls to verify facts. Editors also match stories with accompanying late-breaking photos or graphics and then pull together all the elements into the most up-to-date news publication.

Suggestions for additional reading

American Journalism Review Web site, http://ajr.org.

American Society of Newspaper Editors Web site, http://asne.org.

Borden, Diane L., and Kerric Harvey. *The Electronic Grapevine: Rumor, Reputation, and Reporting in the New On-line Environment.* Mahwah, N.J.: Lawrence Erlbaum Associates, 1998.

Columbia Journalism Review Web site, http://cjr.org.

Editor & Publisher Interactive Web site, http://mediainfo.com.

Jones, Stephen G. *Cybersociety: Computer-Mediated Communication and Community.* Thousand Oaks, Calif.: Sage Publications, 1995.

Newman, Edwin. *Strictly Speaking: Will America Be the Death of English?* New York: Warner Books, 1975.

Newspaper Association of America Web site, http://naa.org.

Newspaper Design: 2000 and Beyond. Reston, Va.: American Press Institute, J. Montgomery Curtis Memorial Seminar, 1988.

Poynter Institute for Media Studies Web site, http://poynter.org.

Society of Professional Journalists Web site, http://spj.org.

Weaver, David H. and G. Cleveland Wilhoit. *The American Journalist in the 1990s: U.S. News People at the End of an Era.* Mahwah, N.J.: Lawrence Erlbaum Associates, 1996.

[Writing] should be treated like a precision instrument: It should be sharpened and it should not be used carelessly.

—*Theodore M. Bernstein*

Using Correct Grammar and Punctuation

LANGUAGE **is the fundamental tool for communicators.** Just as a composer who doesn't care about or understand the sounds of notes can't hope to create an opera, a communicator who doesn't care about words and how they fit together can't aspire to a successful career in mass media or public relations. Some students enter college classes with multiple excuses for their lack of basic language skills. Experienced teachers have heard these laments and others:

▶**"This writing is so different from what I learned in English classes."** This is a false notion. The inverted pyramid organization of news stories (described in Chapter 5) differs from the traditional narrative pattern, and paragraphs are kept artificially short in news stories and press releases, but most other conventions of good writing are unchanged. Besides, newspapers and magazines afford opportunities for writing beyond inverted pyramid news stories. Word usage, grammar and punctuation basics taught in English courses apply also in journalism and public relations courses.

▶**"People today don't know or care whether grammar is used correctly."** This claim applies to a segment of the population but not most people in reading audiences. The constant emphasis on proper English usage is not a form of snobbery. Newspapers, magazines, public relations agencies and Web sites cannot be casual about language usage because precision of language sharpens the meaning of fact. In addition, improper usage damages credibility. Readers question the accuracy of information in a publication containing frequent errors in spelling or language usage.

▶**"I want to write like people talk."** Opportunities may arise to write or edit stories in slang or colloquial language, but, in general, mass media aim to attract the widest possible audience, ranging from people at the fringes of illiteracy to those with maximum literary competence. Because of the extremely diverse audiences, simplicity and clarity are important, so the media use the language familiar to all educated people. Of the four basic types of language—*literary, common, colloquial* and *slang*—*common* is preferred.

▶**"I'm a PR major planning to become a strategic planner, not a technician, so writing and editing aren't all that important to me."** This rationale is faulty even for newly minted PR graduates whose strategically placed friends and relatives might catapult them directly into management positions. Just as novice journalists don't jump from classrooms into editor-in-chief chairs at major daily newspapers, realistic PR graduates should expect to start their careers in entry-level positions, all of which require writing and editing skills. Besides, just as many aspiring newspaper editors and publishers discover that they love reporting or copy editing, aspiring PR strategic planners often fall in love with writing and editing public relations materials and decide to make a career of it. Public relations practitioners who eventually go into management will discover the importance of good language skills in leadership positions and the need to recognize good writing and editing among their staffs.

▶ **"I'm going to be a newspaper reporter (or magazine writer), so I don't need to know grammar and punctuation because the copy desk will correct my errors."** This excuse for not learning basic language skills may work to a point—for those reporters who don't mind being laughed at and derided by their editors—but ultimately weak language skills will derail a successful reporting career.

▶ **"I plan to specialize in page layout and design or work on Web sites."** Designers who want to reach beyond a production specialist job, executing someone else's ideas, must demonstrate word mastery as well as graphic skills; otherwise, they will be passed over by their peers who are also able to express themselves precisely with words.

▶ **"I got through high school without learning good language skills, so why bother now."** Having chosen to study journalism or public relations in college is reason enough. Minimal language skill level might be adequate for some college majors but not for journalism and other communications majors.

Skills for entry-level jobs

People making hiring decisions in public relations, newspapers and magazines consistently rank good language skills at the top of every "desired qualifications" list.

The Commission on Public Relations Education conducted a national survey of PR practitioners and issued a report titled "A Port of Entry: Public Relations Education for the 21st Century." Public relations professionals overwhelmingly rated writing skills as the most desired among all skills or attitudes, especially the ability to write news releases. Fifty-five percent named writing skills as the No. 1 skill required for hiring, while 75 percent of the respondents listed it in the top five (see Figure 2-1).

A national survey of newspaper editors rated knowledge of correct grammar, spelling and punctuation as the most important skill for copy editors. The same editors, representing a cross section of large, medium-size and small dailies, as well as weekly newspapers, ranked accuracy and fact checking a close second in importance. Editing stories for wordiness, clarity and sentence structure was next on the editors' list of important expectations for copy desk personnel. Figure 2-2 presents the ranking of 25 expected knowledge areas and skills for copy editors.

Figure 2-1
A national survey of PR professionals ranked writing as the most desired skill or attitude for entry-level employees and producing print communications as the most highly desired public relations content area. The Commission on Public Relations Education conducted the survey.

Desirable Skills/Attitudes for Entry-Level PR Employees

Rank	Skill or Attitude
1	Writing
2	Critical thinking and problem solving
3	Being a self starter

Most Highly Valued Public Relations Content Areas

Rank	Content Area
1	Planning, writing, producing and delivering print communications
2	Setting goals/objectives/strategic planning
3	Ethical and legal credibility
4	Audience segmentation
5	Publicity and media relations
6	Problem/opportunity analysis

Ranking of Expected Knowledge/Skills Areas for Copy Editors

Rank	Knowledge or Skill
1	Grammar, spelling and punctuation
2	Accuracy and fact checking
3	Editing wordiness, clarity and sentence structure
4	General knowledge
5	Story structure, organization and content
6	Ethical concerns
7	Headline writing
8	Analytical/critical thinking
9	Associated Press style and usage
10	Cutline writing
11	News judgment and story selection
12	Legal concerns
13	Understanding numbers
14	Mechanics of computer editing
15	Layout and page design
16	Photo and art editing and sizing
17	Newsroom procedure and organization
18	Working with wire copy
19	Specific section editing (e.g., Sports)
20	Coaching/working with reporters
21	Software for layout/pagination
22	Typography
23	Information graphics/visual editing
24	Use of color
25	Software for graphics/computer photo editing

Figure 2-2
This ranking of skills that copy editors are expected to have comes from a nation-wide survey of newspaper editors. The research was conducted by Ann E. Auman of the University of Hawaii and Betsy Cook Alderman of the University of Tennessee at Chattanooga and was presented at a national convention of journalism and mass communication educators in Washington, D.C.

A survey of 79 magazine editors asked to list the five most important skills or characteristics for entry-level magazine jobs produced the following results. Carolyn Lepre of the University of Tennessee and Glen L. Bleske of California State University, Chico, conducted the 2005 study.

Desired Skill

1. Writing (listed by 84% of the editors)

2. Interpersonal skills (61%)

3. Editing (60%)

4. Reporting (46%)

5. (tie) Proofreading (34%)

5. (tie) Computer skills (34%)

In recent years, the idea of "math phobia" has received much attention. Quite a few people have said they don't understand math, have never understood it and don't really think an understanding of math is essential to their lives. "Grammar phobia" hasn't been discussed as much, but it does exist.

Some native English speakers say they never understood English grammar until they studied the grammar of a different language. Perhaps that is because little can be accomplished in learning a foreign language without careful attention to its grammar rules and conventions. People who grow up in an English-speaking home or country usually learn to write and speak English without giving careful attention to its grammar. Their understanding of grammar just seems to come naturally, although it is accompanied, in many cases, by incorrect usage, colloquialisms and slang. Most people can get by with this casual knowledge of English grammar, relying on "what sounds right," but one who aspires to become a professional communicator needs more specific knowledge.

A professional writer or editor uses language to enhance communication. Journalists and PR practitioners aren't particularly interested in the ability to label the parts of speech or to diagram sentences. But to use grammar, punctuation and words correctly, they need to understand the parts of speech and how sentences are constructed. Trying to get by on what sounds right is insufficient in the professional world.

So put aside your grammar phobia or, at the other extreme, the notion that you already know everything you need to know about English grammar and spend time carefully going through the rest of this chapter. First we'll review the parts of speech, then sentence structure and, finally, information about how to avoid common grammar and usage problems.

Parts of speech

▶**Verbs** give sentences action or tell the state of being. Verbs serve as predicates of sentences. Examples:

> **Run.**   Expresses action. The subject of this sentence—*you*—is understood.
> She **is** the governor.   Expresses state of being or a condition of the subject *she*.

▶**Nouns** name persons, places or things. Examples:

> **John, player, illness, church, students, dog, girl, boy**

▶**Pronouns** take the place of or substitute for nouns. Examples:

> **he, she, you, it, me, him, her, my, your,**
> **they, them, their, his, hers our, ours**

▶**Adjectives** describe, qualify or limit (modify) nouns and pronouns.

> Descriptive adjectives:
> **pretty** girl, **great** player, **terminal** illness, **intelligent** students
> Qualifying, limiting adjectives:
> **this** boy, **eight** players, **that** dog

▶**Adverbs** describe or limit (modify) verbs, adjectives or other adverbs.

> run **fast**   Modifies a verb
> **very** pretty girl   Modifies the adjective *pretty*
> run **really** fast   Modifies the adverb *fast*

▶**Prepositions** are words that connect their objects (nouns or pronouns) to another word in the sentence. Examples:

> **of, on, at, by, for, from, in, with, into**
> He ran **to** first base.   *To first base* is a prepositional phrase.
> The dog came **into** my house.   *Into my house* is a prepositional phrase.

▶**Conjunctions** also are linking words, connecting words, phrases and clauses. *Coordinating conjunctions* link elements of equal weight. Examples:

Coordinating conjunctions: **and, but, or, nor, yet, so**

Links words   Links phrases

Mary **and** John went to dinner **and** to a
movie, **but** they didn't enjoy the movie.

Links two equal clauses

Subordinating conjunctions connect elements of unequal weight, such as a clause that can stand alone and make sense and a clause that depends on another clause to give it meaning. Examples:

Subordinating conjunctions:

since, because, although, as, as if, before, when, where

Because they arrived late and missed a key
plot theme, Mary and John didn't enjoy the movie.

The subordinating conjunction—*because*—links the subordinate clause—
because they arrived late and missed a key plot theme—to the clause that can
stand alone—*Mary and John didn't enjoy the movie.*

▶**Interjections** express intense emotion. Interjections stand alone without being attached grammatically to other words. They even have their own punctuation, the *exclamation mark*. Examples:

Good grief! Ouch! Yea!

▶**Verbals** aren't classified as a separate part of speech, but to avoid errors in sentence structure and punctuation, it is important to understand their roles. Verbals are verb forms that lack the power of a verb, so they cannot serve as the predicate of a sentence. Instead, verbals act as nouns, adjectives or adverbs. Three categories of verbals are **gerunds** (used as nouns), **participles** (used as adjectives) and **infinitives** (used as either nouns, adjectives or adverbs).

Gerunds, also called **verbal nouns,** usually end in *-ing* and are used as subjects or objects. Examples:

Running is his favorite sport.

Verb form *running* acts as a noun and is the subject of the sentence.

His favorite sport is **running.**

Running completes the state of being verb *is* and refers to *sport.*

Running is used in the sentence as a predicate noun.

He has won many awards for **running.**

The gerund *running* is used here as the object of the preposition *for.*

Participles are verb forms that end in *-ing* or *-ed* and act in sentences as adjectives; that is, they modify nouns or pronouns. Examples:

Thrusting his arms into the air, John
crossed the finish line in first place.

The participle *thrusting* describes John. The subject and verb in the sentence is *John crossed.*

John received a medal **designed** in the style of Olympic medals.

The participle *designed* describes the noun *medal.*

Infinitives are composed of the word *to* plus a verb and may be used as nouns, adjectives or adverbs. Examples:

> **To win** the national championship was John's goal.
>> Infinitive as a noun, subject of the sentence
>
> This victory was the best way **to end** John's running career.
>> Infinitive used as an adjective modifying the noun *way*
>
> John's teammates were happy **to see** him achieve his goal.
>> Infinitive used as an adverb modifying the adjective *happy,*
>> which completes the linking verb and describes *teammates*

Workbook Exercise 1 for Chapter 2 tests your understanding of parts of speech.

Sentence structure

With an understanding of the parts of speech, let's look at how the parts of speech go together to form phrases, clauses and sentences.

▶A **phrase** is a group of related words without a subject and verb. Examples:

> to first base, around the world

▶A **clause** is a group of related words containing a subject and a verb (predicate of the clause). Examples:

> Subject Verb
>
> He ran .
>> The pronoun *he* is the subject; *ran* is the verb to form a clause.
>
> The boat **sailed** around the world.
>> Clause with a subject, verb and prepositional phrase

An **independent** clause can stand alone; it is a complete sentence. A **dependent clause** (also called a **subordinate clause**) has a subject and verb but depends on an independent clause for its meaning, so it cannot stand alone as a sentence. Examples:

> He ran .   Independent clause; can stand alone
>
> Because he **wanted** to win the race,
>> Dependent clause; needs an independent clause to complete its meaning
>
> he ran his fastest time ever.
>> Independent clause completing the meaning of the dependent clause

Dependent clauses can act as nouns, adjectives and adverbs in a sentence. Examples:

> Subject   Verb
>
> That the movie **ranked** No. 1 at the box office last week
> didn't impress John and Mary.
>> Dependent clause used as a noun; the entire clause is the subject of the sentence.

Noun clauses can do anything that nouns can do, serving as subjects or objects.

> The movie, which cost more to produce than any other movie in
> history , is filled with high-tech special effects.
>> Dependent clause used as an adjective modifying *movie*

The dependent clause in the previous example is a *nonessential* or *nonrestrictive clause* because it could be omitted from the sentence. For that reason, it is set off by commas.

> `After Hollywood celebrities gathered for a gala premiere ,`
> `the movie opened nationwide the following day.`
>> Dependent clause used as an adverb

Adverb clauses give information about the sentence's main verb (called the **predicate** of the sentence): when, where, why, under what conditions.

Understanding the various ways that clauses can be combined to form sentences will lead to correct usage and punctuation. Look at the four classifications of sentences.

▶ **Simple sentences** have one independent clause. Example:

Simple sentences may have compound subjects or compound predicates or both and may have modifiers, but they are still classified as simple sentences provided they have only one independent clause. Here is an example of a simple sentence with a compound subject and compound verb.

▶ **Compound sentences** have two or more independent clauses.

> `John Washington won the race , and Harry Markham placed second .`
>> Independent clause linked by a comma and a coordinating
>> conjunction to second independent clause
>
> `John Washington won the 100-meter race , and Harry Markham placed`
> `second , but it was not enough points for the team championship .`
>> Three independent clauses

A semicolon can be used in place of the comma and coordinating conjunction.

▶ **Complex sentences** have at least one independent (main) clause and at least one dependent (subordinate) clause.

> `If another team runner had scored points in the 100-meter race ,`
> `the team would have taken home the championship.`
>> The first clause, introduced by the subordinating conjunction *if,* is the dependent clause; it
>> cannot stand on its own without the information in the second clause—the independent
>> clause—to complete its meaning.
>
> `The team took home second-place honors in the national`
> `championship track meet because John and Harry placed first`
> `and second in the 100-meter race .`
>> The main clause comes first in this example, followed by the dependent clause.

Look back at the "parts of speech" section to review the list of subordinating conjunctions that commonly introduce dependent clauses. Some pronouns, known as relative *pronouns,* can also introduce dependent clauses. Examples:

```
John Washington, who placed first in
100-meter race, is a national champion.
```
> *Who* is used as a relative pronoun, introducing a dependent clause.
> Commas set off the dependent clause because it is nonessential, meaning
> that it could be omitted and the sentence would still be complete.

▶ **Compound-complex sentences** have at least two independent (main) clauses plus at least one dependent clause.

```
The track team was disappointed                Independent clause
because all members had worked hard all season,  Dependent clause
but the coaches congratulated them for the
outstanding effort.                            Independent clause
```

Having the ability to analyze sentences helps writers and editors avoid sentence fragments and run-on sentences. A *sentence fragment* is an incomplete sentence. It may have a dependent clause or a group of related words, but it lacks an independent clause. Examples:

```
Although they won first and second place.
```
> A dependent clause that cannot stand alone

```
Running as fast as possible
```
> A gerund and two prepositional phrases

```
Because he was the national champion,
```
> Another dependent clause without a main clause to complete the thought

A run-on sentence is composed of more than one main clause without proper punctuation or linking conjunctions. Example:

```
They won the final race, another team won the championship.
```
> Two main clauses run together with no conjunction or semicolon

The previous example is called a comma splice. A comma is not enough to link the two main clauses. A conjunction is needed in addition to a comma.

```
They won the final race, but another team won the championship.
```
> The combination of a comma and the coordinating conjunction *but* makes this a good
> sentence.

A semicolon could connect the two main clauses in place of the comma and the conjunction.

Now that the parts of speech and sentence structure have been explained, the next section of this chapter discusses some grammar and usage problems that editors frequently encounter.

Workbook Exercises 2 and 3 for Chapter 2 will test your understanding of sentence structure.

Common pitfalls in grammar and usage

English is not a simple language. Even some professional communicators have never mastered it, making frequent mistakes in grammar, punctuation, spelling, word usage and style. Some common pitfalls are listed and explained in the following pages.

The items are numbered for reference so you and your instructor can refer to each item as you work on the workbook exercises at the back of this textbook.

Subject and verb agreement

The basic rule is that the subject and predicate (or main verb) must agree in number. To apply this rule, first determine the subject of the clause, then determine whether the subject has a singular or plural meaning. Here are some rules concerning subject-verb agreement:

▶**1.** When two or more subjects are connected by the conjunction *and,* use a plural verb:

> An introvert and an extrovert rarely **make** good partners.

Use a singular verb, however, when two parts of a compound subject refer to a single person or thing:

> His friend and partner *(refer to same person)* **is** very patient.

▶**2.** A noun or pronoun subject is not part of a compound subject when joined by phrases that act as prepositions rather than conjunctions. Examples of such phrases are *along with, together with, accompanied by, as well as, including, in addition to* and *no less than.* Identify the subject and then apply the basic rule that the subject and predicate must agree in number:

> John, as well as Jim, **is** going to play on the team.
> The order form, in addition to a money order, **is** required.
> Mary, together with her mother, **is** on the guest list.

▶**3.** When two or more subjects are joined by *or* or *nor,* the verb should agree with the nearest subject:

> Mary or her sisters **are** going to keep the appointment.
> Mary or her sister **is** going to keep the appointment.
> Neither John nor his children **are** required to attend.
> Neither John nor his son **is** going fishing today.

If both subjects are singular, the verb is singular:

> Either Jim or Jack **is** to be at the stadium by 1 p.m.

If both subjects are plural, the verb is plural:

> Neither the boys nor the girls **are** doing well on the agility test.

▶**4.** Don't let words before or between the subject and the verb mislead you. First find the subject of the sentence and then make its predicate agree:

> The last two innings of the game **were** dull.

In this sentence, the prepositional phrase *of the game* comes between the plural subject *innings* and the predicate *were.*

▶**5.** A prepositional phrase between fractions and percentages used as subjects does influence the verb:

> Three-fourths of the students **are** prepared for college.
> Three-fourths of a cup of water **is** needed in the recipe.

If the object of the preposition is a collective noun, follow the principle stated in Rule 7. If the fractional part of the collective is in agreement, use a singular verb.

> One-half of the team **favors** John as captain.

Professional perspective: Edgar Miller

Rule or myth?

Ill-informed English teachers and others have perpetuated the myth that starting a new sentence with a coordinating conjunction—like *and* and *but*—is not acceptable in "proper" English. They are wrong, totally wrong. I would like to lay this idea to rest in your minds, once and for all, so I have done a little research to see what the authorities say about it.

Edgar Miller worked for decades as a newspaper reporter, editor and foreign correspondent. After retiring from United Press International, he edited a magazine in Knoxville, Tennessee, and taught at the University of Tennessee.

■   The Oxford English Dictionary, the ultimate authority on the English language, offers this in its definitions of *and*: "11. Continuing the narration: a. from a previous sentence, expressed or understood. b. from the implied assent to a previous question or opinion." And it says that *but* may be used to introduce "an independent sentence connected in sense, though not in form, with the preceding."

■   The Harbrace Handbook, the bible of many college English departments, says in the 13th edition section 12b: "(3) Begin with a sentence connective—a coordinating conjunction, a conjunctive adverb or a transitional expression." As an example, it gives "Many restaurants close within a few years of opening. But others, which offer good food at reasonable prices, become well established."

Here is what other authorities have to say on the question:

■   "It is a rank superstition that this coordinating conjunction cannot properly begin a sentence. The very best writers find occasion to begin sentences with *and*."

—Bryan Garner, *The Oxford Dictionary of American Usage and Style*

■   "If in the miscellaneous list of good openings for sentences *and* and *but* have been omitted, it is because they deserve special comment. Both have suffered from ignorant prohibition, though it is plain from American and English literature that the most exacting writers use them without hesitation as normal openers."

—Jacques Barzun, *Simple and Direct: A Rhetoric for Writers*

■   "Many of us were taught that no sentence should begin with *but*. If that's what you learned, unlearn it—there is no stronger word at the start. It announces total contrast with what has gone before, and the reader is primed for the change.

—William Zinsser, *On Writing Well*

In general, the same would apply to the other coordinating conjunctions: *or, for, nor, so* and *yet*. I could find no authority that defended the prohibition against starting a sentence with coordinating conjunctions, provided they are used properly and are not overused.

If the fractional part is in disagreement and not working in unity, use a plural verb.

```
One-half of the team are divided
between Bob and Sam as team captain.
```

A way around this unnatural-sounding verb choice is to add the word *members*.

```
One-half of the team members are divided
about the choice of captain.
```

▶ **6.** These pronouns, when used as a subject, always take singular verbs: *it, each, either, anyone, everyone, much, no one, nothing, someone, such.* For example:

```
Each student has lunch money.
```

```
Everyone has lunch money.
No one has money for lunch.
Much has been written about grammar.
Someone is going to meet us at the airport.
It seems like years since we last met.
```

Pay special attention to the placement of *each* in a sentence. As a subject, it takes a singular verb. But as an adjective in apposition with a plural subject, it needs a plural verb:

```
John and Mary each are scheduled to meet
with the president of the company.
```

▶ **7.** Collective nouns take a singular verb when used in the sense of a single unit operating in agreement but take a plural verb when the collective operates as individual units or in disagreement. These are some collective nouns: *jury, team, army, audience, family, faculty, couple, group, staff, club, class, committee, crowd.* For example:

```
The team is going to compete for the championship.
```

The individuals are working together as a single unit operating in agreement, so you would use a singular verb.

The combination of a plural verb with a singular-sounding noun sounds unnatural, although it is technically correct:

```
The team were arguing about their individual
playing assignments and the selection of a captain.
```

The plural verb is used because the team is in disagreement; the individuals are not working as a unit. To avoid the strange sound, most people would probably write or say "The team members were arguing . . ." or "Members of the team were arguing . . ." Another example:

```
The couple were married yesterday and left on
their honeymoon. They will return home next week.
```

Couple takes a plural verb in this example because the word refers to two people.

```
Each couple is going to buy a ticket.
```

In this example the word *couple* refers to a single unit. Some authorities say to use the singular form if the meaning is "the couple" and the plural form when the meaning is "a couple."

```
The couple is planning to attend the banquet.
```

```
A couple are planning to attend.
```

If the subject of an organization's name is a collective noun, treat it as a collective noun: National Association for the Advancement of Colored People, National Council of Churches, National Organization for Women.

```
The National Organization for Women is meeting here Thursday.
```

But if the subject in the organization's name is in plural form, use the plural form of the verb:

```
The United Chicanos of Alameda County are meeting here today.
```

▶ **8.** *Number, majority* and *total* are singular if preceded by *the* but plural if preceded by *a:*

```
The number of convictions is increasing.
```

```
A number of people were convicted on those charges.
```

> The majority **has** voted for Jones.

> A majority of citizens **agree** that the laws should be enforced.

▶**9.** Deciding whether a collective noun is singular or plural is relatively easy, but no similar rule consistently applies for "noncountable" nouns. Most noncountable nouns end in *s*, which makes them appear to be plural, but they are not all plural.

These noncountable nouns ending in *s* always take singular verbs: *apparatus, aesthetics, athletics, civics, economics, linguistics, mathematics, measles, mumps, news, shambles, summons, whereabouts.* Some other noncountable nouns that take singular verbs are *advice, courage, fun, health, information, jazz* and *remainder.*

These noncountable nouns need a plural verb: *assets, earnings, goods, kudos, manners, odds, pants, proceeds, scissors, shears, tactics, thanks, wages.*

These noncountables are either singular or plural, depending on context: *politics, series, gross, headquarters, statistics, ethics, species.* As a study or a science, *politics, statistics* and *ethics* take singular verbs:

> Statistics **is** a required course for business majors.

> Politics **is** not an exact science.

When in doubt, consult a dictionary to see which words ending in *s* need a singular verb or can be either singular or plural.

Workbook Exercise 4 tests your understanding of subject and verb agreement.

Noun and pronoun agreement

The basic rule concerning noun and pronoun agreement is that pronouns agree with their antecedents in person (first, second, third), number (singular, plural) and gender (masculine, feminine, neuter). Let's consider each idea separately.

▶**10.** Pronouns are substitutes for nouns or other pronouns—their antecedents. Be sure that every pronoun has an antecedent and that, if other nouns or pronouns come between the pronoun and its antecedent, readers are not confused: "John introduced Mary to his mother, whom he planned to marry." In this example, the clause beginning with *whom* is misplaced because John planned to marry Mary, not his mother. The sentence should be written this way:

> John introduced **Mary, whom** he planned to marry, to his mother.

▶**11.** Pronouns should agree with their antecedents in person:

> **I** asked for **my** money.

> **He** asked for **his** money.

▶**12.** Pronouns should agree with their antecedents in number. Singular nouns take singular pronouns (*he, she, it, him, her, his, hers, its*):

> **John** lost **his** books.

> The **woman** said **she** would compete in the race.

Plural nouns take plural pronouns (*they, them, their, we, us, our*):

> The **men** said **they** would go on strike.

> **John and Mary** received **their** new bicycles today.

> The **women** asked that **they** be given equal pay for equal work.

> The Tennessee **Titans** won **their** division.

Pronouns and collective nouns that take singular verbs (see Rules 6, 7 and 8) also take singular pronouns:

> **Tennessee** won **its** division.
>
> The **team** defended **its** championship.
>
> The **National Organization for Women** announced
> **its** position on the proposed legislation.
>
> **Either** of the boys should receive **his** prize.
>
> The **faculty** expressed **its** displeasure with the salary proposal.
>
> **Each** of the girls received **her** invitation in the mail.

The position of *each* in a sentence determines whether a later noun is singular or plural (see the comment about *each* in Rule 6). If *each* is in apposition with a plural subject, the later noun is plural. But if *each* is the subject, the noun should be singular. For example:

> The girls **each** receive **invitations.**
>
> **Each** of the girls receives an **invitation.**

Pronouns and collective nouns that take plural verbs (see Rules 7 and 8) also take plural pronouns:

> **All** of the students have **their** pencils.
>
> A **majority** of voters cast **their** votes for Jones.

▶ **13.** Pronouns should agree with their antecedents in gender. If the antecedent is male, the pronoun should be masculine (*he, him, his*); a feminine pronoun (*she, her, hers*) is used for female antecedents; a neuter pronoun (*it, its*) is used for neuter antecedents.

This rule is straightforward, but problems arise with *either . . . or* and *neither . . . nor* constructions in which one subject is masculine and one is feminine. In that situation, the pronoun should agree with the antecedent that follows *or* or *nor*:

> Neither Mary nor **John** has applied for **his** visa.
>
> Neither John nor **Mary** has applied for **her** visa.

In this example, the plural pronoun *their* would be incorrect because *neither* is singular. However, the phrase *for a visa* would be better in both cases.

Another consideration in choosing pronoun gender is to attempt to avoid sexism in journalistic writing. Traditionally, masculine pronouns have been used to refer to a singular antecedent that included both males and females, but most newspapers now try to avoid sexist terms (as well as racist and ageist terms). One way to avoid excluding women is to use the expressions *he or she* and *his or her*. A better way is to use plural forms and plural pronouns. Compare the following:

> A **journalist** should edit **his or her** copy carefully.
>
> **Journalists** should edit **their** copy carefully.

Reflexive and intensive pronouns

Reflexive and intensive pronouns, the *self* pronouns, are used when a noun acts on itself or when a noun must be emphasized.

▶ **14.** Reflexive pronouns should not be used alone without referring to a noun or pronoun earlier in the sentence:

> The store manager **himself** waited on customers.
>
> I **myself** don't mind working hard.
>
> John injured **himself.**

The following usage is incorrect: "Sarah and myself will work hard"; "He divided the work between John and myself."

Pronoun case

***Case* refers to the use of a pronoun in a sentence. *Nominative case* is used for subjects of sentences and as predicate nominatives. *Objective case* is used for objects,** such as direct objects, indirect objects, objects of prepositions, participles, gerunds and infinitives. The objective case is also used as the subject of an infinitive. Possessive case shows ownership.

▶ **15.** Pronouns agree with their antecedents in person (first, second, third), number (singular, plural) and gender (masculine, feminine, neuter), but they take their case from the clause in which they stand.

Figure 2-3 shows the person, number, case and gender of personal pronouns.

Figure 2-3
The choice of personal pronoun depends on the person, number and gender of the antecedent and on the case indicated by the pronoun's position in the clause.

Person	Case		
	Nominative	*Objective*	*Possessive*
SINGULAR			
First	I	me	my, mine
Second	you	you	your, yours
Third: *Masculine*	he	him	his
Feminine	she	her	her, hers
Neuter	it	it	its
PLURAL			
First	we	us	our, ours
Second	you	you	your, yours
Third	they	them	their, theirs

The relative pronoun *who* also has a different form for each case: *Who* is nominative case, *whom* is objective case, *whose* is possessive case.

People have little problem distinguishing the proper case in simple sentences. But as sentence structure becomes more intricate, more effort is required to determine the role of each pronoun in each clause. The relative pronouns *who, whom* and *whose* are generally the most troublesome. In the following example, the relative pronoun is used as the subject of the sentence and thus needs the nominative case:

    Who is coming?

In this example, the object of the preposition takes the objective case:

    To **whom** should we address the letter?

The following example is more complicated:

    He gave advice to **whoever** asked for it.

The subject of the dependent clause is *whoever,* although the entire dependent clause is used as the object of the preposition *to.* Here, again, the nominative case is correct:

    Jones, **who** I always thought was unapproachable, gave me advice.

Who is the subject of the dependent clause *who was unapproachable.*

In this case, *whom* is the object of the preposition:

> We tried to discover to **whom** the gun belonged.

The final example clearly calls for the possessive case:

> **Whose** gun is this?

> **Workbook Exercise 5** tests your understanding of pronoun cases.

▶ **16.** Unlike all other subjects, which are in the nominative case, the subject of an infinitive is in the objective case. Transposing the sentence usually can remove doubt about the correct form. In the first example, the pronoun *him* is the subject of the infinitive *to be:*

> They declared the culprit to be **him.**

If you transpose the sentence, you can clearly see that *him* is the direct object:

> They declared **him** to be the culprit.

▶ **17.** Do not confuse *who's,* the contraction for *who is,* with the possessive form *whose.* The contraction for *it is* is *it's;* the possessive form is *its.* For example:

> **Who's** going to ride in our car? **Whose** book is this?
>
> **It's** unusually warm today. The dog lost **its** collar.

An analysis of how the relative pronoun is used is the best way to determine the correct case. However, you can also try substituting *he* for *who* and *him* for *whom* to see whether the substitute sounds right. With intricate sentences, this system is not foolproof.

> **Workbook Exercise 6** tests your understanding of noun-pronoun agreement and pronoun case.

Essential and nonessential clauses

Both *that* and *which* are relative pronouns used to introduce clauses that refer to an inanimate object or an animal without a name. The use of *that* or *which* depends on whether an essential or a nonessential clause is being introduced.

A *nonessential clause* gives additional information about the noun or pronoun it modifies. Because a nonessential clause could be eliminated from the sentence without altering its meaning, the clause is set off with commas.

An *essential clause,* on the other hand, is necessary because it gives the sentence the intended meaning; thus, it is not set off from the rest of the sentence.

▶ **18.** *That* should be used to introduce an essential clause; *which* is correct for nonessential clauses. In the following example, the clause is essential because it restricts or identifies the car:

> This is the car **that** won the race.

The meaning of the sentence would be incomplete and unclear if the essential clause were omitted.

In the next example, the clause adds nonessential information:

> John Smith's 2003 Ford, **which** won the race last weekend, is for sale.

The car that is for sale is sufficiently identified or restricted by the modifiers *John Smith's 2003 Ford.*

Compare how the use of *that* and *which* affects the meaning of the sentences in the next three examples:

```
Leave the package on Cherry Street at the
house that has a white mailbox.
```

You can expect to find only one house on Cherry Street with a white mailbox because the dependent clause is not set off with commas. The next example assumes that at least three Cherry Street houses have white mailboxes, so you need to bypass the first two and leave the package at the third one with a white mailbox.

```
Leave the package on Cherry Street at the
third house that has a white mailbox.
```

In the next example, the house is restricted to the *third* house. And as additional but nonessential information, we're told that third house has a white mailbox.

```
Leave the package on Cherry Street at the third house,
which has a white mailbox.
```

Note that commas set off nonessential clauses from the rest of the sentence.

Workbook Exercise 7 tests your understanding of essential and nonessential clauses.

Possessive nouns

The possessive form of a noun is used to show ownership.

▶**19.** Most nouns form their possessive by adding an *'s* to the singular form:

```
girl's book, John's glove, horse's saddle
```

▶**20.** If a noun ends in an *s* sound and is followed by a word that begins with *s*, form the possessive by adding an apostrophe alone:

```
for appearance' sake        for conscience' sake
```

▶**21.** If the singular form ends in *s*, add *'s* unless the next word begins with *s*, in which case just add an apostrophe to the singular form:

```
the hostess's invitation, the hostess' standards,
the witness's testimony, the witness' story
```

▶**22.** To form the plural possessive, first make the noun plural; then add an *'s* if the plural noun does not end in *s*:

```
woman  Singular      women  Plural      women's  Plural possessive
```

▶**23.** If the plural form ends in *s*, add only an apostrophe:

```
boy  Singular        boys  Plural        boys'  Plural possessive
```

▶**24.** For compound words, add an *'s* to the word closest to the object possessed:

```
the major general's decision     Singular
the major generals' decisions    Plural
```

▶**25.** To show that two people own something jointly, use a possessive form after only the last word. If the objects are individually owned, use a possessive form after both nouns:

> **John and Mary's** home   Joint ownership
>
> **John's** and **Mary's** projects   Individual ownership

▶**26.** For descriptive phrases, no apostrophe is needed for a word ending in *s*. To determine whether the word or phrase is used in a descriptive sense, try using *for* or *by* rather than *of*. The following is correct:

> New York Yankees pitcher

In this case, the phrase *New York Yankees* is descriptive, meaning that the person is a pitcher *for* the New York Yankees.

▶**27.** Use *'s* for a plural word that does not end in *s*:

> **women's** hospital, **men's** team

▶**28.** For corporations or organizations with a descriptive word in their name, use the form that the group uses:

> **Writer's** Digest, the **Veterans** Administration, **Diners** Club

Journalistic style cautions against excessive personalization of inanimate objects. Often a phrase referring to an inanimate object is clearer if an *of* construction is used rather than a possessive form:

> mathematics' rules, the rules of mathematics

Personal pronouns and relative pronouns have separate forms for the possessive and do not need an apostrophe: *my, mine, our, ours, your, yours, his, her, hers, its, theirs, whose.* The exception is *one's,* the possessive form for *one*.

Workbook Exercise 8 for Chapter 2 tests your understanding of plurals and possessives.

Sequence of tenses

The tense of a verb describes the time of the action. News writing commonly uses past tense to report what has already happened. But confusion about the proper verb tense often arises when journalists paraphrase and attribute information.

▶**29.** The basic rule is to select the verb tense that describes the time of the action and to stick with that tense unless a shift is needed to show a change in time. Do not shift tenses unnecessarily. In this example, all actions are in the past tense:

> The Senate **passed** the tax bill, **defeated** the food
> stamp proposal and **sent** the defense measure back to
> the appropriations committee.

Now let's shift the tense from past to past perfect to indicate that the House action took place before the Senate action:

> The Senate **defeated** the food stamp proposal,
> which **had been approved** by the House of Representatives.

A shift from past to future tense again indicates different timing of the action:

> The Senate **sent** the defense measure back
> to the committee, where it **will be amended.**

▶**30.** Grammarians agree on the basic rules for consistency in verb tenses, but neither grammarians nor newspaper editors agree on the importance of a rule governing the sequence of tenses in reported speech. That rule states that when reported speech is used, the verb of attribution governs subsequent verbs in the sentence.

Journalistic work often involves reporting what has happened in the recent past and what sources have said, so journalists commonly use reported speech, which can be distinguished from direct speech and parenthetical speech:

> "I **disagree** with the mayor's policies, but I
> **don't confront** him about them," Jim said.   Direct speech
>
> Jim **disagrees** with the mayor's policies,
> he said, but he **doesn't confront** him.   Parenthetical speech

Note that in parenthetical speech the quote is paraphrased and the attribution is in the middle of the paraphrase. In reported speech, in contrast, attribution is at the beginning of the sentence:

> Jim **said** he **disagreed** with the mayor's policies,
> but he **didn't confront** the mayor about them.   Reported speech

In this example, the verb of attribution is in the past tense, so other verbs are in the past tense as well.

It can be argued convincingly that reported speech confuses readers. Does Jim still disagree with the mayor, or is the disagreement a thing of the past? Strict proponents of following the sequence of tenses in reported speech can argue that the job of the newspaper is to report what the source said at the time the reporter received the information ("Jim disagrees with the mayor") rather than being concerned about whether the source changed his mind between the time he said it and the time the article was published. Of course, one way to avoid the problem is to use a present-tense verb of attribution ("Jim *says* he disagrees"), but typical usage in news stories calls for past-tense attribution.

The rule for sequence of tenses in reported speech requires that the verb used in direct speech should be changed one degree: from present to past (*disagrees* to *disagreed*), from past to past perfect (*disagreed* to *had disagreed*), from future to future perfect (*will disagree* to *would disagree*).

Some grammar books omit entirely the sequence-of-tenses rule for reported speech, and many editors pay no attention to it. Other editors are rigid in their adherence to the rule. The late Theodore M. Bernstein, for many years a wordsmith at The New York Times, devoted six pages to an explanation of sequence of tenses in his book "Watch Your Language." He ended his discussion with this suggestion: "Normal sequence of tenses is desirable except when it produces obscurity or ambiguity." So even Bernstein, who stood firmly by the rules of sequence of tenses for reported speech, would allow a variation for perpetual truths, referred to as "exceptional sequence." Thus, this sentence would be correct:

> She **said** that the Earth **revolves** around the sun.

Irregular verb forms

Irregular verbs change the middle of the word to create the past tense instead of adding *ed, t* or *en* at the end, as is the pattern for regular verbs.

▶ **31.** Check a dictionary when you are uncertain about forming the past and past participle forms of a verb. These are the principal parts (present, past, past participle) for frequently misused irregular verbs:

awake, awoke, awakened

be (am, is, are), was (were), been

bear, bore, born

bite, bit, bitten

broadcast, broadcast, broadcast

burst, burst, burst

catch, caught, caught

cling, clung, clung

do, did, done

drink, drank, drunk

drive, drove, driven

drown, drowned, drowned

eat, ate, eaten

find, found, found

fly, flew, flown

fly, flied, flied *(for a baseball)*

forsake, forsook, forsaken

get, got, got (gotten)

go, went, gone

hang, hanged, hanged *(as in "execute someone")*

hang, hung, hung *(as in "hang a picture")*

hide, hid, hidden

hit, hit, hit

know, knew, known

lay, laid, laid *(transitive verb meaning "to place")*

lead, led, led

leave, left, left

lie, lay, lain *(intransitive verb meaning "to recline")*

mean, meant, meant

pay, paid, paid

ring, rang, rung

rise, rose, risen *(not to be confused with transitive verb* raise*)*

say, said, said

set, set, set *(transitive verb meaning "to place")*

shake, shook, shaken

shine, shone, shone

show, showed, showed (shown)

shrink, shrank, shrunk

sit, sat, sat *(intransitive verb)*

spring, sprang, sprung

steal, stole, stolen

strive, strove, striven

swear, swore, sworn

swim, swam, swum

swing, swung, swung

tear, tore, torn

weave, wove, woven

wring, wrung, wrung

write, wrote, written

Pay particular attention to the correct meanings and principal parts of *lie/lay*, *sit/set* and *rise/raise*. Lie and lay are particularly troublesome because the past tense of *lie* is the same as the present tense of *lay*. *Set*, *lay* and *raise* are transitive verbs and need direct objects. Here are examples of correct usage:

Please **sit** here.	No direct object
Please **set** the book here.	*Book* is direct object..
Lie on the sofa.	No direct object
Lay the baby on the sofa.	*Baby* is direct object.
She **lay** on the sofa.	Past tense of *lie*
She **laid** the baby on the sofa.	Past tense of *lay*

Workbook Exercise 9 for Chapter 2 tests your understanding of troublesome verb tenses.

Subjunctive mood

Grammarians today disagree on the relevance of the subjunctive mood. Some usage experts argue that the subjunctive mood is dead or is dying and has little practical use. Other grammarians say that the subjunctive mood is alive and necessary.

▶ **32.** Use the subjunctive mood to express a condition that is either contrary to fact or is purely hypothetical:

If I **were** president of the company, I would give
workers a salary increase.

Were is used instead of *was* because the condition is contrary to fact; I am not president of the company.

Except for forms of *to be,* the present tense of the subjunctive mood is the infinitive without the *to.* That verb form is the same as the indicative mood for the first and second persons but not for the third-person singular:

Indicative	**Subjunctive**
I run	*I run*
you run	*you run*
she runs	*she run*

```
If Jennifer were in shape to run faster, the coach would
not have asked that I run the final leg of the relay.
```

Misplaced and dangling modifiers

Modifiers, used to make writing more descriptive and interesting, should refer clearly and logically to some specific word in the sentence. Modifiers that aren't attached grammatically are called "misplaced" or "dangling" modifiers. They can bring a humorous picture to mind, as in this example:

```
Running down the road, my nose got cold.
```

You have a couple of options for correcting this dangler:

```
Running down the road, I felt my nose getting cold.

As I ran down the road, my nose got cold.
```

▶ **33.** Modifiers must be attached grammatically to the word they modify to avoid reader confusion. Consider this sentence: "*To grow strong, good diet is important.*" What is to grow strong? Not the diet. The infinitive phrase has no word to modify in this sentence. Give it a logical noun or pronoun to modify:

```
To grow strong, children need a good diet.
```

Prepositional phrases often cause problems when misplaced or left dangling. Here's an example of the problem: "*As a member of Congress,* I want to get your views on alleged ethics violations by some of your colleagues." The reporter is not a member of Congress. The sentence could be written correctly in several ways. Here are two:

```
Because you are a member of Congress, I want to get your views on
alleged ethics violations by some of your colleagues.

I want to ask you, a member of Congress, about your views on alleged
ethics violations by some of your colleagues.
```

The word *only* as a modifier is frequently misplaced in sentences, leading to ambiguity. An omitted article (*a/an* for indefinite reference, *the* for definite reference) often causes the confusion with *only.* In these examples, the placement of *only* has a considerable effect on the meaning:

```
He gave the hungry children only money.

He gave only the hungry children money.

He gave the hungry children the only money.
```

Double negatives

A negative word is one that expresses the idea of *no*. The rule prohibiting the use of double negatives—two negative words in a row—has been drilled into us since elementary school. It is so fundamental that the Associated Press Stylebook and Libel Manual does not even include it.

▶ **34.** Avoid double negatives. "He *don't* know *nothing*" is a construction that no journalist would use. Still, a double negative sometimes slips past, particularly in long sentences and especially when the adverbs *hardly, rarely* and *scarcely* are used. Consider the following pairs of examples:

> She **never hardly** studies.
>
> She **hardly ever** studies.
>
> The store **doesn't** have **but** one brand.
>
> The store **has but** one brand.

But, when used as an adverb, is also a negative.

Negative adjectives (those with the prefixes *im, in, ir, non* and *un*) may be used with negative adverbs. Therefore, the following are correct:

> It is **not impermissible** to use negative adjectives
> with negative adverbs.
>
> It is **not incorrect** to say it this way.

Authorities have mixed opinions on usage of the phrase *cannot help but,* as in

> Workers **cannot help but feel** the effect of the wage freeze.

Bernstein, Flesch and the American Heritage Dictionary accept this usage; the Random House Dictionary says it is common usage but frowned on. To avoid the argument, omit *but* and use the present participle:

> Workers **cannot help feeling** the effect of the wage freeze.

Workbook Exercise 10 tests your understanding of misplaced modifiers and double negatives.

Parallel construction

Lack of parallel construction is another common pitfall in writing. Parallelism helps give a sentence balance, rhythm and symmetry.

▶ **35.** Use the same grammatical patterns to express equal ideas in a sentence. Here, along with improved versions, are examples of sentences that hinder understanding because they lack parallel construction. The first set demonstrates that the objects of a preposition should both be either gerunds or nouns:

> Cardiovascular health is promoted by **exercising**
> frequently and a good **diet.**   Not parallel
>
> Cardiovascular health is promoted by frequent
> **exercise** and a good **diet.**   Parallel
>
> Cardiovascular health is promoted by **exercising**
> frequently and **eating** a good diet.   Parallel

Changing the two examples immediately above from passive voice to active voice (discussed later in this chapter) would improve them.

> Frequent exercise and a good diet promote
> cardiovascular health.   Active voice

Don't mix two kinds of verbals:

> Velcro is popular for **fastening** shoes and
> **to keep** compartments in handbags shut.   Not parallel
>
> Velcro is popular for **fastening** shoes and
> **keeping** compartments in handbags shut.   Parallel

In a series, don't mix verbals and nouns:

> He was charged with drunken **driving, carrying** a
> weapon, **resisting** arrest and **possession** of cocaine.   Not parallel

> He was charged with drunken **driving, carrying** a
> weapon, **resisting** arrest and **possessing** cocaine.   Parallel

Not only should be followed by *but also:*

> She **not only** sold some of her possessions, she took a
> second job to earn money to pay the hospital bills.   Not parallel

> She **not only** sold some of her possessions **but also** took
> a second job to earn money to pay the hospital bills.   Parallel

Don't mix nouns and a dependent clause in a series:

> They elected him because of his **knowledge,**
> **honesty** and **because** he was personally appealing.   Not parallel

> They elected him because of his **knowledge,**
> **honesty** and **personal appeal.**   Parallel

Active and Passive Voice

Active voice means that the subject of the sentence performs the action expressed by the verb. The sentence pattern is subject-verb-object.

> Police arrested five suspects.

In passive voice, the subject receives the action expressed by the verb. Verbs in passive voice sentences take the form of a "to be" verb (*am, is, was, were, are, be, being* and *been*) plus a past participle (usually, but not always, ends in *-ed*). As in the following example, the actor in the sentence often becomes the object of the preposition *by.*

> Five suspects were arrested by police.

Active voice makes writing more vigorous and concise than passive voice, which often leads to wordiness through overuse of prepositional phrases. Sentences in active voice are more direct and specific, as shown in these examples.

> There are more suspects expected to be arrested
> by police in the raids.   Passive
> Police expect to arrest more suspects in the raids.   Active

Copy editors should rework sentences beginning with *there* plus a form of a "to be" verb. The *there is* gives no additional meaning to the sentence. To change a passive-voice sentence to active voice, find the person or thing doing the action (usually in a *by the . . .* phrase). Rewrite to make the actor the subject of the sentence and change the verb to the correct form, creating a subject-verb-object sentence structure. If a *by the . . .* phrase is not used in the passive voice sentence, the actor usually is inferred in the context of the paragraph.

> More fatal car crashes are caused by 16-year-old
> drivers than by any other age group, research shows.   Passive

> Sixteen-year-old drivers cause more fatal car
> crashes than any other age group, research shows.   Active

> Research shows that 16-year-old drivers cause
> more fatal car crashes than any other age group.   Active

Avoid shifting from active to passive voice; consistency in voice speeds reading and aids comprehension:

> Congress **passed** the tax-reform legislation,
> but the minimum-wage increase **was defeated.**   Not parallel
>
> Congress **passed** the tax-reform legislation
> but **defeated** the minimum-wage increase.   Parallel

Passive voice is not grammatically incorrect and may be preferred in these instances:

1. When the agent performing the action is obvious or unimportant. The object rather than the actor is emphasized in these examples:

> Nine votes were needed to pass the ordinance.
>
> Retaining walls were built around the perimeter of the property.

2. When the actor is unknown or the writer wants to avoid naming the agent, as in these examples:

> Important documents were missing from the safe.
>
> Mercury and other pollutants had been dumped into the river.

Workbook Exercises 4 through 11 for Chapter 2 will test your understanding of fundamental grammar principles. Unless your instructor directs you otherwise, use the copy editing symbols in the workbook to complete the exercises.

Punctuation

A good copy editor, knowing the purpose for each punctuation mark, never relies simply on "what sounds right." Understanding the rules of punctuation requires a good knowledge of grammar and sentence structure. After studying the grammar section in this chapter and completing the related exercises at the end of the book, you should be ready to review the basic punctuation rules presented here. If you need a more thorough study of punctuation, consult a basic grammar and punctuation book or a reference guide such as the AP stylebook.

Correct punctuation is essential for clarity. Consider the potential for confusion in this sentence:

> Go to the parking lot and get on the second bus
> that displays "stadium" as its destination.

Following those directions, one might walk past many buses before arriving at the second one with the "stadium" designation. Change the punctuation, and it becomes clear that the second bus in the parking lot is the one to board. The information after the comma is simply additional information.

> Go to the parking lot and get on the second bus,
> which displays "stadium" as its destination.

Punctuation in these sentences makes clear how many doctors are in the house:

> The doctor, who is my sister, will see you now.
>   Only one doctor who happens to be my sister
>
> The doctor who is my sister will see you now.
>   More than one doctor; one of them is my sister

The most common punctuation marks are the ampersand, apostrophe, colon, comma, dash, exclamation point, hyphen, parentheses, period, question mark, quotation marks and semicolon.

▶ **Ampersand.** Do not use the ampersand (&) in place of *and* in body copy or in headlines, except when it is part of a company's formal name.

▶ **Apostrophe.** Use an apostrophe to form the possessive. Refer to Rules 19 through 28 in this chapter for information on using apostrophes to make nouns possessive.

Use an apostrophe to indicate omitted letters in contractions: *I'm, doesn't, rock 'n' roll, it's* (*it is,* not to be confused with the pronoun *its*). Contractions reflect informal speech and should be used only in that context in journalistic writing.

Use an apostrophe to indicate omitted figures: *the celebration of '90, the '20s* (no apostrophe needed before the *s*). Also use an apostrophe to make the plural of a single letter: "She made 3 *A's* and 2 *B's* on her report card," "The Oakland *A's* won the World Series." Do not use an apostrophe with multiletter plurals or with the plurals of numbers: "This is the section for *VIPs,*" "The company ordered new *747s.*"

▶ **Colon.** Use a colon at the end of a sentence to introduce lists, tabulations or texts: "These bills passed during the legislative session:" (the list follows, often in separate paragraphs, each introduced with a dash, bullet or some other typographical device).

The part of the sentence before the colon should be an independent clause. It is incorrect to use a colon after a *to be* verb or words like *such as* or *including.* Avoid this use of the colon: "The items stolen were: a television set, ring and watch." The word after a colon should *not* be capitalized unless it is a proper noun or the beginning of a complete sentence: "The police report listed these stolen items: a television set, ring and watch." But: "She told her students this: If you work hard, you will succeed in this class." Use a colon to introduce a direct quotation of more than one sentence that remains in one paragraph:

```
The coach said in his resignation letter: "It is with
regret that I leave this university. We've had a long,
successful run, and I expect that my successor will
maintain the winning tradition of this great institution.
It's time for me to turn to other opportunities."
```

When used with quotation marks, a colon goes outside the quotation marks unless it is part of the quotation itself.

Use a colon to introduce a single item for emphasis: "His thoughts were concentrated on one thing: revenge." Use a colon in time designations, except for the even hour: *1:30 a.m., 2:15 p.m.* (but *7 a.m.*).

Use a colon to separate the main title and subtitle of a book or an article, a chapter and verse in the Bible, and sections of statutes: *The Truth Hurts: A Critique of a Defense of Defamation; John 3:16; Tennessee Code 5:2.*

Use a colon in a headline to replace a verb of attribution if the speaker is at the beginning of the headline:

Jones: 'Taxes are too high'

▶ **Comma.** The comma is the most misused mark of punctuation, probably because of its frequency.

Use commas to separate the elements in a series. But note that news-service practice, observed on most U.S. newspapers, omits the comma before the conjunction in a simple series:

```
She ordered a hamburger, fries and orange juice.
```

But use a comma before the conjunction in a series if an integral element of the series requires a conjunction:

> She ordered orange juice, toast, and ham and eggs.
>
> Today's copy editors should be able to write headlines, edit stories quickly and thoroughly, and lay out pages.

Use a comma to separate a series of equal adjectives. If the adjectives can be separated by *and* without changing the sense, they are equal:

> an old, bent tree; a slow, deliberate manner.

Use commas to set off nonessential phrases and clauses:

> His mother, on the other hand, lived in New York City.
>   Nonessential phrase
>
> His mother, who is an artist, lives in New York City.
>   Nonessential clause

Nonessential phrases include such items as hometowns, ages and political affiliation. All should be set off with commas.

Use a comma to set off a dependent clause that introduces a sentence:

> Because of his appeal to elderly voters, he was considered a sure bet to win re-election to the Senate.

These examples show how the use of commas with essential and nonessential clauses can affect the meaning of sentences:

> Staff members **who** were required to work on Christmas Day will receive extra pay.

Not all staff members will receive extra pay, so the essential clause restricts the extra pay only to those who were required to work. No commas are used. If the clause were set off with commas, the sentence would mean that all staff members were required to work and all will receive extra pay.

> Staff members **who** have children at home refuse to work on Christmas Day.

Not all staff members refuse to work on Christmas, but those with children refuse; thus, the clause is essential and is not set off with commas. The following example specifies or restricts the staff members to those at a particular hospital, so the dependent clause becomes nonessential and is set off with commas.

> Children's Hospital staff members, **who** have children of their own at home, want to be with their patients on Christmas Day.

Without the commas in the previous example, the sentence would be changed to mean that staff members with children want to be with their patients. The assumption might be that staff members without children of their own do not want to be with their patients on Christmas.

Use a comma to set off a long introductory phrase. But no comma is needed after a short introductory phrase unless its omission would slow comprehension:

> In the morning she will feed her cats.
>
> Across the street, lives my sister.   Comma helps comprehension

Use a comma before the conjunction in a compound sentence:

> The mayor unveiled her plan for redevelopment of a downtown park, but each member of the city council expressed concern about the estimated cost of the project.

Use a comma to set off a direct quotation from its attribution. For quotations that are more than one sentence long within a single paragraph, use a colon to set off the attribution:

```
He said, "Let's go now."

"Let's go now," he said.

He said: "Let's go now. It will be dark soon, and the headlights on
my car are not working properly."
```

A comma setting off attribution after a direct quotation always goes inside the quotation marks.

Commas are not used to set off attribution in paraphrased quotations or partial quotations:

```
He said he wanted to leave immediately.

He said that it was "of utmost importance" that they leave.
```

Use a comma to set off nouns of direct address and *yes* and *no* at the beginning of a sentence:

```
James, please pay attention.

Yes, I will pay the bill.
```

Set off the name of a state if the state name follows a city; separate the names of the city and the state:

```
Nashville, Tenn., is a music-publishing center.
```

Note that newspaper style is to abbreviate state names when they are used with a specific city but not when they stand alone in a sentence:

```
Nashville, Tenn., is a book- and music-publishing center.

Tourism is a major source of state revenue in Tennessee.
```

Use commas to set off conjunctive adverbs:

```
It is essential, therefore, that we pay the bill.
```

News services and most newspapers use commas for figures of 1,000 or more because the comma speeds comprehension. This rule would not apply for figures of more than 1 million or those that are part of a street address, room number, serial number, telephone number or year.

▶**Dash.** Use dashes in a sentence to denote an abrupt change in thought or an emphatic pause: "His selection as chairman—*much to the surprise of the committee*—was based on political favors rather than merit." Also use dashes to set off a list or parenthetical material that contains commas: "The notice listed the qualifications—*80 wpm typing speed, knowledge of computers, good writing skills*—that the successful applicant must have." Use a dash in a headline to replace a verb of attribution if the quotation comes before the name of the speaker:

'Taxes are too high'—Jones

Use a dash before an author's or composer's name at the end of a quotation:

```
"Despite its cost, the children need the school lunch program."
—Mayor Jane Doe
```

Use a dash after the dateline at the beginning of a story:

```
KNOXVILLE, Tenn. (AP)—A $75 million complex opened . . .
```

▶**Exclamation point.** Use an exclamation point after an expression of surprise, incredulity or other strong emotion, but avoid overuse. A comma rather than an exclamation point is used after mild interjections, and mildly exclamatory sentences should end with a period.

When used with quotations, the exclamation point goes inside the quotation marks when it is part of the quoted material:

> "Stop!" he shouted.

The exclamation mark goes outside the quotation marks when it is not part of the quoted material:

> We loved the movie "Pirates of the Caribbean: Dead Man's Chest"!

▶**Hyphen.** One use of hyphens is to join words that form a single idea. Use a hyphen between two or more words that form a compound modifier placed before the word they modify:

> She took a photograph of the **moss-covered** tree.
>
> **Out-of-date** merchandise was on sale.
>
> He is a **part-time** teacher.

To test whether two words form a single idea, try using them individually with the word they modify and see whether the result makes sense. In the first example here, would "moss tree" make sense? Would "covered tree" have the same meaning? No, because the two words need to go together to convey the message of "moss-covered tree." Consider these examples:

> She wore a cheap fur coat.
>> No hyphen. *Cheap* modifies *fur.*
>
> She wore a new, blue coat.
>> *New* and *blue* are equally ranked modifiers of *coat,* so a comma is correct rather than a hyphen.
>
> He looked good in his military-issue coat.
>> The words *military-issue* form a single idea. They are a compound adjective modifying *coat.*

Combinations that are hyphenated before a noun are not hyphenated when they come after the noun.

> He teaches part time.
>> No hyphen; modifier comes after the word it modifies, *teaches*

However, after a form of the verb *to be,* such combinations are generally hyphenated to avoid ambiguity:

> His second novel was **second-rate.**
>
> They are **top-notch.**

Do not use a hyphen after adverbs that end in *ly* or after the adverb *very.*

Some publications use a hyphen to designate dual heritage: *Japanese-American, Mexican-American.* Not all stylebooks agree on this point, however, so follow the style used at the publication where you work. These terms do not refer to dual heritage and are therefore not hyphenated: *Latin American, French Canadian.*

For the use of hyphens in prefixes, consult a dictionary. The general rule is that a hyphen is used if a prefix ends in a vowel and the word that follows begins with the same vowel: *re-elect, pre-election, anti-intellectual, pre-empt, pre-exist.* Use a hyphen to attach a prefix to a proper noun: *anti-American.*

Use a hyphen between numbers that express odds, scores, some fractions and some vote tabulations:

> The odds of her winning are **5-4.**
>
> The Yankees beat Boston **3-2.**
>
> **Two-thirds** of the books were sold.
>
> He won by a **five-vote** margin.

To avoid confusing adjectival forms, the Associated Press style is to use the word *to* for vote totals involving more than 1,000 votes on a side.

> The incumbent mayor won re-election by a vote of **8,479 to 7,020.**

The Associated Press instructs that the word *to* seldom is necessary for odds, but when it appears it should be hyphenated in all constructions:

> **4-to-1** odds   odds of **3-to-2**   The odds were **3-to-2.**

AP uses *to* and hyphens for ratios unless the word *ratio* follows the numbers.

> The ratio of water to sugar is **2-to-1.**
>
> Use a **2-1** ratio of water to sugar.
>> Numbers precede the word *ratio,* so *to* is not used.

Use a hyphen to spell out two-word numbers when the first word ends in *y: forty-five, twenty-two, fifty-one.* The usual newspaper style is to use figures rather than spell out numbers greater than nine, but numbers that begin a sentence should be spelled out.

Two prefixes may be linked to one word by using suspensive hyphenation:

> She accepted the deal on a **one- to three-month** trial basis.
>
> Those selected had a **50- to 90-vote** margin.

▶**Parentheses.** Use parentheses to set off an aside, information that explains or qualifies but is not essential to the sentence. Journalists use parentheses sparingly. The AP stylebook indicates that the temptation to use parentheses is a clue that the sentence is becoming contorted; suggested solutions are to rewrite the sentence or, if the sentence must contain incidental material, to use commas or dashes.

If the material enclosed in parentheses comes at the end of a sentence but the enclosed material is not a complete sentence, put the period outside the closing parenthesis. If the enclosed material is a complete sentence, include the period at the end of the sentence within the closing parenthesis:

> She is an excellent reporter (and a fine writer).
>
> (If you don't know French, you might not like the movie.)

▶**Period.** Use a period at the end of a declarative sentence and at the end of a mildly imperative sentence:

> She is coming to the party.   Declarative
>
> Please come here.   Mildly imperative

Use a period in many abbreviations—B.A. degree; Baton Rouge, La.; U.N. headquarters; U.S. military—and as a decimal point in figures—$1.8 million, 4.6 miles, $3.25.

Periods, like commas, always go inside quotation marks:

> The speaker told the crowd, "Our government should help us."

Three spaced periods are used to form an ellipsis, which is used to indicate the deletion of one or more words in condensing quotations, texts and documents. If an ellipsis comes at the end of a sentence, put the required mark of punctuation—period, question mark or exclamation point—and then a space before typing the ellipsis: "My administration will uphold the law. . . ."

▶**Question mark.** Use a question mark at the end of an interrogative: "Who is responsible for this mess?" Do not use a question mark to indicate the end of indirect questions: "He asked who was responsible for the mess." Question marks go inside or outside quotation marks, depending on the meaning. If the quotation is a question, the question mark is included within the quotation marks. But if the quoted material is not a question, the question mark goes outside the quotation marks:

```
She asked, "Are you ready to go?"
Who wrote "War and Peace"?
```

Do not use a comma before the attribution in a direct quotation if a question mark is needed to end the quoted material:

```
"Are you ready to go?" she asked.
```

▶**Quotation marks.** Surround the exact words of a speaker or writer when reporting them:

```
"I think it is important to finish quickly," Jones said.
```

Running quotations—those that continue for more than one paragraph—should not have a close-quote mark at the end of the first paragraph if the quoted material is a complete sentence. However, open-quote marks are needed at the beginning of the second paragraph to indicate that the quotation is continuing:

```
Jones said, "I think it is important to finish quickly
to make up for unavoidable delays caused by bad weather.

"Our credibility is at stake here because we promised
to have the job finished before July 1."
```

If the first paragraph of a continuing quotation ends with a partial quotation, close-quote marks should be used at the end of the partial quotation and open-quote marks should be used at the beginning of the next paragraph:

```
Jones attributed the delays to "bad weather."

"Our credibility is at stake here because we promised
to have the job finished before July 1."
```

Do not use quotation marks with a question-and-answer format. Each speaker's words should start a new paragraph:

```
Q: Who was responsible?
A: John Smith.
```

Use quotation marks around a word or phrase that is used in an ironic sense or that is unfamiliar on first reference:

```
The "doctor" treated people for two years
before being exposed as a fake.
```

To save space, single quotation marks are used for direct quotations in headlines:

**'I will campaign
for re-election,'
Rep. Jones says**

Use single quotation marks around a quotation within a quotation:

```
She testified, "John never told me
specifically, 'I plan to kill my boss.' "
```

Note that three quotation marks—a single quote and double-quote marks—are used when, as in the last example, two quoted elements end at the same time.

Follow the style used by your publication regarding the use of quotation marks with titles of books, plays, movies, television shows, poems, songs and works of art. Some publications have switched from quotation marks to italics for such titles, as computers allow newspapers and magazines to use italics with relative ease, whereas insertion of italics was more time-consuming with previous typesetting technology.

News-service style is to put quotation marks around the titles of all books, movies, operas, plays, poems, songs, television programs, lectures, speeches and works of art—except for the Bible and books that are primarily catalogs of reference material, including almanacs, directories, dictionaries, encyclopedias, gazetteers, handbooks and similar publications.

The period and comma always go within the close-quote marks. Other punctuation marks go within the quotation marks when they apply to the quoted matter only. They go outside the quotation marks when they apply to the whole sentence.

▶**Semicolon.** In general, use the semicolon to indicate a greater separation of thought and information than a comma can convey but less than the separation that a period implies. In a compound sentence, for example, a comma is insufficient separation between the two independent clauses. A comma and a coordinating conjunction can be used between the two clauses, or a semicolon alone can be used.

```
The city has committed $500,000 to the project,
and private developers will also put money into it.

The city has committed $500,000 to the project;
private developers will also put money into it.

The city has committed $500,000 to the project;
however, private developers will pay most of the cost.
```

Use semicolons to separate elements of a series when individual segments contain material that must also be set off by commas:

```
Club members elected Jane Smith, president;
Robert Blake, vice president; Sam Brown, secretary.
```

Be sparing with semicolons. To many readers, a semicolon signals a difficult passage and becomes a point at which to exit the story. Well-regarded authors have written entire novels without a single semicolon.

Workbook Exercises 12 and 13 for Chapter 2 will test your punctuation skills.

Editing on computers or hard copy?

Few newspaper or online copy editors deal with copy on paper these days, as reporters in the field, freelancers, letter-to-the-editor authors and public relations personnel typically submit material as e-mail attachments or by other electronic means. Some magazine editors and other communicators without daily deadlines prefer hard copies of articles to track fact-checking and editorial changes on paper rather than using a computerized tracking system to move copy through the editing process. Some people feel more confident about catching errors if working from text on paper.

Chapter 1 explained the copy editing process at major newspapers: how copy goes from writers to assigning editors, to copy desk chiefs, to copy editors, back to copy desk chiefs and eventually to design desks for pagination. Typically, the story goes through that process electronically.

As every student today knows, computer access to World Wide Web sites and their billions of pages of research material and interactive search features beats trips to a library. The same computer convenience appeals to copy editors when fact-checking stories. Chapter 4 discusses fact-checking tips and ways to find specialized Web sites and databases quickly and easily. But a couple of other matters need attention before ending this chapter and moving on to Chapter 3 on style and correct language usage.

Is copy editing the same as proofreading? The men and women who sit at copy desks and know everything about some thing and something about everything or where to find out quickly are *copy editors*, not *proofreaders*. Don't call them proof-readers although they may read proof these days in addition to their editing duties. While copy editors help improve and polish writing, devise creative headlines, write photo captions and often lay out pages, the purpose of proofreading is to catch ty-pographical errors. Material edited on paper must be re-keyboarded into printers' typefaces, creating the possibility of typing errors.

An editor works at a networked personal computer. When she finishes editing the story and writing a headline for it, she will insert computer codes that specify the desired type style, size, width and amount of leading for the copy. If the publication is using paste-up to plate for printing, production personnel will paste the computer-generated type into place, according to an editor's layout. Most newspapers and magazines today skip the paste-up stage by paginating pages with computer software so that the copy desk chief reviews the editing and headline and then sends the story electronically to design editors, who will transfer it to a page. Copy editors at some publications decide how each page will look, draw a dummy layout and send the layout to a person skilled with pagination software.

Galley proofs are typeset material before it is placed onto pages. Page proofs are copies of complete pages. Because computerized pagination has replaced the paste-up production method at most communication organizations, page proofs are more common today than long strips of galley proofs. Digital pagination has led also to the disappearance of the official job title of proofreader. Now copy editors often look at pages before press operators take over.

How should page proofs be checked? Whether someone with the job title of proofreader or copy editor performs the task, following are some tips for checking page proofs.

▶**Use appropriate symbols.** Whereas copy typed on paper is double- or triple-spaced, allowing space for editors to make corrections in pencil between the lines of type, proofs have no such extra line spacing, so special proofreading symbols showing corrections must be written in the margins.

▶**Use a proper writing instrument.** When proofing pasted-up pages rather than photocopies of a page, use a special blue pencil that will not appear when the page is photographed. Corrected lines will be substituted for erroneous lines, leaving the rest of the paste-up page intact with blue-penciled proofreading symbols still showing in the page margins. On the other hand, for digital pages, the paginator will print a copy for proofreading or perhaps more than one copy so that several people can proof a page at the same time. The type of pen or pencil for proofreading won't matter in this situation.

▶**Ensure that the body text on the proof is large enough to read easily.** Copy editor bloggers complain about page proofs being too small to read. Popular pagination software such as QuarkXPress® and InDesign® permits reduction of broadsheet pages to typing-paper size. If the body text on such proofs is too small, plead with the paginator to print a larger copy or try enlarging the page with a photocopying machine.

▶**Avoid the impulse to read with eye toward improving writing.** It's too near deadline time for that at the proofreading stage. Time may allow correction only for major errors, especially errors in display type like headlines and other type larger than the size for story text.

▶**Double-check every headline and other display type elements on the page.** Read each line of each headline separately to catch typos, double meanings, juxtapositions of headlines and unrelated photos that might make the publication appear insensitive or stupid.

▶**Check captions.** Are names in captions spelled the same as those in related stories? Make sure captions fit their space, and, if time permits for correcting, double-check whether line spacing appears awkward in captions.

▶**Look carefully at the date and page number.** A publication with yesterday's or last year's date or incorrect page numbers will cause embarrassment and perhaps angry words from a supervisor.

▶**Make sure section-front stories that continue to inside pages have a jump line telling readers where to find the rest of the story.** Then, check to ensure that the rest of the story is indeed on the page indicated.

▶**Check that each story fits its space—not too long or too short.** Extra leading can be used between lines or paragraphs for stories that are only several lines too short. For larger holes in the layout, a second headline deck, a pullout quote within the story, a larger photograph or even another story may be necessary. For stories too long to

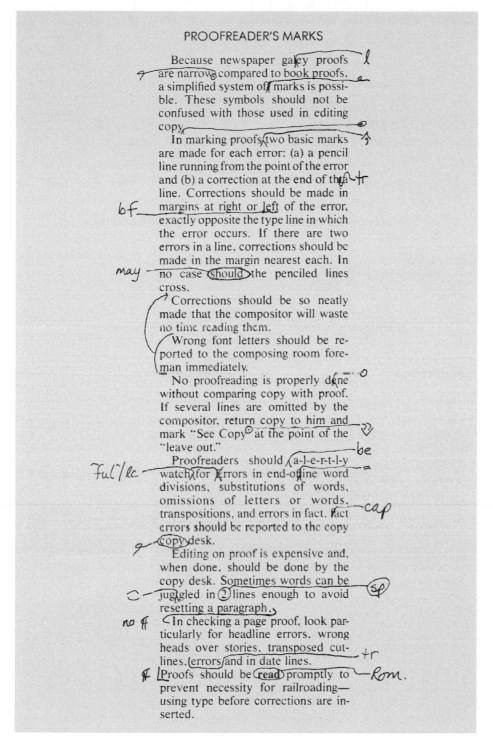

Figure 2-4
Proofreading symbols are written in the margins of typeset copy. This method of proofreading applies to newspapers and magazines. A slightly different approach is used in book publishing.

fit, sentences from the end can be eliminated for stories written in inverted-pyramid style. For other stories, try to find a repetitious quotation or sentences that don't advance the story in significant or interesting ways.

Figure 2-4 shows proofreading symbols. Copy editing symbols are in the workbook section of this textbook, handy for use in completing the exercises found there. Instructors may direct students to complete some or all workbook exercises in pencil on the paper versions. The exercises are available also in electronic format at the Thomson Wadsworth Web site for this textbook.

Suggestions for additional reading

Bernstein, Theodore M. *The Careful Writer: A Modern Guide to English Usage.* New York: Atheneum, 1965.

———. *Watch Your Language.* Great Neck, New York: Channel Press,1958.

———. *More Language That Needs Watching: Second Aid for Writers and Editors, Emanating from the News Room of The New York Times.* Great Neck, New York: Channel Press, 1962.

Brooks, Brian S., James L. Pinson, and Jean Gaddy Wilson. *Working With Words: A Concise Handbook for Media Writers and Editors,* 6th ed. New York: St. Martin's Press, 2006.

Cappon, Rene J. *The Associated Press Guide to Punctuation.* Cambridge, Mass.: Perseus Publishing, 2003.

Darling, Charles. *Guide to Grammar and Writing.* Online. http://grammar.ccc .commnet.edu/grammar.

Glenn, Cheryl, Robert K. Miller, Suzanne Strobeck Webb, and Loretta Gray. *Hodges' Harbrace Handbook,* 15th ed. Belmont, Calif.: Wadsworth, 2004.

Goldstein, Norman (ed.). *The Associated Press Stylebook and Libel Manual.* Reading, Mass.: Addison-Bacon, 1998.

Kessler, Lauren, and Duncan McDonald. *When Words Collide: A Media Writer's Guide to Grammar and Style,* 6th ed. Belmont, Calif.: Wadsworth, 2004.

Strunk, William, and E.B. White. *The Elements of Style,* 4th ed. Allyn & Bacon, 2000. Available online at http://sut1.sut.ac.th/strunk/ and at http://www .bartelby.net/141/.

Truss, Lynn. *Eats, Shoots & Leaves—The Zero Tolerance Approach to Punctuation.* London: Profile Books Ltd., 2003.

Zinsser, William. *On Writing Well,* 30th anniversary ed. New York: HarperCollins, 2006.

> Every misused word revenges itself forever upon a writer's reputation.
>
> —Agnes Repplier

Consistent Style and Correct Words

Consistency and precise word usage are important in communication. Research indicates that readers are irritated when they find, for example, *advisor* in one paragraph and *adviser* in another or *street* spelled out in one address and abbreviated in another. Readers notice when writers and copy editors confuse *effect* with *affect* or write *biannual* when they mean *biennial*.

Readers wonder whether a publication careless about style and proper language usage can be trusted to be accurate and fair about its more substantive content. This chapter will introduce common style conventions used by most U.S. newspapers and for press releases submitted to newspapers. The second half of this chapter will call attention to frequently misused words in written and spoken English.

Consistent style for carefully edited publications

All good publications adopt consistent style policies, and all employees are expected to adhere to that style for material they disseminate to the public. Particular style guidelines that publications use vary with the intended audience and the purpose of the material, but consistency is the primary goal.

Many academic disciplines, businesses and organizations, for example, use the *American Psychological Association Publication Manual.* Book publishers commonly use *The Chicago Manual of Style,* now in its 15th edition and nearly 1,000 pages long. The current style bible for the legal profession is the 17th edition of *The Bluebook: A Uniform System of Citation,* published by the Harvard Law Review Association. College students generally are familiar with Kate Turabian's *A Manual for Writers of Term Papers, Theses, and Dissertations.*

Some journalistic publications compile their own stylebook, but most use the one published by The Associated Press. In addition, newspapers generally develop supplementary style guides to incorporate information particular to their city and state. Besides being a guide for capitalization, abbreviation, punctuation, spelling, numerals and other usage matters, the AP stylebook has evolved into a valuable reference source for its range of general information.

Associated Press style

Journalism and public relations teachers commonly require students to use the AP stylebook for all written assignments. Don't panic, thinking that the book contains too much to ever learn. Although it isn't nearly as long as some of the other style manuals mentioned, not all experienced copy editors have committed the entire volume to memory. But through study and frequent use, they have become thoroughly familiar with all the basic style points.

Time is money in journalism and public relations work, so to save time, writers and editors commit to memory commonly used style matters. In addition, experienced copy editors are familiar with the types of information contained in the stylebook to enable them to find specific facts quickly. They don't waste time consulting a variety of reference books or searching the Internet for information contained in the handy AP stylebook.

▶**Contents of the AP Stylebook.** The stylebook, edited by Norm Goldstein, includes guidelines on spelling, capitalization, grammar, punctuation and usage, with special sections on business and sports. It also outlines some basic principles of media law, with practical guidelines on libel law, privacy, copyright and access to places of information.

Recent editions contain Internet and computer terms to specify consistent capitalization and spelling, such as Web site and e-mail, and correct style for URLs and "cyber-" prefixes. A separate section of the stylebook offers Internet searching tips and cautions.

In addition to the special sections, the stylebook contains individual entries on a wide range of subjects such as geography, religion, governmental agencies and popular culture. A fully searchable Web-based version of the Associated Press Stylebook is available for a $20 annual subscription. AP editors update the online version as needed instead of waiting for new editions of the printed book.

▶**Organization of the stylebook.** Like a dictionary, entries are in alphabetical order. Want to know whether *AAA* is acceptable usage? Look under the *A* entries. Need to know whether *C* or *K* is correct spelling for *Keystone Kops*? Look under the *C* entry, and, not finding it there, go to *K* entries.

Finding some style points, however, requires a bit more thought from users. To learn whether to write *street* or *st.,* for example, sends users to the "abbreviations and acronyms" section. To discover whether quotation marks enclose song titles takes one to the entry for "composition titles." Many entries appear with cross-references to other entries.

One section of the "numerals" entry deals with whether numbers should appear as figures or words, followed by multiple separate entries, including items such as act numbers, court names, earthquakes, highway designations, ratios and spacecraft designations.

It's a good idea to examine the "Stylebook Key," one of the first pages in the book. It shows the format of entries and how boldface and italics are used throughout the book. Users need to be aware that examples of both correct and incorrect style are shown in italic type. Read the accompanying section to avoid confusion. The use of italic type for examples does not mean that those words (newspaper names, for example) should be written in italics.

This chapter focuses on style points that appear in most news stories, press releases and other public relations materials. Reporters and copy editors should memorize these. You should not have to refer to the stylebook each time you encounter these style matters.

Numerals

Consider the following leads from news stories and press releases. What type of information do they have in common?

News story leads:

```
A city council committee approved pay raises of up to 28 percent for
council members and some other elected officials yesterday. Under
the proposal, a council member's base salary would go to $70,000,
from $55,000, and the mayor's salary would rise to $165,000 from
$130,000.
```

Fred Smith, 521 Oak Ave., won the high-point trophy in the Holiday Masters Open Swimming Championships yesterday. The 74-year-old Smith took first place in the 50, 100, 200 and 500 freestyle events and the 50-yard backstroke.

Undefeated Austin-East, down 40-39 at halftime, came back for a 69-63 victory Saturday night over previously unbeaten Chattanooga Brainerd. Andrea Fenderson's 21 points led the way for the 8-0 Roadrunners.

Just nine days before Christmas, fire destroyed a warehouse containing an estimated $1 million worth of goods meant to be distributed by one of the city's largest charities.

More than 100 firefighters battled the blaze Friday night at the four-story building at 4400 Western St. Crews were still pouring water on the persistent flames at noon Saturday, some 17 hours after the fire was first reported.

Press release leads:

Lexus announced today that the RX 350, the top-selling luxury SUV, is now available with a savings of $900 on its most popular option packages. The new RX 350, available as both front-wheel drive (FWD) and all-wheel drive (AWD) models, features a powerful 3.5-liter V6 engine that improves both performance and fuel efficiency.

July is heating up and so is Mega Millions. Friday's Mega Millions drawing produced more than 345,000 winning tickets from coast to coast. That includes five tickets that came within a heartbeat of hitting the jackpot. Since no ticket matched all six numbers to win the $12 million jackpot, the jackpot for the Tuesday, July 25, 2006, drawing grows to an estimated $15 million.

Over 120 Hooters Girls from Taiwan to New York are heading to Las Vegas to compete for $150,000 in cash and prizes at the 10th Annual Hooters International Swimsuit Pageant.

America's favorite talent show, American Idol, is heading to the New Jersey Meadowlands to hold auditions for its upcoming 6th season. The Meadowlands, home to some of the most prominent sports franchises in the region and a major tourism destination, is expected to swell with thousands of people during the days leading up to the August 14th audition.

The common ingredient in these leads is numbers, including numbers used for addresses, ages, dates, distances, dollar amounts, sports scores, telephone numbers, speed and time. Numbers should be used in a consistent pattern throughout a publication. Note that some the press release examples above do not follow AP style, which decreases their chances of being used in the media.

The following lists define some AP stylebook rules regarding the use of numbers. The general rule is to spell out the numbers one through nine; use numerals for 10 and higher: "The couple has four cats and two dogs"; "She needs 10 more tickets to win."

Use numerals for:

- Addresses and streets numbered 10 and higher: *15th Avenue, 12th Street*

- Ages of people and things: *the 8-year-old prodigy, in their 60s, the car was 3 years old*

- Dates and time: *January 1, 2008; 7 p.m.*

- Decimals and percentages: *cost of living rose 5 percent, unemployment down 0.5 percent, $2.5 million*

- Decisions, rulings and votes: *The Supreme Court ruled 5–4*

- Dimensions and measurements: *a 4-foot fence*

- Exact dimensions and measurements: *The star player is 6 feet 4; The puppies each weighed 2 pounds, 5 ounces; The rug is 9 by 12 feet*

- Fractions contained in numbers greater than one: *5 1/2 inches*

- Geographical and political districts: *5th Congressional District*

- Monetary units: *5 cents, $5, $500, $5 million*

- Numerical ranking: *No. 1 choice*

- Recipe amounts: *2 cups of flour*

- Speeds: *5 mph*

- Sports scores, standings and odds: *5–3 victory, 2–1 odds*

- Temperatures except zero: *70 degrees; minus 5 degrees; The temperature stood at zero at midnight*

Use words for:

- Addresses and streets below 10: *Fifth Avenue*

- Distances below 10: *five-mile race*

- Fractions smaller than one: *one-half inch*

- Indefinite or approximate figures: *Thanks a million; We walked about five miles; A thousand times no!*

- Numbers used at the start of a sentence, except for a numeral that identifies a calendar year: *Five hundred people protested; 1990 was a good year*

Abbreviations

Abbreviations are used to save space, especially in headlines, and to improve readability. They should not be overused or used if they are unfamiliar or confusing.

Most all-capital abbreviations are spelled without periods: *FBI, CIA, ABC, AFL-CIO, NASA.* But all-capital abbreviations of places and of the United Nations take periods: *U.S., U.N.* Most other abbreviations take periods: *c.o.d., Inc.* An exception: *55 mph.* Abbreviations should not be used at the beginning of a sentence.

▶**Acronyms.** Acronyms may be used after the first reference if they are well-known. Some commonly used acronyms may be used on first reference: *NASA, radar, NATO, AIDS.* Do not follow an organization's full name with an abbreviation or acronym either in parentheses or set off by dashes. If an abbreviation or acronym would not be clear on second reference without this arrangement, do not use it.

▶**Addresses.** Use the abbreviations *Ave., Blvd.* and *St.* only with numbered addresses: *1600 Pennsylvania Ave.* Spell them out and capitalize when they are part of a formal street name without a number: *Pennsylvania Avenue.* Do not abbreviate *Circle, Court, Drive, Highway, Lane, Road, Place* and so on.

▶**Businesses and organizations.** Abbreviate *Co., Corp., Ltd.* and *Inc.* when used at the end of a business's name: *The New York Times Co.* Spell out *Association, Bureau, Department* and *Division.*

▶**Dates and times.** Abbreviate *Jan., Feb., Aug., Sept., Oct., Nov.* and *Dec.* only when they are used with specific dates: *Jan. 25, 1947.* Spell out *March, April, May, June* and *July. A.D., B.C., a.m.* and *p.m.* take periods; *PDT, MDT, EST* and so on don't.

▶**Military.** Abbreviate military ranks before names on first reference *(Gen. Irene Smith)*; do not use rank after the first reference *(Smith).* Some common abbreviations are *Gen., Col., Maj., Capt., Lt., Sgt.* and *Pfc.* See the complete listing of military ranks in the AP stylebook.

▶**States.** Spell out *United States* when used as a noun; abbreviate *U.S.* as an adjective: "The U.S. plan failed." Most state names are abbreviated when they follow the name of a town or city. The correct abbreviations are as follows:

Ala.	Ga.	Minn.	N.J.	Tenn.
Ariz.	Ill.	Miss.	N.M.	Va.
Ark.	Ind.	Mo.	N.Y.	Vt.
Calif.	Kan.	Mont.	Okla.	Wash.
Colo.	Ky.	N.C.	Ore.	Wis.
Conn.	La.	N.D.	Pa.	W.Va.
D.C.	Mass.	Neb.	R.I.	Wyo.
Del.	Md.	Nev.	S.C.	
Fla.	Mich.	N.H.	S.D.	

Do not abbreviate Alaska, Hawaii, Idaho, Iowa, Maine, Ohio, Texas or Utah. Use two-letter Postal Service abbreviations only with full addresses, including ZIP codes.

▶**Titles.** Abbreviate *Gov., Lt. Gov., Sen., Rep., Dr.* and the *Rev.* before a name on first reference. Do not use titles after the first reference. Do not abbreviate *Attorney general, Controller, Detective, District attorney, Officer, Professor* or *Superintendent.*

▶**Other abbreviations.** *AWOL, GI, POW, SOS* and *TV* are acceptable on first and succeeding references. Do not use periods in plane or ship designations: *USS Enterprise, SST.*

Capitalization

In addition to capitalizing the first word of a sentence, you should capitalize the following:

▶**Academic degrees.** Capitalize the abbreviation for but not the formal names of degrees: *B.A., M.S., Ph.D.,* but *bachelor of arts, master of science, doctorate.* Lowercase general references: *bachelor's degree, master's degree.*

▶**Geography.** Capitalize regions: *West Coast, East Coast, the South, the West, Pacific Coast, the Northwest.*

Capitalize natural features: *Blue Ridge Mountains, Gulf Stream, Continental Divide.* Capitalize popular names of natural features: *Deep South, Bible Belt, Texas Panhandle.* But lowercase plurals and general directions: *western, the coasts, boat on the bay.*

▶**Government.** Capitalize full names and short forms: *the U.S. Postal Service, Postal Service; the Federal Reserve Board, the Fed.* Lowercase general terms: *delayed at customs, the post office.*

Capitalize city as part of a formal name: *Kansas City.* Lowercase city elsewhere: *the city of Seattle, a Missouri city.*

Capitalize formal names of committees: *the Senate Appropriations Committee.* Lowercase informal names of legislative committees and names of subcommittees.

▶**Politics.** Capitalize political organizations or movements: *the Democratic Party, Republicans, Communists.* Lowercase political philosophies: *socialism, communism, democracy.*

▶**Religion** Capitalize all recognized faiths and their members: *Protestants, Catholics, Jewish faith.*

▶**Titles.** Capitalize official titles before names, unless they are simply job descriptions: *Pope John Paul III* (but *the pope*), *Professor Mary Purswell, Officer Jay Brown, engineer Mary Jones, coach Barb Smith.*

▶**Trade names.** Capitalize trade names when their use is necessary: *Kleenex, Jell-O, Band-Aid.* Generic references are preferred: *tissue, gelatin, bandage.*

▶**Other capitalization.** Capitalize the names of official and historical documents, doctrines, legal codes and laws. Capitalize designating terms before figures and letters: *Room 222, Section 8, Title 9, Channel 60.* Lowercase the seasons: *winter, spring, summer, fall.* Lowercase academic departments unless they are proper nouns or adjectives: *journalism department, department of journalism; English department, department of English.*

Time

- A specific time should precede the day, and the day should precede the place: "The production will begin at 8 p.m. Friday at the Opera House."

- Use *noon* and *midnight*, not *12 a.m.* and *12 p.m.*

- Avoid redundancies: *5 p.m. tomorrow,* not *5 p.m. tomorrow night.*

- Use *today, this morning, tomorrow* and the like as appropriate. Use the day of the week elsewhere. Use *Monday, Tuesday* and so on for days of the week within seven days before or after the current date. Use the month and a figure for dates beyond this range. Avoid redundancies such as *last Thursday* or *next Friday;* the verb tense should denote usage. *The event was Tuesday. The event will be Tuesday.* Always spell out days of the week.

- Use an apostrophe for omitted figures in years: *events of '07.*

- Use figures for decades, with an apostrophe for omitted figures: *the 1990s, the '90s.*

- Lowercase the word *century* and spell out century numbers below 10: *the third century, the 21st century.*

Cities and datelines

The general rule is that names of towns and cities in the United States should be followed by the abbreviation of the state: Norman, Okla.; Salem, Ore. Exceptions are the names of states that should never be abbreviated: Alaska, Hawaii, Idaho, Iowa, Maine, Ohio, Texas and Utah. Thus, cities and towns in those states are followed by the unabbreviated name of the state: Athens, Ohio; Austin, Texas; Provo, Utah; Bangor, Maine.

Cities and towns in the state in which a newspaper is published generally stand alone. For example, a newspaper published in Tennessee would not follow the name of a city within Tennessee with the abbreviation Tenn.: Morristown, Franklin, Chattanooga. If, however, it is not clear from the context of the story that a home state city is meant instead of an out-of-state city with the same name, then use the name of the state: Athens, Tenn. (to distinguish from Athens, Ohio, or Athens, Ga.).

Another exception to the general rule is the list of cities designated by the Associated Press as standing alone without the name of the state. Generally, these are large cities that appear frequently in the news and are not likely to be confused by readers. They are capitalized here as in a dateline. The following are the U.S. cities that can stand alone:

ATLANTA	HOUSTON	PHILADELPHIA
BALTIMORE	INDIANAPOLIS	PHOENIX
BOSTON	LAS VEGAS	PITTSBURGH
CHICAGO	LOS ANGELES	ST. LOUIS
CINCINNATI	MIAMI	SALT LAKE CITY
CLEVELAND	MILWAUKEE	SAN ANTONIO
DALLAS	MINNEAPOLIS	SAN DIEGO
DENVER	NEW ORLEANS	SAN FRANCISCO
DETROIT	NEW YORK	SEATTLE
HONOLULU	OKLAHOMA CITY	WASHINGTON

These international cities stand alone:

BEIJING	KUWAIT CITY	OTTAWA
BERLIN	LONDON	PARIS
DJIBOUTI	LUXEMBOURG	QUEBEC CITY
GENEVA	MACAU	ROME
GIBRALTAR	MEXICO CITY	SAN MARINO
GUATEMALA CITY	MONACO	SINGAPORE
HAVANA	MONTREAL	TOKYO
HONG KONG	MOSCOW	TORONTO
JERUSALEM	NEW DELHI	VATICAN CITY

Stories that do not originate locally should have a dateline at the beginning. A dateline should contain a city name, entirely in capital letters, followed in most cases by the name of the state, country or territory in which the city is located. The style at many newspapers is to follow the dateline with the abbreviation of the news service in parentheses, followed by a dash and then the lead paragraph of the story.

```
TULSA, Okla. (AP) -- Heavy winds and rain . . .

WASHINGTON (AP) -- The cost of living rose . . .
```

See the "dateline entry" in the AP stylebook for the correct style for island nations, territories and overseas territories. It includes information about date selection and how to cite other cities within the body of a datelined story.

Other style issues

In addition to knowing correct style for numerals, abbreviations, capitalization, time, cities and datelines, copy editors must know correct style for the following:

▶**Long titles.** Avoid their use before a name. Use *John Jones, assistant undersecretary for the interior,* rather than *Assistant Undersecretary for the Interior John Jones.*

▶**Time zones.** Capitalize the names of time zones in formal usage: *Eastern Standard Time, Pacific Daylight Time, EST, PDT.*

▶**Weather terms.** Following are some of the terms defined by the National Weather Service and listed in the *AP Stylebook.*

- A *blizzard* has winds of 35 mph or more and considerable falling or blowing snow, with visibility near zero.

- A *cyclone* is a storm with strong winds rotating about a moving center of low atmospheric pressure.

- A *funnel cloud* is a violent, rotating column of air that does not touch the ground.

- *Gale winds* are sustained winds within the range of 39 to 54 mph (34 to 47 knots).

- A *hurricane* is a warm-core tropical cyclone in which the minimum sustained surface wind is 74 mph.

- A *tornado* is a violent, rotating column of air forming a pendant and touching the ground.

- A *knot* is one nautical mile (6,076.10 feet) per hour. To convert knots into approximate statute miles per hour, multiply knots by 1.15. Always use figures to express the result: "Winds were at 7 to 9 knots."

▶**Temperatures.** Use figures for all except zero: "The low today was minus 10." Temperatures get higher or lower, not warmer or cooler. The temperature scale generally used in the United States is Fahrenheit rather than Celsius. In the Fahrenheit scale, the freezing point of water is 32 degrees and the boiling point is 212 degrees. To convert a Fahrenheit temperature to Celsius, subtract 32 from the Fahrenheit figure, multiply by 5, and divide by 9 ($77 - 32 = 45$; $45 \times 5 = 225$; $225 \div 9 = 25$ degrees Celsius).

▶**Internet terms.** World Wide Web is often shortened to Web (capitalized), and we write about Web sites (capitalized and two words). Electronic mail is usually referred to as e-mail (a hyphenated word).

In addition to the frequently used style matters discussed in this chapter, the AP stylebook is crammed with useful information for reporters and copy editors. Keep it handy. Use it often.

Correct word usage

The English language, particularly the U.S. version of it, changes constantly. New words, many associated with evolving technology, enter the language, and some words and phrases once reserved for spoken but not written language eventually become commonly accepted for both forms of communication. Copy editors and other wordsmiths should recognize the evolutionary nature of the language but, at the same time, work to protect it from barbarisms that detract from clear, concise communication.

Students often balk at grammar and word usage drills, arguing that incorrect usage should stand, on the basis that "it's the way people say it." A purist might ask *What people?* and question why professional communicators should let nonprofessionals assume the role of experts. Spoken English is not the same as written English, and even the most careful and graceful writer may lapse into imprecision when speaking extemporaneously.

The remainder of this chapter will consider word usage problems that copy editors must guard against, including frequently misused words.

▶ **Words to eliminate.** If these words are part of either your written or spoken vocabulary, quit using them: *alright, irregardless, towards, wreckless.* The correct version is *all right. Regardless* or *irrespective* should be used in place of *irregardless.* Unless you are writing for a British publication, *toward* is the correct word. One might have occasion to use *wreckless* in the sense of a place where no wrecks occur—a *wreckless* intersection perhaps—but usually the writer intends *reckless,* as in *reckless* behavior.

▶ **Crutch words.** These words seem to run in cycles. A few years ago, *hopefully* was a crutch word, seemingly used to steady a speaker or writer who was about to launch into a sentence, as in "Hopefully, I will make an A on the exam." The correct phrase in these example sentences is *I hope* because *hopefully* is an adverb that should modify verbs, adjectives or other adverbs, not nouns or pronouns. "He looked into her eyes *hopefully* as he proposed marriage." *Basically, like* and *you know* have become crutch words, particularly in spoken English, as in "Basically, I think like I deserve an A because, like you know, I studied like 10 hours the night before the exam, you know."

▶ **Redundant phrases.** Eliminating a few dozen redundant phrases in each issue of a newspaper provides space for another story. Perhaps enough space could be saved to run another obituary if the redundancies *funeral service, autopsy to determine the cause of death, died suddenly* and *fatal killing* were eliminated from obits.

Copy editors should use the delete key on these redundant expressions:

acute crisis	few *in number*	*possibly* might
bald-*headed*	first *annual*	reason is *because*
basic essentials	follow *after*	*regular* weekly meeting
climb *up*	*free* gift	rise *up*
commute *back and forth*	*general* public	*self*-confessed
completely destroy (*completely* with eliminate, empty, full, finished, true)	*hot*-water heater	*sworn* affidavits
	invited guest	*total* operating costs
	kept watch	*underground* subway
consensus *of opinion*	large *in size*	*very* unique (*really* unique, *most* unique)
dead body	*new* record	
depreciate *in value*	*noon* luncheon	whether *or not*
end result	*pair of* twins	8 a.m. *this morning*
entirely new (*entirely* with original, complete)	plan *for future* (plan *ahead, in advance*)	*12* noon (midnight)

▶ **Wrong words.** Experienced police reporters know that *burglary, robbery* and *theft* must not be used interchangeably. It is common newspaper practice, however, to assign rookie reporters, who may not know the precise meanings of these words, to the "cop shop." As always, copy editors must be on guard. Here are some commonly misused words:

- **according to:** Use *according to* as an attribution if the intent is to cast doubt on the speaker's credibility, not as a synonym for *said*: "According to Jones, he was at home in bed at the time the crime happened."

- **alleged and allegedly:** Other misusages common to police stories, these words do not afford the legal protection that some reporters associate with them. In addition, production errors could lead to the word being dropped. Rather than writing, "Jones *allegedly* assaulted the woman," it is better to write, "Jones has been charged with assault."

- **because, since:** These words are not interchangeable. Use *because* to denote a specific cause-effect relationship: "They canceled the company picnic *because* it rained." *Since* is acceptable in a causal sense when the first event in a sequence led logically to the second but was not its direct cause: "They wore casual clothes to work *since* a company picnic was scheduled for the afternoon." *Since* can be used as an adverb, preposition or conjunction. "He has since graduated from college." (adverb) "I have known him since our college years." (preposition) "I haven't seen him since he graduated." (conjunction)

- **burglary, robbery, theft:** A *burglary,* as defined by common law, means forcible entry with intent to commit a crime. *Robbery* means stealing with force or threat of force; *theft* means stealing without force or threat of force. A holdup is a robbery; shoplifting is theft.

- **convince, persuade:** People are *persuaded* to do or believe something; they become *convinced,* meaning they feel secure about a decision of principle. *Convince* should not be followed by an infinitive, rather by *that* or *of.* "She *persuaded* her father to allow her to attend the party." "He was *convinced* that it was the right thing to do."

- **execute:** In the sense of killing, this word should be reserved for the taking of life by due process of law. Terrorists or gangsters do not execute people, although they may engage in execution-style murder.

- **feel, believe and think:** Although some usage experts have abandoned efforts to preserve the distinctions, *feel, believe* and *think* have different meanings. *Believe* is used to express ideas that are accepted on faith: "She said she *believes* in God." Use *think* when mental processes and reason, rather than emotion, work to form an opinion: "Researchers said they *think* their studies will lead to medical advances." To describe emotional or physical sensations, *feel* is the correct word: "She says she *feels* sad." "He said he *felt* the prick of the needle."

- **fewer, less:** In comparing quantities, use *fewer* if the items can be counted or separated easily: *fewer* dollars, *fewer* inches of rain. Use *less* for items that cannot be counted or separated easily: *less* money, *less* rain.

- **figuratively, literally:** *Figuratively* is an adverb describing an action that is not in its usual or exact sense or is metaphorical, as in *a figure of speech. Literally* means exactly, actually, precisely as stated. When used to mean a display of great emotion or anger, it is incorrect to say he *literally* hit the ceiling. He did not actually hit the ceiling. What is meant is that he *figuratively* hit the ceiling.

- **if, whether:** To introduce a condition, use *if,* as in, "*If* it rains, the picnic will be canceled." To express an alternative, use *whether,* as in, "He asked *whether* the picnic had been canceled." The word *whether* includes the idea that something may or may not exist, so it is redundant to say *whether or not.*

- **like, as:** If a conjunction is needed to join two parts of a sentence, *as* is the correct word. "The women look *as though* they might be sisters." Use *like* if a preposition is needed: "The women look *like* sisters."

- **over, more than:** For spatial relationships, *over* is the word to use, as in, "The cow jumped *over* the moon." For figures, *more than* is the preferred usage: "*More than* 40,000 people gathered to watch the cow jump over the moon."

- **refute:** This is another troublesome word that is sometimes mistakenly used to indicate disagreement as a synonym for *deny, contradict, reject, rebut* or *dispute.* For something or someone to be *refuted,* it must be proved to be false or mistaken. If there is any question about the success of the argument, *refute* is not the proper word. *Disprove* is a correct substitute for *refute.*

- **verbal, oral:** A person's ability to use language, either spoken or written, is referred to as *verbal* skill. *Oral* skills are spoken, not written. A person who gives a speech makes an *oral* presentation.

▶ **Words that sound alike.** Writers and editors sometimes misuse words that sound alike and are spelled similarly but have different meanings. Following are examples:

- **all together, altogether:** The two-word expression means in a group, *altogether* means thoroughly or entirely. "Let's go *all together* in one car." "The idea is *altogether* ridiculous, as 10 adults won't fit into the small sports car."

- **allude, elude, illusion:** To refer indirectly to something is to *allude* to it; *elude* means to escape a pursuer. "The author *alluded* to his previous bouts with alcoholism." "The criminal *eluded* the police." The word *illusion* comes from the Latin, meaning "to mock." An *illusion* is a false idea or conception, or it can refer to the act of deception by creating illusory ideas. "The magician created the *illusion* of sawing his assistant in half."

- **carat, karat, caret, carrot:** *Carat* is the unit of weight (200 milligrams) for measuring precious stones and metals. *Karat* is used to express the proportion of pure gold used with an alloy. Pure gold is 24 karat gold, while something containing half gold and half an alloy is 12 karat gold. *Caret* is an editing mark used to indicate an insertion. *Carrot* is a vegetable.

- **compose, comprise:** The parts *compose* the whole; the whole *comprises* its parts. The consensus among usage experts is that the expression *is comprised of* should be avoided. "The U.S. government *comprises* the executive, legislative and judicial branches." *Comprised* is a transitive verb, so it needs a direct object. These usages are correct: "Nine players *compose* the team." "The team *comprises* nine players."

- **credible, creditable, credulous:** Something that can be believed is *credible,* as *a credible story. Creditable* means deserving credit or praise. "His service to the community was *creditable.*" A *credulous* person is one who tends to believe too readily, is gullible.

- **eminent, imminent:** *Eminent* is an adjective describing something that is high, lofty, prominent, renowned. "An *eminent* person will be the best candidate for the university presidency." Something that is likely to happen without delay, that is impending, can be said to be *imminent.* "The appearance of the sky indicates that a storm is *imminent.*"

- **farther, further:** Use *farther* to refer to physical distances. "She ran *farther* than I did." *Further* means to a greater extent or degree, as *investigate the matter further. Further* also can mean in addition. "*Further,* I will not do as you ask because your plan is unethical."

■ **imply, infer:** The speaker or writer *implies;* the listener or reader *infers.* "In her speech, the company president *implied* that major policy changes were forthcoming." "After listening carefully, I *inferred* that the policy changes would not involve my department."

■ **incidence, incidents:** *Incidence* refers to the rate of occurrence, as in *the incidence of a particular disease in the United States.* An *incident* is an occurrence. The word does not mean attack or violence, although those adjectives might apply to an incident. "It was an *incident* that he would remember fondly for the rest of his life."

■ **levee, levy:** A *levee* is an embankment to prevent a river from flooding bordering land. "*Levees* failed in New Orleans, flooding the city." *Levy* as a noun is an imposed tax or fine; as a verb it means to impose a tax or fine. "The state legislature will *levy* an income tax." "The amount of the *levy* has not been determined."

■ **naval, navel:** *Naval* pertains to a navy. *Navel* is the small scar on the abdomen where the umbilical cord was attached to the fetus; also *navel orange.*

■ **pore, pour:** *Pore* as a transitive verb means to study carefully, to ponder. It is used with *over,* as *to pore over books.* Used as a noun, *pore* is a tiny opening, as in skin and plant leaves, for absorbing or discharging fluids. Neither meaning is related to the verb *pour,* which means to cause to flow in a continuous stream. "I will *pour* the drinks."

■ **stationary, stationery:** An object that does not move is *stationary.* One uses *stationery* when writing a letter.

■ **tortuous, torturous:** *Tortuous* means full of twists and turns, crooked, deceitful or tricky, as *a tortuous act* or *tortuous path. Torturous* pertains to torture.

▶**Frequently misused words.** Yes, the preceding list is long and here comes another long list. English is not an easy language for those who wish to use it correctly and carefully. Successful copy editors, as well as good reporters, know how to use these terms. A few of the words on the next several pages have fallen into such common misusage that even language experts debate the merits of maintaining the original distinctions. But to professional writers and editors who want to say exactly and concisely what they mean, the distinctions are important. See Figure 3-1 on page 65 for interesting misuse, termed *eggcorns,* of some common words.

Exercises 13 through 20 for Chapter 3 in the workbook section test your knowledge of these words.

adverse, averse *Adverse* means unfavorable: "Adverse weather delayed our departure." *Averse* means opposed or reluctant and is used with *to:* "She was averse to her daughter's choice of friends."

advice, advise *Advice* is a noun: "His advice to students who failed the exam was to study harder." *Advise* is a verb: "He advised the student to study harder."

affect, effect *Affect* is a verb: "Did studying this long list of words *affect* your skill in writing and editing?" *Effect* is a noun: "The effect of your learning to use words correctly will be to make you a better job candidate." *Effect* may also be used as a verb meaning to bring about: "Your knowledge will effect change in your career advancement."

afterward Preferred usage in the United States. The British use *afterwards.*

aggravate, irritate The distinction between these two words may be lost, as many authorities say they are now interchangeable. Traditionally, *aggravate* means to make an existing situation or condition worse, and *irritate* means to annoy or to provoke to anger: "He aggravated his knee injury and was unable to play football, which irritated him."

altar, alter An *altar* is a table or platform used for sacred ceremonies; *alter* means to change: "They said their wedding vows at the altar. They altered the traditional wedding vows."

annual Something that happens every year. It is incorrect to write *first annual.*

appraise, apprise *Appraise* means to set a value on: "The bank wants to appraise the property before granting a loan." *Apprise* means to notify or inform: "Please apprise me of your progress on the project."

ascent, assent A climb is an *ascent;* the verb form is *ascend:* "They will ascend the stairs"; "The trip to the top of the hill was a steep ascent." *Assent* is a noun or verb meaning "an agreement" or "to agree to": "I want their assent before I continue this program."

awhile, a while *Awhile* is an adverb and *a while* is an article plus a noun: "We fished for a while, but the fish weren't biting, so we swam awhile."

bail, bale *Bail* refers to dipping water out of something or posting a bond. To *bale* something is to tie it into bundles, as to bale old newspapers to take them to a recycling plant.

balance, remainder Do not use these words interchangeably. Use *balance* in fiscal contexts to report the equality of debits and credits or the difference between them (to balance a checkbook). Use *remainder* for what is left when a part is taken away. "We spent the remainder of the day studying."

baloney, bologna *Baloney* refers to nonsense; *bologna* is a type of meat.

bazaar, bizarre One might buy odd *(bizarre)* items at a *bazaar.*

beach, beech One vacations at the *beach. Beach* may also be used as a verb meaning to run aground (as in beaching a ship). *Beech* trees are not associated with beach areas.

because of, due to *Due to* is an adjective and should modify a noun: "The accident was due to carelessness." *Because of* explains why something happened: "Because of my good work, I received a salary increase."

berth, birth A resting place is a *berth:* "The captain guided the boat into its berth." *Birth* is the act of bringing forth offspring or of being born: "She gave birth to a girl."

beside, besides "The cat lay beside her." *Besides* means in addition to: "Besides the professional musicians, the show will include high school choirs."

better, bettor One who gambles is a *bettor.* It is *better* not to gamble.

biannual, biennial Something that happens twice a year is *biannual (semiannual* is a synonym); a *biennial* event occurs once in two years. If you are confused by *bi-* words, they probably confuse readers also, so it is better to spell it out as *twice a year* or *every two years.*

bloc, block A *bloc* is a coalition of people or a group with a single purpose or goal: "Farmers were a powerful voting bloc in the last election." *Block* is a different word, with about 40 dictionary definitions.

boar, boor, bore A male hog is a *boar.* An insensitive person is a *boor:* "His behavior at the party shows that he is a boor." *Bore* refers to someone who is boring; *bore* as a verb means to drill: "We like our neighbors, but they are such bores that it is difficult to stay awake when visiting with them."

born, borne A baby is *born. Borne* is the participle of the verb *bear,* meaning carry: "She has borne great responsibilities during her husband's illness"; "She has borne three children."

bouillon, bullion *Bouillon* refers to broth; *bullion* is gold or silver that has been cast into bars or some other convenient shape: "After working with the bullion all morning, the workers stopped for a lunch of chicken bouillon and sandwiches."

breadth, breath, breathe *Breadth* means width: "The river's breadth is nearly a quarter mile." *Breath* is a noun meaning air taken into the lungs and then let out; *breathe* is the verb form: "I took a deep breath"; "It is unpleasant to breathe smoke-filled air."

Britain, Briton The country is Great Britain; an inhabitant of Britain is a Briton. *Britain* is acceptable usage for reference to Great Britain, which is an island comprising England, Scotland and Wales. The United Kingdom is Great Britain plus Northern Ireland. *The British Isles* applies to the United Kingdom and the islands around it: Scilly to the southwest, the Isle of Man to the west, the Channel Islands to the east, and the Orkneys and the Shetlands to the north of Scotland.

broach, brooch To *broach* is to start a discussion or to make a hole in so as to let out liquid; as a noun, *broach* can refer to a tapered bit for drilling holes. A *brooch* is a large ornamental pin with a clasp: "She wore her favorite brooch that night because she planned to broach the subject of whether they had a future together."

burro, burrow A *burro* is a donkey. *Burrow* as a noun refers to a hole in the ground, usually dug by an animal; as a verb, *burrow* means to dig a hole in the ground.

callous, callus Both words come from the same Latin word meaning hard skin. A *callous* person is one who is unfeeling, who is hardened. *Callus* refers to a thickened place on the skin: "The guitar player has calluses on his fingers."

Calvary, cavalry *Calvary* is the biblical place where Jesus was crucified. *Cavalry* means combat troops mounted originally on horses but now often on motorized armored vehicles.

canvas, canvass *Canvas* is a type of cloth. To *canvass* is to go through places or among people to ask for votes, opinions or orders: "We will canvass this neighborhood in support of our political candidate."

capital, capitol The city is the *capital;* the building is the *capitol. Capital* means principal or chief and also refers to money. A capital letter should be used when writing about specific state capitols, such as the Tennessee Capitol, or about the Capitol in Washington, D.C., but Washington, D.C., is the capital of the United States.

cement, concrete *Cement* is a powdered substance made of lime and clay that is mixed with water and sand or gravel to make *concrete. Cement* may also be used as a verb, meaning to bind.

cemetery Not *cemetary.*

censor, censure, censer *Censor* and *censure* both come from a Latin word meaning to judge, and both can be used as either nouns or verbs. *Censor* means to prohibit or suppress; *censure* means to disapprove or sharply criticize. A book or film may be censored (suppressed, prohibited) or censured (sharply criticized), but a person is censured, not censored: "The Senate formally censured Sen. John Doe." *Censer,* unrelated to the other two words, is a noun meaning a container in which incense is burned.

cession, session A *cession* is a ceding or giving up to another: "The treaty provided for the cession of individual rights to the territory." A *session* is a period of activity of some kind. A legislative session, for example, might include many meetings and extend for several weeks or months.

childish, childlike *Childish* is a disparaging description of an adult who is silly or foolish: "His childish behavior was inappropriate at the office." *Childlike* means of or like a child in the sense of innocent and trusting: "Her childlike manner made her a delightful companion."

chord, cord A *chord* is a combination of three or more tones sounded together in harmony. *Cord* refers to a string or a measure of wood; it is also the word to apply to vocal cords or the spinal cord.

cite, sight, site One *cites* (names, gives credit) a source or receives a citation ordering a court appearance. *Sight* refers to seeing: "The man was out of my range of sight"; "He carefully aligned the rifle sights with the target." A *site* is a place: "This is the site for our new house."

climactic, climatic *Climactic* refers to the final culminating element in a series, the highest point of interest or the turning point of action: "The climactic scene in the movie was the death of the title character." *Climatic* pertains to weather, as in climatic conditions.

collide Two objects must both be in motion before they can collide. A car might smash into or hit a fence but not collide with it.

commensurate, commiserate The first word means equal in measure or size: "She wants a salary commensurate with her value to the company." To *commiserate* is to feel pity or sympathy for, to condole: "We commiserate with the family during this sad time."

compare with, compare to *Compare with* means to note both differences and similarities, and this is usually the intended meaning: "Jim compared his report card with John's." *Compare to* means to note similarities alone.

complacent, complaisant One who is *complacent* is self-satisfied, contented, unconcerned: "She was complacent with her role at the company." *Complaisant* means eager to please or obliging: "He was *complaisant* regarding his mother's wishes."

complement, compliment As a verb, *complement* means to complete; as a noun it refers to that which completes or perfects: "The sauce complemented the main dish." *Compliment* means praise, and it too can be used as either a verb or a noun: "He complimented her work." "He gave her a compliment on her work."

complementary, complimentary These are the adjective forms of *complement* and *compliment*: "The service department is complementary to the sales department." *Complimentary* can also mean free or given as a courtesy: "He received complimentary tickets."

comprehensible, comprehensive That which is *comprehensible* is understandable: "Now that I know the whole story, his actions are comprehensible." *Comprehensive* means inclusive, wide in scope: "The exam at the end of the semester will be comprehensive."

connotation, denotation A word's *connotation* is its suggested or implied meaning; the *denotation* is the actual meaning or dictionary definition of a word: "The denotation of this word is neutral, but it has a negative connotation."

conscience, conscious, consciousness *Conscience* is an awareness of right and wrong: "Let your conscience be your guide." *Conscious* is an adjective meaning awake; *consciousness* is a noun meaning awareness: "He was conscious throughout the ordeal." "She quickly regained consciousness."

contagious, infectious A *contagious* disease is spread by contact, whereas an *infectious* disease is transmitted by the presence in the body of certain microorganisms. An infectious disease may also be contagious.

contemptible, contemptuous A thing deserving scorn or contempt is *contemptible*. "His behavior was contemptible." Something is *contemptuous* when it expresses contempt, as a contemptuous remark.

continual, continuous Something that is repeated often at intervals (intermittent) is *continual*: "The rain today was continual" (meaning that it rained off and on during the day). *Continuous* means going on without interruption, or incessant action: "The rain was continuous today" (meaning that it never stopped raining today).

council, counsel, consul A *council* is a group called together for discussion, as in a city council. A *counsel* is one who gives advice or is a lawyer. A *consul* is a diplomat.

councilor, counselor A *councilor* is a member of a council. A *counselor* is an adviser or an attorney.

couple of The *of* is necessary: "A couple of dollars should be enough."

crochet, crotchet, crotchety *Crochet* is a type of needlework; to crochet is to do such needlework. *Crotchet* is a noun meaning "a particular whim or stubborn notion"; thus a crotchety person is one who is stubborn or cranky.

croquet, croquette, coquette *Croquet* is an outdoor game. A *croquette* is a small meat or fish patty. *Coquette* is a French word meaning a flirtatious girl or woman.

cue, queue A *cue* is a stick used in billiards or pool to strike a ball. A *queue* is a pigtail or, in Britain, a line, as of persons waiting to be served: "The queue was quite long when we arrived at the restaurant." *Queue* is also used as an intransitive verb with *up*, as in "We queued up to wait for a table at the restaurant."

currant, current A *currant* is a small seedless raisin from the Mediterranean area. *Current* means at the present time or circulating (as electricity): "On our current visit to the Mediterranean, we have been enjoying the currants."

cymbal, symbol A musician uses a *cymbal*, a circular brass plate that makes a ringing sound when hit. A *symbol* is an object used to represent something abstract; a mark or letter standing for a quality or process, as in music or chemistry; or an editing mark.

cypress, Cyprus A *cypress* is an evergreen tree. *Cyprus* is the name of an island country in the east end of the Mediterranean. A citizen of Cyprus is a Cypriot.

Figure 3-I
Copy editors must be alert to erroneous words that appear in copy as a result of reporters' (or their sources') poor hearing or spelling. A group of linguists who write the blog Language Log (http://itre.cis.upenn.edu/~myl/languagelog/) have coined the word *eggcorn* to refer to a nonstandard reshaping of words that go beyond a homophone substitution and to some degree make sense. Not knowing how to spell "acorn," perhaps some anonymous writer reasoned that an acorn is more or less shaped like an egg, and it is a seed, just like grains of corn. Ergo: *eggcorn*.

Watch out for falling *eggcorns*

Here are a few eggcorns that have appeared more than once in journalistic writing and even more frequently in blogs:

The critic accused Lindsey Lohan of *lipsinging*. He said she had *lipsang* on earlier occasions. (*Lip-syncing* is the practice of pretending to sing by synchronizing your lip movements with a vocal soundtrack.)

His suggestions really got my *dandruff* up. (The idiom "get one's dander up" refers to becoming angry.)

I don't like the new magazine. It's *boggled* down with too many pages of advertising. (The correct term is *bogged down,* as what might happen to one who falls into a wet, muddy bog.)

She speaks French with a *floorless* accent. (She would prefer to speak without flaw or *flawless*.)

I turned on MTV, and it looked like a documentary on *marsh* pits. (The term comes from the slam-dancing sense of *mosh* and *mosh* pit.)

Wind *turbans* could supply environmental-friendly energy. (Cloth goes round and round one's head to produce a turban, but the wind turns a *turbine* to produce energy.)

He accepted a *10-year-track* position at the university. (*Tenure* usually is earned within six years, or the teacher must leave the position.)

After Hurricane Katrina, the Red Cross was a *god's end* for many people on the Gulf Coast. (God may have sent the Red Cross, which was a *godsend* for people.)

For these and more than 500 other eggcorns, see The Eggcorn Database, http://eggcorns.lascribe.net/.

---

defective, deficient   Something that has imperfections or is faulty is *defective*: "The car had defective brakes." *Deficient* means incomplete, lacking in some essential or inadequate in amount: "The doctor said her diet was deficient in vitamin C."

demolish, destroy   These words mean that something is done away with completely, so it is redundant to say *completely demolished* or *totally destroyed.*

demur, demure   To *demur* is to hesitate because of doubts or to have objections; *demur* is also a noun meaning an objection: "The lawyer filed a demur with the court." To be *demure* is to be affectedly modest or coy: "She wore a demure dress for her appearance in court."

deprecate, depreciate   To *deprecate* is to express disapproval of, to belittle: "He deprecated her efforts." To *depreciate* is to lessen in value: "A car depreciates rapidly."

desert, dessert   To *desert* is to abandon, to forsake, as to leave a military post without permission and with no intent to return. *Desert* also refers to a dry, barren, sandy region, such as the Sahara Desert. A *dessert* is the final course of a meal.

detract, distract   To *detract* is to take away: "Unattractive landscaping detracts from the appearance of a house." To *distract* is to draw the mind in another direction, to divert, to confuse or bewilder: "The child's crying distracted the man from his work."

different from   Not *different than:* "Mary's political views are different from those of her sister." *Differ with* indicates disagreement: "I differ with her political views."

dilemma   A choice between two alternatives, both bad. *Dilemma* should not be used to mean a choice from among more than two or a choice between a good alternative and a bad one: "To leave the car and walk toward town during the blizzard or to wait for help that wasn't likely to come before daybreak: that was his dilemma." (both are bad alternatives)

disapprove, disprove   To *disapprove* is to have or express an unfavorable opinion: "She disapproved of John's behavior." To *disprove* is to prove to be false: "He disproved the belief that the earth is flat."

disburse, dispense, disperse   To *disburse* is to pay out, as in disbursing wages. To *dispense* is to give out or distribute, as with medicine or justice: "The judge will dispense justice." *Disperse* means to break up and scatter: "Police ordered the crowd to disperse."

disinterested, uninterested   One who is *disinterested* is impartial or unbiased, as in a disinterested judge. An *uninterested* person is indifferent or lacks interest. The distinction between these two words is being lost in common usage, so a writer or speaker might prefer to use *impartial* instead of *disinterested.*

distinctive, distinguished Something that is *distinctive* is different or characteristic. It is not necessarily good or bad, just different. *Distinguished* means excellent, outstanding. A teacher who wears unusual clothes, stands on her desk and shouts at students can be said to have a distinctive teaching style, but it may or may not be considered distinguished: "He had a distinctive speaking style. Later he became a distinguished diplomat."

dose, doze A *dose* is an amount of medicine to be taken at one time; to *doze* is to sleep lightly or nap: "He took a dose of medicine and then sat in front of the television set to doze."

drier, dryer *Drier* is the comparative form of *dry:* "A desert is drier than a river valley." A *dryer* is a person or thing that dries, such as an appliance for drying clothes.

drown No need for an auxiliary or helping verb unless the victim was helped in the drowning. Just say "He drowned," not "He was drowned."

drunk, drunken Use *drunken* as a modifier before a noun, as in drunken driver. Use *drunk* as a predicate adjective, as in "He was drunk."

dual, duel *Dual* means something composed of two, a double, as in "The car has dual headlights." A *duel* is a prearranged fight between two people armed with deadly weapons.

each other, one another The consensus among grammatical experts is to use these interchangeably instead of applying *each other* when the meaning is limited to two and *one another* when more than two are involved.

eager, anxious Experts are divided about whether these may be properly interchanged. *Anxious* refers to foreboding; *eager* means to look forward to: "She was anxious about the surgery." "She was eager for the vacation trip."

ecology, environment *Ecology* refers to the relationship between organisms and their environment. It is not a synonym for *environment.*

eek, eke out *Eek* is an exclamatory expression: "Eek! There's a snake!" *Eke out* means to get something with great difficulty: "During the Depression, they barely managed to eke out a living."

elder, eldest; older, oldest Some dictionaries make a distinction, applying *elder* and *eldest* to people and *older* and *oldest* to either things or people. At what age these terms should be applied to people is highly subjective. The AP stylebook cautions that they should not be used to describe anyone younger than 65 and should not be used casually in referring to anyone beyond that age. *Elderly* is appropriate in generic phrases that do not refer to specific individuals, as in concern for the elderly or a home for the elderly. If the intent is to show that an individual's faculties have deteriorated, the AP stylebook says to cite a graphic example: "His memory fades." "She walks with a cane."

elicit, illicit *Elicit* is a transitive verb meaning to draw forth or evoke (a response): "The teacher sought to elicit answers from her students." *Illicit* is an adjective describing something that is unlawful, improper or prohibited, as in an illicit affair.

emigrant, immigrant One who leaves a country is an *emigrant;* one who comes into a country is an *immigrant.*

ensure, insure The consensus among usage experts is that these terms may be used interchangeably to mean make certain, but AP style is to use *ensure* for that meaning: "Additional testing will ensure quality control." *Insure* is the correct word to mean guarantee against loss, as in to insure your automobile (buy insurance).

epithet, epitaph An *epithet* is a word or phrase characterizing a person or thing; in common usage it has come to be associated with derogatory descriptions. An *epitaph* is an inscription, as for a tombstone, in memory of a dead person.

erasable, irascible A pencil mark is *erasable,* meaning that it can be erased or rubbed out. An *irascible* person is one who is easily angered or is hot-tempered.

especially, specially *Especially* means to an outstanding extent or particularly: "I am especially happy about the good news." *Specially* means for a special purpose: "She bought the dress specially for the party."

every day, everyday *Every day* is an adverb: "She wore a suit every day to work." *Everyday* is an adjective meaning usual, common or suitable for everyday use: "She wore an everyday dress rather than her best suit."

evoke, invoke To *evoke* is to call forth, to elicit: "His soothing voice evoked memories of her father." To *invoke* is to call on a higher authority, such as God or the Muses, for blessing or help; to resort to (such as a law or ruling) as pertinent; to conjure, beg for, implore. The noun form is *invocation.*

exalt, exult *Exalt* is to raise in status or dignity, to praise or glorify, to fill with joy or pride, as in exalted ruler. *Exult,* an intransitive verb, means to rejoice greatly or to glory; the noun form is *exultation:* "They exulted in the news of their victory."

excite, incite *Excite* means to make active, to stimulate, to arouse emotionally; *incite* means to urge to action. A speaker might excite a crowd, for example, without inciting the crowd to take action, but generally a crowd will not become incited without first becoming excited: "The sound of a doorbell excites the dog and causes it to bark"; "The dynamic speaker incited the inmates to begin fighting the guards."

exercise, exorcise *Exercise* pertains to physical activity, as in an exercise class to promote good health. *Exorcise* means to expel (such as evil spirits) by incantations or to free from such spirits; noun forms are *exorcism* and *exorcist.*

expose To lay open, generally to something undesirable, such as danger or attack: "The worker was exposed to radiation"; "The revelations exposed the candidate to political attacks from his opponents." *Expose* should not be used in the sense of making known, as in "Our travels abroad exposed us to new cultures."

extant, extent *Extant* means still existing: "This is the oldest extant structure in North America." *Extent* means space, amount, degree to which a thing extends, size, scope, limits: "The child tested the extent of his mother's patience."

facetious, factious, factitious, fictitious *Facetious* means joking or amusing, as in a facetious comment. *Factious* refers to creating dissent, especially in political matters: "The trade legislation was factious in this congressional session." *Factitious* means forced or artificial. *Fictitious* means of or like fiction, imaginary, false, assumed for disguise not necessarily with the intent to deceive, as in a fictitious account or a fictitious title.

fact A reality, a truth. It is redundant to say *true fact, real fact* or *actual fact.*

feat, fete *Feat* describes an accomplishment of unusual daring or skill: "Few of Babe Ruth's feats have been matched." A fete is a festival, entertainment or lavish party: "The fete honored her 100th birthday."

ferment, foment *Ferment* means to undergo fermentation by the addition of some substance, such as yeast: "Grapes ferment to become wine." *Foment* means to stir up (such as trouble), to incite: "He sought to foment trouble among the workers."

fiancé, fiancée Despite efforts toward a gender-neutral language, this distinction remains. General usage and AP style reserves *fiancé* for males and *fiancée* for females.

fiscal, physical *Fiscal* means financial, as in the nation's fiscal policy.

flack, flak *Flack* is a slang term for a press agent or public relations practitioner. It is often used in a derogatory sense. *Flak* was first used during World War II as an acronym for a German antiaircraft gun and the shells fired by the gun. It has come to mean criticism: "He took a lot of flak for his stand on the issue."

flagrant, fragrant *Flagrant* means obviously evident and connotes outrageous or shocking conduct: "He was flagrant in his disregard for rules and regulations." Something that is *fragrant* smells good.

flaunt, flout To *flaunt* means to show off proudly or in an ostentatious manner: "She flaunted her wealth." *Flout* means to defy, mock or scorn: "His behavior flouts authority."

flier, flyer The news-service stylebooks prefer *flier* for both aviators and handbills. Other usage guides prefer *flyer* for handbill. *Flyer* is the proper name for some trains and buses: the Western Flyer.

flounder, founder In addition to denoting a variety of fish, *flounder* means to struggle awkwardly or to speak or act in an awkward, confused manner: "He floundered in the deep snow." *Founder* as a verb means to stumble, fall or go lame, as in "The horse foundered." *Founder* as a verb also means to fill with water and sink, as in to founder a ship.

forbidding, foreboding *Forbidding* is an adjective meaning difficult or looking dangerous or disagreeable, as in a forbidding climb to the top of a mountain. *Foreboding* as a noun means a prediction, usually of something evil: "She believed that the dream was a foreboding of doom."

foregoing, forgoing *Foregoing* is something previously said or written, as in the foregoing paragraph of the speech. *Forgoing* is the present participle form of the verb *forgo,* meaning to do without, to abstain: "He will forgo eating meat."

fortuitous, fortunate *Fortuitous* means happening by luck or chance: "Our meeting here is fortuitous because I want to talk with you." *Fortunate* means having good luck: "She was fortunate throughout her career."

funeral service A redundant phrase. A funeral is a service.

gantlet, gauntlet A *gantlet* was a punishment in which the offender ran between two rows of men who struck him ("running the gantlet"). Now *gantlet* is used to mean a series of troubles. Originally, *gauntlet* meant a knight's armored glove. Throw down the gauntlet meant to challenge to combat. Opinion is divided on whether modern usage correctly allows these terms to be used interchangeably. Several dictionaries indicate that they are the same, with *gauntlet* the preferred spelling.

genteel, gentle *Genteel* means polite or well bred, with modern usage referring to affectedly refined or polite: "His genteel mannerisms seemed out of place in his current state of homelessness on New York City streets." *Gentle* means refined, courteous, tame, not harsh or rough, as in a gentle man or a gentle animal.

gorilla, guerrilla A *gorilla* is the largest and most powerful of the apes native to Africa. A *guerrilla* is a member of a small defensive force of irregular soldiers.

gourmand, gourmet Both terms refer to someone who likes good food and drink, but *gourmand* is used in the sense of eating or drinking to excess, as a glutton would: "John is a gourmand and weighs 350 pounds." *Gourmet* connotes one who is an excellent judge of fine foods and drinks, a connoisseur: "June is a gourmet cook."

grisly, gristly, grizzly *Grisly* means horrible or gruesome, as in a grisly crime. *Gristly* means having gristles, as in gristly meat. *Grizzly* means gray or streaked with gray, having gray hair; it is also a type of bear.

half brother, stepbrother If they have one parent in common, they are *half brothers;* if they are related by the remarriage of parents, they are *stepbrothers.* Because in some cultures it is considered insensitive to identify family members as *half brother, half sister, stepmother* and so on, some newspapers do not specify such family relationships except when germane to a story or specified by the people involved.

half-mast, half-staff Flags on ships or at naval stations are lowered to or flown at (but not raised to) *half-mast.* Flags in other places are lowered to *half-staff.*

hangar, hanger A *hangar* shelters airplanes. A *hanger* is used to support clothes or other objects.

hardy, hearty *Hardy* is an adjective meaning bold and resolute, robust, or vigorous, as in a hardy species of plants. *Hearty* means warm and friendly, jovial, unrestrained, as in a hearty laugh.

head up Incorrect usage. A person heads a committee, perhaps.

healthful, healthy Something that is conducive to good health is *healthful:* "Exercise is healthful." Something that has good health is *healthy:* "The healthy man exercises daily." Today, *healthy* is commonly used in both senses.

historic, historical *Historic* means important to history, as in a historic battle. *Historical* means of or concerning history: "It is a historical novel."

holey, holy *Holey* means full of holes: "Throw the holey socks in the trash." *Holy* refers to sacred things: "He considered his work to be a holy duty." Neither word should be confused with *wholly,* which means entirely.

hopefully One of the most commonly misused words. It should be used as an adverb to describe the way the subject feels; it should not be used as an adjective. Thus, it is incorrect to write "Hopefully, he will make an A in the course." The correct wording is "He hopes he will make an A." To describe his feelings, write "He looked hopefully at his grade report."

impassable, impassible *Impassable* means not capable of being passed, as in an impassable obstacle. An *impassible* person is one who is incapable of showing emotion: "He was impassible as the judge sentenced him to prison."

inapt, inept *Inapt* (also *unapt*) means inappropriate or not suitable: "To wear a hat at the dining room table is inapt behavior." *Inept* is sometimes used in that sense, but usually it refers to something that is foolish or incompetent: "Mary is a computer expert, but she is inept in diagnosing problems with her car."

incite, insight To *incite* is to urge to action, as in to incite violence (see entry *excite, incite*). *Insight* is a noun meaning the ability to see and understand clearly the inner nature of things, especially by intuition: "She had a keen insight into the situation."

incredible, incredulous Something that is unbelievable is *incredible; incredulous* means skeptical: "I was incredulous when I heard about his feats on the basketball court, but when I saw him perform, I realized that he was capable of incredible plays."

ingenious, ingenuous An *ingenious* person is inventive; an *ingenuous* person is honest or open to the point of being naive: "We know that Benjamin Franklin was ingenious, but he was probably not ingenuous."

insoluble, insolvable, insolvent An *insoluble* substance cannot be dissolved. An *insolvable* problem is one that cannot be solved. A person who cannot pay debts is said to be *insolvent.*

interment, internment To *inter* is to put into a grave or tomb, so *interment* is a burial. *Internment* means detention, as in internment camp.

interstate, intrastate *Interstate* means between states: "The truck was used for interstate commerce." *Intrastate* means within a single state.

intestate Not having a will: "He died intestate."

into, in to The preposition *into* is not interchangeable with the adverb *in* followed by the preposition *to*: "The firefighter ran into the burning building"; "The escaped convict turned himself in to the police."

irrespective An adjective meaning regardless. Do not use *irregardless.*

judicial, judicious *Judicial* refers to a judge or court or their functions, as in a judicial system or the judicial branch of government. *Judicious* means having or showing sound judgment: "His actions demonstrate that he is judicious."

lam, lamb *Lam* is a slang expression for a headlong flight, as in fleeing. A person in this situation is said to be on the lam. A *lamb* is a baby sheep.

lama, llama A priest or monk in Tibet or Mongolia is a *lama.* A *llama* is an animal found in the South American Andes.

leach, leech To *leach* is to wash a solid substance with a filtering liquid or to extract from some material. A *leech* is a bloodsucker, originally a bloodsucking worm; now the term is also applied to a person who clings to another to get what he or she can.

leak, leek *Leak* is a verb meaning to let fluid in or out accidentally or, as a noun, meaning a hole: "The boat had a leak"; "Water leaked into the boat." A *leek* is an onionlike vegetable.

lie, lay See Rule 31 in Chapter 2.

lightening, lightning *Lightening* means making something less heavy or less dark, as in lightening the color of paint or lightening the load. *Lightning* is a flash of light in the sky caused by the discharge of atmospheric electricity.

like, as *As* is a conjunction; *like* is a verb or a preposition: "She looks like her sister." "The two women look as though they might be sisters." Use *as though* or *as if* when what follows is a clause; a conjunction, not a preposition, is needed to join the dependent clause and the main clause.

linage, lineage *Linage* is the number of written or printed lines on a page. In journalism, advertising linage refers to the number of lines of advertising matter in an issue. *Lineage* means descent from an ancestor: "She traced her lineage to the Pilgrims."

loath, loathe *Loath* is an adjective meaning reluctant; the expression *is loath to*: "She is loath to give a speech before a large audience." *Loathe* means to dislike intensely: "She loathed her boss because of his sexist behavior."

locate To fix the position of, to situate or become situated, to discover. *Locate* is not a synonym for *find;* "She located her car keys" is incorrect. Correct usage: "The city council decided to locate the new city hall at Fourth and Main streets."

Magna Carta, Magna Charta In the United States, *Magna Carta* is the preferred spelling.

majority, plurality More than half is a majority. A plurality is less than half but is the largest number. For example, if the votes of 11 people were 5 for, 4 against, and 2 undecided, you could say that a plurality voted in favor. At least 6 of 11 people would have to vote the same way before there would be a majority. Do not use *majority* in place of most or many or when numbers are not involved. Do not use *majority* in the comparative sense, as in greater majority or greatest majority.

marshal, marshall *Marshal* is the correct word for the verb form (marshal the forces) or the noun (fire marshal, parade marshal). *Marshall* is the usual spelling for a proper noun (John Marshall).

masterful, masterly *Masterful* means domineering: "She feared her masterful teacher." *Masterly* means skillful or expert: "It was a masterly performance." *Masterful* is often misused in the latter sense, perhaps because there is no adverbial form of *masterly*.

may be, maybe *May be* is a verb, as in "I may be selected for the job." *Maybe* means perhaps, as in "Maybe I will be selected for the job." *Maybe* should not be used as an adjective: a maybe fun party.

mean, median *Mean* is a synonym for *average*, referring to the sum of all components divided by the number of components. The *median* is the middle number, meaning that half the components are larger and half are smaller. "The test scores were 95, 85, 70, for a mean of 83.33, but the median grade was 85." Some authorities object to using *average* to mean common or ordinary, as in an average person.

media, medium *Media* is plural: "The media are business enterprises." *Medium* is singular: "The artist's medium was watercolor."

motor, engine An *engine* develops its own power, usually through internal combustion or the pressure of air, steam or water passing over vanes attached to a wheel: an airplane engine, an automobile engine, a jet engine, a missile engine, a steam engine, a turbine engine. A *motor* receives power from an outside source: an electric motor, a hydraulic motor.

nauseated, nauseous A person becomes *nauseated* because of something that is *nauseous*, which means causing nausea. It is wrong to say a person who is ill is nauseous: "While on the trip, she was nauseated because she suffers from motion sickness."

negligent, negligible To be *negligent* is to be careless, inattentive or neglectful: "This place will shelter the children of negligent parents." *Negligible* refers to that which can be disregarded, a trifling: "At the end of the week, the amount of work left to do on the house was negligible."

odious, odorous *Odious* means hateful, disgusting or offensive, as in an odious task. Something fragrant is *odorous*, as in odorous flowers.

palate, palette, pallet The *palate* is the roof of the mouth. Although the taste buds are not located there, in common usage the word *palate* applies to taste. An artist uses a *palette* for mixing paints. A *pallet* is a small, simple bed or a low platform for moving and stacking materials, as in a warehouse.

parlay, parley To *parlay* is to bet an original wager plus its earnings on another race or game: "He parlayed $10 into $1,000." *Parley* comes from *parler*, the French word for speak, and means to confer, especially with an enemy.

partially, partly Most dictionaries list these words as synonyms in the sense of part of the whole. *Partially* can also mean showing favoritism. If there is room for ambiguity, use *partly*: "The work was partly done."

pedal, petal, peddle You *pedal* a bicycle. A flower has *petals*. When selling something, you *peddle* it.

pendant, pendent A *pendant* is an ornamental hanging object, such as a locket or earring: "She wore a silver pendant." *Pendent* means suspended, overhanging, undecided or pending.

perquisite, prerequisite A *perquisite* is something in addition to the regular pay for one's work: "A perquisite of the position is the use of a health club." A short form of *perquisite* is *perk*. A *prerequisite* is something required beforehand as a necessary condition. In education, for example, a student must complete basic courses as prerequisites to more advanced courses.

persecute, prosecute To *persecute* is to afflict constantly so as to injure or distress, particularly for reasons of race or religion: "The Jewish people were persecuted by the Nazis." To *prosecute* is to conduct legal proceedings against one accused of a crime: "The state will prosecute those arrested for selling illegal drugs."

perspective, prospective *Perspective* refers to the appearance of objects as determined by their relative distance and position; it also refers to a sense of proportion: "The artist's paintings have unusual perspective." It has come to be used as a synonym of viewpoint: "What is your perspective on this matter?" *Prospective* is an adjective meaning expected or likely: "Jones is the prospective candidate for the job."

podium, lectern A speaker stands on a *podium* or dais. The speaker stands behind a *lectern*.

populous, populace A thickly populated place is *populous*: "The cost of living is usually high in such populous places as New York City." *Populace* refers to the common people, the masses: "The politician was admired by the populace."

precede, proceed To *precede* is to come before something or someone: "The attendants will precede the bride down the aisle." *Proceed* means to go ahead or to continue some action: "He proceeded to read the newspaper." The plural noun *proceeds* refers to the yield derived from a commercial or fund-raising venture.

predominant, predominate As an adjective, use *predominant*, and use *predominate* as a verb. Both refer to having influence over others or being dominant in frequency: "The New York Yankees were the predominant baseball team during the 1950s." "The teams predominated the American League."

prescribe, proscribe *Prescribe* means to order, as a medicine is prescribed by a doctor. *Proscribe* means to prohibit, outlaw or denounce: "Drunken driving is proscribed behavior."

pretense, pretext A *pretense* is a false show, an overt act intended to conceal personal feelings: "My profuse compliments were a pretense." A *pretext* is a motive or reason for action offered in place of the true one: "She was accused of tardiness, but that was only a pretext for sexism."

principle, principal A guiding rule or basic truth is a *principle* (a noun): "He followed the principle 'live and let live.'" *Principal,* which can be used as either a noun or an adjective, means first, dominant or leading thing. A memory aid taught to schoolchildren is "The principal is your pal" because the dominant person at most schools is the principal. In the early years of a home mortgage, most of the monthly payments are applied to the interest on the loan rather than the *principal* (the dominant amount).

reckless Heedless or rash. It is *reckless* (not wreckless) driving that often causes automobile accidents.

recur, reoccur Copperud (American Usage and Style) found that most experts see no distinction between these forms. Of the language authorities he consulted, only one said that *reoccur* suggests a single repetition. The consensus is that *recur* and *recurrence* are preferred.

regardless Not *irregardless.*

reluctant, reticent *Reluctant* means that someone does not want to act: "She was reluctant to audition for the play." *Reticent* means disposed to keep silent: "He was reticent about his failed marriage."

remediable, remedial Something that can be fixed is *remediable.* Something that is meant to be a remedy is *remedial:* "The student enrolled in remedial reading."

repairable, reparable Both words mean that something can be fixed. *Repairable* is used for physical items: "The child's toy is repairable." *Reparable* is used with nonphysical things: "I hope that the damage to the group's morale is reparable."

rise, raise See Rule 31 in Chapter 2.

rye, wry *Rye* is grass. *Wry,* from an Old English word meaning to turn, is used in the sense of twisted, distorted or ironic, as in wry humor.

say, said The most serviceable words of attribution. Other verbs of attribution, including *stated, declared, admitted, screamed, yelled, shouted* and *cried,* have meanings different from *said* and should not be used unless they accurately describe the speaker's demeanor. Sources don't *grin, frown, smile* or *giggle* their comments to a reporter.

seasonable, seasonal *Seasonable* means timely, suitable to the season: "A wool suit is seasonable for winter." *Seasonal* means depending on the season: "Fresh vegetables are seasonal."

shear, sheer *Shear* means to cut off, as in shear wool from sheep. *Sheer* as a verb means to turn aside or cause to turn aside, to swerve: "The truck sheered from the mountainside." As an adjective, *sheer* refers to very thin, transparent material, as in sheer curtains. It can also mean absolute or utter, as in sheer folly.

similar to Not *similar with.*

sit, set See Rule 31 in Chapter 2.

sleight, slight *Sleight* means skill with the hands, especially in deceiving onlookers, as in magic: sleight of hand. To *slight* is to treat as unimportant; as a noun *slight* can refer to the condition of being treated as unimportant: "The slight was unintentional." As an adjective, *slight* can mean light, slender in build, frail or fragile, as in the slight man.

sniffle, snivel *Sniffle* means the act or sound of sniffling or, as a verb, to sniff repeatedly. *Snivel* means to cry and sniffle or to complain and whine.

spade, spayed A *spade* is a shovel. To *spay* is to sterilize a female animal by removing the ovaries. *Spayed* is the past tense of *spay.*

strop, strap The leather band for sharpening razors is a razor *strop,* not *strap.*

supersede To replace or succeed: "The agency issued guidelines that supersede those adopted in 1988." *Supersede* is often misspelled. It is the only word in the English language that ends in *sede.* Three words end in *ceed: succeed, exceed* and *proceed.* The others end in *cede.*

supposed to The correct form (not *suppose to*) in the sense of *expected to:* "I am supposed to attend training sessions this week."

tack, tact In addition to being a short nail, a **tack** is a course of action or the direction a ship goes in relation to the position of the sails: "He decided to use a different tack to reach his goals." *Tact* means a delicate perception of the right thing to say or do without offending: "Mending the relationship will require tact." *Tactful* is the adjective form, as in a tactful person.

teem, team *Teem* means to be prolific, to abound, to swarm. The present participle form is *teeming,* not *teaming:* "The room was teeming with flies."

tempera, tempura *Tempera* is used in painting, *tempura* in cooking.

temperatures They get higher or lower, but they don't get cooler or warmer.

tenant, tenet A *tenant* is one who pays rent to occupy land or a building. A *tenet* is a principle, doctrine or belief held as a truth: "Doing unto others as you would have them do unto you is a tenet of Christianity."

that, which See Rule 18 in Chapter 2.

there Generally, sentences should not begin with *there,* as in *there is, there was, there were.* Rather than writing "There were four touchdowns scored in the game," write "The team scored four touchdowns." Get to the real subject rather than using a false subject. Examples abound of good writing with sentences beginning with *there,* especially when the idea is to downplay the true subject, but more often in common usage *there* at the beginning is a signal of lazy thinking.

tort, torte *Tort* is a legal term referring to a wrongful act or damage not involving a breach of contract for which a civil action can be brought: "Libel is an example of a tort." A *torte* is a rich cake.

toward Correct usage in the United States; the British prefer *towards*.

translucent, transparent When looking through something that is *translucent*, one can see light but cannot see objects on the other side; one would be able to see through a *transparent* glass or fabric: "He installed translucent windows in the office to provide privacy."

trooper, trouper A *trooper* is a member of the cavalry, a mounted police officer or a state police officer. A *trouper* is a member of a troop of actors or singers. *Trouper* is also used to refer to a veteran entertainer.

type Use as a noun, not an adjective. Incorrect: "He is a studious type person." Instead, say "He is a studious type." *Type* with a hyphen is acceptable in technical uses, as in B-type blood.

unique Something that is unique is one of a kind, so expressions like *more unique, most unique* and *very unique* should be avoided.

up Avoid its use as part of a verb, as in *stood up, beat up, paired up* and *stirred up*.

venal, venial *Venal* means open to or characterized by corruption or bribery, as in a venal government official. *Venial* means that which may be forgiven or is pardonable, as in a venial sin.

veracious, voracious To be *veracious* is to be habitually truthful or honest: "A veracious person is not likely to become a thief." *Voracious* comes from a Latin word meaning devour. It means greedy, ravenous or very eager, as in a voracious reader.

viral, virile *Viral* means of or caused by a virus, which is an organism that causes certain diseases: "He is ill with a viral disease" (not with a virus). *Virile* means of or characteristic of a man's ability to function sexually. Alternatives to *virile* that can refer to both sexes include *energetic, vigorous, strong, dynamic* or *bold*.

waist, waste *Waist* is correct for referring to part of the human body: "He put his arm around her waist."

wangle, wrangle To *wangle* is to get or cause by contrivance or tricks: "Can you wangle an invitation to the party?" To *wrangle* is to argue or quarrel. As a noun, *wrangle* means an angry, noisy dispute. A *wrangler* is a ranch hand who herds livestock, especially saddle horses.

well-known, widely known Journalistic usage prefers *widely known* to describe someone whose name or work is known by many people: "The actor Brad Pitt is widely known, but few of his fans have ever met him, so they do not know him well."

who's, whose See Rule 17 in Chapter 2.

wholly Entirely: "The incorporated village was wholly within the city."

wreak, wreck *Wreak* means to inflict: "The storm will wreak havoc on our new plants." To *wreck* is to damage.

Common spelling errors

Most word processing programs for computers now have spell-check functions, but as the following poem shows, they are far from foolproof.

Spell Checker Blue It

I have a spelling checker;
It came with my PC.
It plane lee marks four my revue
Mistakes I cannot sea.
I've run this poem rite threw it.
I'm sure your pleas to no,
Its letter perfect in it's weigh.
My checker tolled me sew.

As useful as computerized spell-checker programs are, they are not designed to catch correctly spelled but misused words, so a good copy editor would never rely entirely on such an aid. Following are a few commonly misspelled words. Keep in mind that in some cases there are alternative correct spellings (*advisor, good-bye*) but that these are the preferred ones.

a lot	business	embarrass	immediately	nickel
acceptable	caffeine	employee	inevitable	niece
accessible	calendar	envelop	innocence	ninth
accidentally	canceled	envelope	inseparable	occasion
accommodate	cancellation	equipped	jewelry	occurred
accumulate	category	erroneous	judgment	offered
acknowledgment	cellar	exaggerate	knowledgeable	omitted
across	cemetery	experience	laid	ordinarily
adviser	chief	familiar	legitimate	parallel
alleged	Cincinnati	February	leisure	pastime
allotted	commemorate	fierce	liaison	percent
already	commitment	financial	lieutenant	personal
Alzheimer's disease	committee	foreign	lightning	personnel
anoint	comparable	fortunate	likable	physician
apparent	compatible	forty	loose	pigeon
appearance	conceive	fraudulent	lose	possession
appellant	criticize	gauge	lovable	potato
arctic	desirable	goodbye	mantel	potatoes
argument	dilemma	grammar	mantle	practically
assistant	disappoint	grievance	marshal	prairie
attendance	discipline	guarantee	medicine	preferred
bachelor	doughnut	harass	mischievous	preparation
beggar	drowned	height	misspell	pretense
beginning	drunkenness	heir	naive	prevalence
broccoli	eighth	illegitimate	necessary	preventive

Professional perspective: Poynter Institute faculty

Spelling tips

The faculty at the Poynter Institute, a school for journalists, future journalists and teachers of journalism, suggests these tricks for spelling tricky words.

accommodate	Everything is double except a DATE.	innovate	The INN has to innovate to survive.
all right	Two words. Associate with "all wrong."	memento	They hold MEMories, not moments.
attendance	At ten dance—be there.	millennium	Double all consonants.
Believe	You can't believe in a LIE.	occasion	Don't be an *ass*.
capitol	It has a dome.	questionnaire	There are always at least two questions on a questionnaire.
compliment	Is what *I* like to get.	stationary	This word means stAnding.
definite	A FINITE thing.	stationery	This is for writing letters. Or E for
dependable	All ABLE workers are.		envelope.
desert	The Sahara has one *s*; so does this.	tragedy	Every AGE has a tragedy.
Dessert	Strawberry sundae—SS.	vaccine	Measured in Cubic Centimeters.
fluorescent	He got the FLU looking for the ORE that has no SCENT.	villain	He has a *villa in* the country.
graffiti	Funky Frank takes his graffiti seriously. (Two f's, one t)		
hear	With my *ear*.		

For more tips on "Doing Journalism," see the Poynter Institute Web site, http://www.poynter.org.

professor	resistance	sergeant	sophomore	tournament
quantity	responsibility	sheriff	succeed	truly
questionnaire	rhyme	siege	successful	ukulele
readable	rhythm	signaled	superintendent	usable
receipt	ridiculous	similar	supersede	vacuum
receive	sacrilegious	sincerely	surprise	veterinary
recommend	schedule	sizable	surveillance	villain
recur	scissors	skier	tendency	weird
referee	seize	skiing	thoroughly	wherever
religious	seizure	soldier	tobacco	X-ray
repetitious	separate			

For spellings not covered in the *Associated Press Stylebook, Webster's New World College Dictionary* is the authority.

Suggestions for additional reading

Barzun, Jacques. *Simple & Direct.* New York: HarperCollins, 2001.

Brooks, Brian S., James L. Pinson, and Jean Gaddy Wilson. *Working With Words: A Concise Handbook for Media Writers and Editors,* 6th ed. New York: St. Martin's Press, 2006.

Burchfield, R.W. *The New Fowler's Modern English Usage,* 3rd ed. Oxford, England: Oxford University Press, 1998.

Darling, Charles. *Guide to Grammar and Writing.* Online. http://grammar.ccc .commnet.edu/grammar.

Glenn, Cheryl, Robert K. Miller, Suzanne Strobeck Webb, and Loretta Gray. *Hodges' Harbrace Handbook,* 15th ed. Belmont, Calif.: Wadsworth, 2004.

Kessler, Lauren, and Duncan McDonald. *When Words Collide: A Media Writer's Guide to Grammar and Style,* 6th ed. Belmont, Calif.: Wadsworth, 2004.

Maggio, Rosalie. *Talking About People: A Guide to Fair and Accurate Language.* Phoenix, Ariz.: Oryx, 1997.

Miller, Casey, and Kate Swift. *Handbook of Nonsexist Writing,* 2nd ed. New York: Harper & Row, 1988.

Purdue University Online Writing Lab, http://owl.english.purdue.edu.

Schwartz, Marilyn. *Guidelines for Bias-Free Writing,* 2nd ed. Bloomington, Ind.: Indiana University Press, 1995.

Strunk, William, and E.B. White. *The Elements of Style,* 4th ed. Allyn & Bacon, 2000.

Truss, Lynn. *Eats, Shoots & Leaves—The Zero Tolerance Approach to Punctuation.* London: Profile Books Ltd., 2003.

University of Wisconsin-Madison Writing Center, http://www.wisc.edu/writing.

Zinsser, William. *On Writing Well,* 30th anniversary ed. New York: HarperCollins, 2006.

Checking Facts

"If your mother says she loves you, check it out!" This adage has been around newsrooms for decades, serving as a reminder of the importance of journalistic accuracy and the role skepticism plays in achieving accuracy. Another newsroom notion holds that the ideal copy editor knows everything about something and something about everything. Language is the "something" that a perfect copy editor would know "everything" about. Reference materials provide the sources for editors to know "something about everything." Assigning editors should detect gross inaccuracies and holes in a story and return it to the reporter who wrote it instead of sending it forward to the copy desk.

Yet, copy editors must always be alert to errors, discrepancies and illogical statements in copy. Much of the skill in checking facts exists in sensing which specific facts to question because the sheer volume of copy a newspaper editor handles under deadline pressure does not allow the luxury of checking every single fact in each story. Editors dealing with online copy face even greater deadline pressure, as Web sites are revised frequently each day. Editors at public relations firms and magazines, where the pace tends to be less hectic, should double-check each fact in every story. Magazines typically hire fact checkers for this purpose. The most frequent errors in news stories are in names, dates, locations and descriptions of past events.

When copy editors question facts in a story, four courses of action are open to them:

1. If the question can be answered by a reference source, the verification or correction can be made rather easily, provided the copy editor is facile at using reference materials.

2. If the writer is readily available, the question can be referred to that person.

3. If it is a question of company policy, taste or consistency, copy editors should know the policy, but if they have doubts, they must consult the chief copy editor or a managing editor.

4. If the fact is not vital and cannot be checked before deadline, it can be deleted from the story. Of course, this is the last resort, not merely an easy way out of a difficulty. A fact that is essential to the story must be checked at all costs, even if the story is held until a later edition.

To achieve the goal of being 100 percent accurate, copy editors need a librarian's working knowledge of reference materials in both printed and electronic format. This chapter provides overviews and lists of electronic reference materials on general and specialized topics, emphasizing those most useful for quick fact checking common to copy desk work.

To work efficiently, editors need to know when to consult a standard reference work, probably within reach on the copy desk or just a few keystrokes away on the Internet, and when a specialized book or electronic database is needed. Here is a sampling of questions that regularly send copy editors scrambling for answers:

- Was the architect for the General Motors Building in Detroit Albert Kahn or Louis Kahn?

- When did Pakistan become a republic?

- What is the name of the highest point in Australia?

- Which is the correct name: Southwestern Baptist Theological Seminary or Southwest Baptist Theological Seminary? Is it in Dallas or Fort Worth?

- In what year was Hillary Rodham Clinton born?

- How many stars does the flag of Honduras have?

- What were the top five U.S. companies in terms of advertising expenditures in 2000?

- Who is the mayor of Omaha, Neb.?

- According to the Bureau of Labor Statistics, what two occupations were projected to be the fastest growing during the next decade?

Experienced copy editors recognize that an up-to-date copy of *The World Almanac and Book of Facts* answers all these questions. With practice, copy editors and other fact checkers gain enough familiarity with these sources to know where to go for specific types of information and how to find it fast.

Although previous editions of this textbook included exhaustive lists of standard reference works, this fifth edition focuses on Internet resources. Many reference book publishers issue both print and online versions, usually accessible by subscription only, and more libraries are opting now for online versions to save shelving space and labor. Users of this textbook will need to use their university or employer Web portal to gain use of those fee-based databases, but most of the resources listed in this chapter are free.

Reliability of reference sources

Journalists must exercise good judgment before relying on any information source, whether it comes from a personal interview or a printed or electronic document. This caution applies particularly to materials posted on the World Wide Web. Whereas subject-matter specialists edit and review standard print reference works and their online counterparts, other documents floating around cyberspace are the electronic equivalent of over-the-transom manuscripts that may or may not be worthwhile or accurate. Anyone with a rudimentary knowledge of HTML (Hyper-Text Markup Language) or Web authoring software and access to space on a server can post documents to the Web. Editors must decide what is reliable and what is junk. Publishers of standard reference works have established reputations for accuracy and can be trusted to maintain similar rigor in their online publications and electronic databases.

Not all references are created equal. No foolproof method exists to distinguish reputable Internet publishers from untrustworthy amateurs, but understanding Internet domains and recognizing the purpose of individual Web pages can help editors assess the accuracy of online information. To determine the domain, examine the URL (Uniform Resource Locator) of the particular information. Figure 4-1 explains how to break down e-mail and Web site addresses.

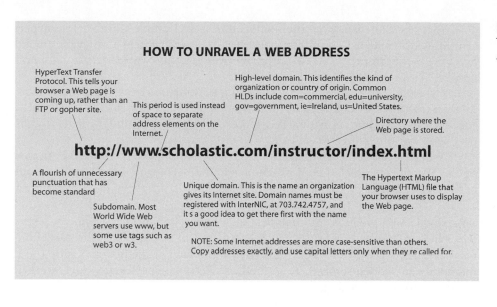

Figure 4-1
The anatomy of a Web address.

Generic top-level domains in operation since the 1980s are as follows:

- **mil** = military agency (U.S.)
- **gov** = government institutions (U.S.)
- **edu** = educational institutions
- **org** = nonprofit organization
- **com** = commercial
- **net** = networks
- **de, uk,** etc. = two-letter, nation-specific designations (for example, **de** is Germany, **uk** is United Kingdom)

Additional top-level domains that have become operational more recently are as follows:

- **aero** = aviation industry
- **arpa** = Address and Routing Parameter Area domain, designated exclusively for Internet-infrastructure purposes
- **biz** = businesses
- **cat** = Catalan linguistic and cultural community
- **coop** = cooperatives
- **info** = all uses
- **int** = domain registering organizations established by international treaties between governments
- **jobs** = human resource managers
- **mobi** = consumers and providers of mobile products and services
- **museum** = museums
- **name** = individuals
- **pro** = certified professionals and related entities
- **travel** = travel industry

Fact checkers can learn the name, address and phone number for owners of unique domains for nonmilitary and non-U.S. government top-level domains by going to the InterNIC Registration Services at http://www.internic.net/whois .html.

Generally, information in the .gov and .edu domains ranks higher on reliability than that in other domains, but this is not a hard-and-fast rule. After all, many educational institutions provide server space to all faculty, staff and students with no peer review or other attempts at verifying what is posted.

When assessing the reliability of online information, also consider the purpose of the Web site on which the information is found. Web pages usually fall into one of these categories:

▶**Personal.** *Pages published by an individual who may or may not be affiliated with a larger institution.* Personal pages may reside on any of the domains; the most common are .net or .com, and .edu for students and faculty members. A tilde (~) is frequently embedded somewhere in the URL. Personal pages vary widely in their usefulness for fact checking.

▶**Advocacy.** *Pages promoting ideas and trying to sway public opinion.* These typically reside in the .org domain. As with printed materials, editors must consider the source and know the agenda of the organization sponsoring the page.

▶**Informational.** *Pages for the purpose of presenting factual information.* The URLs frequently end in .edu or .gov because educational institutions or government agencies sponsor them, but commercial information brokers using a .com domain also post material on the Web.

▶**Marketing.** *Pages created to sell products and services.* These exist primarily on the .com domain and their sponsors range from Fortune 500 companies to scam artists.

▶**News.** *Pages with the primary purpose of providing current information.* News organizations generally sponsor these pages, with URLs also used in the .com domain.

What about Wikipedia? This online interactive encyclopedia far exceeds any other encyclopedia in its number of entries, which are updated daily by anyone who wants to participate. But this is a situation where bigger and democratic may not be better.

"Wikipedia is a combination of manifesto and reference work," wrote The New Yorker in a July 2006 article. Author Stacy Schiff wrote:

> It is also no more immune to human nature than any other utopian project. Pettiness, idiocy, and vulgarity are regular features of the site. Nothing about high-minded collaboration guarantees accuracy, and open editing invites abuse.

Exemplifying this characterization are entries that Wikipedia's five-person staff periodically close to editing: God, Galileo, George W. Bush, Al Gore, Frédéric Chopin, poodles and oranges.

Examples of inaccuracies in Wikipedia abound, but one that particularly resonated with journalists was the vile biography of John Seigenthaler, a former president of the American Society of Newspaper Editors, founder of the First Amendment Center and a 50-year news veteran. In a brief sojourn from journalism during the administration of President John F. Kennedy, Seigenthaler served as administrative assistant to Attorney General Robert F. Kennedy, specializing in civil rights. Instead of portraying Seigenthaler as a friend and colleague of the Kennedy brothers, Wikipedia's biography cast him as a suspect in their assassinations.

Figure 4-2 provides a checklist for evaluating the merit of Web pages.

Accuracy: Does the page list the author and institution that published the page and provide a way of contacting the author?

Authority: Does the page list the author's credentials and is its domain a preferred domain (.edu, .gov)? Is the information cited correctly? Are citations to reputable sources? Are there links to related sources, and are the linked sites authoritative?

Objectivity: Does the page provide accurate information with limited advertising, and does it present information in an objective manner rather than as advocacy or opinion?

Currency: Is the page current, and is the date of the most recent update indicated on the page? Are links (if any) also up-to-date?

Coverage: Are accompanying links evaluated and do they complement the document's theme?

Expert evaluation: Check a reputable directory for evaluations of the page. Directories that provide evaluations include Academic Info at http://www.academicinfo.net/, Infomine at http://infomine.ucr.edu/ and Librarians' Internet Index at http://www.lii.org/.

Figure 4-2
When fact-checking material, copy editors should apply these guidelines to evaluate the credibility of Web pages.

E-mail is a tool more helpful to reporters than to copy editors working under deadline pressure. E-mail discussion lists can be good sources for opinions, but better electronic sources exist for fact checking. Discussion lists and those of special interest to journalists and public relations practitioners will be discussed later in this chapter.

Internet search tools

The Internet is like a gigantic research library without a card catalog or a shopping mall without locator maps or directional signs. Widespread adoption of the World Wide Web in the 1990s simplified Net navigation. Then came search tools to help users find information, but, thus far, no single search can ferret out everything on the Internet about a particular topic.

Estimates vary, but Google reportedly indexes somewhere around 9 billion Web pages, only a fraction of existing pages. It's such a wonderful tool that lowercase *google* has become part of the English language (Figure 4-3), but Internet sources cited in this chapter lead to more efficient searches without wading through pages of results irrelevant to copy editors' need for specific facts.

An Internet search is a process, requiring several stages, much like using reference books in a library. Many search tools use Boolean logic, a way to combine terms using AND, OR, AND NOT and sometimes NEAR. All terms must appear in a record if AND is used. OR retrieves records with either term. AND NOT excludes terms. Parentheses may be used to sequence operations and group words. Almost all search tools on the Web display a Help icon, and the few minutes it takes to read the search tips for that particular tool will speed the search in the long term.

The word *google* with a small *g* has been added to the Merriam-Webster online dictionary as a verb. The definition is "to use the Google search engine to obtain information . . . on the World Wide Web," as in, "Let me google that."

Figure 4-3
While Google, Yahoo! and others index billions of Web pages, billions more pages exist that search engines do not find.

These are three types of Internet search tools:

- Search engines

- Metasearch engines, also called all-in-one searches, parallel searches or metacrawlers

- Lists of databases or hypertext links indexed by subject, sometimes called "webliographies," to correspond with bibliographies of printed resources

Search and metasearch engines and all-in-one pages

Some search engines are *crawler-based,* meaning that they use computer programs called "spiders" to scan the Internet continually. Examples are Yahoo! and Google. Everything the spider finds goes into the search engine index, sometimes called the catalog. Other search engines are more correctly referred to as human-powered *directories* like Open Directory, which rely on humans to build listings to describe Web sites. Still other search engines are *hybrids* or *mixed results* in that they return results that combine crawler-based and human-powered listings.

Metasearch engines, also called *metacrawlers,* send searches to several search engines at the same time. The results from each engine are then blended to form one page for the user. Some experts recommend using an all-in-one engine at the beginning of the search; other experts like to begin with a single engine before conducting a metasearch. Drawbacks of metasearches are the slight increase in retrieval time and the lack of precision in syntax allowed on individual search engines.

All-in-one search pages, unlike metacrawlers, do not send your query to many search engines at the same time. Instead, they generally list a wide variety of search engines and allow you to search at your choice without having to go directly to that search engine.

Search engines vary widely in their range of search features and in the way they index and present their search results. Some index complete Web pages or page titles; others add material selectively and review sites based on content; still others present subject indexes for users to browse by keywords. Some Web site administrators include coding that instructs indexing robots to omit particular pages from search results.

Another difference in search engines is that most guarantee pages will be included in their index in exchange for a fee. Google is an exception to this business model. All rely on advertising for revenue, but some engines maintain separate "editorial" services. This isn't to imply that paid listings don't contain worthwhile information on the Web pages, but search engine users aren't always informed about which results lead to editorial material rather than advertisements in disguise. An analogy would be a newspaper or TV station that did not delineate between news content and advertising messages.

Previous editions of this textbook contained names and URLs for popular search engines. Rapid changes in Internet technology and the financial instability of many Internet-based companies threaten long-term accuracy of such a list. Consequently, readers are directed instead to **Search Engine Watch** at http://www .searchenginewatch.com, a Web site that stays abreast of developments in the world of search engines—which ones are most usable, are most popular, possess special features or require payment for listings. In addition, this site offers Web searching tips and reviews, ratings and tests about how well individual engines perform. The site links users to all the major search engines, popular metasearch engines, kid-safe services and others. This site was created and is maintained by Danny Sullivan, an Internet consultant and journalist with no potentially compromising entanglements with the search engine industry.

The Computing and Technology section of About.com, now owned by The New York Times Company, provides information, tips, tricks and tutorials on search engines and links to at least 100 of them, compiled by Wendy Boswell (http://websearch.about.com/od/enginesanddirectories/).

The invisible Web

Valuable as it is, Google catalogs approximately 4 percent of the Web, according to mid-2006 estimates. Combine those results with other popular search engines, and all those robot spiders and metacrawlers may reveal as much as 10 percent of online pages. The "invisible" or "deep" Web comprises the other 90 percent of pages that search engines can't detect because the pages are stored not as static web pages but as on-demand database content, most of it free. These pages are dynamic, meaning that they exist only when readers request answers from a large, often modified database and then only temporarily. Academic institutions or government agencies compile many of these databases, so the information is more trustworthy than much of the other Internet fare.

So how do copy editors and others find hidden Web resources? It often involves a two-step process: First, locate a database on the desired topic, and then go to the database to dig into specific information. Finding a database appropriate to a topic often is as easy as typing the topic plus the word *database* into Google or another search engine. Here is a comparison of the number of results returned from Google searches:

Search Term	Number of Results
immigration	About 512,000,000 pages
immigration database	About 25,400,000

This eliminates many of the general news articles about immigration, but yields still a huge number of results to skim through. Try narrowing the search, while continuing to use the term *database*.

Search Term	Number of Results
student immigration database	About 8,170,000 pages
US student immigration database	About 7,570,000
US student immigration database + financial aid (using Google)	About 1,960,000
US student immigration database + financial aid (using Google Scholar)	About 3,420 pages

To limit the search further, one can use Google Scholar, which searches a subset of Google focusing on scholarly literature. With about 3,420 results from the narrowed search for information about this topic, fact-checking copy editors still face a daunting task, but these databases contain high-quality information, not single articles. Perhaps the copy editors will get lucky, finding a reliable answer to their queries in the first database on the result list.

The remainder of this section provides resources that may bypass the first step of finding databases hidden from Web search engines. Web experts have already completed that first step and compiled lists of their findings in subject categories that they share with the world.

To stay abreast of developing invisible Web tools, Gary Price's two sites are worth bookmarking. Price, who established a reputation for extraordinary Web research while a reference librarian at The George Washington University, became director of information resources at Ask.com in 2006. Two sites that he manages in that position are as follows:

▶ **ResourceShelf,** a daily update of resources and news for information professionals, journalists and educators, among others. http://www.resourceshelf.com/

▶ **DocuTicker,** Price's selection of resources, reports and publications from government agencies, NGOs, think tanks and other public interest organizations. http://www.docuticker.com/

Here are some of the other sites that lead to hidden Web resources:

▶ **Academic Index.** Maintained by a librarian in Texas, it indexes research-quality reference and information sources. www.academicindex.net/

▶ **BUBL Catalogue.** Covers all academic subject areas; uses the Dewey Decimal Classification system as the primary organization structure. From the Centre for Digital Library Research, Strathclyde University, Glasgow. http://bubl.ac.uk/

▶ **CompletePlanet.** Home page says the site contains more than 70,000 searchable databases and specialty search engines. http://www.completeplanet.com/

▶ **Directory of Open Access Journals.** From Sweden's Lund University Libraries, free access to the full text of more than 2,300 journals and 105,000 articles in science, humanities and social sciences with continual additions to the directory. http://www.doaj.org/

▶ **FindArticles.** Searchable article Web archive, claiming to search more than 10 million articles from leading academic, industry and general-interest publications. http://www.findarticles.com/

▶ **HighWire Press.** A division of the Stanford University Libraries, it claims to host the largest repository of free, full-text, peer-reviewed content. http://highwire.stanford.edu/

Web sites listed in subject categories later in this chapter include other database directories from the invisible Web.

Blogs

Never rely on blogs for fact checking. A problem with blogs (short for weblogs), as a journalism professor in South Africa noted in his blog, is that there is nothing that separates the wheat from the chaff. Plenty of good stuff lurks in blogs; indeed, some subject-matter experts choose that avenue to disseminate their specialized knowledge. But plenty of opinion and just plain wrong information also populates the blogosphere.

Reporters can find good story leads on blogs, and a copy editor's Internet search may lead to a blog, but double-check anything claimed to be factual there. To repeat, don't rely solely on blogs for fact checking, even if the blogger works in one's own newsroom or PR agency. In July 2006 The Pew Research Center for the People & the Press released a report on its in-depth survey and study of blogging in the United States. Figure 4-4 summarizes some of the study's findings, and the entire report can be read at http://www.pewinternet.org/PPF/r/186/report_display.asp.

Figure 4-4
Here is a summary of major conclusions of a multistage telephone survey of bloggers in the United States that The Pew Research Center for the People & the Press conducted in late 2005 and early 2006. Complete results are available on the Center's Web site.

Bloggers: Summary of Findings at a Glance
Blogging is bringing new voices to the online world.
Telephone surveys capture the most accurate snapshot possible of a small and moving target.
Contrary to the impression created by the press attention on political blogging, just 11% of bloggers say they focus mainly on government or politics.
The blogging population is young, evenly split between women and men, and racially diverse.
Relatively small groups of bloggers view blogging as a public endeavor.
The main reasons for keeping a blog are creative expression and sharing personal experiences.
Only one-third of bloggers see blogging as a form of journalism. Yet many check facts and cite original sources.
Bloggers are avid consumers and creators of online content. They are also heavy users of the internet in general.
Bloggers are major consumers of political news and about half prefer sources without particular political viewpoint.
Bloggers often utilize community and readership-enhancing features available on their blogs.
Source: Lenhart, Amanda and Susannah Fox. *Bloggers*. Washington, DC: Pew Internet & American Life Project. July 19, 2006.

Weblogs inside and outside of newsrooms have triggered changes in news operations, bringing transparency to some news operations so readers better understand the process of gathering, editing and distributing news. Blogs of media criticisms have led to some retracted or corrected stories and occasionally more aggressive pursuit and in-depth coverage of news. In addition, blogs on news Web sites offer opportunities for readers to interact with news organizations.

Like consolidation in the mainstream media, or MSM in blog speak, as blogging became popular, networks of blogs quickly sprang up to offer more eyeballs to potentially lucrative advertising markets. One of those networks, Weblogs Inc., attracted enough page views to lead to an AOL buyout in late 2005 for reportedly between $20 million and $35 million and a CEO position for the its originator.

How to find blogs. These sites help readers find blogs about particular subjects:

▶**Blog Search Engine.** Claims to search more than 10 million weblogs. http://www.blogsearchengine.com/

▶**Blogwise.** A directory of blogs, grouped by keyword and country. Intends to be a guide to blogs around the world. http://www.blogwise.com/

▶**Technorati.** In addition to claiming to track almost 50 million blogs, this site lists topics that users are searching and bloggers are writing about most often. http://technorati.com/

To find blogs written by journalists, some expounding on their beats or news jobs and others about personal interests, go to the list at the Cyberjournalist.netWeb site: http://www.cyberjournalist.net/cyberjournalists.php.

Blogs for copy editors. The blogs in the following list focus on copy editing. Scores of other blogs cover the media in general or specific aspects of media work.

▶ **A Capital Idea.** Covers grammar and newspapers; written by Nicole Stockdale, a copy editor at The Dallas Morning News. http://nstockdale.blogspot.com/

▶ **Common Sense Journalism.** Written by Doug Fisher, former AP news editor for South Carolina who now teaches journalism at the University of South Carolina. http://commonsensej.blogspot.com/

▶ **Copy Massage.** "Muses on the copy, the editing and the quirky rules that make folks despise us," according to its writer, Clay McCuistion, who says he edits copy at "a Tampa Bay paper." http://copymassage.blogspot.com/

▶ **The Editor's Desk.** Discusses editing and writing, with an emphasis on the concerns of the newspaper copy desk; written by Andy Bechtel, a former copy editor who now teaches journalism at the University of North Carolina. http://editdesk .blogspot.com/

▶ **NewsDesigner.com.** Emphasizes newspaper design and features photos of newspaper pages; written by Mark Friesen, a news designer at The Oregonian. http://www .newsdesigner.com/blog/

▶ **The Slot.** Springs from Washington Post copy desk chief Bill Walsh's Web site where he has posted excellent resources for copy editors since 1995. http://theslot.blogspot .com/

Web sites for communicators

Subject-area experts compiled the lists in this section especially for journalists and public relations practitioners and students preparing for careers in communications. Copy editors may find it easier to bookmark one of these lists for launching search tools rather than bookmarking dozens of individual reference sources. The sites included here inform communicators about developments and current topics in their specialized fields and provide training materials. If the URL indicated here has changed since publication of this textbook, look for the site by entering its name into a search engine. The following sites are listed in alphabetical order:

▶ **CyberJournalist.net.** Focuses on how the Internet, convergence and new technologies are changing the media. The site offers tips, news and commentary about online journalism, citizen's media, digital storytelling, converged news operations and using the Internet as a reporting tool. http://www.cyberjournalist.net

▶ **EditTeach.org.** In addition to tips for improving news content and editing skills, this site, operated by the Knight Ohio Program for Editing and Editing Education at Ohio University, provides exercises for students and professionals to test their skills. http://www.editteach.org

▶ **A Journalist's Guide to the Internet.** The name may be misleading because this site provides annotated links to Internet resources on a variety of material for public relations practitioners and journalists. http://reporter.umd.edu

▶**The Journalist's Toolbox.** Features thousands of Web sites helpful to the media and other researchers. The site includes information from a variety of journalistic beats and news industry–related topics and has a separate page with links to editing resources. Begun by Mike Reilley, who spent 10 years reporting and copy editing at the Los Angeles Times and the Chicago Tribune, this site is now owned by the American Press Institute. http://www.americanpressinstitute.org/pages/toolbox/

▶**Megasources.** Includes links for finding expert human sources, basic Internet reference materials and gateways for a variety of special topics, compiled by Dean Tudor, emeritus professor at the School of Journalism, Ryerson Polytechnic University, Toronto, Canada. http://www.ryerson.ca/~dtudor/megasources.htm

▶**Power Reporting Bookmarks.** Compiled by Bill Dedman, Pulitzer Prize winner and former director of computer-assisted reporting for The Associated Press; includes thousands of free research tools organized in easy-to-use categories. http://powerreporting.com

▶**The Writers' Well.** Provides links to multiple dictionaries, encyclopedias and other reference materials of special interest to writers. It also includes links to e-zines, online versions of print magazines and sites devoted to many famous authors. Ink Magazine sponsors this site. http://www.hellskitchen.com/well.htm

See Figure 4-5 for a list of Web sites of professional organizations of interest to journalists, public relations practitioners and others in communication-related fields.

American Copy Editors Society: http://www.copydesk.org
American Society of Newspaper Editors: http://www.asne.org
Associated Collegiate Press: http://studentpress.journ.umn.edu
Associated Press Managing Editors: http://www.apme.com
The Freedom Forum: http://www.freedomforum.org
Investigative Reporters and Editors: http://www.ire.org
National Association of Black Journalists: http://www.nabj.org
National Association of Broadcasters: http://www.nab.org
National Association of Hispanic Journalists:
    http://www.nahj.org/home/home.shtml
National Press Club: http://npc.press.org
National Press Photographers Association: http://www.nppa.org
National Scholastic Press Association: http://studentpress.journ.umn.edu
Online News Association: http://www.cyberjournalist.net
Organization of News Ombudsmen: http://www.newsombudsmen.org
The Poynter Institute: http://www.poynter.org
Public Relations Society of America: http://www.prsa.org
Public Relations Student Society of America: http://www.prssa.org
Reporters Committee for Freedom of the Press: http://www.rcfp.org
Society for News Design: http://www.snd.org
Society of Professional Journalists: http://spj.org
Society of Publication Designers: http://www.spd.org
The Student Press Law Center: http://www.splc.org

Figure 4-5
Many professional associations, foundations and institutes host Web sites with content related to communications, and most contain links to related sites. Here is a sampling.

Internet discussion groups

Although more useful for reporters in gathering information for stories than for editors, Internet discussion groups, also called *listservs* and ***mailing lists,*** can be helpful for fact checking when copy editors aren't facing immediate deadlines.

Members of discussion groups exchange opinions and information via e-mail with people who share common interests. With an e-mail account established, it is simple to join such a group. First, decide which group or groups are of interest, and then send an e-mail message to the central computer serving those particular groups.

To communicate with other group subscribers, send an e-mail message to the list address (not the same as the subscription address), and the message will be circulated automatically to all members. The list of discussion groups numbers in the thousands, dealing with almost every subject imaginable. Some groups discuss highly specialized academic-related topics; others focus on popular culture, sports, recreational activities and hobbies.

Keep a listserv's initial return message that acknowledges a subscription and explains how that particular list operates. This information includes instructions about how to quit the group temporarily or permanently. It will also explain whether the list has a digest or index feature or is archived. Some discussion lists generate multiple messages each day, rather quickly filling electronic mailboxes.

The initial acknowledgment message also may include important notes about proper etiquette observed by members. Despite a sense of anonymity offered by the Net, segments of the Internet, including discussion groups, operate like social or professional gatherings and individual communities. One doesn't want to become an unwelcome presence in the community. Newcomers to a discussion group should "lurk" awhile, meaning that they should read mail from other members for a few days before sending their own messages.

Another caution: Many, if not most, messages posted to discussion lists are opinions, not facts. Don't accept material from discussion lists as factual without verifying the information. In addition to real experts, these lists attract self-proclaimed experts who may transmit inaccurate statements. It's wise to "unsubscribe" from lists that turn out to be uninteresting or generate too many messages.

Here's another piece of advice, particularly for students: Don't post questions to a discussion group that can be answered by using readily available reference sources. No member wants to spend time or money reading a message from someone who appears too lazy to go to a library or to conduct online searches. A request to discussion group members for help on a term paper or other research project is appropriate only after other resources have been exhausted. Summarize sources already consulted and information already known about the topic, and then frame a specific, narrow question for members to address.

To find discussion lists and addresses for subscribing, use an Internet browser to search this site:

▶**CataList:** This is the catalog for a commercial discussion list manager, LISTSERV™. This page enables users to browse any of the public discussions managed by LISTSERV lists, search for mailing lists of interest, and get information about LISTSERV host sites. This information is generated automatically from LISTSERV's LISTS database and is always up-to-date. At the time of this writing, CataList included information on 81,093 public lists. http://www.lsoft.com/lists/listref.html

Usenet newsgroups

Usenet newsgroups have been called the water coolers of the Internet. They are similar to discussion groups in that they contain messages from people worldwide and are grouped by interest, but users gain access to groups and read messages via the

World Wide Web instead of e-mail. Newsgroups tend to be much less scholarly than discussion lists, but content varies according to academic disciplines. Thousands of Usenet newsgroups exist and new ones are created daily.

Newsreaders, a feature of Internet browsers and most Internet service providers, offer access to newsgroups, although ISPs usually narrow the list somewhat instead of trying to carry all of them. Online files accompany browsers and ISP newsreader programs to help users configure their computers to the specifications of individual newsreaders. The next step is to determine which newsgroups to read. Here one needs to understand how newsgroups are organized in hierarchies.

Newsgroup hierarchies begin with the major subject area, followed by several words, each separated by a dot, describing subareas. For example, *rec.sports* is a newsgroup about sports; *rec.sports.basketball.women* is a more specialized rec.sports group about women's basketball. The following are the major newsgroup hierarchies:

▶**alt** (alternate). Anything goes in this category, and almost any one person can add a newsgroup to the alt group. Some ISPs don't carry the alt newsgroup because of the huge number of them and because the content of many is objectionable to ISP customers.

▶**comp** (computers). These range from highly technical geekspeak to discussions of the merits of individual computer manufacturers.

▶**misc** (miscellaneous). These are the topics that either don't fit in any of the other hierarchies or that are too general to fit a specific one.

▶**rec** (recreation). Here people discuss topics such as sports, hobbies, outdoor activities, games and television. Each hobby, game and television show may spawn a separate newsgroup.

▶**sci** (science). Discussions here get fairly technical. The group is subdivided into various scientific disciplines such as sci.physics.

▶**soc** (social). All sorts of societal and cultural issues are aired here. Social topics may subdivide further to focus on an individual country, state or city, for example.

▶**talk.** Here the talk is frequently about controversial, often emotional topics such as politics and religion.

The search engines listed earlier in this chapter can lead to newsgroups.

Commercial electronic databases

Much information on the Internet is free, particularly most databases containing government records, but, increasingly, news organizations and other information brokers have begun to charge fees for information as they attempt to recoup their expenses and make a profit. Some database vendors have been in the information-selling business for many years and recently adapted their services to electronic technology, offering duplicate or similar services in both print and electronic versions. Other vendors concentrate solely on computerized databases. Online versions generally have a search feature.

Costs of many electronic databases are prohibitive for most individuals and small publications or public relations firms. DIALOG, LEXIS/NEXIS, H.W. Wilson and Dow Jones News Retrieval are four of the large commercial electronic database providers that university libraries and major news organizations subscribe to. Each offers search services and full-text articles from hundreds of newspapers, magazines and other publications. To minimize search time and online fees for using these services, many publications now hire librarians trained to use electronic databases rather than allow reporters and editors to conduct their own searches. Likewise, college students may need to work with librarians who know how to go online and find materials quickly. Some commercial databases, such as LEXIS/NEXIS, offer abbreviated versions (LEXIS/NEXIS Academic, for example) to educational institutions for a cheaper subscription rate than the rate paid by for-profit firms.

CD-ROMs have become an increasingly popular medium because of the vast amount of information contained on easily portable discs. CD readers have become standard equipment on personal computers. As thousands of compact discs enter the marketplace, printed directories have emerged to catalog these products, including *Gale Directory of Databases* and *CD-ROMs in Print: An International Guide to CD-ROM, Multimedia & Electronic Book Products,* published by the Meckler Corporation.

A sampling of online reference works

In addition to print versions of standard reference works available in university libraries and major newspaper libraries, many such standard works are now available online. This section categorizes a sampling of those materials. Most of the sites in the list that follows are free or commonly subscribed to by university and large public libraries. Some universities allow public access to their online subscription services, while others require authentication, as noted in the lists here. Remember, the Internet is not static, so use a search engine if the URL cited here is nonfunctional.

General reference materials

▶**Infoplease.** Site includes a world almanac, atlas, a dictionary, thesaurus, background about current events, Columbia Encyclopedia and other features. http://www.infoplease.com/index.html

▶**Martindale's Reference Desk.** Large collection of links to reference resources, including language centers, calculators, maps and science tables. http://www.martindalecenter.com/

▶**refdesk.com.** Indexes and provides links to hundreds of free online reference resources. http://www.refdesk.com/index.html

▶**Reference.com.** Includes materials similar to those on the *Infoplease* site and a Web directory listing multiple reference sites. http://www.reference.com/

Biographical information

▶**Anthropology Biography Web.** Brief descriptions of anthropologists and other scientists who have direct influence on the discipline of anthropology. http://www.mnsu.edu/emuseum/information/biography/

▶**Biography.com.** A&E Television Networks operates this site. http://www.biography.com

▶**Biography-Center.** Provides a search of biography sites. http://www.biography-center.com/

▶**Biographical Dictionary.** Entries are one-sentence identifications. http://www.s9.com/

▶**Biographical Directory of the United States Congress 1774–Present.** Years of service and other political offices held, a brief and an extended bibliography, and references to collections that contain the papers or other information on the subject of the biography. http://www.nysl.nysed.gov/reference/bioref.htm

▶**Catalog of the Scientific Community in the 16th and 17th Centuries.** Detailed biographies of scientists of this period. http://galileo.rice.edu/lib/catalog.html

▶**Distinguished Women of Past and Present.** Biographies of women from many time periods and ethnic groups. http://www.distinguishedwomen.com/

▶**Mathematician Biography Index.** Features brief biographies for the most important mathematicians in history; the site is operated by the School of Mathematics and Statistics at the University of St. Andrews, Scotland. http://www-history.mcs.st-andrews.ac.uk/BiogIndex.html

▶**Rulers.** Lists of heads of state and heads of government of countries and territories, usually going back to at least 1900. http://rulers.org

Book reviews

▶**Publishers Weekly Book Reviews.** A review database for any review that has appeared in Publishers Weekly or its Web site since 1987. http://www.publishersweekly.com/bookReviews.html

▶**Book Review Digest.** The subscription-based online version of this reference, published by H.W. Wilson, is a subscription service available through major university database gateways.

▶**JSTOR: The Scholarly Journal Archive.** This is a fully searchable, full-text database containing the back issues of several hundred scholarly journals in the humanities, social sciences, mathematics, music, ecology and botany, business, and other fields. Book reviews are a part of many such journals. Often available through university gateways.

Factual data and statistics

▶**Census of Population.** Summarizes census data for the United States. http://www.census.gov/

▶**Demographic Yearbook.** The United Nations publishes this volume, which gives world population data and statistics on topics such as mortality, marriage and divorce. http://unstats.un.org/unsd/demographic/products/dyb/dyb2.htm

▶**Economic Indicators.** A huge selection of online business and economics databases compiled by Columbia University Libraries. www.columbia.edu/cu/lweb/indiv/business/guides/ecind.html

▶**Historical Statistics of the United States.** This publication gives comparative historical statistics since 1878 in areas such as U.S. agriculture, labor, migration and population. http://www.census.gov/prod/www/abs/statab.html

▶**Regional Economic Information System.** Contains personal income and employment estimates for states, counties and MSAs. http://www.bea.gov/bea/regional/data.htm

▶ **Statistical Abstract of the United States.** A digest of data collected by all the statistical agencies of the U.S. government and by some private agencies. Much of the data can be downloaded in Excel spreadsheets. http://www.census.gov/compendia/statab/

▶ **Yearbook of Immigration Statistics.** A compendium of data on foreign nationals who, during a fiscal year, were granted lawful permanent residence, were admitted into the United States on a temporary basis, applied for asylum or refugee status, or were naturalized. http://www.uscis.gov/graphics/shared/statistics/yearbook/index.htm

▶ **The World Factbook.** Produced annually by the Central Intelligence Agency; contains information about the geography, people, economy, industry, government, transportation and defense of the countries of the world. https://www.cia.gov/cia/publications/factbook/index.html

Government

▶ **GPO Access.** The catalog of U.S. Government Publications; finding tool that includes descriptive records for historical and current publications and provides direct links to those that are available online. http://catalog.gpo.gov/

▶ **Congressional Record.** The official record of the proceedings and debates of the U.S. Congress is published daily when Congress is in session. http://www.gpoaccess.gov/index.html

▶ **Governments on the WWW.** Comprehensive database of governmental institutions on the World Wide Web: parliaments, ministries, offices, law courts, embassies, city councils, public broadcasting corporations, central banks, multigovernmental institutions and political parties. http://www.gksoft.com/govt/en/

▶ **National Security Archive.** Independent nongovernmental research institute and library located at The George Washington University; publishes declassified documents acquired through the Freedom of Information Act. http://www.gwu.edu/~nsarchiv

▶ **Public Affairs Information Service.** Indexes books, documents, pamphlets and periodicals relating to public policy issues. Subscription required. http://www.pais.org

▶ **Thomas.** Official source of United States federal legislative information, including the latest floor actions and the status of bills. http://thomas.loc.gov

▶ **U.S. Senate Virtual Reference Desk.** General information on the Senate, the legislative branch and process, and other aspects of the federal government. http://www.senate.gov/pagelayout/reference/b_three_sections_with_teasers/virtual.htm

▶ **Urban Affairs Abstracts.** This weekly service of the National League of Cities includes abstracts of articles related to urban affairs. Subscription service available through gateways at major libraries.

Law

▶ **ABA LawInfo.org.** Consumer legal information organized by topic from the American Bar Association. http://www.abalawinfo.org/

▶ **American Law Sources On-Line (ALSO).** Comprehensive compilation of links to online sources of law in the United States, Canada and Mexico that are available without charge. http://www.lawsource.com/also

▶**FindLaw.** Overview of the legal world, including constitutional, intellectual property and labor law, law schools, U.S. Supreme Court cases; organized by topics. http://www.findlaw.com

▶**Internet Law Library.** A gateway site containing links to U.S. laws and treaties, laws of other nations, legal directories, and other legal topics. http://www.lawguru.com/ilawlib/refdesk.htm

▶**The Legal Information Institute.** Published by the Cornell Law School; collection of recent and historic Supreme Court decisions, the U.S. Code, U.S. Constitution, federal rules of evidence and civil procedure, recent opinions of the N.Y. State Court of Appeals, and commentary on them. http://www.law.cornell.edu

Newspapers and magazines

▶**The Internet Directory of Publications.** A free directory of publications: journals, newspapers, magazines, newsletters. Data comes from Ulrich's International Periodicals Directory. http://www.publist.com

▶**The Directory of Publications.** Brief description of the editorial content, plus editorial and subscription addresses, e-mail addresses and phone numbers for more than 1,500 U.S. and international magazines, newspapers and journals. http://www.proquestk12.com/lsm/sirs/sks-help/pubs.html

▶**NewsLink.** Provides links to newspapers, magazines and broadcast station Web sites around the world. http://newslink.org/news.html

▶**Topix.** A news search engine and news aggregator claiming to draw from more than 10,000 sources; creates topically driven, specific news Web pages and populates each with links to stories from news sources about that particular topic. http://www.topix.net/

People Finders

▶**Pretrieve.** Search engine specifically geared toward finding public records relevant to a person, business or address. http://www.pretrieve.com/

▶**The Virtual Chase.** Includes access to public records as well as other Web-based, people-finding tools. http://www.virtualchase.com/people/index.html

Politics

▶**America Votes.** Contains election statistics for all U.S. states in presidential, gubernatorial and congressional races. http://americavotes.org

▶**Annenberg Political Fact Check.** Monitors the factual accuracy of what is said by major U.S. political players in the form of TV ads, debates, speeches, interviews and news releases. http://www.factcheck.org/default.html

▶**National Political Index (U.S.).** Links to political groups and organizations. http://www.politicalindex.com/sect8.htm

▶**Political Information.** A search engine for politics, policy and political news. http://www.politicalinformation.com/index.html

▶ **Political Resources on the Net.** Links to worldwide political parties, organizations, governments and media, sorted by country. http://www.politicalresources.net/

Quotations

▶ **Bartlett's Familiar Quotations.** Collection of passages, phrases and proverbs traced to their sources in ancient and modern literature. http://www.bartleby.com/100

▶ **The Quotations Page.** Quotations from famous people and literature; searchable by authors or subjects. http://www.quotationspage.com/

Science

▶ **Scirus.** The most comprehensive science-specific search engine on the Internet, searching more than 250 million science-specific Web pages. http://www.scirus.com/srsapp/

Just as printed periodicals alter their content from issue to issue and occasionally alter their formats, the Internet changes constantly. This continual state of flux makes the Internet an exciting place to explore again and again and an invaluable resource for communicators.

Suggestions for additional reading

Bausch, Paul. *Yahoo! Hacks.* Sebastopol, Calif.: O'Reilly Media, 2005.

Berkman, Robert I. *Find It Fast: How to Uncover Expert Information on Any Subject Online or in Print,* 5th ed. New York: Harper Resource Book, 2000.

Biersdorfer, J.D., and David Pogue. *The Internet: The Missing Manual.* Sebastopol, Calif.: O'Reilly Media, 2006.

Biersdorfer, J.D., Rael Dornfest, Matthew MacDonald, and Sarah Milstein. *Google: The Missing Manual,* 2nd ed. Sebastopol, Calif.: O'Reilly Media, 2006.

Calishain, Tara. *Web Search Garage.* Indianapolis: Prentice Hall, 2004.

Gralla, Preston. *Internet Annoyances: How to Fix the Most Annoying Things About Going Online.* Sebastopol, Calif.: O'Reilly Media, 2005.

Hansen, Kathleen A., and Nora Paul. *Behind the Message: Information Strategies for Communicators.* New York: Allyn & Bacon, 2003.

Library staff. *Finding Information on the Internet: A Tutorial.* Berkeley, Calif.: University of California, 2006. http://www.lib.berkeley.edu/TeachingLib/Guides/Internet/FindInfo.html

McFarlane, Nigel. *Firefox Hacks.* Sebastopol, Calif.: O'Reilly Media, 2005.

Poremsky, Diane. *Google and Other Search Engines: Visual Quickstart Guide.* Berkeley, Calif.: Peachpit Press, 2004.

Powers, Shelley, and Cory Doctorow. *Essential Blogging.* Sebastopol, Calif.: O'Reilly Media, 2002.

Sherman, Chris, and Gary Price. *The Invisible Web: Uncovering Information Sources Search Engines Can't See.* Medford, N.J.: Information Today Inc., 2001.

> The White Rabbit put on his spectacles. "Where should I begin, please, your majesty?" he asked. "Begin at the beginning," the King said, very gravely, " and go on till you come to the end; then stop."
>
> —*Lewis Carroll, Alice in Wonderland*

Editing Stories

O<small>NCE</small> **copy editors** understand their role, their audiences, the correct use of grammar and punctuation, style conventions, and proper word usage, they may be ready to begin the daunting task of improving the story on the computer screen before them. All writers, no matter the medium in which they publish (books, newspapers, magazines, newsletters, radio, television, the Internet) and regardless of the level of their experience, require a good editor. Rarely does a piece of professional news copy make it into print or on the Web without being subjected to the skills of a copy editor. At the best-edited publications, policy demands that at least two copy editors examine each piece of copy.

When editing a story, copy editors must not only remember to pay attention to spelling, grammar, punctuation and style but also look beyond these details and answer the following questions:

- Is the story balanced, accurate and fair?

- Are there any legal or ethical implications?

- Is the lead appropriate and not buried later in the story?

- Does the story contain the essence of the event or issue and does it leave information holes or gaps?

- Has the writer developed the story structure properly?

- Does the reporter understand numbers or statistics, attribute information and use direct quotations correctly?

- Does the story contain redundancies or superfluous information?

Good copy editors develop over a period of years, and the best pay strict attention to answering these questions. Beginning editors might be well-served to keep the list nearby.

Editing leads

Writers learn to write leads in one of several formats. Hard-news leads take a different form, for example, than feature or delayed leads, and the lead on a news broadcast differs from the lead in a press release. It is the copy editor's role to understand the difference and to balance the need for reader understanding with the writing style of the author. Most hard-news leads are written on the basis of a formula that incorporates the traditional five W's and H (who, what, when, where, why and how). Reporters learn to use the answers to a combination of these six lead elements to craft a hard-news or direct lead.

News judgment comes directly into play when making the decision to write these leads. For example, given the following set of facts, which of the six lead elements are the most important, and which should be included in the lead?

Facts for lead:

1. At a city council meeting tonight (Tuesday) in San Diego, council members voted unanimously to put a bond issue on next month's election ballot.

2. The bond issue will ask voters for authority to sell $33 million in bonds.

3. Proceeds from the bonds would be used to finance a performing arts complex for San Diego. Plans reviewed by the city council depict an impressive facility with two theaters, one seating 2,600 people and the other 400. Everyone is excited about the prospect for such a complex.

4. The mayor, a woman named Frances Howard, said following the council's vote: "I've lived in San Diego all my life, and this is the most exciting civic opportunity I've seen. If the good citizens of San Diego will build this center, we will become known far and wide as the biggest supporters of the arts in the state."

To determine the relative importance of the six lead elements, the reporter and the editor must bring the traditional news values mentioned in Chapter 1 to bear: timeliness, proximity, prominence, relevance, unusualness, conflict, human interest. In this set of facts, two time elements should be considered: first is that the city council meeting was tonight (Tuesday night, if writing for a morning newspaper), and second is that the bond issue will be placed on next month's ballot. Which is more important? In this case, voters probably would want to know more about the future action (the ballot issue *next month*) than the past action (council meeting *Tuesday night*). The WHEN question, then, has just been answered and should be included in the lead.

The answer to the WHO question could be both the city council, which took the action, and the voters, who will be affected by the action. Most often the people affected by the action should be included in the lead. The WHAT is the placing of the $33 million bond issue on the ballot. The WHERE question is not relevant for this lead, as no location is included in the set of facts and the editor assumes the story is local. The WHY is to finance a new performing arts complex. The answer to the HOW question, not included in this set of facts, is usually left for later in the story. The answers to both the WHAT and WHY questions are significant for the lead because they have an impact on readers.

Part of the direct-lead writing formula also includes using only a few of the news elements in the lead to keep it to one sentence and making certain that the number of words in the sentence is between 25 and 35. With all these rules in mind, the lead might be written this way:

```
San Diego voters will be asked next month to approve a $33 million
bond issue to build a 3,000-seat performing arts complex.
```

If the reporter or the editor wanted to add a little color to this direct, hard-news lead, the lead could be written this way:

```
San Diego voters will be asked next month to approve a $33 million
bond issue to build a 3,000-seat performing arts complex, which
Mayor Frances Howard said could make San Diego residents "the
biggest supporters of the arts in the state."
```

For a copy editor, the task is to balance the desire to satisfy the reader's need for clear and concise information with the reporter's right to write the story in a distinct, personal style. Direct leads that include the reporter as observer are to be avoided at all costs. For example, "As I approached the scene of the fire, I noticed that more than four engines and 20 firefighters had responded" should be rewritten to delete the reporter's personal observation. Thus: "More than four engines and 20 firefighters responded to the fire."

As mentioned previously, however, the style for the lead depends on the nature of the story. If the reporter is writing a feature story or an in-depth analysis of a major issue, then he or she should be allowed more freedom to pursue an individual style. The key is to make sure the copy is understandable to busy readers. Here's an example of a feature lead from The San Diego Union-Tribune; notice that it breaks some of the rules for direct leads (too many words, no WHEN or WHERE), but it still tells what the story is about: "The iconography is familiar: The Virgin Mary is ascending to heaven. Lisa Venditelli's version of it even has the look of an aging tapestry. But somehow, it's hard to imagine an artist of any era except ours weaving such an image from pasta." Copy editors learn how to balance hard-news and feature leads through day-in-and-day-out interaction with the reporting staff and with the news.

For public relations practitioners, the lead on a press release is so crucial that it alone may determine whether the event or product receives the free publicity desired. If, after reading the first paragraph, the editor of the target publication or broadcast doesn't understand what the PR story is about and why it is important, the subsequent paragraphs never will be read. In addition, the editor may determine that the story is worth only a brief mention, and information from the lead paragraph of the press release may be the only information that makes it into print or on the air.

Most press releases use a summary lead, which wraps up the main point of the PR story. Veteran writers of press releases follow the same rules of lead writing previously outlined. They recognize that the more their press release reads like a news story, the more likely it will be used in the newspaper or on the air. When considering a press release, however, editors always must remember the difference between publicity and news and remain vigilant about deleting adjectives, jargon and exaggeration from stories based on press releases.

Editing story structure

The most often used news story structure remains the inverted pyramid, which asks the reporter to assemble the factual information for the story in descending order of importance or significance. Unlike the telling of a fairy tale, for example, the news story begins with the climax or the most important fact, then compiles the rest of the information in a way that would allow the story to be trimmed from the bottom. In addition, an inverted pyramid story includes within the first three or four paragraphs a direct quotation from one source in the story.

Here is a classic example of the inverted pyramid structure:

```
WASHINGTON--A plastic surgeon who had been jailed for more
than two years for refusing to let her daughter visit the girl's
father was released yesterday on a judge's orders.
```

The lead answers the WHO, WHAT and WHEN questions, often considered the most significant in a hard-news story, and is 29 words long.

```
Dr. Elizabeth Morgan emerged from jail wearing a prison jumpsuit
and carrying a dozen yellow roses.
    "I feel very happy and very grateful to everyone who has helped
me," she said. "I will probably cry when I say this, but I want to
thank God for every angel on Earth."
```

The third paragraph includes the first direct quotation.

```
She said she spent her 760 days behind bars thinking of "my
daughter and the people I love."
    Morgan's release was ordered by District of Columbia
Superior Court Judge Geoffrey Alprin--as directed by the
district's Court of Appeals under a law passed by Congress
and signed by President Bush last week.
```

This paragraph answers the WHY question but is less important than the WHO, WHAT or WHEN and thus comes later in the inverted pyramid.

```
    Morgan, 41, went to jail voluntarily in August 1987 on civil
    contempt charges after refusing to produce the couple's 7-year-old
    daughter, Hilary, for court-ordered visits with the girl's father,
    Dr. Eric Foretich, Morgan's former husband.
        The case has received international attention and has been
    adopted by a number of groups, including the National Organization
    for Women, as a classic example of a mother fighting for her child's
    mental and emotional well-being against an unresponsive judiciary.
        Morgan has alleged that Foretich sexually abused the child;
    Foretich has consistently denied the charges. Morgan is Foretich's
    third wife. His second wife has also accused him of sexual abuse of
    their daughter, Heather, 9. Foretich denies those charges as well,
    and has charged that the two women have acted in collusion.
```

These three paragraphs include background and chronology of the story, answering the HOW question and providing context and detail that can be placed after the hard-news elements.

The inverted pyramid form continues to be widely used, but more and more publications are employing alternative writing styles. The narrative approach (storytelling), or the personalized approach, has been transformed into an art form by the staff of The Wall Street Journal. These feature-writing formats allow writers to break out of the rigid breaking-news formula and create stories that can be emotionally compelling as well as informative. Good editors understand the differences among the various writing forms and learn to respect an author's choice. Generally, editors give more leeway to authors who choose a literary form, as long as that form is appropriate to the subject matter. For example, a feature writer may decide to use present-tense verbs in the story to lend a more folksy tone. As already mentioned, in most news stories verbs are expressed in the past tense. Editors may leave the present-tense verbs in the feature story but double-check to confirm the writer did not switch back and forth to past tense. The rules of good grammar, punctuation and spelling always should be front and center in the editor's mind.

Using transitions

Although many other forms of writing can be found within the print media, including storytelling and use of anecdotes, the inverted pyramid is still used at most news publications as a way to structure a hard-news story. Copy editors must be alert to the form of news-telling at their publication. But it is the copy editor's job to ensure that the story flows logically from one paragraph to the next, using good transitions that move the reader through the story chronologically or that take readers on a journey in search of a solution to a particular problem or puzzle. Good transitions are essential to the flow of any story, regardless of its form.

Transitional techniques—including chronology, journey and problem solving— move readers along in this story by Don Williams, a staff writer for the Knoxville (Tenn.) News-Sentinel. The story, published on the 20th anniversary of the first human space flight to the moon, develops a local angle on that momentous event.

```
    Joan Trolinger waits for a rocket engine to speak thunder and roll a
    brand new cloud into the sky.
        Few rocket tests are conducted here at the Redstone Arsenal,
    where Wernher Von Braun brought a ragtag band of scientists and a
    few leftover German V-2 rockets after World War II and launched
    America toward the stars.
```

> Ever since Trolinger was a child she wanted to be part of that movement into space, a movement rife with glamor, but also with tedium and terror, as she would discover.
>
> Growing up in Morristown, the daughter of Jim and Sarah Gose, she was 6 years old when she watched Neil Armstrong take his small step/giant leap onto the moon.
>
> Later she made spacesuits for her dolls and suspended rocket models from her ceiling. Children were doing much the same thing throughout America.
>
> These days, at 26, Trolinger drives daily past real rockets on display in Huntsville--rockets named for gods--Jupiter, Atlas, Titan, Saturn.
>
> Trolinger still has a model of the Starship Enterprise hanging from her ceiling, but her interest in space has matured.

In addition to using chronology, journey and problem solving to move a story along, a writer can achieve continuity by

- repeating a key word of the preceding paragraph.

- using a synonym to refer to a key word in the preceding paragraph.

- referring to a fact or idea in the preceding paragraph.

- elaborating details in logical sequence.

- using words and phrases as transitional devices.

The first several paragraphs of this news story by Eric Vreeland of the Knoxville News-Sentinel staff illustrate the first three methods of achieving transition:

> The Knoxville Food Policy **Council** last week waded into the fray over where to locate a farmers' **market**. The **council** lobbied Gov. Ned McWherter to pick Knox County over Sevierville or White Pine.
>
> However, the **council** added a new wrinkle--advocating that, regardless of where the main **market** is built, **inner-city** Knoxville should be developed as a retail satellite **market**.
>
> The idea is that poor **inner-city** residents suffer by not having adequate food outlets near them. Since 1979, eight super**markets** and about 30 independent grocers have closed in the **inner city,** says Bill **Powell**, a staff member with the **council**.
>
> **Powell** is a Mechanicsville resident and die-hard historical preservationist. He thinks he has the perfect candidate in mind for housing that retail **market:** the Western Avenue Market.

The remainder of the story also used the technique of elaborating details in logical sequence, as the reporter described the details of Powell's proposal for refurbishing and promoting the old market.

Writers can use a variety of words and phrases as transitional devices:

- **To show time:** then, meanwhile, shortly, thereafter, now, later, soon, all this time, formerly, previously, at last, finally

- **To cite examples:** for instance, thus, for example, to illustrate, an illustration

- **To indicate emphasis:** indeed, moreover, in particular, especially, in addition to, similarly, furthermore

- **To show change of viewpoint:** however, but, nevertheless, of course, also, seriously, in another way, in a lighter view, in addition, in general, on the other hand

Handling quotations

One key part of an editor's job is to make sure the reporter or writer has clearly identified the source of information in a story. Careless handling of attribution, especially in quotations, can result in cluttered, ambiguous and awkward sentences.

One guideline is to grammatically join a direct quotation to the speaker. A direct quotation is one that reports the exact words of the speaker. Don't make the reader guess the source:

> *Wrong:* Clark boasted about the salaries. "I'm proud to be in a city where librarians are paid decently, and I'll never back away from that."

> *Right:* "I'm proud to be in a city where librarians are paid decently, and I'll never back away from that," Clark said.

Attribution is important, but it can be overdone. A continuous, or multisentence, quotation needs only one attribution, placed after the first break in the first sentence or at the end of the first sentence:

> *Wrong:* "Modernizing our facilities has always been a priority," Clark said. "This is a city that loves its libraries," she continued. "I know that voters will approve construction of the new building," she added.

> *Right:* "Modernizing our facilities has always been a priority," Clark said. "This is a city that loves its libraries. I know that voters will approve construction of the new building."

When two or more sentences of direct quotation run continuously in a paragraph, the speaker should be identified in the first sentence. Don't make the reader wonder who is talking. In the preceding example, the attribution is placed after the first sentence instead of at the end of the three-sentence paragraph. Quote blocks ordinarily shouldn't be more than two paragraphs; quote blocks should be separated by a transition.

What the speaker said is generally more interesting and important than who said it, so put the quotation first, followed by the attribution:

> *Wrong:* Clark said, "Modernizing our facilities has always been a priority. This is a city that loves its libraries. I know that voters will approve construction of the new building."

> *Right:* "Modernizing our facilities has always been a priority," Clark said. "This is a city that loves its libraries. I know that voters will approve construction of the new building."

This rule cannot be followed if a second speaker is quoted because readers will be misled into thinking that the original speaker is continuing:

> *Wrong:* "Modernizing our facilities has always been a priority," Clark said. "This is a city that loves its libraries. I know that voters will approve construction of the new building." "I wish the library would buy more books instead of constructing new buildings," Jane Smith, president of the writers union, said.

> *Right:* "Modernizing our facilities has always been a priority," Clark said. "This is a city that loves its libraries. I know that voters will approve construction of the new building." Jane Smith, president of the writer's union, said, "I wish the library would buy more books instead of constructing new buildings."

Start a new paragraph when a different speaker is quoted, as in the previous example. Direct quotations from two speakers should not be included in the same paragraph, even if the quotations are extremely brief.

Inexperienced reporters sometimes write in *stutter* quotes; that is, they paraphrase what the speaker said and then use a direct quotation that says the same thing:

> ***Wrong:*** Clark said that voters care about modernizing the libraries and predicted that they would approve new facilities. "This is a city that loves its libraries," Clark said. "I know that voters will approve construction of the new building."

> ***Right:*** "Modernizing our facilities has always been a priority," Clark said. "This is a city that loves its libraries. I know that voters will approve construction of the new building."

Rarely is it necessary to tell the reader what question was asked. The question generally is obvious from the phrasing of the answer in either a direct or an indirect quotation:

> ***Wrong:*** When asked about modernizing the city's libraries and whether voters would approve new facilities, Clark said, "Modernizing our facilities has always been a priority. This is a city that loves its libraries. I know that voters will approve construction of the new building."

The trick is to summarize what the speaker said, without using the exact words, and then use the direct quotation as strong follow-up dialogue:

> Clark is unapologetic about her belief in the city's residents to do what she believes is the right thing. "Modernizing our facilities has always been a priority," she said. "This is a city that loves its libraries. I know that voters will approve construction of the new building."

In general, avoid fragmentary, or partial, quotes. If a speaker's words are clear and concise, favor the full quotation. If cumbersome language can be paraphrased fairly, use an indirect construction, reserving direct quotations for sensitive or controversial passages that must be identified specifically as coming from the speaker. Unless a particular word or phrase has special significance or is used in an unusual or colorful sense, do not enclose it in quotation marks as a partial quotation:

> ***Weak use of partial quotes:*** To conserve energy, Americans began "turning off" lights and "turning down" thermostats, the official said.

> ***Good use of partial quotes:*** Referring to his quick pitching style, the major leaguer said he pitched "like my hair was on fire."

Punctuate direct quotations correctly. Refer to the AP stylebook, a grammar handbook or Chapter 2 for rules on punctuating direct quotations.

Should a reporter or an editor correct grammatical errors in direct quotations? Many newspapers have the policy of making such corrections, unless, of course, the source's speech patterns are important to the story. The AP stylebook, however, notes that quotations should never be altered even to correct minor grammatical errors or word usage. AP style is to use ellipses to remove casual or minor slips of the tongue, but only with extreme caution. AP recommends that if journalists have a question about a quote, either do not use it or ask the speaker for clarification.

Do not routinely use abnormal spellings, such as *gonna,* in attempts to convey regional dialects or mispronunciations. Such spellings are appropriate, however, when they are relevant or help to convey a desired effect in a feature story.

Space limitations usually preclude extensive use of direct quotations from an interview or speech. However, writers should paraphrase and use sufficient background information to preserve the context of direct quotations, especially startling remarks. It isn't always possible for editors to detect out-of-context quotations that distort the speaker's meaning, but editors should question reporters and writers about context when especially surprising or strong quotations are used. In addition, the manner of delivery is sometimes part of the context. Reporting a smile or a deprecatory gesture may be as important as conveying the words themselves.

Copy editors should pay careful attention to verbs of attribution. *Said* is the most common verb of attribution and usually the most appropriate. But reporters, in their reluctance to repeat *said,* often resort to other verbs of attribution. Note that terms such as *pointed out, noted* and *claimed* are not synonymous with *said* and convey editorial opinion. *Stated* and *declared* are too stilted for informal speech.

Pointed out and *noted* should be reserved for attribution when the speaker said something that is a verifiable fact: " 'New York City is the largest city in the United States,' she *noted.*" It would be incorrect to use *pointed out* or *noted* as the verb of attribution if the speaker said, "New York City is the best city in the United States" because that statement is arguable, not generally accepted as fact. *Claimed* as a verb of attribution connotes doubt about the speaker's credibility. Reserve *claimed* for an assertion of legal rights by the speaker: " 'Roger is innocent of the crime,' he *claimed.*" Or, "She *claimed* that the property belonged to her."

Verbs that describe the speaker's tone or mood more specifically than *said* may be used: " 'The house is on fire,' he *yelled.*" " 'I wouldn't do that for all the money in the world,' she *snapped.*" " 'Please be quiet,' she *whispered.*" But use such verbs accurately. A copy editor should question a reporter who has someone whispering that the house is on fire, or hissing a greeting or reprimanding a loud talker.

Remember, reporters can report what sources said, not what they thought or believed or felt. Reporters aren't mind readers. They know only what the source said or did:

> *Wrong:* `The convicted murderer felt remorse.`

> *Right:* `The convicted murderer said he felt remorse.`

Another way to handle this idea would be to describe the convicted murderer's actions or comments that would indicate a feeling of remorse.

> `At his sentencing hearing, the convicted murderer sobbed as he`
> `listened to a mother describe one of his victims.`

Including essential information

After copy editors make certain the lead is the best it can be and that the story structure is appropriate, they next turn to the essence of the rest of the story and look for "holes" that need to be filled in for the reader, as well as make certain that numbers are accurate, that words are not misused and that redundancies are avoided. The copy editor should always ask: Is all the essential information included in this story? Does the story make sense?

The copy editor should be able to spot whether a paragraph of vital background information is missing, or whether the first name of a source was left out, or whether too much jargon is left in.

Accuracy in numbers

Copy editors are charged with ensuring that all the numbers in a story make sense. So, besides a computer and a dictionary, the editor's tool kit should include a calculator. Making numbers easy to understand is part of the editor's job. For example, a city budget in the millions of dollars means little to readers. The story should provide a breakdown by budgetary categories and should report percentages allocated for major items. In reporting sources of revenue for the budget, the story should show how these numbers affect individual residents: How much will property taxes be raised? What is the percentage of increase? Based on these figures, the story should report the dollar increase for property taxes on the average-priced home in the community. Are automobile registration fees increasing? If so, how much?

Stories often need to report raw numbers, but those numbers will be more easily understood if the percentage of increase or decrease is also reported. Percentages are derived this way:

$$\% \text{ increase or decrease} = \frac{\text{New figure} - \text{Original figure}}{\text{Original figure}}$$

For example, if enrollment in the school district was 30,200 students last year and is 33,100 students this year, enrollment has increased 9.6 percent:

$$\frac{33,100 - 30,200}{30,200} = \frac{2,900}{30,200} = .0960 = 9.6\%$$

Another example: If the number of burglaries decreased this year from 3,196 to 3,005, the percentage of decline is 5.97 (which may be rounded off to 6 percent):

$$\frac{3,005 - 3,196}{3,196} = \frac{-191}{3,196} = -.0597 = -5.97\%$$

Remember, the percentage of change is based upon the original number and the change from the original number.

Percent and *percentage points* do not mean the same thing. If interest rates increase from 10 percent to 12 percent, they have increased 2 percentage points, but it is an increase of 20 percent:

$$\frac{12 - 10}{10} = \frac{2}{10} = 20\%$$

Similarly, "two times as much" does not mean the same thing as "two times more than." For example, two times as much as $10 is $20 ($10 $\times$ 2 = $20), but two times more than $10 is $30 ($10 + $10 $\times$ 2 = $30).

Copy editors should be especially alert in handling stories that include ages, box scores, infographics, results of opinion polls and information about property taxes.

▶**Ages.** Use common sense in editing stories that include a person's date of birth, dates of accomplishments and ages. An alert copy editor should spot the inconsistencies, for example, in an obituary published in 1999 that reports the age of the deceased as 67 if the birth date is listed as 1922 or that reports this person graduated from a university in 1932. Was she 77 when she died, or was she born in 1932? Did she graduate from the university at age 10, or is the graduation date a typographical error?

▶**Box scores.** Add the number of points scored by each player to be sure that the totals for each team equal the final score.

▶ **Informational graphics.** Check the numbers. Do they add to the total reported in the graphic? Check that the percentages add to 100. If they don't, an explanation should be included.

▶ **Property taxes.** The single largest source of income for cities and counties generally is the tax charged on property. The tax is formally known as a *mill levy*. A *mill* is 0.1 cent (one-tenth of a cent). Generally, the property tax is expressed as the number of mills levied for each $100 in assessed valuation of the property. For example, if the mill levy is 1.5, property owners will pay 15 cents for each $100 of assessed value or $1.50 for each $1,000 of assessed value.

Stories about property taxes should include an example of how much tax will be levied on a representative home in the community. Using a mill levy of 1.5 for a home assessed at $50,000 (note this is assessed value, not market value), the property tax would be $75 ($1.50 × 50). If several governmental units within the community have taxing power, a story about the city tax rate should not mislead readers into thinking that this will be their total property tax bill. The story should include the rates that other governmental units have levied or note that the budget is not complete and thus the mill levy has not been determined.

Reporting survey results

A story based on a public-opinion survey should provide information that helps readers understand how to interpret the poll results correctly. Too often, stories present the results from a hastily conducted survey at a shopping mall in the same manner as polls conducted by scientific norms. This doesn't mean that person-on-the-street polls lack entertainment value, but readers should be told the difference.

When handling a story or a press release reporting that 53 percent of the people support one candidate for governor and 47 percent support another candidate, a copy editor should insist that the story answer these questions:

- Who conducted the survey? (Was it a company that specializes in scientific polling, campaign workers, reporters?)

- Who paid for the survey? (Did a news organization or some other disinterested party hire a survey-research firm, or did one of the candidates pay for it?)

- Who was interviewed for the survey? (Respondents who aren't eligible to vote in the gubernatorial election—such as out-of-state tourists or minors—produce meaningless results for this survey.)

- How were people selected to be interviewed? (Was it a random sample? Did people from all sections of the state have an equal chance of being selected? Did the sample reflect the state's population according to demographic factors, such as race and ethnicity, gender, age, religious affiliation and occupation?)

- What was the margin of sampling error for this particular survey? (In a scientific survey, the size of the sample influences the margin of error. In this example of 53 percent versus 47 percent, a 3 percent margin of error would mean that one candidate could have as much as 56 percent or as little as 50 percent support, and the other candidate's support could range from 44 percent to 50 percent. In this case, the race is too close to call.)

- How was the survey conducted? (By telephone? In private interviews? Or did respondents answer in the presence of co-workers, friends or other people?)

■ When was the poll conducted? (In a political campaign, events can cause opinions to change quickly. The story should indicate whether such an event happened between the time the survey was conducted and its results were published.)

■ What questions were asked during interviews, and what was the order of questions? (Unless the wording is controversial or central to issues in the campaign, the exact text does not have to be included in the story, but copy editors should be sensitive to the potential for bias.)

Accuracy in word usage

Chapter 3 lists words that often are misused in both written and spoken English. A few are homonyms (words that have the same sound and often the same spelling but differ in meaning) that are unlikely to be confused except by people uneducated in the language. Others are word substitutions that literate people commonly but erroneously make. A few of these words have fallen into common misusage to the extent that even the experts debate the merits of maintaining the original distinctions. To professional writers and editors who want to say exactly and concisely what they mean, the distinctions are important.

Eliminating redundancies

Journalistic editing often requires that sentences and paragraphs be short and concise, using as few words as possible to tell the story because space (news hole) or time (on the air) is at a premium. One way to achieve conciseness is to make each word meaningful and avoid jargon and redundancies. In his book *The Word: An Associated Press Guide to Good News Writing,* Rene Cappon said:

> To say things clearly and concisely takes skill and, above all, vigilance. Bloated language is all around us. Government pumps gaseous bureaucratese into the environment. Other institutions, corporate headquarters, the professions and the social sciences diligently contribute to the effusion of jargon.

He goes on to illustrate his point by suggesting that a person who resigned her position in order to replenish her financial resources more appropriately quit to make more money, or that the Air Force's struggling to minimize the aircraft's engine capability problems could be put more concisely as struggling to fix the plane's engine.

Alert copy editors will spot the most frequently used redundancies. Here is a list published by the Minnesota Newspaper Association:

absolutely necessary	enclosed you will find	reasonable and fair
advance planning	fall down	redo again
ask the question	first and foremost	refer back
assemble together	friend of mine	right and proper
at a later day	gathered together	rise up
attached hereto	honest truth	rules and regulations
at the present time	important essentials	send in
canceled out	necessary requirements	small in size
carbon copy	open up	still remain
city of Chicago	other alternative	temporarily suspended
close proximity	patently obvious	totally unnecessary
consensus of opinion	plain and simple	true facts
continue on	postpone until later	various and sundry
each and every		

Shortening stories

Tight, fast-paced writing characterizes both the print and online versions of most publications today. See Figure 5-1 for an example of a wire-service story that has been edited on a computer. Hurried readers, perhaps on the verge of information overload, want more information than broadcast newscasts typically provide, but they want it in concise packages. USA Today set the standard in this regard for newspapers, using short news stories and high-impact graphics. Online news sites demand brevity and conciseness because long passages download slowly and are tedious to read on a computer screen. An order to cut 2 or 3 inches from an already short 10-inch story is not uncommon on copy desks today. Editing stories for online publication will be discussed in a later segment of this chapter.

Figure 5-1
Here is an example of how one copy editor edited a wire-service story on a computer.

Wild pigs

1-1-1-1-1-1-1

~~Titusville, Florida AP~~ TITUSVILLE, Fla. (AP) -- The wild pigs ~~which~~ that have been giving Kennedy Space Center officials headaches for years are now ending up on the menu at the ~~Bravard~~ Brevard County ~~j~~Jail.

Sheriff Jake Miller ~~says~~ said the pigs are goodies from heaven~~.~~

I m constantly looking for food sources for that jail , Miller said.

The plan to trap the animals is the latest of several ideas by Miller to cut down on the food bill for the jail s ~~two hundred and fifty~~ 250 inmates. His efforts ~~are apparantly~~ apparently are paying off.

The jail s meal budget for the upcomming fiscial year is $260,000 ~~thousand dollars~~, the same as in the current fiscial year. ~~Its~~ It is the first time anyone can remember the food bill not going up. The National ~~Auronautics~~ Aeronautics and Space Administration gave Miller permission about ~~2~~ two months ago to trap the porkers, whose population was estimated recently at ~~over~~ more than 5,000 and multiplying fast.

NASA officials are afraid the pigs could threaten the space shuttle and other craft by wandering onto the space center's runway. In addition, the ~~porkers~~ pigs cause traffic accidents, dig near underground cables, and endanger other wildlife by hogging food supplies.

The pig~~s~~ began multiplying after they were abandoned by homeowners displaced in the 1960 s, when NASA bought their property to build the space center.

At first, Miller's traps came up empty when he tried baiting them with corn, which the wild pigs barely noticed. Once trappers switched to leftovers from the jail and other goodies to give the bait an odor, the hogs couldn't resist, the sheriff said. ~~About 6~~ Six hogs were slaughtered last week and are in the jail's freezer waiting to be cooked.

Jail Administrator Frank Billings ~~says~~ said he ~~hopes~~ hoped eventually to keep about ~~twenty-five~~ 25 or ~~thirty~~ 30 ~~porkers~~ pigs at the prison farm to serve as a constant supply of meat.

\#\#\#

Estimating story length

Before copy editors begin cutting a story to fit a desired length for layout purposes, they must first estimate its current length. In most modern newsrooms, or public relations firms, computers are programmed to provide story length with a simple keyboard or menu command. Programs vary from publication to publication because the width of standard columns varies from publication to publication and within single publications. Stories are measured in column inches; thus, wide columns require more copy to fill a space one column wide and 1 inch deep than do narrower columns.

Copy editors working without the copy-fitting aid of a computer can determine copy length by measuring at random several inch-long samples set in the desired column width and then counting the number of words in each sample. Averaging these word-count samples gives a fairly accurate idea of the number of words in a column inch of body copy. For layout purposes the editors divide this average into the total number of words in a story to derive an estimated length for that particular story.

Editing with precision

The reduction of story length generally falls within three broad categories: (1) trimming, a tightening of the story; (2) boiling, a more drastic process of paring most of the sentences and sacrificing minor facts; and (3) cutting, which eliminates all but the most important facts. Copy editors should be careful when reducing any story's length to ensure that elimination of facts or descriptions does not leave readers with a false or misleading impression.

▶**Trimming.** A mark of good writing is economy of language. This maxim is most eloquently stated in *Elements of Style* by William Strunk and E.B. White:

> Vigorous writing is concise. A sentence should contain no unnecessary words, a paragraph no unnecessary sentences, for the same reason that a drawing should contain no unnecessary parts. This requires not that a writer make all his sentences short, or that he avoid all detail and treat his subject only in outline, but that every word tell.

The duty of the copy editor is to delete all words and phrases that do not contribute to the clarity and conciseness of the news story. A carelessly written story must be pulled together to be compact and readable. By deleting nonessentials, the copy editor artfully turns an overwritten piece into a story with impact.

Strong writing depends on nouns and verbs. Deleting unnecessary adjectives, avoiding redundancies and using active rather than passive verbs can help strengthen the story's message.

▶**Boiling.** In boiling a story with more than one angle, copy editors may be forced to remove one or more angles completely and to concentrate on developing the remaining angles fully. When a story presents several sides of an issue, however, all sides must be represented fairly.

An informational graphic might offer another possibility for copy editors faced with the need to eliminate one or more angles from a story. Consider whether a graph, chart, map or other graphic device might convey part of the story effectively and concisely. Be sure to coordinate such a move with personnel responsible for laying out the page and for executing graphics. A graphic approach to reducing copy length requires time and planning. It isn't a deadline-time option. (Information graphics are covered in Chapter 10.)

▶**Cutting.** Most of the time, stories are cut because they need to fit a specified space, usually determined by a layout editor. Because surveys have shown that readers prefer short news stories and because space is at a premium in print publications, today's copy editors are often asked to cut a few long stories to accommodate more short ones.

When cutting a story, the copy editor should try to preserve the essential facts and enough detail to answer the reader's pressing questions. The copy editor should never assume that a story can be chopped off anywhere; cutting a story requires a great deal of skill. The broad outline of the story should be preserved when the story is not written in the routine inverted pyramid style. The flavor or tone of the story should be maintained. This is especially true for feature stories using narrative or personalized writing approaches.

After the copy editor completes the cuts, he or she should read the new version with care, making certain that transitions are clear and the copy flows past the cuts. For routine stories written in the inverted pyramid style, chopping the story from the bottom up is usually the easiest and quickest way to get the desired length. However, bad editing can result. The copy editor must make sure no news story ends with a line like this: "In other action, the council decided . . ."

Copy editors must use common sense, as well as good judgment, in cutting stories for publication.

Editing news-service copy

In this age of mass-media marketing, editors of print media continually try to determine "what sells." That is to say, editors base their judgments about what kinds of content to publish on many factors, including results of reader surveys, demographic profiles of readers and potential readers and desires of advertisers.

Although the percentages vary from city to city, most research indicates that readers of daily newspapers want a variety of news topics from a variety of geographic locations. The same is true of news magazines. Some readers may be very interested in news about transportation, science and education; others may be interested in news about politics, sports and business. Some read local news with vigor. Others prefer national and international news.

Selecting and publishing news that appeals to the diverse interests of readers is imperative if a media product is to survive. But only the most widely circulated newspapers and magazines can afford to situate reporters in offices outside their primary market area. Most U.S. newspapers, magazines, broadcast stations and Internet news sites, therefore, rely on the news services to provide wide-ranging, nonlocal coverage.

People who travel across the United States and notice the news products in the cities and towns they visit may note the similarities in this country's press accounts. Magazines such as Time and Newsweek often publish the same topic on their covers, network news broadcasts often announce the same stories each night and appear to use the same format, and daily newspapers resemble each other in content and design.

Some have called this important, and many would argue, disturbing insight into U.S. mass media of the past 100 years the "blanding" of American journalism. Researchers and media scholars continue to try to define the reasons why this is so. One significant reason is that the mass media are increasingly becoming merged into the same huge corporations, which often dictate the ways their "products" will read and look. Others argue that the nature of journalistic "routines," such as accepting news from the same known sources (government officials, business leaders, and so on) and publishing on 24-hour cycles, creates these resemblances. Still others suggest that the uniform profile of media workers necessarily contributes to uniformity in content. One other reason for the quality of sameness is that many of the nation's media use the same reports from the primary news services.

Primary news services

Three primary news services offer broad coverage of world events, without direct governmental support. They are The Associated Press of the United States, Reuters of Great Britain and Agence France Presse of France. Agence France Presse is not directly subsidized, but French government ministries pay handsomely to subscribe, an arrangement one AFP official admitted "could be called a disguised [governmental] subsidy."

The Associated Press, the largest supplier of breaking news in the world, has been in existence for more than 150 years. Six New York City publishers created the wire service in 1848 to save news-gathering costs by sharing information with each other in a cooperative, not-for-profit arrangement. According to its Web page, the AP now serves 1,700 U.S. newspapers and more than 5,000 U.S. radio and television stations, a steady stream of news totaling more than 20 million words and 1,000 photos a day (see Figure 5-2).

Although AP is the only news service in the United States that attempts to provide a full range of coverage in the nation and around the world, many supplemental, or "designer," news services offer specialized coverage, focusing on the important stories of the day, analysis pieces, feature reports and opinion columns. Most metropolitan newspapers and national magazines subscribe to several services, while most small and midsize dailies subscribe only to AP and perhaps one or two of the supplementals.

United Press International, which was created in 1907 as a competing news service, no longer serves large numbers of daily U.S. newspapers but does sell its content to U.S. broadcast stations and international subscribers.

Supplemental services

The nation's mass media may also purchase content from among dozens of supplemental news services and hundreds of syndicated feature services. One of the best supplemental services, The New York Times News Service, has for many years focused on in-depth stories and analysis of news from around the world. Subscribers get a daily report from the news pages of The New York Times, as well as background pieces, opinion columns, sports columns, feature stories, photos and computer graphics from The Times and from 11 news-service partners, including the Boston Globe, Cox News Service and Hearst Newspapers.

In addition to the supplemental services, more than 350 syndicated feature services sell to media clients thousands of political cartoons, comic strips, astrology columns, crossword puzzles, games and quizzes, advice and humor columns,

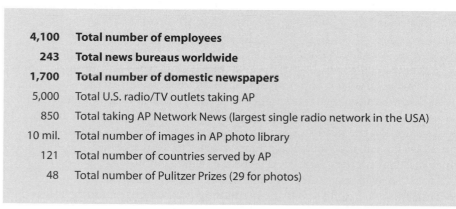

4,100	**Total number of employees**
243	**Total news bureaus worldwide**
1,700	**Total number of domestic newspapers**
5,000	Total U.S. radio/TV outlets taking AP
850	Total taking AP Network News (largest single radio network in the USA)
10 mil.	Total number of images in AP photo library
121	Total number of countries served by AP
48	Total number of Pulitzer Prizes (29 for photos)

SOURCE: HTTP://WWW.AP.ORG FEBRUARY 2007

Figure 5-2
The Associated Press is a worldwide organization with considerable assets for gathering and disseminating the news.

commentary pieces, television listings, business features, entertainment and sports features, maps and charts, and computer graphics packages.

The public relations industry offers a wire service of sorts that distributes press releases. PR Newswire (http://www.prnewswire.com) provides "electronic distribution, targeting, measurement, translation and broadcast services for 30,000 organizations worldwide that seek to reach the news media, the investment community and the general public. Established in 1954, PR Newswire has offices in 11 countries and distributes customer press releases to outlets in 135 countries in 40 languages. PR Newswire is a subsidiary of United Business Media, a company based in London.

Handling copy

Most news media throw away far more news copy than they use, generally because of space limitations. In addition, a focus on local news generally requires that national and international news stories be condensed or digested. More and more editors are spending their time merging news-service stories, compiling bits and pieces of information from several sources to create a unique story for their publications. To help busy editors keep pace with the vast quantity of copy, the news services have developed coding systems that enable editors to route stories easily and efficiently.

Priority codes, which appear at the top of all news-service stories, help assure that stories move over the news-service wires according to their urgency. Editors often use the codes to help decide order of importance. See Figure 5-3 for the principal priority codes used by AP.

Figure 5-3
AP priority codes used on news budgets and at the top of the story indicate a story's urgency.

f:	Flash, highest priority. Seldom used, except for stories of the utmost importance, such as presidential assassination
b:	Bulletins, first adds to bulletins, kill notes
u:	Urgent, high-priority copy, including all corrections. Must be used on all stories determined to be urgent; may be used on stories that are not urgent but require urgent transmission
r:	Regular priority. Used for advisories, digest stories, other late-breaking stories and special fixtures, such as People in the News
d:	Deferred priority. Used for spot-news items that can be delayed if more urgent material is available
a:	Weekday advances. Intended to be used more than 12 hours after transmission (hold-for-release stories transmitted for use in less than 12 hours carry priority code **d**)
s:	Sunday advances. Designed for use more than 12 hours after transmission

REPRINTED WITH PERMISSION OF THE ASSOCIATED PRESS

Category codes, which also appear at the top of all news-service stories, are designed to help editors sort copy into the equivalent of electronic stacks—for example, one stack for Washington news, another for sports stories, another for entertainment and so on. Before computer editing, copy editors performed the same function by hand, separating the news stories into paper stacks to make the editorial selection process as efficient as possible. Computer systems have streamlined the process. The principal category codes used by AP appear in Figure 5-4.

In addition to using category codes and priority codes, the news services supply other information helpful to busy news editors. News *budgets,* for example, digest the

Figure 5-4
Category codes are used to indicate the type of story coming across AP wires.

a: Domestic general news items. Excludes news from Washington

b: Special events

d: Stories about food and diet. Primarily advance features

e: Selected entertainment stories. Movie reviews, television reviews and columns, etc.

f: Stories for use on business and financial pages (Editors are advised, however, that an important story of financial interest is routed to both the financial and news desks.)

i: International news items. Includes stories from all foreign datelines, the United Nations, U.S. possessions and undated roundups keyed to foreign events

j: Lottery numbers

k: Commentary

l: Selected lifestyle stories

n: State and regional items with domestic datelines (If the dateline is foreign, the **i** category code is used. If the dateline is Washington, the **w** category code is used. If the story is written primarily for the business pages, the **f** category code is used.)

o: Weather tables

p: National political copy. Used only in election years

q: Results or period scores of a single sporting event

s: Sports stories, standings and results of more than one event

t: Travel copy

v: Advisories about any stories or photos transmitted on the news-service wires. Designed for news digests, news advisories, lists of advance stories and indexes

w: Stories datelined Washington, D.C. (If a subsequent lead shifts the dateline to another city, the category code changes to **a** or **b**.)

stories considered the most important by the news service. The service transmits a budget at the beginning of each publication cycle, and one for both cycles; AP editors transmit the one for morning newspapers about noon Eastern time and the one for afternoon newspapers at about midnight. The AP also updates budgets during each news cycle. In addition to a budget, subscribers to The New York Times News Service also receive a list of the stories The New York Times plans to use on its Page One the following morning. Figure 5-5 is an example of just a small part of an updated AP budget for morning newspapers; the sample came over the wires at a newspaper on the West Coast.

As you read through the news digest, you will notice that the news service uses other keywords to tell editors more about the stories. For example, note that AP will transmit graphics with some stories, such as the one about the Florida earthquake in Figure 5-5. Some stories are "developing" (still being reported and written); others "may stand" or "should stand," meaning the information probably won't change very much, and the news service probably won't do much updating or rewriting. Because of increasingly sophisticated computer technology, even developing stories are transmitted whole, rather than piecemeal, as was previously the case. In addition, many stories are transmitted for both cycles (BC), meaning they may be used in both morning and afternoon publications.

Figure 5-5
An AP news budget, called a news digest, is an overview of what AP editors believe are the most significant events of the day. This example is just a small part of an updated AP budget for both morning and evening publication cycles (BC), which moved on the wires of a newspaper on the West Coast.

```
BC-AP New Digest
The World at 7 a.m.
Eds: All times EDT

HEADLINES:

-- Nation marks 9/11 fifth anniversary with
somber reflection

-- Bush honors Sept. 11 anniversary with visits
at each of the three crash sites

-- Iran considering suspending uranium
enrichment for up to 2 months, diplomats say

-- Hurricane Florence barrels toward Bermuda

-- Series of attacks kill at least 29 Iraqis

-- Survey: Americans more spiritual and active
in religious groups than previously thought

-- Blair's trip to Lebanon draws protests from
Shiite Muslims

-- Anti-incumbent sentiment could mean job
losses on Election Day

NEWS AND DEVELOPING:

-- SPACE SHUTTLE: Hatch opening and handshake
set for 7:52 a.m., removal of the P3/P4 truss
segment from shuttle at 9:18 a.m. and the
hand off to the space station's robotic arm
at 10:42 a.m.

-- TROPICAL WEATHER: Next advisory at 8 a.m.

-- SEPT 11 RDP: Ground zero ceremony scheduled
to begin 8:40 a.m.

MULTIMEDIA:

Notable Photos:

-- SEPT 11 FREEDOM WALK: DCNW111, Marchers
participating in a Sept. 11 Freedom Walk to
honor the nearly 3,000 victims of the terror
attacks on America five years ago are given a
tour of the Pentagon in Washington.

-- SEPT 11 BUSH: NYJD112, Mayor Michael
Bloomberg, President Bush, first lady Laura Bush,
New York Gov. George Pataki and former New York
City Mayor Rudolph Giuliani descend into ground
zero for a memorial ceremony.

Interactives:

-- ANGRY AT INCUMBENTS: An interactive map
with audio interviews in wdc/restive -- voters
folder; interactive maps on congressional and
gubernatorial races in wdc/house, wdc/senate and
wdc/governors folders.

-- TROPICAL WEATHER: hurricanetracker05 folder.

-- US OPEN: tennis/usopen folder.

-- RYDER CUP: Course tour,

-- sports/golf2006/ryder/ryder06 -- course folder.
```

```
ALSO GETTING ATTENTION:

-- FLORIDA EARTHQUAKE -- Earthquake in Gulf of
Mexico sends shock waves from La. to Fla.; no
damage reported. AP Graphic FLORIDA EARTHQUAKE.

-- HEWLETT-PACKARD-DIRECTORS -- Hewlett-Packard
Co.'s board adjourned an emergency phone
conference Sunday without announcing whether it
would oust Chairwoman Patricia Dunn for ordering
an investigation that may have used illegal
means to spy on colleagues and journalists.

-- SKYDIVING DDEATHS -- 2 skydivers fall to
their deaths in southern New Jersey; pair was
making tandem jump. AP Photos NJCAM101-102.

TOP STORIES:

SEPT 11 RDP

NEW YORK -- Five years after terrorists wrought
death from clear skies, the nation began to
observe a solemn anniversary Monday, with plans
for silent reflection and fresh mourning for
the nearly 3,000 lost on Sept. 11, 2001. By AP
National Writer Erin McClam. AP Photos planned.

NUCLEAR-IRAN

VIENNA, Austria -- A senior U.S. envoy on Monday
welcomed progress at talks meant to defuse a
standoff over Iran's nuclear defiance, but said
the U.N. Security Council still intends to "move
forward" toward sanctions if Tehran refuses to
freeze uranium enrichment. By George Jahn.
AP Photos VIE101-102,110-112.

HURRICANE FLORENCE

HAMILTON, Bermuda -- Hurricane Florence barreled
toward Bermuda, forcing residents of the wealthy
British enclave to abandon their yachts and
championship golf courses for the shelter of
their thick-walled homes. By Elizabeth Roberts.
AP Photos: SJU101, SJU104.

IRAQ

BAGHDAD, Iraq -- A mini bus explosion outside
an army recruiting center, a parked car bomb in
eastern Baghdad and a string of other attacks
on Monday left at least 29 Iraqis dead and more
than a dozen wounded. A U.S. soldier also died
over the weekend, the military said. By Sinan
Salaheddin. AP Photos BAG101-109.

AMERICAN FAITH, HFR

UNDATED -- More Americans are active in
religious groups than previously thought, and
many others without ties to congregations still
believe in God or a higher power, according to
a broad survey of faith in America released
Monday. By Religion Writer Rachel Zoll. HOLD FOR
RELEASE until 9:30 a.m.
AP Graphic AMERICAN FAITH.
```

Figure 5-5 *(continued)*

```
INTERNATIONAL:

MIDEAST-BLAIR

BEIRUT -- British Prime Minister Tony Blair
heads to Beirut after nudging Israeli-
Palestinian peace efforts forward during talks
in Israel over the weekend. But the trip to
Lebanon is drawing harsh words from Shiite
Muslims, who accuse Britain of backing Israel
during the summer's fighting. AP Photos: LON139,
JRL121


AFGHAN-COCA COLA

KABUL, Afghanistan -- A Coca-Cola plant opens
in Kabul with snipers perched on the roof,
highlighting the dangers facing this major
American symbol in Afghanistan where violence
has reached its deadliest proportions since
the ouster of the Taliban. By Paul Garwood.
AP Photos KAB101-113


NATIONAL.

DESIGNER BEEF-CHICAGO

CHICAGO -- Fashionistas who want the latest in
couture can go to Paris, but for cow-ture, the
place to be is Chicago. The city once known for
its stockyards is at the center of a hip food
trend: designer beef. By Don Babwin. AP Photos
CX301-303.
```

```
-- SPACE SHUTTLE -- CAPE CANAVERAL, Fla. --
The space shuttle performed a back-flip Monday
so crew on the international space station
could photograph any signs of damage on the
belly of Atlantis, which carried the first new
addition to the space lab in 3 years. AP Photos
TXDC101-110.


SPORTS:

TEN-US OPEN

NEW YORK -- Roger Federer and Tiger Woods broke
open two bottles of Dom Perignon and toasted
-- to a growing friendship, greatness and Grand
Slams. With his new best pal watching from a
corner box, Federer won his third straight U.S.
Open title in convincing fashion. By National
Writer Ben Walker. AP Photos XNYF149. XNTF174,
XNYF228.


FBN-ON FOOTBALL-THE MANNINGS

EAST RUTHERFORD, N.J. -- Being neutral didn't
come easy to Archie Manning, as he watched sons
Peyton and Eli quaterback the Colts and Giants
on Sunday night. The Colts won 26-21, but there
was no joy for Archie -- it would have been just
as hard on him if the result had gone the other
way. By Football Writer Dave Goldberg.
AP Photos ERU101-103, ERU105-106.
```

▶**Keyword or slug.** Names the story and is repeated on all subsequent versions. Editors use this slug throughout the editing process, including on page layouts (see Chapter 11).

▶**Cycle designator.** Indicates that morning publications have first use of the story (AM), afternoon publications have first use of the story (PM), or the item is available to both cycles (BC).

▶**Word count.** Estimates the length of the story.

▶**Story version vocabulary.** Reveals the following:

- Whether the story is one of the news schedules (budgets) for that day (Bjt)

- Whether the story is the first version—first lead (1st Ld)—or a later version (2nd Ld, 3rd Ld, and so on)

- Whether the transmission is simply advising or alerting editors (Advisory)

- Whether the transmission is an advance story (Adv 01)

Here is other information supplied by the news services to help find and sort the copy:

- How many takes (a take, or a page, usually does not exceed 450 words) the story is (2 takes)

- Whether the transmission is an addition to the first take (1st Add, 2nd Add, and so on), an insert to the story (Insert), a substitution for part of the story (Sub), a correction (Correction) or a complete rewrite of the story, including all inserts, substitutions and corrections (Writethru)

Before computer technology, news editors had to collect all these bits of information as they were transmitted—at a very slow 33 words per minute on teletype machines—and literally cut and paste them all together into a cohesive story to send to the composing room for typesetting. Today, ultra-high-speed computers perform the cut-and-paste function, and most later versions of a story are transmitted as a write-through.

The wire editor's job

The person who oversees copy from the news services is commonly known as the wire editor because in the years before satellite transmission, news services sent their stories by telegraph and later telephone wires. The wire editor is the news editor's link to events of the day outside the primary circulation area of the publication or viewing area of the broadcast station. The wire editor is responsible for providing the news editor with complete wire budgets (digests), updated news stories and advisories on breaking news. The news editor prepares advance copy (stories to be used in future editions) and edits stories. Communication is the key to the wire editor's job. Working closely with the news editor results in a well-packaged and informative news report.

At a morning newspaper with several editions, published in a metropolitan area with competing papers, the job of the wire editor begins around 2 p.m. He or she reads the competing publications, paying close attention to the AP stories that their editors chose to use.

Before the wire editor left work the night before, he or she told a copy aide to leave the final edition on the wire editor's desk. Doing so helps the night news editor, who may not have seen the last edition, and also helps the wire editor refresh his or her memory about the previous day.

The news editor will mark a copy of the wire budget, which is the news service's list of stories that will be transmitted during the AM cycle. The stories selected should be processed first.

To make certain of what is in the computer system for the day, the wire editor begins to scan the *queues,* computer files of news-service stories sorted according to broad categories. The news editor also scrolls through the queues periodically. These are the broad categories used to organize the queues:

NA: National stories
FO: Foreign (international) stories
CA: California stories (this category varies, of course, with the state)
NX: New York Times and other supplemental news services
AV: Advance stories from supplemental services
AD: Advance stories from AP

The wire editor scans the queues for stories that can be "killed," or thrown away—multiple write-throughs of the same story or versions for morning papers. The wire editor checks the morning version before killing any story in case the morning version is better than the afternoon version. The editor may decide to use a morning version if the competition hasn't already used it.

Moving through the queues, the wire editor keeps in mind the news editor's plan, suggests stories that can be grouped together in a content package and makes sure the news editor knows whether a story is expected to change.

The wire editor is on the lookout for stories that are important. The news editor needs to know about developing stories that will be transmitted later in the day and about fresher versions of a story that appeared earlier in another form. One way to keep the news editor informed is to use the *slug field* space at the top of the computer screen. A "good" or "wow" message there will tip off the news editor.

The news editor must have clean copy that can be sent to the copy desk with minimal effort; speed is essential. The wire editor can help reduce the time the news editor spends with each story by doing the following things:

▶ **Remove all news-service labels and numbers at the top of each story.** Anything that should not appear in print should be deleted. Only the news-service credit line, byline and dateline should remain. Many publications omit news-service bylines unless the story is a particularly important news story, a feature, an analysis or an op-ed piece. A story in which the writer exhibits personal flair usually warrants a byline.

▶ **Make certain the credit line is correct.** For example, a story transmitted by AP should not be published with the credit line for another news service.

▶ **Remove the news-service instructions at the bottom of the story.** Unless removed, these extra lines will be reflected in the total length of the story, which will cause problems when page layouts are drawn.

Increasingly, the wire editor or a copy editor rewrites news-service stories to get a better angle or, when possible, to give the story a local angle. With important international and national stories, more and more copy desks are combining stories from a variety of news services to save space and avoid duplication. For example, often stories on the Consumer Price Index and on other governmental economic or employment statistics can be combined. The newspaper, magazine, or Internet news site may add local figures as well. Stories about U.S. Supreme Court decisions, several of which may be handed down on the same day, also can be combined into one story.

John Brewer, former president of The New York Times Syndicate and later the publisher of a daily newspaper in the Pacific Northwest, says modern wire editing is "finding good stuff from the zillion news-service sources available these days and packaging it effectively." He adds that this kind of editing "takes news judgment, a good sense of design and a desire to Make It Count."

The story conference

Wire editors for morning newspapers usually prepare for the afternoon story conference, or budget meeting, while they process news-service copy for the first edition. They do this by jotting down the sluglines of stories that are expected to develop during the afternoon and evening. AP is good about keeping member papers advised of developing stories, and many such stories are obvious. For example, a two-sentence story at 11 a.m. about a plane crash can grow into a lead story as information about the crash becomes available. Another key as to what news is developing is the afternoon advisory that AP moves about noon, which lists stories the AP expects to "top"—send new leads for—during the day.

Those who attend the story conference usually include the managing editor, metro editor, wire editor, section editors (sports, business, features) and photo chief. Some publishers ask marketing and circulation people to sit in as well. At this time the editors discuss stories that are ready or will be ready shortly for the next day's editions and decide which stories will get Page One treatment. The news editor or wire editor may suggest local angles that staff reporters could develop as sidebars or additions to news-service stories. Decisions about the use of photographs or other art or graphics are made during this brief meeting.

During and after the crunch

The times between multiple editions of a morning newspaper are critical. Often the deadlines come no more than an hour apart. The wire editor must work quickly and work closely with the news editor to put out a successful follow-up to the first edition.

After the budget meeting, any stories requested by other editors are sent to the news editor. The wire editor will check frequently with the news editor to make sure that needed copy is in the queue. The wire editor will notify the news editor when stories are updated to see whether they should be re-edited. Minor changes may not be worth the trouble.

By 9 p.m. the bulk of the wire editor's work for the day's editions is usually completed. During lulls, feature and advance copy moves to the proper departments.

By 10 p.m. the wire editor should have all the queues clean, taking out advisories that are intended for editors and printing copies for the managing editor, the assistant managing editor and the news editor.

Copy editors who handle news-service material are responsible for sorting and then distributing stories to various newspaper sections and for avoiding the publication of duplicated stories, for choosing the best version of a story from among several news services and for merging several versions into one story. They also help the news editor decide the top national and international stories of the day.

The wire editor must also work closely with those responsible for the publication's computer systems to determine the most efficient way to retrieve, sort and store the vast volumes and variety of news-service material transmitted each day.

Editing for the Web

In the 1990s, many editors and publishers predicted that Web sites would result in the demise of the traditional print media. Instead, Web sites have become the next evolutionary phase for print journalism, and a way for newspapers and magazines to compete with the broadcast media as the public's dominant source of information. The Web is a medium that can move beyond the practice of placing text around static images on a page with a 24-hour lag time. It allows news organizations to cover events in greater depth and with greater speed than before and allows them to employ multimedia to tell the story in a way neither broadcast nor print media, individually, can.

Online journalism is not without its own unique set of perils. The printing press no longer determines breaking news deadlines, and accuracy is threatened in the rush to post a story 15 seconds before a competitor. But just who is the competition on the Internet? The answer is: everyone and anyone. Yet, readers and viewers who want to be certain the information they glean from the Web is credible will continue to rely on the name brands: the newspapers, magazines and broadcast stations they depended on in the past. Readers of The New York Times, for example, trust that the information contained there is accurate because the newspaper has established its credibility over decades. Users have come to rely on nytimes.com in the same way they rely on the traditional news publication.

News Web sites are an amalgamation: They can resemble a wire service in that editors continually update stories with new information. They also can resemble a bulletin board as all content from that day's print edition is posted there. Finally, they can resemble their parent products as reporters will be sent out to write stories that are going to appear only online. But news Web sites are more than a wire service, a bulletin board or a traditional news-gathering operation. They are a resource of information that cannot be found in print editions, alone, or on news broadcasts, alone. News Web sites combine text, graphics, video and audio into a brand new form of information delivery, a form that requires an increasingly savvy cadre of editors.

One such editor, Matthew Lee, a former senior sports producer at washingtonpost .com, says his online newsroom was organized according to news units, or pods, each with different responsibilities. People who worked in the breaking-news pod, for example, occupied workstations in the center of the office and were responsible for building and updating the home page (the first page of the Web site users see when they visit washingtonpost.com). "By midmorning, the online newsroom was near full capacity," he said. "Each section was monitoring the wires for any news that may arise. Each was also working on long-term projects or maintenance of individual sections." Editors working on news packages will develop audio clips, streaming video highlights, interactive photo galleries and a long archive of past articles related to the content of the package.

For people who develop content for the Web, graphics, animations and multi-media applications still attract a lot of attention, but Web sites and the Internet as a whole continue to be heavily text-based. Lessons in this chapter about editing leads, including essential information in stories, handling quotations, shortening stories and editing news-service copy apply to the Web as well as traditional print-media editing. The Web's hypertext structure and the glut of information it offers, however, require copy editors to give special attention to these considerations:

- How much text will appear at any one time on the reader's computer screen?

- How easy will it be for readers to get key information quickly without necessarily reading the complete text?

- How is the story broken into segments?

Keep it short

Web Review quotes a "cool site" judge as saying, "If a site works, I'm going to read what they have to say," commenting further that the quality of the text was a major criteria in evaluating sites. The first part of his quote—*if a site works*—is a key to getting Web users to read the copy. Despite nifty navigational tools, the site won't work unless text is well-edited and brief.

Research by John Morkes and Jakob Nielsen indicates that Web users do not like long, scrolling pages; they prefer the text to be short and to the point. Other Nielsen research suggests that reading from computer screens is about 25 percent slower than reading from paper. Readers report that they suffer eyestrain and lack of patience when reading online material. This may change as more high-resolution monitors become affordable; meanwhile, the lesson for copy editors is to keep Web copy brief. In "Data Smog: Surviving the Information Glut," David Shenk writes that in an information-saturated world, journalists become consumers' first line of defense in trying to tame the information tide. News companies and journalists understand better than newcomers to the information society that "less is more" in the Internet news business. That journalistic standby, the inverted pyramid style, works well to communicate succinctly in the online environment.

Make it skimmable

For the same reasons that bulleted lists, informational graphics and other condensed information formats are popular in traditional media, certain factors compel their use in the online world. Such "skimmable" content, also referred to as "scannable" material, helps prevent eyes from tiring while reading from a computer screen. Additionally, Nielsen and other Internet researchers speculate that readers approach the Web with the mind-set that they must be active while online, frequently moving a mouse around a page or surfing from one site to another. To sit and read a long passage seems unproductive to most online users.

The sheer volume of Internet material—that data smog Shenk describes—compels users to move from page to page, unwilling to commit much time to any single item because the next download might contain more valuable or easier-to-grasp information. These devices can help readers skim Web pages:

- Clear, informative headlines either standing alone or followed by one or two sentences with a link to the full story

- Lists of key ideas, highlighted by bullets or other typographical elements

- Paragraphs with a single idea

- Colored type to emphasize words or phrases

- Hypertext anchors, which appear on the screen in color and often underlined

- Quotes or other key passages pulled from the text and set in a different size, style or color type or highlighted by borders

- Frequent subheadings within the text

Link it

Scientists and military researchers used the Internet for a quarter of a century before Tim Berners-Lee at the CERN physics laboratory in Switzerland developed the concept of the World Wide Web in the late 1980s. The Web, based on a hypertext networked information system that made the Internet simple for everyone to use, caused Internet growth to explode in the mid-1990s, both in the number of users and the amount of information linked by computers. The term *hypertext* describes text containing links to other text. *Hypermedia* refers to the joining of a variety of media, such as text, video and sound, which the Web makes possible. HyperText Transfer Protocol (the "http" that forms the beginning of most Web addresses) is used by Web browsers such as Netscape Navigator and Internet Explorer to build pages held on computer servers at distant sites.

This linking capability provides writers and editors the advantages of a non-linear approach to communication. Participants in Morkes and Nielsen's Web readability study made these comments about hypertext:

> The incredible thing that's available on the Web is the ability to go deeper for more information.

> Links are a good thing. If you just want to read the page you're on, fine, you're not losing anything. But if you want to follow the links, you can. That's the great thing about the Web.

> I might be searching for one document, but I might find 15 other related things that pique my interest. It's very useful. I really enjoy that.

To determine the most reader-friendly ways to link related material, copy editors must abandon traditional linear ways of thinking. The best use of hypertext is not simply to chop a long story into separate linked pages, an online counterpart to jumping a newspaper or magazine story from Page One to an inside page. This approach discourages readers by adding to download time and complicating printing, should readers desire a hard copy of the article.

Editors must think of each story as a package of separate components and structure the package with hypertext links that readers can choose to follow or ignore according to their own needs or interests at a particular time. It is important that editors give readers specific information about what they will find if they decide to follow a link. Readers don't want a surprise after waiting for a page to download. This is not the place for teaser words or phrases.

Hot spots, another term for hypertext links, can be incorporated within a sentence, displayed as colored and often underlined words. In addition, links can be listed as headlines or perhaps just labels in a separate column or box alongside the main story. Each link can lead to pages with still other links about the subject.

Material published on previous days can likewise be linked into an archive of stories, allowing readers to review the unfolding of a particular news story. A section about Web page design in Chapter 11 further describes how hypertext links are used.

Figure 5-6 shows how ESPN.com handled links to its package of stories about the then-dominant players in women's tennis, Venus and Serena Williams, as they prepared for another U.S. Open tournament.

The lead item on the ESPN.com home page is a strong, active photograph of older sister Venus. The cutline provides concise, basic information about the sisters and advances the tournament. Included are three highlighted and underlined hyperlinks: "U.S. Open," "beginning Monday," and "all but impossible." A mouse click on the first link leads to a package of stories and photos about the U.S. Open, including even more links to information about the tournament. The "beginning Monday" link leads to the tournament draw, a list of all of the matchups in the first round. Finally, the "all but impossible" link leads to a story headlined, "The princess and the warrior," a feature story about the differences in how Venus and Serena Williams play tennis.

Figure 5-6
The lead story, headlined "Court Of Law," in this screen capture of an ESPN.com home page, shows links to stories about the 2002 U.S. Open tennis tournament.

Professional perspective: Matthew Lee

Online editing

Q: Is editing for the Web different than editing for traditional print and media? Why or why not?

A: The basics of editing for a newspaper Web site are no different than editing for the traditional print newspaper. Correct spelling, proper grammar and adherence to the various stylebooks are a constant, regardless of the medium. However, the newspaper copy editors work directly with reporters and edit articles, whereas at most newspaper Web sites, the online staff generates only limited content. The majority of a newspaper Web site editor's time is devoted to enhancing the newspaper's content.

Q: How can print editors work effectively with Web editors to present their content?

A: As with most successful working relationships, communication is key. Having a basic understanding of how each medium operates and a common ground are always very helpful communication tools. On a technological level, many newspaper organizations are searching for and developing publishing systems that allow content to easily be reconfigured for use in the newspaper as well as on the newspaper's Web site.

Q: How does emerging technology affect the job of an editor?

Matthew Lee received a bachelor's degree in communication in 1999 from George Mason University in Fairfax, Va. He worked as a senior sports producer for washingtonpost.com.

A: Internet-capable cell phones and handheld computers (PDAs) are making it increasingly easy to be wired nonstop. With this emerging technology comes a certain added pressure to be on top of breaking news stories. The Washington Post Company has always put an emphasis on being right about the facts of a breaking news story rather than simply being first to report something. However, the implication of new technologies is clear: Our readership looks to us for accurate, timely news regardless of the time of day or night. Also, as broadband Internet access becomes more widely available, the use of multimedia to enhance stories on newspaper Web sites becomes crucial.

Suggestions for additional reading

American Copy Editors Society, http://www.copydesk.org.

Associated Press, http://www.ap.org.

Berner, R. Thomas. *Language Skills for Journalists,* 2nd ed. Boston: Houghton Mifflin, 1984.

Bernstein, Theodore M. *Dos, Don'ts and Maybes of English Usage.* New York: New York Times Books, 1999.

————. *Watch Your Language.* Great Neck, New York: Channel Press, 1958.

Biagi, Shirley. *Media/Impact: An Introduction to Mass Media,* 5th ed. Belmont, Calif.: Wadsworth, 2002.

Brooks, Brian S., and James L. Pinson. *Working With Words: A Concise Handbook for Media and Editors,* 3rd ed. New York: St. Martin's Press, 1996.

Cohn, Victor, and Lewis Cope. *News and Numbers: A Guide to Reporting Statistical Claims and Controversies in Health and Related Fields.* Ames, Iowa: Iowa State Press, 2001.

Desmond, Robert W. *Windows on the World: World News Reporting 1900–1920.* Iowa City, Iowa: University of Iowa Press, 1980.

Emery, Edwin, and Michael Emery. *The Press and America: An Interpretive History of the Mass Media,* 6th ed. Englewood Cliffs, N.J.: Prentice Hall, 1988.

Folkerts, Jean, and Dwight L. Teeter Jr. *Voices of a Nation: A History of Mass Media in the United States,* 2nd ed. New York: Macmillan College Publishing Co. Inc., 1994.

Gans, Herbert J. *Deciding What's News: A Study of CBS Evening News, NBC Nightly News, Newsweek and Time.* New York: Vintage Books, 1980.

Meyer, Philip. *Precision Journalism: A Reporter's Introduction to Social Science Methods,* 4th ed. Lanham, Md.: Rowman & Littlefield Publishers, 2002.

Morkes, J., and J. Nielsen. (1998). "Applying Writing Guidelines to Web Pages," Online. http://www.useit.com/papers/webwriting/rewriting.html, January 10, 1999.

Murray, Donald Morison, and Donald M. Murry. *The Craft of Revision.* New York: Harcourt Brace, 1997.

Reuters, http://www.reuters.com.

Rosewater, Victor. *History of Cooperative News-Gathering in the United States, 1865–1935.* New York: Appleton-Century-Crofts, 1930.

Schudson, Michael. *Discovering the News: A Social History of American Newspapers.* New York: Basic Books, 1979.

Schwarzlose, Richard A. *The Nation's Newsbrokers—Volume 1: The Formative Years, from Pretelegraph to 1865.* Evanston, Ill.: Northwestern University Press, 1989.

———. *The Nation's Newsbrokers—Volume 2: The Rush to Institution, from 1865 to 1920.* Evanston, Ill.: Northwestern University Press, 1989.

Shenk, David. *Data Smog: Surviving the Information Glut.* New York: HarperCollins, 1998.

Tuchman, Gaye. *Making News: A Study of the Construction of Reality.* New York: Free Press, 1978.

United Press International, http://www.upi.com.

Wilhoit, G. Cleveland, and David H Weaver. *Newsroom Guide to Polls and Surveys.* Bloomington, Ind.: Indiana University Press, 1990.

Legal Concerns

THE **First Amendment** to the U.S. Constitution provides, among other things, that the people may speak and write free of censorship from the federal government. Colonial history and subsequent Supreme Court interpretations of the First Amendment make it clear, however, that the First Amendment is not an absolute. Competing societal interests limit the unbridled exercise of free expression.

Like the idea that "your right to throw a punch ends where my nose begins," the press's practice of First Amendment rights must accommodate other people's rights, including the following:

- The right to the reputation that one has built

- The right to be left alone if one wishes to be left alone

- The right to a fair trial for a criminal defendant

- The right not to receive unsolicited obscene material

- The right to profit from one's intellectual or artistic creations

- The right not to be cheated by false or deceptive advertising

Editors are expected to understand legal topics that directly concern the editorial process, including prior restraint, libel, privacy and copyright. This chapter provides an overview of these topics, as well as rights of the college press.

Prior restraint

The Supreme Court has held that raw governmental censorship in the form of **prior restraint,** or telling the press what types of information it cannot publish, is inconsistent with the guarantees of the First Amendment. Nevertheless, the court has ruled that the government, in the interests of national security, has a right to protect its secrets. Determining what information falls into that category is not always clear-cut.

The U.S. Supreme Court provided guidance in the 1971 Pentagon Papers case. The court held in that case that The New York Times, The Washington Post and other publications could publish the secret Pentagon study of U.S. involvement in the Vietnam War because the government was unable to prove that publication would cause "direct, immediate and irreparable harm" to the national security. The Court was clear that government assertions alone that particular information endangers national security are not sufficient. The government has the burden of providing evidence to prove that all three parts of the legal test are met:

1. A direct link between publishing the information and a specified harm (death or injury to soldiers, for example)

2. That the harm will come immediately after publication, not at some far distant time in the future

3. That the nature of the harm will be irreparable (death, injury, destruction of property)

The First Amendment applies to Congress, but through the due process clause of the Fourteenth Amendment, states are now forbidden from passing laws that abridge free expression. These amendments do not grant the mass media any special rights; they apply to all individuals. Communication companies, like other businesses, are subject to laws governing such matters as antitrust, labor, contracts, taxation and postal services. Reporters and copy editors are not expected to have specific knowledge of these matters, which are generally handled by corporate attorneys, but journalists are expected to know how their publications can function as a watchdog on government and how to avoid violating the individual rights of the people they cover.

Competing personal interests

Our society places high value on freedom of expression, but society likewise values other personal rights, such as the right to enjoy a good reputation once it has been earned and the right to be left alone. Property rights, including the right to profit from intellectual creations, have legal protection. As noted previously, the First Amendment is not an absolute, so laws concerning libel, privacy and copyright are not considered inconsistent with First Amendment guarantees.

Sometimes these various interests clash. That is, the media may publish information they think is protected expression, but individuals may think the published statements infringe on personal rights. Individuals who think their reputations have been damaged may choose to "suffer in silence," doing nothing to correct the perceived wrong. Or offended people may seek redress by asking the media to publish a clarification, correction or retraction.

Professional perspective: Mary Kay Martire

Legal advice for copy editors

Mary Kay Martire, a partner with the Chicago law firm of Hopkins & Sutter, gave the following advice for copy editors at an Inland Press seminar:

- Engage in regular training on defamation and libel law. Annually review employees' strengths. Work with employees on weaknesses.

- Apply record-retention policies consistently. Make sure the newsroom uses the same policy throughout. The policy on retaining reporters' notes does not matter—newspapers can keep them all, throw them all away or keep them for a certain amount of time. The consistent application of whatever policy is chosen is what helps protect newspapers.

- If an error is made, print a retraction—a newspaper limits its damages by doing so.

- Copy editors should have an awareness of the framework of the U.S. libel laws. They should have an idea of the standards for judging public and private figures, for instance.

- Check sources—elementary, but too often overlooked.

- Take particular care with headlines and cutlines. Small errors in these small parts of an overall story package can result in large jury verdicts.

- Take the same care with online material as with print material.

A retraction is not a libel defense, but it may be sufficient to ward off a lawsuit or mitigate damages if a lawsuit is successful. A conversation with the editor or publisher or perhaps with the publication's attorney may persuade upset people that they would be unlikely to prevail in a libel or privacy lawsuit.

If informal attempts to resolve a conflict over rights are unsuccessful, a civil lawsuit may result. The party with the complaint files a lawsuit and becomes the ***plaintiff.*** The party being sued becomes the ***defendant.*** One of several things might happen at this point. For example, the parties might decide to settle out of court, in which case the defendant might pay an agreed-on amount of money for damages. Most defendant news organizations, however, are extremely reluctant to take this approach because it could invite frivolous lawsuits.

The following sections of this chapter look at the elements that the plaintiff must prove and the legal defenses for libel, invasion of privacy and copyright infringement lawsuits.

Libel

Libel is a false statement that exposes people to hatred, ridicule or contempt; lowers them in the esteem of their colleagues; causes them to be shunned; or injures them in their business or profession.

Plaintiff's burden of proof

A person who sues for libel must prove the following:

- The statement was published.

- The plaintiff was identified in the statement.

- The statement was defamatory.

- The statement caused injury.

- The publisher was at fault in publishing the statement.

Publication is usually obvious in cases involving the mass media. Strictly speaking, publication has occurred when at least one person other than the defamed person has received the material. In media cases, courts typically rule that publication has not occurred until the material reaches its intended audience. In other words, media personnel can discuss a potentially libelous item during the production process without fear of a successful libel lawsuit.

Identification may be established even though the plaintiff is not named in the story if people reasonably understand that the statement refers to the plaintiff. An address, job title or description might be sufficient for people to identify the plaintiff.

Individuals cannot sue successfully just because they are members of a large group that has been defamed. For example, the statement "All lawyers are crooks" would not be sufficient identification for an individual lawyer to bring a lawsuit. But an attorney might be able to prove individual identification and harm by the statement "All lawyers at the XYZ Law Firm are crooks."

Although published statements may identify and damage the memory of a deceased person, the dead cannot sue, and relatives may not sue on their behalf.

Defamation is another part of the plaintiff's burden of proof. The plaintiff must persuade the court that the offending statement carried a "sting," meaning that it harmed the plaintiff's reputation. Evidence about a plaintiff's reputation before and after publication is admissible. In a few instances, courts have decided that plaintiffs were "libel-proof" because their reputations were already tarnished beyond the possibility of further damage.

In most cases involving the mass media, the plaintiff must also prove that the offending statement was *false.* True statements that harm someone's reputation are not actionable as libel, although they may be actionable as an invasion of privacy. Thus, the accurate claim that someone has been arrested and charged with murder is not actionable, even though the person may subsequently be acquitted of the charge.

Minor inaccuracies will not defeat the defense of truth as long as the part of the statement that carries the sting is true. For example, a libel case would not be decided on inaccurately reporting the place of arrest of a murder suspect as long as the suspect was accurately identified and the charge accurately reported.

Some words and phrases are particularly dangerous if applied falsely to an identifiable person. These words have sparked numerous lawsuits for slander or libel; therefore, copy editors should be particularly alert when dealing with copy containing any "red flag" words and expressions listed in Figure 6-1.

Injury to the plaintiff may take the form of general harm to reputation such as losing friendship and trust. Some plaintiffs seek "special damages," meaning that they can show proof of monetary loss such as loss of their job, opportunity for promotion in their job, customers, clients or contracts.

Fault joined the list of elements that public official libel plaintiffs had to prove following the 1964 Supreme Court ruling in *New York Times v. Sullivan.* Noting the need to promote public debate about public affairs and potential for error, the court determined that the U.S. Constitution protects defamatory statements published without fault. Before then, once a libel plaintiff had established publication, identification and defamation, the burden of proof shifted to the defendant, who then had to offer a defense.

In some states, public officials were using libel suits to intimidate news organizations—primarily The New York Times—that chronicled the civil rights movement. The Supreme Court's new fault standard worked to lessen the chilling effect of such lawsuits. Today all libel plaintiffs must prove some degree of fault, with public officials or figures needing to meet a tougher burden than private people who sue. The fault standards will be discussed later in this chapter.

Defenses against libel

Media defendants attempt to persuade the court that they should not have to pay damages for a statement claimed to be libelous because its publication is protected by the U.S. Constitution or by a traditional common-law defense.

Figure 6-1
Here are some "red flag" words and phrases that require special care.

adulteration of products	collusion	illegal gambling	perjurer
adultery	corruption	illegitimate	scoundrel
altered records	coward	illicit relations	shyster
atheist	criminal	incompetent	sneak
attempted suicide	crook	infidelity	sold influence
bad moral character	deadbeat	Jekyll-Hyde personality	sold out
bankrupt	double-crosser	kept woman	spy
bigamist	drug addict	Ku Klux Klan	stuffed the ballot box
blackmail	ex-convict	liar	suicide
brothel	fool	mental disease	swindle
bribery	fraud	Nazi	unethical
brothel	graft	peeping Tom	unprofessional
buys votes	has AIDS		villain
cheats	hypocrite		

▶**The constitutional defense.** A full-page advertisement in The New York Times in 1960 led to a case that profoundly altered libel law. A group of civil rights leaders placed the ad, which criticized tactics used by police and public officials in several Southern cities to disrupt the civil rights movement. The ad asked for contributions to pay bail for Martin Luther King Jr. and other movement leaders who had been jailed for their protest activities. The accusations made in the advertisement were true for the most part, but the copy also contained several rather minor factual errors. Although he was not named in the advertisement, L.B. Sullivan, police commissioner in Montgomery, Ala., sued the Times for libel. Sullivan won $500,000 for damages in the state courts of Alabama, but in 1964 the U.S. Supreme Court overturned the damage award.

In *New York Times v. Sullivan,* the Supreme Court reasoned that public officials must live with the risks of a political system in which there is "a profound national commitment to the principle that debate on public issues should be uninhibited, robust, and wide-open, and that it may well include vehement, caustic, and sometimes unpleasantly sharp attacks on government or public officials." Further, the court said that "erroneous statement is inevitable in free debate, and . . . it must be protected if the freedoms of expression are to have the breathing space that they need to survive."

In effect, the Supreme Court was saying that the U.S. Constitution protects false, defamatory statements about public officials as long as the defendant does not show reckless disregard for truth or knowingly publish falsehoods. On the basis of that ruling, public officials accusing the media of libel became obligated to prove that a media defendant published with **actual malice.** Actual malice was defined by the court as knowledge of falsity or reckless disregard for truth.

Soon after the decision, the court determined that public figures, in addition to public officials, should have to prove that the defendant published with knowledge that the defamatory statements were false or with reckless disregard for truth.

Since a 1974 Supreme Court decision, all libel plaintiffs now must prove some measure of fault on the part of the defendant. The court held that state laws could no longer impose liability without proof that the defendant was at fault in publishing the offending statement. States were free to set the standard of fault to be met in their individual jurisdictions, and most states have set **negligence** as the fault standard. A finding of actual malice would be necessary to award **punitive damages,** those more costly monetary awards designed to punish the guilty party.

Negligence is defined somewhat differently from state to state. Some states use the "reasonable publisher" definition of negligence: Would a reasonable publisher in the same community or a similar community under similar circumstances have published the defamatory statement? Other states use a "reasonable person" definition: Would a reasonable person have published the statement under existing circumstances?

Here are examples of situations in which state courts have ruled that the press was negligent:

■ Relying on a source whom local police described as not reliable in the past

■ Failing to examine a public court record when writing about a criminal case

■ Publishing a negative, one-sided story about a teacher, based primarily on complaints of parents who had ill will toward the teacher

Public or private libel plaintiff

The fault standard to be used in the case depends on the status of the plaintiff. Thus, the outcome of a libel case often hinges on whether the plaintiff is considered a public official or figure or a private person. That determination is not always easy to make, leading appeals courts to sometimes overturn libel verdicts because the status of the plaintiff was misjudged, leading to the wrong fault standard being imposed.

In a series of cases debating this issue, the courts have set down guidelines for deciding the status of the plaintiff.

A *public official* is one who has, or who the public perceives to have, substantial responsibility for, or control over, the conduct of governmental affairs or someone whose qualifications for a position are of public interest. Not all government employees are necessarily public officials because not all occupy policymaking positions. Candidates for public office and applicants for policymaking government positions are considered public officials in the context of a libel suit because the public is interested in their qualifications for the job.

The Supreme Court has distinguished two types of *public figures:*

- **All-purpose public figures:** These are people who achieve such pervasive fame or notoriety or who occupy a position of such pervasive power and influence that they are considered public figures for all purposes and in all contexts within their community. An all-purpose public figure usually, but not always, possesses a high degree of name recognition in the community.

- **Limited public figures:** These people, by their public statements and actions, have projected themselves into the arena of public controversy and into the vortex of a question of pressing public concern in an attempt to influence the resolution of an issue.

Few public figures are all-purpose public figures, involved in all aspects of public life. Instead, most are limited public figures; they voluntarily become involved in just a few, perhaps only one, controversy. For example, someone who becomes involved in the public debate about whether abortion should be legal in the United States would be a public figure in a libel lawsuit concerning that controversy. However, if that same person filed a libel lawsuit about a private matter or about a public controversy in which he or she had not become involved voluntarily, that person would be classified as a private person. In another example, a person involved in a highly publicized divorce case was held to be a private person in a libel case that originated when a magazine misstated the grounds for granting the divorce. The court held that divorce was a private matter, not a public controversy.

Finally, a *private person* is one who may be widely known in the community but who has no authority or responsibility for the conduct of governmental affairs and has not thrust himself or herself into the middle of an important public controversy.

Reporting and writing techniques are examined to determine whether the defendant acted with fault. Before and during the trial, copy editors, reporters and other newsroom personnel might be interrogated about procedures used to produce the story, including this information:

- The number and credibility of sources

- Deadline pressures involved in gathering information, writing and editing the story

- The reasonable probability that the information was accurate

- News personnel's doubts about the story's truth

Neutral reportage is the practice of accurately and disinterestedly reporting that a responsible, prominent person or organization has made false, defamatory statements about a public official or public figure. In a few jurisdictions, neutral reportage is recognized as having constitutional protection in a libel action. Most courts have not considered a case dealing with this defense or have refused to recognize it, and the Supreme Court has not decided the issue.

The several courts that have recognized neutral reportage as a libel defense accepted the argument that such accusations about public figures are newsworthy. The courts also accepted that the First Amendment does not require the press to ignore newsworthy statements made by one prominent person about a similarly situated person just because the press cannot verify them or because the reporter has doubts about their truth.

It is important to note that in cases in which the doctrine of neutral reportage has been accepted, the stories included denials or explanations from the defamed parties. Both legal and ethical concerns require careful adherence to this practice. Such stories should also alert readers to the fact that the defamatory charges are debatable and have not been independently verified. Copy editors should insist that such information be included in this type of story.

▶ **Common-law defenses.** Defendants in both criminal and civil cases typically argue every defense that potentially applies. Libel defendants advance the constitutional defense if the published statement is false but was published with insufficient fault. In addition, one or more of these common-law defenses might be argued:

- Fair comment

- Qualified privilege

- Truth

Fair comment protects opinion about matters of public interest or things that have been put on public display. The doctrine of fair comment allows reviewers, for example, to publish scathing reviews of plays, movies, books, restaurants and so on.

Copy editors should ensure either that opinion in a story is based on generally known facts or that the factual basis for such opinion is stated in the story. Copy editors must eliminate opinion that relies for its support on the existence of undisclosed information unless the editor knows that such information is accurate. For example, it is protected opinion to say that an actor gave a poor performance in a play, but to falsely state or imply that the poor performance can be attributed to the actor's use of alcohol or illegal drugs is an unprotected statement of fact.

Publications, broadcast stations and Web sites are responsible for what they publish, which includes letters to the editor. Copy editors must edit editorial page material with the same care as other stories. Expressions of opinion can often imply the existence of facts that may turn out to be false and defamatory and thus actionable. Like editorials, the letter writer's opinions are protected, but the facts that underpin opinions are not protected if they are false and defamatory. This letter, which actually appeared in a newspaper, should not have left the copy desk (identifying names have been changed for the purposes of this illustration):

To The Sentinel:

I was stopped at the corner of Victoria and Water Streets when Officer Smith's cruiser hit my vehicle. He hit me. The dent and blue paint on the driver's side door proves it. (He can't drive.)

Because of one cop's stupidity Jonesville just lost another cruiser (myself a car). This is his sixth cruiser he zeroed, and I don't drive with my lights off.

Smith is a Wyatt Earp who likes to assault perpetrators (allegedly). He muscled me with both hands handcuffed, lying in a hospital bed (a real man). He's done it before, and will do it again to you.

Assistant City Attorney John Doe has numerous complaints on the
matter of Smith.

Eh, what's happening Jonesville? Go to sleep. Don't get involved.

[Signature]

[Address]

EDITOR'S NOTE: Attorney Doe denies he has received complaints about
Patrolman Smith, except from the author of this letter with regard
to his recent arrest.

The editor's note did little to remedy the situation. And the "letters policy" statement, which the newspaper published with its letters column, increased the potential for a libel lawsuit in connection with the letter: "The reader's column is for your opinions. . . . We do not publish letters we feel to be libelous . . . or that make allegations we are unable to verify independently."

Ed Williams, former editorial page editor for The Charlotte (N.C.) Observer, gave these instructions to editorial page writers and editors at his newspaper:

- Get the facts straight.

- Be sure facts are facts and opinions are opinions.

- Read it on the page proofs.

- Talk with the paper's lawyers before publication if the subject matter is touchy.

Qualified privilege, another common-law defense, allows the media to cover privileged situations. But the privilege is conditioned on an accurate and fair account of the proceedings. Usually, to be considered privileged, the proceeding must be open to the public, or the information must be available for public inspection. Public meetings and public records are examples of privileged situations.

It is this common-law defense that allows the media to cover damaging and false statements that are made during trials, for example. Even if it is later revealed that a witness lied during testimony, the media are not held liable for repeating those lies. Copy editors must keep in mind, however, that the privilege applies only to those comments made during the proceedings, not to comments made by public officials or other parties outside the proceedings.

To rely on the qualified privilege defense, journalists must be certain that records used as sources are indeed public records. Because reporters sometimes gain access to information that is not a matter of public record, copy editors should be on guard against nonpublic information that is the basis for a potentially actionable story.

Truth is the best common-law defense against libel because falsity is an integral part of the definition of libel. Unfortunately, truth is not always easily proved. When the offending statement concerns public matters, the plaintiff has the burden of proving falsity—certainly a heavy burden—but the defendant will try to convince the jury that the published statements were true.

The truth must be as broad as the charge. To support a published charge that the plaintiff is a crook, it is not enough to prove, for example, that the plaintiff once shortchanged someone. Likewise, it is not sufficient to prove that the plaintiff was convicted of a misdemeanor shoplifting charge if the published statement said the plaintiff was a convicted felon. Again, copy editors must be especially alert when handling stories that make accusations.

Courts usually allow truth to stand as a defense even though the story contains minor inaccuracies that do not carry the "sting" of the statement. For example, to

Figure 6-2
Here is a summary of the plaintiff's burden of proof, the requirements for summary judgment and potential defenses for a libel suit.

Overview of a Libel Case

Plaintiff must prove:

1. publication
2. identification
3. defamation
4. injury
5. publisher at fault

Summary judgment?

A judge may award judgment to the defendant without a trial if

1. both parties agree on the facts involved in the case
2. plaintiff can't meet burden of proof with "convincing clarity"

Defendant may argue:

Common-law defenses

1. truth
2. fair comment and criticism
3. qualified privilege

Constitutional defense

- Although the published statement was false, it was not published with the required standard of fault.
- Public plaintiff fault standard is "actual malice," that is, the publisher acted with reckless disregard for truth.
- Private plaintiff fault standard is usually "negligence."

Some states define negligence as not exercising due care as measured by a reasonable person.

Other states measure negligence as the amount of care that other publishers would exercise when operating in similar circumstances to that of the defendant publisher.

publish that someone was arrested on Aug. 1 instead of Aug. 2 is unlikely to defeat the truth defense unless other circumstances make the exact date important to the case. Figure 6-2 summarizes key points about libel as discussed in this section of this chapter.

Privacy

Privacy has been defined as the right to be left alone and the right to be free from unwarranted publicity. The information explosion, the increasing amount of personal information that the U.S. government collects about its citizens and the ease with which computers allow access to that data have all contributed to legal and ethical problems for the mass media.

Journalists sometimes have ethical qualms about publishing information that they have a legal right to publish. Public opinion polls in recent years indicate a decline in media credibility, which to some extent can be traced to the public perception that some media outlets occasionally use objectionable news-gathering techniques or publish information about individuals that should remain private.

Difficult ethical questions arise as responsible journalists attempt to perform their watchdog function: How much does the public need to know about the private lives of candidates for public office to make wise voting decisions? Should people know that a co-worker suffers from AIDS or any other disease? Should the public know that a man who thwarted an assassination attempt on the president is gay? Chapter 7 deals with ethical dilemmas posed by such questions; this section discusses the legal aspects of invasion of privacy.

Unlike libel laws, which protect reputational interests, privacy laws are meant to give legal redress for mental anguish and suffering caused by an invasion of personal privacy. Most states recognize four distinct legal wrongs under the broad heading of invasion of privacy:

- Intrusion into a person's physical solitude

- Publication of private information that violates ordinary decencies

- Publication of information that places a person in a false light

- Appropriation of some element of a person's personality, name or likeness for commercial purposes

Intrusion upon physical solitude can take several forms, such as trespassing upon private property and using hidden cameras or microphones to eavesdrop on private conversations. Unlike libel actions, publication is not a prerequisite for an intrusion lawsuit. The act of trespassing constitutes the legal wrong.

Embarrassing actions that take place in public view can be photographed or reported without invading privacy. But the media may not invade someone's "zone of privacy," either physically or with mechanical or electronic devices.

Courts have held that property owners have the legal right to request that journalists leave public places such as restaurants when the journalists' purpose does not coincide with the primary purpose of the public place—to dine, for example.

Publication of private information involves publicizing a private matter that would be highly offensive to a reasonable person and is not of legitimate concern to the public. Published information that is embarrassing or upsetting to a plaintiff is not sufficient to support a privacy claim; the information must be highly offensive to a reasonable person in the community.

The information must be private, not public. If embarrassing and offensive information becomes a matter of public record, then a privacy action will not succeed. Embarrassing information such as that sometimes published in "looking back into history" columns—for example, that a person with good standing in the community served a prison sentence years ago—generally is not actionable if based on information available in public records. Unlike the law of defamation, truth is not a defense for this type of privacy lawsuit if the offensive information is indeed private and not newsworthy.

False light is like libel in that it involves falsity, and if the matter is of public concern, this type of invasion of privacy requires the plaintiff to show that the publisher knew the information published was false or that the publisher had reckless disregard for truth (actual malice). As in libel law, truth and privilege are defenses for this aspect of privacy. Some courts have required that the false light statement also be judged as highly offensive to a reasonable person.

Picture captions and file photographs used to illustrate stories can be particularly troublesome. For example, a couple filed a false-light privacy lawsuit against a magazine that published a picture showing their child being hit by a car. The use of the picture in the newsworthy context of an accident would have been permissible if the caption had been accurate. However, the magazine used the picture to illustrate a story titled "They Ask to Be Killed," which concerned careless or negligent actions through which people cause themselves harm. Because the accident had involved no carelessness or negligence on the part of the child or the parents, the family won the lawsuit.

Appropriation is the unauthorized use of a person's name or likeness for commercial gain—for example, using someone's name or picture in an advertisement without permission. The argument is made that such use causes the plaintiff mental anguish. A better argument may be that a "right of publicity" is involved, in that unauthorized use deprives people of the right to decide how their name or picture will be used and the right to profit from such use.

Appropriation more often concerns the advertising department rather than the editorial department of a publication. Permission is not needed to use a person's name or picture for news purposes, assuming that no illegal news-gathering techniques were used. On the other hand, written consent should be obtained from people whose name or picture is used for advertising purposes.

▶**Invasion of privacy defenses.** Legal defenses for invasion of privacy lawsuits vary. Truth, for example, is a defense for false-light invasion of privacy but not for the other three categories of privacy cases. If truth cannot be established in a false-light case and the subject matter is of public concern and not purely personal, the defendant can try to establish that the falsity was not published with actual malice.

The only legal defense for trespass is consent, either explicit or implied. One who allows a reporter to enter private property or who does not object to the presence of visible cameras or recorders, for example, has consented. Consent is also the defense for appropriation. For commercial use, rather than news, the consent should be written.

Faced with a lawsuit claiming publication of private information, a defendant can argue newsworthiness and claim that the published material is not highly offensive to a reasonable person.

Copyright

Copyright law provides the right to control or profit from a literary, artistic or intellectual production. In preventing material from being copied without permission of the copyright owner, copyright law both protects and restricts the mass media.

A key principle of copyright law is that facts and ideas cannot be copyrighted. No person or news organization can "own" the facts concerning a newsworthy story or the idea of covering a particular subject. But the manner of expression used to tell the story or discuss the idea—the specific patterns of words and images—can be copyrighted and thus protected from infringement by others. Plagiarism is both illegal and unethical.

Many publications may use the same article through contractual agreements with news services and other suppliers of syndicated material. Members of The Associated Press, for example, agree to send to AP all spontaneous local news stories, and AP members have the right to use such "spot news" stories verbatim. The AP contractual agreement specifies that stories resulting from individual enterprise and initiative and copyrighted by the originating news organization cannot be used by fellow AP members without permission and credit.

Current copyright law protects original works of authorship fixed in any tangible medium of expression, now known or later developed. Categories of such works include literary works; musical works, including any accompanying words; dramatic works, including any accompanying music; pantomimes and choreographic works; pictorial, graphic and sculptural works; motion pictures; and other audiovisual works and sound recordings. A copyright now lasts for the lifetime of the owner plus 70 years, after which the work becomes part of the public domain.

Under the *work-made-for-hire* doctrine, unless specific contractual agreements establish otherwise, the publication, rather than an individual employee, owns the copyright on published material. Unless the employer gives permission, reporters or photographers cannot sell or give away copies of their work or authorize some other publication to use it. The duration of copyright protection for works made for hire is 95 years from the date of first publication or 120 years from the date of creation, whichever expires first.

The same principle applies for public relations firms: the employer owns work produced by employees. When a public relations firm produces material for a client, the PR firm retains ownership of the material and may reuse elements for future campaigns unless the two parties specify that the client will own all of the material. Under such a contract, the PR firm's work for the client would be considered a work made for hire.

Freelance journalists retain ownership of their work unless they expressly sign away such rights. A freelancer can agree to give or sell specific rights to a work and retain all other rights. For example, an author can sell "first serial rights," which allow a publication to publish the work one time anywhere in the world; "first North American rights" allow publication of the work one time in North America only. After losing a court battle against freelance writers, major newspapers and magazines in the late 1990s began requiring that freelancers permit republication of their work for the publications' online outlets.

A defense against copyright infringement is *fair use.* This defense allows publications to use brief quotations from a copyrighted work for the purposes of critical reviews or scholarly work. Key ideas behind the fair use doctrine are that the person who copies must add substantial independent work and that such copying should be in the public interest. Despite the protests of producers of television shows, the Supreme Court ruled that the copying of off-the-air television shows for noncommercial use is "time shifting" for the convenience of viewers rather than copyright infringement.

Because no formula exists for determining how much copying is permissible under the fair use doctrine, copy editors should give careful scrutiny to stories that contain verbatim passages from copyrighted material. Several paragraphs may be acceptable in some circumstances, whereas a single line from a poem or song may be grounds for a successful infringement lawsuit. Much depends on the amount and nature of the material that the copier adds to the original work.

Trademarks

In addition to copyrighted works, other legally protected types of intellectual property include trademarks, service marks and trade names. A *trademark* is defined by statute as "any word, name, symbol or device or any combination thereof, adopted and used by a manufacturer or merchant to identify its goods and distinguish them from those manufactured or sold by others." The term *service mark* is used for distinctive identifiers for a service rather than a product. A *trade name* is defined by statute as "any name used by a person to identify his or her business or vocation."

Proctor & Gamble, for example, is the trade name of a business that identifies its products with many different trademarks, including Ivory soap, Tide detergent and Crest toothpaste. A single word—*Sears,* for example—may be used for all three purposes: to identify products and services and the name of the company that produces those products and services. Examples of trademark symbols are the peacock feathers identifying the National Broadcasting Company and McDonald's golden arches.

In addition to identifying sources of goods and services, trademarks function to warrant that goods coming from a particular source will be of consistent and desirable quality. The instant recognition value of trademarks permits companies to use shortcuts in advertising their products and services. Companies recognize the tremendous value of their trademarks and work zealously to protect them from infringement and from falling into generic use.

Some trademarks have become generic because they were used by the public to designate the genus of the products. King-Seeley Thermos Co., for example, originated the term *thermos* for vacuum-insulated containers during the 1920s, but the term fell into general use, leaving King-Seeley unsuccessful in its attempts to prevent Aladdin Industries from referring to its vacuum-insulated products as "thermos" bottles. Other examples of former trademarks that are now generic nouns are *aspirin*, *cellophane* and *yo-yo*.

To protect their marks from falling into generic use, trademark owners take steps—such as using advertisements—to educate the public that the mark should not be used in a generic sense. Companies also write warning letters to journalists and others who use trademarks incorrectly, such as using them as a noun or verb, as in "Xerox this document" or "make a Xerox." Correct usage for trademarks is as an adjective followed by a noun: Xerox copier, a Xerox copy, Kleenex tissue, Teflon coating, Jeep vehicle, Weed Eater trimmer.

Trademarks should be differentiated typographically from words around them. AP style is to capitalize a trademark, but the stylebook directs that a generic term should be used unless the trademark name is essential to the story. In its alphabetical entries, the AP stylebook includes many trademarks, together with generic equivalents. Plural forms should not be used, such as "She uses Kleenexes." The correct form is "She uses Kleenex tissues." Trademarks should not take the possessive form, as in "the Jeep's windshield." Instead, write "the windshield on a Jeep sport utility vehicle."

College press rights

In general, college and university student journalists enjoy the same First Amendment rights as the professional press and face the same responsibilities. Younger journalists, however, encounter greater oversight from school administrators. The Supreme Court in a 1988 case (*Hazelwood School District v. Kuhlmeier*) empowered high school officials to exercise editorial control over school-sponsored media to the extent that such editorial direction contributes to the learning process, which courts have interpreted rather broadly.

Legally, school censorship does not extend to content that is simply embarrassing to administrators or critical of school policies, although some school officials routinely violate this legal principle, arguing that the school district is the publisher of the material and can exercise editorial control. This is not within the meaning of the Supreme Court's *Hazelwood* decision, but school officials know that students rarely have the legal and financial resources to challenge such censorship.

Several states enacted laws that effectively grant high school students greater rights than specified by that 1988 Court ruling, and policies in some school districts allow students editorial authority over school-sponsored student media.

Student media produced independent of school sponsorship, such as alternative newspapers or individual student Web sites, remain free from school censorship unless evidence shows that such productions will cause "substantial disruption or material interference with school activities." Officials can exercise reasonable time, place and manner restrictions on the distribution of such media on campus.

Thus far, most college student media, despite battles on several fronts in recent years, remain free of direct school censorship. An exception is in the states of Illinois, Indiana and Wisconsin because in a 2005 case (*Hosty v. Carter*), the Seventh Circuit Court of Appeals applied the high school standards from the Hazelwood case to a college newspaper in Illinois. Despite a petition for certiorari filed by the Student Press Law Center, joined by other press rights groups, the Supreme Court refused to consider the case.

The Student Press Law Center, a nonprofit, nonpartisan organization, has operated for more than 30 years to educate high school and college journalists about the rights and responsibilities embodied in the First Amendment and to help the student news media cover important issues free from censorship. The Center provides free legal advice and educational materials for student journalists on a wide variety of legal topics. Figure 6-3 provides the SPLC's most frequently asked questions from college journalists.

Figure 6-3
These are frequently asked questions that college journalists submit to the Student Press Law Center and the responses from SPLC attorneys.

Top 10 FAQ's about college press rights

Q: Do students at a public college or university have First Amendment rights?

A: Emphatically, yes. As the United States Supreme Court said back in 1969, "It can hardly be argued that either students or teachers shed their constitutional right to freedom of speech or expression at the schoolhouse gate." As agents of the government, public school officials are prohibited by the First Amendment from censoring most student speech. Students at a public school have the right to voice their opinions and write about the issues that concern them just like every other American. But because the First Amendment only prohibits government officials from suppressing speech, it does not prevent censorship by private school officials. Nevertheless, a state constitution or statute—or even a school policy protecting free speech—may give private school students important free press protections.

Q: But if school officials or student governments fund a student publication, radio or television station, can't they censor it like any other publisher or owner could?

A: Not at a public school. The courts have ruled that if a school creates a student news or information medium and allows students to serve as editors, the First Amendment drastically limits the school's ability to censor. Among the censoring actions the courts have prohibited are confiscating copies of publications, requiring prior review, removing objectionable material, limiting circulation, suspending editors and withdrawing or reducing financial support.

Q: But what about the *Hazelwood* decision?

A: The U.S. Supreme Court's 1988 *Hazelwood* decision, which gave school officials significant power to censor some school-sponsored student expression, only dealt with high school student publications. While a few college officials have tried to extend *Hazelwood's* reach to their campuses, courts have rejected every such attempt except for the Seventh Circuit in the 2005 *Hosty v. Carter* decision.

Q: What about underground or independent student publications? Are they protected from censorship, too?

A: Absolutely. Schools can establish reasonable restrictions as to the time, place and manner of distribution, but non-school-sponsored student publications are entitled to at least as much First Amendment protection as school-sponsored student publications.

Q: Can a student publication be sued for libel, invasion of privacy or copyright violations?

A: Yes, and on rare occasions they are. In such cases the individual reporter who produced the story, the editor of the publication and the publication itself if it is separately incorporated can always be held liable if money damages are awarded. Court decisions suggest that a school that does not exercise content control over the publication will not be held liable for what students publish. In any event, most cases are dropped or settled before they ever get to court.

Q: Can student reporters protect confidential news sources or information when they receive a court subpoena asking that they turn it over?

A: In most cases, yes. Some states have "shield laws" and others have court-created reporters privileges that protect journalists from having to reveal this kind of information. Most states have never explicitly applied these laws to student journalists, and the language of a few of these might not protect students. You should check your state law.

Q: How can I make use of freedom of information laws?

A: Freedom of information, or "sunshine" laws, require that government agencies such as public schools and police departments open to the public most of their official records and meetings. These laws, which vary from state to state, are usually simple to use and often require that a journalist simply make an informal request. Every newsroom should have a copy of their state's open records and open meetings laws.

Q: Since freedom of information laws only apply to the records or meetings of government agencies, are private school students out of luck in getting information about their school?

A: Not necessarily. There are a number of state and federal laws that now require private schools to reveal certain information. One of the most important access tools for private school journalists is the institution's federal informational tax return, the Form 990, which the law says must be available at your school's business office for public inspection. The form provides information about where your school gets its money and where it spends it.

Figure 6-3 *(continued)*

Q: One of our star student athletes has been accused of stealing thousands of dollars of school computer equipment. Rather than going to the local court system, the school has decided to try the case before the University Judicial Board, or campus court. They have said the proceeding is closed and they refuse to release any information about the case's outcome. What can I do?

A: This is one of the hottest—and most important—issues confronting the student press today. Many schools claim that these proceedings are "educational" in nature, and that releasing information about them will unfairly invade students' rights to privacy. Student journalists (and many commercial journalists as well) believe that schools are simply using campus courts to control or bury information that hurts the school's reputation. They argue that when these proceedings involve charges of criminal rather than academic activity, the public has a right to know what goes on behind closed doors. College students, they argue, are adults. And they should be treated as such. The public routinely has a right to attend criminal proceedings in public courts. Public access ensures fairness and accountability, both to the accused and to the system and victims. Where schools take on the responsibility of a public criminal court they must be held to the same standards of openness and accountability. Invoke the power of your state's open records and open meetings law. If you are still denied access, appeal. Also, let your readers and other media know what the school is doing.

Q: Where can I go for more information about my rights and responsibilities as a student journalist?

A: The Student Press Law Center at http://www.splc .org/legalresearch.asp.

Techniques for avoiding lawsuits

A copy editor reviewing a story for libel, privacy or copyright problems has four choices:

- Publish the story because it has no legal problems
- Kill the story because it is libelous, invades privacy or infringes copyright
- Skillfully edit the story to remove offending passages
- Expect a lawsuit, but publish the story because we'll win if we're sued

The decision to publish a dangerous-but-defensible story must not be made lightly and must not be made by a copy editor acting alone. As noted in Chapter 1, the copy desk is the last line of defense. If a dangerous story has made it through the reporter and the assigning editor to the copy desk, it is up to the copy editor to notify a supervising editor. The story may then be subjected to review by the chain of command at the publication, and attorneys may become part of the decision-making process.

Cost of a lawsuit

The tremendous cost of lawsuits—even those that publishers can win—is a factor in deciding whether to publish. A lawsuit depletes the time and energy needed to go about the business of publishing. A small staff may be unable to meet deadlines if personnel are occupied with lawyers and with sitting in a courtroom day after day during pretrial motions, jury selection and a trial.

In addition to time and energy, monetary costs are a tremendous burden. In 2005 the Media Law Resource Center reported that although media defendants won most of the lawsuits against them during the previous year, the average damage award for libel, privacy and related claims against the press was $3.4 million. These figures do not include legal fees and court costs for defending those lawsuits.

Dealing with complaints from the public

The most desirable outcome for the newspaper or other publication is to publish the important, dangerous-but-defensible story without being sued. Assuming that the story is accurate, fair and balanced, the publisher may be able to persuade the would-be plaintiff that a lawsuit is a waste of time and money.

Unfortunately, the publisher or publisher's representative may never get an opportunity to placate an angry person if newsroom personnel fail to exercise common courtesy. Anyone who calls the newsroom with a complaint, with a story tip or for any other reason should never be passed around from one person to another or treated with the "Hey-we've-got-a-crazy-on-the-line" approach.

Three professors at the University of Iowa interviewed more than 700 people who had sued the media for libel. The majority told the researchers that they were more upset about reputational harm and emotional distress than financial damage. Plaintiffs told researchers that after becoming distraught about something they read or heard broadcast, they first contacted the offending publisher or broadcaster—usually by telephone. Rudeness encountered during that initial contact provoked many respondents to anger; then came the call to a lawyer.

The media can't be expected to satisfy all agitated complainers, even if the publisher or station manager was willing to yield to every demand. But media personnel can be expected to refrain from rudeness. The Iowa researchers recommended that newsroom managers take the following actions:

- Insist that everyone in the newsroom understands the power that the press has to hurt people and that everyone gives courtesy a high priority.

- Assign one person the responsibility for dealing with complaints. Many newspapers employ a "reader representative," sometimes called an *ombudsman,* who serves in this capacity.

- Develop written policies and procedures for addressing complaints, and make sure that everyone in the newsroom knows what they are.

- Deal harshly with any employee who stifles a complaint and doesn't direct it to the designated person.

Two trends during the past few years show that newspapers and their online sites treat reader complaints seriously: More regularly publish corrections columns, and more have created the position of ombudsman or reader representative. Readers can talk back to newspapers and magazines through letters to the editor, of course, but most are not motivated to spend time and effort writing letters. Many readers will take the time to phone or to send an e-mail to report errors, and people who do this seem to appreciate the opportunity to contact someone specially designated as the reader representative. Where questions of news judgment and standard journalistic practices are concerned, the reader representative can often satisfy angry readers simply by explaining why journalists do certain things.

Smaller newspapers and broadcast stations rarely have someone on the payroll to serve solely as a reader representative, but small news organizations, like their larger counterparts, often publish corrections columns. Newspapers vary in their policies about what kinds of errors they acknowledge and the prominence they give to corrections columns. Some give the corrections column prominent treatment in the front section; others relegate the column to a less noticeable spot in a back section.

Along with the corrections, some papers and Web sites tell readers how each error was made, such as "incorrect information supplied by a source," "a reporting error" or "a copy editing error." Regularly published corrections columns serve as one more quality-control device and can help enhance credibility with readers. Including reporters' e-mail addresses with stories facilitates corrections.

Prepublication cautions at the news-gathering stage

The work of avoiding libel, invasion of privacy and copyright infringement should begin at the reporting stage so that copy editors don't have to deal with such legal problems. But in reality, copy editors sometimes need to question reporters aggressively about their news-gathering techniques and the credibility of their sources. Both legal and ethical concerns may be at stake.

Reporters must understand that they can defame someone at the news-gathering stage, even before a story is written. Making a defamatory statement about someone to a third party constitutes *slander,* so the old reporter's ploy of pretending to know more than he or she does to gain information can be dangerous.

Dangerous: "We already know that Jones is a dishonest cop. We just want your comments."

Safer: "We're looking into Jones' conduct as a police officer, and we'd like to get your comments."

As noted earlier in this chapter, privacy can also be invaded during the news-gathering stage. Hot pursuit of a story does not excuse intrusion or trespassing. Reporters have no legal right to enter private property or use hidden microphones or cameras without consent, even if the purpose of the story is to expose wrongdoing. Journalists have no legal right to accompany protesters onto private property—a nuclear power plant, for example—to get a story. The power plant operators may legally restrict reporters and cameras to a particular "viewing" area, although better pictures might result from the vantage point of the protesters.

Most states allow one-party consent to recording a telephone conversation; that is, the reporter may record a telephone interview without telling the source. Some states require both parties to give consent for taping, so it is essential that copy editors know the law in their state.

Prepublication cautions at the copy desk

Generally, an assigning editor reads stories before sending them to the copy desk, but copy editors must not assume that the assigning editor was alert to all potential legal problems. As always, accuracy is essential. In addition, copy editors should take special care to ensure that stories are fair and balanced. Stories involving reluctant sources or confidential sources, as well as stories about lawsuits, can be particularly dangerous.

▶ **Accuracy, fairness and balance.** Accuracy cannot be overemphasized. Attention to accuracy must start at the very beginning of the news-gathering process—when the idea for a story is conceived. The copy editor must be alert to stories that reporters approached with preconceived notions. Copy editors shouldn't hesitate to question reporters about whether they examined all angles of a story and relied on the most credible sources.

To head off lawsuits, copy editors must check stories for fairness and balance, ensuring that reporters have included evidence from interviews and from record searches to support generalizations and have contacted those who might be damaged by the story. Denials, if made, should be included in the story.

Remember that truth is a defense for libel but not a defense for three of the four types of privacy cases. Private information that is highly offensive to a reasonable person is actionable as an invasion of privacy, even when the information is true. Also, truth is often difficult to prove in a libel lawsuit. Although the plaintiff has the burden of proving the falsity of a story about a public matter, the publication will also present arguments to support the accuracy of the story because the burden of proof often poses a difficult distinction for juries.

Literal accuracy is not always enough to defend against a libel lawsuit because literal accuracy is not necessarily the same as truth. One newspaper faced a libel suit after it published a story stating that a woman shot her husband when she found him in the company of another woman. The statement was literally accurate, but it falsely implied adultery. The truth was that the woman entered a residence in which her husband was sitting in the living room in the company of several other people, including the "other woman's" husband.

A story that accurately reports that someone made a false and defamatory statement about someone else may become grounds for a successful libel action. Unless the charge is made during a privileged situation, such as a public meeting, it is not safe to republish defamatory statements unless the news organization operates in one of the few jurisdictions recognizing neutral reportage as a libel defense. The general rule is that anyone who republishes a defamatory quotation is just as guilty of libel as the original defamer.

▶**Reluctant sources.** If a person who might be damaged by a story is reluctant to talk to a reporter and avoids phone calls, copy editors should not let such stories go with a simple "Jones was unavailable for comment." Tell readers what attempts were made to contact the reluctant source.

The copy editor should work with the assigning editor to make sure that the reporter tries repeatedly to talk with the person. Establish a record of attempts to get the source to talk. These extra efforts may be important if the publication is sued for libel. Repeated attempts to reach the person and obtain information from sources close to him or her may help show a lack of fault on the part of the press.

If particular conditions were imposed on an interview and the reporter agreed to those conditions, copy editors should be prepared to honor them. If the news organization decides to violate agreements that a reporter made with a source, such a decision should be the responsibility of supervising editors rather than a copy editor.

▶**Confidential sources.** Anonymous sources should be avoided in most instances. Some news organizations have adopted a policy of allowing anonymous sources only in exceptional circumstances, noting that readers deserve to know who said what. If a story becomes the basis for a libel suit, the publisher has a better legal case if all sources were identified.

Many states lack shield laws strong enough to protect confidentiality between reporters and their sources, and at this writing, legislation to enact a federal shield law is under consideration in Congress but has not passed. Source credibility is one factor used in determining actual malice. If the jury does not know the identity of the source, credibility cannot be judged.

When a publication is faced with a story of Watergate magnitude, an anonymous source may be the only way to get the story, such as meeting Deep Throat in the parking garage in the dark of night. But too often the use of anonymous sources seems to readers to be an excuse for "weasel" journalism and sloppy, lazy reporting. The use of anonymous sources can be an invitation for sources to exaggerate, embellish, slant or take a cheap shot.

Information supplied by an anonymous source should be verified independently by at least one other source, preferably more than one. If the decision is made to use an anonymous source in a story, explain to readers why the identity is being withheld. Give readers enough information to establish the source's authority to speak on the subject. Of course, this is sometimes difficult to do without revealing the source.

▶**Stories about lawsuits and crime.** Be especially alert to libel and privacy dangers when editing stories about civil or criminal lawsuits. Never let a story leave the copy desk saying that someone "may" or "plans to" file a civil lawsuit. Be sure that the lawsuit has been filed and, depending on state law, that some action has been taken on the lawsuit. Make sure that the complaint is accurately quoted or paraphrased once the lawsuit is filed.

In criminal cases, double-check all key facts: the name of the accused, address and specific charge. Use middle names or initials for the suspect to avoid confusion with someone who has a similar name. Be aware that manslaughter and murder are not the same charge.

Let courts, not your publication, judge the guilt or innocence of defendants. The word *alleged,* as in "alleged ax murderer John Jones," does not always get the publication off the libel hook. Grammatically, the description *alleged ax murderer* could be understood to mean that Jones is an ax murderer who also happens to be accused, which is hardly what the writer meant, unless the writer does not accept the innocent-until-proved-guilty principle of American jurisprudence.

Don't let defamatory out-of-court statements by police or attorneys find their way into stories. If the police chief says, "We've got an airtight case against this killer John Jones," don't go to press with the statement unless the police chief says it in a privileged, public situation, such as in court during a trial. When reporting what was said during an open court session or other privileged situation, be sure to restate it accurately and to present a fair account of what happened during the privileged proceeding.

Consult the Associated Press Stylebook or previous explanations in this textbook for correct usage of such words as *assault, burglary, robbery, manslaughter* and other terms in stories about crimes.

In the interest of fairness, the outcome of both civil and criminal cases—especially if the criminal defendant is acquitted—should be published as prominently as the story about the defendant's arrest or indictment.

▶**Headlines and quote boxes.** The copy editor's task doesn't end with the story. Once the story is "lawsuit-proof," the editor must take care not to libel someone or invade privacy in the headline. Quote boxes can be problematic also because quotations taken out of context may be damaging.

Guarding against libel and other legal problems ranks among the most important duties of copy editors. (Refer to Chapter 1 for a list of duties of copy editors.) The copy desk often becomes the last line of defense against costly and credibility-damaging lawsuits. While copy editors aren't expected to possess detailed knowledge, they should understand basic media law well enough to avoid unnecessary restraint in stories and to know when to consult their company's legal staff.

Some journalistic and public relations practices that fall within the law may raise ethical questions. Legal does not always equate to ethical. The next chapter will discuss ethical concerns of journalists and other communicators.

Suggestions for additional reading

Carter, T. Barton, Marc A. Franklin, and Jay B. Wright. *The First Amendment and the Fourth Estate: The Law of Mass Media,* 9th ed. New York: Foundation Press, 2004.

Communication Law Writers Group. Wat Hopkins (ed.). *Communication and the Law,* 2007 ed. Northport, Ala.: Vision Press, 2006.

Corn-Revere, Robert L., Robert M. Frieden, Charles H. Kennedy, and Harvey
     L. Zuckman. *Hornbook on Modern Communications Law.* Mineola, N.Y.:
     Thomson West, 1999 (with updates).

Hiller, Janine, and Ronnie Cohen. *Internet Law and Policy.* Englewood Cliffs, N.J.:
     Prentice Hall, 2002.

Middleton, Kent, and William E. Lee. *The Law of Public Communication,* 2007 ed.
     White Plains, N.Y.: Longman, 2006.

Moore, Roy. *Mass Communication Law and Ethics,* 2nd ed. Hillsdale, N.J.: Lawrence
     Erlbaum Associates, 1999.

Overbeck, Wayne. *Major Principles of Media Law,* 2007 ed. Belmont, Calif.:
     Wadsworth, 2006.

Pember, Don R., and Clay Calvert. *Mass Media Law,* 2007–2008 ed. Boston:
     McGraw-Hill, 2006.

Teeter, Dwight L., and Bill Loving. *Law of Mass Communications: Freedom and
     Control of Print and Broadcast Media,* 11th ed. New York: Foundation Press,
     2004.

> **Green light ethics would pay more attention to virtues and heroes than to vices and villains.**
>
> —*Roy Peter Clark, senior scholar, Poynter Institute*

Editing and Ethics

As more and more news operations develop multiple ways (print, broadcast and online) to transmit their content, and as search-engine corporations such as Yahoo! and Google begin to create digital news content, questions arise about whether traditional journalistic values will survive in a multimedia world. More than one in three Americans routinely use the Internet for their news, and studies suggest that users seem to trust the information they find online, especially at the sites of traditional news operations such as The New York Times or The Washington Post.

"Despite the controversy over news gathering techniques employed by some Internet sites, those who go online generally give Internet news operations high marks for believability," according to a study conducted by the Pew Research Center in 2000. "In fact," the study said, "the online sites of such well-known news organizations as ABC News get better ratings from Internet users than the ratings accorded the traditional broadcast or print outlets."

J.D. Lasica, a leading authority on grass-roots media and senior editor of the Online Journalism Review, suggested two reasons for this surprising discovery. First and foremost, he said, "print journalists, by and large, have successfully transferred their greatest assets—their long-standing values and standards of accuracy, balance, credibility, fairness and trustworthiness—to the online medium." At the same time, "online journalists are taking advantage of some of the Web's key assets: its nonlinear nature (users like to call up stories, or drill down to related stories on their own time frame); its instantaneity and convenience (breaking news lies only a mouse click away); its authentication value (reporters can point to source documentation rather than tell readers to just trust us); and its interactivity (though this is still greatly underused)."

Lasica added: "One could make a strong case that online journalism thus hews to an even higher standard than traditional news media, given that we link to original documentation to buttress our reports and that we can correct mistakes after publication."

While some might argue with this conclusion, the fact is that journalistic credibility is vital to the survival of every news medium and can be built only over time. During periods of societal distress, people seek out those newspapers, magazines and broadcast stations they have relied on in the past for fair, accurate and thorough reporting.

The generally outstanding news coverage of the terrorist attacks on Sept. 11, 2001, as well as the coverage of Hurricane Katrina in 2005, may have begun to help repair a decades-long credibility gap between the media and their audiences. Yet, the gap does exist. The disconnection reached such crisis proportions in the 1980s that editors and publishers thought it warranted some action. Some began to respond by remembering the basics:

- Practice journalistic principles of fairness, accuracy and completeness.
- Respect people's feelings.
- Become aware of sensitive topics.
- Broaden issues of coverage.

Others, such as The Oakland (Calif.) Tribune, instituted policies to handle corrections and clarifications and revised local stylebooks to include sections on how to address issues of poor taste, profanity and violence.

But many believe that the credibility "challenge," among other factors, has had a negative effect on the financial health of traditional news media. Newspaper circulation rates, for example, although increasing in raw numbers, have failed to keep up with population growth. Network news share has also continued to slip.

Nationwide surveys taken in 2004 revealed that the public believes that the news media are not believable and that a media source's credibility was influenced by various factors, including a consumer's age and political affiliation.

In June 2004 the Pew Research Center for the People & the Press released the results of an important research project called the "Media Consumption and Believability Study." The survey indicated that, among other things, the U.S. public is skeptical about news outlets and those people who run them. More than half of people agreed with the statement, "I often don't trust what news organizations are saying." In fact, in a subsequent (2005) study also conducted by the Pew Research Center, only 54 percent of those surveyed said they could believe most of what was printed in their local newspaper. In 1985 that percentage was 84 percent. Tom Rosenstiel, director of the Project for Excellence in Journalism, and Bill Kovach, chairman of the Committee of Concerned Journalists, wrote a commentary on the study and had this reasoning for the decline in the public's faith in the news media: "There is evidence . . . that the new declines in confidence reflect a sense that the press is not aggressive enough in its coverage of major issues." Rosenstiel and Kovach also speculated that the survey results revealed the public's frustration with what they perceived as the increasingly partisan nature of the press, as well as aggravation over excessive coverage of "tabloid"-type stories, such as the Michael Jackson child molestation trial or the dating habits of celebrities such as Britney Spears and Brad Pitt.

Today, in the first decade of a new millennium, media ethics must be discussed within the context of negative perceptions of journalists, as well as within the context of emerging media technologies, such as digital photo imaging and online information sources. Should editors, for example, digitally manipulate a news photograph to delete obtrusive details in the foreground or to change the color of a person's clothing or jewelry? Should editors link, in any way, online editorial content with advertising? Should print publications report on "cybergossip" without checking all the facts? (See discussion of these issues later in this chapter.)

At the same time, other mass communicators, including public relations practitioners, are developing codes of ethics to help them navigate an increasingly complex moral landscape.

Journalists and journalism educators are pondering the role of the press in the 21st century. In the mid-1990s, newspaper journalists began forging the concept of public journalism or civic journalism. Jay Rosen, associate professor of journalism at New York University, and Davis "Buzz" Merritt, editor and senior vice president of The Wichita (Kan.) Eagle, were leaders in defining the reform movement known as ***public journalism.*** This movement calls on the press to "take an active role in strengthening citizenship, improving political debate and reviving public life." In addition, nearly 150 daily newspaper editors and educators participated in the ASNE-sponsored Journalism Values Institute, a multiyear project to define journalism values. The editors issued a series of reports in the late 1990s that focused on how to stay true to core journalism principles—news judgment, balance, accuracy, leadership in the community, accessibility and credibility—in the age of new media.

Just as journalists are engaged in nationwide conversations about how to undertake a fundamental reassessment of the basic mission of the press, so, too, should journalism students enter into a robust and earnest discussion of media ethics on their campuses.

How to decide questions of ethics

The stereotypes of journalists as cynical, conniving and unprincipled hacks who believe that a scoop is sacred persist in the popular culture. But what kind of decisions do real journalists make? Here are three newsroom scenarios that editors might face:

- Your magazine's summer intern discovers that the death of a prominent celebrity occurred because of complications associated with AIDS. You're the senior editor on duty, and your magazine goes to press in two hours. Should you publish the cause of death?

- As your publication's online sports producer, you believe your audience wants to read stories about all the games, both home and away, of the professional football franchise in your area. Your publication cannot afford to send you to the away games, but the owners of the football team will allow you to travel with the team, free of charge, and will grant you exclusive interviews with the star players as well. Should you accept the team's offer?

- Your newspaper's photographer returns from an assignment with a dramatic photo of an accident scene. In the foreground, a child's covered body, turned away from the camera, lies in the street; in the background, traffic stands still and passersby look on. As the editor who is laying out tomorrow's Page One, you must decide whether to use the photograph.

People who are in the business of editing and judging the news face such ethical questions as a matter of routine. Often journalists must find answers within hours or even minutes—because of the harsh deadlines of publication or broadcast.

What are the benefits of publishing the story about the celebrity dying of AIDS? Does the magazine have a policy calling for inclusion of the cause of death in obituaries? Would a great public good be served by publication? Should respect for the privacy of the relatives and friends of the deceased be considered? What personal values do you bring to bear on your decision?

In the case of the online sports producer, the question is whether traveling with the football team legitimately adds value to the Web site's reporting or to readers' understanding of the sport. Or might the sports producer simply be submitting to a form of bribery and risking conflict of interest?

What news values in the accident photograph warrant its use? Is the photo a sensational exploitation of the senseless death of a child, or is it a legitimate portrayal of a newsworthy event?

Few ethical decisions are clear-cut, and many are quite complicated. Most of the time, journalists have no detailed ground rules to guide them in making such decisions.

Some groups of professionals are able to turn to rules and principles for help in solving ethical problems. Law students, for example, study the ethics of their profession along with court procedure. Medical students study the ethics of medicine along with anatomy. Both know that the ethical code of their profession is universal and that individual practitioners will be policed by their own colleagues, who have the power to take away their licenses to practice.

Journalists, however, have no such procedures or universal rules of conduct. For them, the signs are, at best, blurred and, at worst, nonexistent. Restraints are few, and a policing agency like the American Bar Association or the American Medical Association doesn't exist. Most journalists are acutely aware of the need for ethical performance, and most attempt to respect standards for responsible journalism codified by national press organizations. Still, ethics remains a trial-and-error proposition.

What is ethics?

In popular usage, one meaning of **ethics** is "a set of principles of conduct governing an individual or group." One writer said that ethics refers not only to statements about our conduct and the conduct of others but also to statements of what that conduct ought to be. People embrace certain ethical standards of conduct because of the moral education provided by their culture—their family, school, church, friends and peers—and because of an inner commitment to culturally defined moral standards.

Ethics, therefore, is personal. It is determined and enforced by each of us individually, and it can provide us with certain basic principles by which we can judge actions to be right or wrong, good or bad, responsible or irresponsible. Because of this background, we make many moral judgments without much thought or deliberation. Most of us, for example, would not hesitate to say that we value telling the truth.

Once in a while, an ethical decision involves more than one moral rule. For example, most of us have been taught that stealing is wrong; we have also been taught that human lives are highly valued. What if a loved one required medication to live and we had no money to buy that medication? Would we hesitate to steal the medicine from the pharmacy? Would we be morally justified in doing so? Does the value of a human life outweigh the harm done by stealing the medicine? Or is stealing always wrong, regardless of the motivation?

Philosophical principles

When we are looking for a way to balance conflicting ethical rules, we are seeking moral standards, philosophical principles we can invoke to help us justify our decision. Immanuel Kant is one philosopher we might call on to help justify our decision about stealing the medicine. Kant's **categorical imperative** is based on a conviction that as human beings we have certain moral rights and duties and that we should treat all other people as free and equal to ourselves. Our actions are morally right, then, only if we can apply our reasoning universally—that is, only if we would be willing to have everyone act as we do, using the same reasoning in any similar situation. Kant's view is an **absolutist** view: Right is right and must be done under even the most extreme conditions. Thus, we cannot justify stealing the medicine unless we are willing to let anyone steal medicine under similar circumstances.

The argument that a greater good would be served by saving the life of our loved one than by not stealing the medicine might be justified by John Stuart Mill's **principle of utility.** His utilitarian theory is very influential in journalism today. It is based on the notion that our actions have consequences, and those consequences count. The best decisions, the best actions have good consequences for the largest number of people possible. The **utilitarian** principle prescribes "the greatest happiness for the greatest number." In media situations, this maxim often translates into "the public's right to know." In the example, utilitarians might argue that more good consequences would flow from stealing the medicine and thus saving the life than from any other act we could perform in that situation. Therefore, we would be morally justified in stealing the medicine.

A third philosophical principle, Aristotle's **golden mean,** holds that moral behavior is the mean between two extremes—at one end is excess and at the other deficiency. Find a moderate position, a compromise, between these two extremes, and you will be acting with virtue. In this case, the moderate and ethical position between the two extremes—stealing the medicine or allowing the loved one to die—might be to offer to work for the pharmacist in return for the medicine.

The philosophical principles of Kant, Mill and Aristotle are just three among many that can be used to help justify ethical decisions. At first these three approaches may seem inapplicable to today's fast-paced newsrooms. But on closer examination, we can sense how they might hold value for today's editing processes. At the very least, the use of philosophical principles allows us to step back for a moment and ponder the situation more than we might ordinarily do in the rush to publish. In addition, invoking a theory or philosophical principle helps us frame our approach toward solution of the ethical issue. In other words, it helps us see the problem in a broader light rather than isolate it from any historical, social or economic context. Unfortunately, in the day-to-day scramble to publish and broadcast, journalists rarely take time to reason carefully through a thorny ethical problem.

How to use the Potter box

Media professionals would benefit from a framework for thinking and reacting ethically to the myriad situations they face every day. In "Media Ethics: Cases and Moral Reasoning," the authors describe a model of moral reasoning called the Potter box (see Figure 7-1). Formulated by Dr. Ralph Potter of the Harvard Divinity School, the Potter box helps dissect a situation requiring an ethical response by introducing four dimensions of analysis: definition, values, principles and loyalties. To make a decision, we move through each dimension—from defining the situation to considering values to appealing to an ethical principle to choosing loyalties—eventually reasoning our way toward a solution.

To see how this method of moral reasoning works, let's look at a scenario that an increasing number of journalists face in this, the age of the 24-hour news cycle. You are editor of the Daily Bugle, a midsize newspaper in Hampshiretown. Word has leaked out that a town official is going to be arrested tomorrow in connection with an Internet child pornography ring that was being investigated by a federal task force. The problem is no one knows who the official is or what time the arrest will take place. Your newsroom team is poised to stake out Town Hall in the morning to try to find out who the official is, but by then other media probably will have the story and you will be scooped by online, television and radio competitors.

Then, the anonymous call comes into the newsroom. According to the source, the town's vice mayor is the one being arrested and the arrest will happen at his office at 10 a.m.

Figure 7-1

The Potter box can be used to analyze the dimensions of an ethical problem for journalists. The first step is defining the situation. It is followed by outlining the possible values at work and determining the relevant moral principles to apply. The next step is choosing loyalties. After the four-stage analysis, the final step is to make an ethical decision about whether to publish.

You put your two best reporters on the story, and they call every city official, including the vice mayor, but can't get in touch with anyone. You also have received another anonymous call that confirms the information from the first call, but no one will go on the record with the information. This is a big story with broad political ramifications for the town, involving a well-known public official and a child pornography task force that has been in the paper a lot recently.

Daily Bugle investigative reporter Dora Wallace got the call with the first anonymous tip. She strongly believes that the paper should run with the information, posting a story today on the Daily Bugle's Web site and in tomorrow's print edition. She also believes the story should be displayed prominently on Page One.

You know you must get some questions answered before you make a decision. You linger to talk to Mike Modular, the news editor, before deciding what to do. Modular tells you that the newspaper's police reporter has learned that, indeed, the rumors are true about the arrest happening in the morning

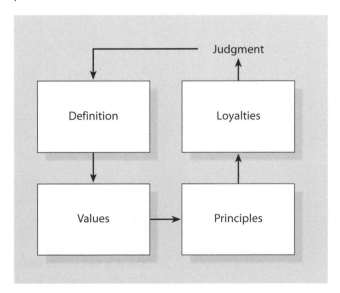

and that the public official is male, but then again, all of the town's top officials are male, so it could be anyone. Modular is hesitant to go with the story, particularly since the charges are quite serious and wrongly accusing someone of being involved with child pornography could seriously damage a person's reputation and ability to lead the community.

The Potter box can help you decide whether to publish the story without on-the-record verification of the information, as the reporter who received the tip wishes, or to not publish it, as the news editor wishes.

▶ **Step 1 is to define the situation.** Reporter Wallace might define the situation as this: The town's vice mayor is involved with a child pornography ring and the Bugle is the only news source with information on who the official is and when he will be arrested. News editor Modular might define the situation as this: The newspaper has information from an anonymous source about the potential arrest of a city official, and the information has not been verified by anyone willing to go on the record.

▶ **Step 2 is to identify the values underlying the choices.** This part of the exercise asks you to define the costs and benefits of publication. What are the positive and negative values that reflect your own personal ethics?

In this case, reporter Wallace might identify these positive values as benefits of publishing the story:

■ The news tip is about an issue (child pornography task force) that has pervaded the Bugle's newspaper pages and most broadcast news programs for many months.

■ In addition, the man who has been named by the source is a well-known city official, adding to the newsworthiness of the story.

■ The information is also, from what is known, exclusive to the Daily Bugle, and nothing has been uncovered to contradict what the anonymous tips detail.

News editor Modular, on the other hand, might identify these negative values as the costs of publishing the news based on an anonymous tip:

■ The information is potentially very damaging to the city official in question, and if the tip is wrong, the story could irreparably damage the vice mayor's reputation and that of his family.

■ The newspaper's unwritten policy is not to publish information attributable only to unnamed sources, except in extremely rare cases.

▶ **Step 3 is to appeal to a moral principle to help justify your decision.** If you were to agree with Wallace and decide to publish the story, you might call on Mill to help justify your decision. The utilitarian principle would argue that the public has a right to know about this newsworthy event and the more the newspaper can educate the public about this problem, the more unlikely it is that further crime of this kind will continue. "The greatest good for the greatest number" would suggest publication.

Conversely, if you agree with Modular and decide not to publish the story, you might call on Kant to help justify your decision. The absolutist view would argue that you should follow the newspaper's policy not to publish information from anonymous sources, no matter what. Right is right, and wrong is wrong. And publishing such potentially damaging information like this is wrong.

▶ **Step 4 is to choose loyalties.** This last step is very significant and often the most agonizing because direct conflicts arise among competing obligations. To whom is the highest moral duty owed? Is the first loyalty to yourself, to the newspaper, to the family of the victims, to the city official, to the readers, to your colleagues or to society?

Wallace might argue that the ultimate loyalty is to society and to readers. The newspaper has a social obligation to inform and educate the public about the crackdown on peddling child pornography and on its consumers, and this story could be part of that campaign. Wallace also might argue that a secondary loyalty would be to herself; publication of the story would help her earn currency with her peers, who would admire her for getting such a scoop, and the story could even win a journalistic award.

Modular, however, might argue that the ultimate loyalty should be to the newspaper and its policies regarding publication of information from anonymous sources. Or he might argue that the highest moral duty is owed the city official in question and that the story should not be published until it can be verified because it would hurt the vice mayor, perhaps permanently, if the story published turns out to be false.

After reasoning your way through the four dimensions of the Potter box—definition, values, principles and loyalties—you should be able to reach a responsible and ethical decision. The questions become more focused as the discussion proceeds through each quadrant. In the end, bringing your personally defined ethics to bear, what would you decide? Would you publish the story?

Unfortunately, reporters and editors do not often use such methods to make moral judgments. They either react instinctively, hoping that they will make the right decision and that the negative consequences will not be too overpowering, or they try to find answers in a professional code of ethics. It is in situations such as the one just posed that media professionals should fall back on the guidance provided by the Potter box or other ethical guidelines and leave instinct for finding the best stories or taking the best photos.

Codes of ethics

The Society of Professional Journalists has compiled generalized statements about well-known unethical behaviors. This code of ethics provides little substantive guidance to help journalists balance conflicting moral rules. But it does provide a starting point for defining an ethical problem that needs to be resolved. The SPJ code appears in Figure 7-2. The Public Relations Society of America has developed a code of ethics for public relations practitioners. This code uses examples to help clarify some of the values. The PRSA code appears in Figure 7-3.

In addition to these general codes of ethics, individual publications have developed their own codes or policy statements, most of which address such issues as acceptance of gifts and junkets or conflicts of interest. Here is a sampling, culled from daily newspapers around the United States:

▶ **Paying for news**

- We pay our own way. If an event is newsworthy, we can afford it. When purchasing a reserved seat is impossible or impractical, exceptions should be brought to the attention of a supervisor in advance. [Milwaukee (Wis.) Journal Sentinel]

- We barely pay reporters, let alone sources.

  Be wary of anyone offering information for money. We never pay for news, and the very attempt to solicit payment raises questions about truthfulness and motives.

  We do, of course, pay material costs such as copying expenses for documents. [Tampa (Fla.) Tribune]

- We do not offer money, favors or anything of value for news. [Kansas City (Mo.) Star]

Figure 7-2

This version of the Society of Professional Journalists' Code of Ethics was adopted in September 1996.

Preamble

Members of the Society of Professional Journalists believe that public enlightenment is the forerunner of justice and the foundation of democracy. The duty of the journalist is to further those ends by seeking truth and providing a fair and comprehensive account of events and issues. Conscientious journalists from all media and specialties strive to serve the public with thoroughness and honesty. Professional integrity is the cornerstone of a journalist's credibility. Members of the Society share a dedication to ethical behavior and adopt this code to declare the Society's principles and standards of practice.

Seek Truth and Report It

Journalists should be honest, fair and courageous in gathering, reporting and interpreting information.

Journalists should:

- Test the accuracy of information from all sources and exercise care to avoid inadvertent error. Deliberate distortion is never permissible.
- Diligently seek out subjects of news stories to give them the opportunity to respond to allegations of wrongdoing.
- Identify sources whenever feasible. The public is entitled to as much information as possible on sources' reliability.
- Always question sources' motives before promising anonymity. Clarify conditions attached to any promise made in exchange for information. Keep promises.
- Make certain that headlines, news teases and promotional material, photos, video, audio, graphics, sound bites and quotations do not misrepresent. They should not oversimplify or highlight incidents out of context.
- Never distort the content of news photos or video. Image enhancement for technical clarity is always permissible. Label montages and photo illustrations.
- Avoid misleading re-enactments or staged news events. If re-enactment is necessary to tell a story, label it.
- Avoid undercover or other surreptitious methods of gathering information except when traditional open methods will not yield information vital to the public. Use of such methods should be explained as part of the story.
- Never plagiarize.
- Tell the story of the diversity and magnitude of the human experience boldly, even when it is unpopular to do so.
- Examine their own cultural values and avoid imposing those values on others.
- Avoid stereotyping by race, gender, age, religion, ethnicity, geography, sexual orientation, disability, physical appearance or social status.
- Support the open exchange of views, even views they find repugnant.
- Give voice to the voiceless; official and unofficial sources of information can be equally valid.
- Distinguish between advocacy and news reporting. Analysis and commentary should be labeled and not misrepresent fact or context.
- Distinguish news from advertising and shun hybrids that blur the lines between the two.
- Recognize a special obligation to ensure that the public's business is conducted in the open and that government records are open to inspection.

Minimize Harm

Ethical journalists treat sources, subjects and colleagues as human beings deserving of respect.

Journalists should:

- Show compassion for those who may be affected adversely by news coverage. Use special sensitivity when dealing with children and inexperienced sources or subjects.
- Be sensitive when seeking or using interviews or photographs of those affected by tragedy or grief.
- Recognize that gathering and reporting information may cause harm or discomfort. Pursuit of the news is not a license for arrogance.
- Recognize that private people have a greater right to control information about themselves than do public officials and others who seek power, influence or attention. Only an overriding public need can justify intrusion into anyone's privacy.
- Show good taste. Avoid pandering to lurid curiosity.
- Be cautious about identifying juvenile suspects or victims of sex crimes.
- Be judicious about naming criminal suspects before the formal filing of charges.
- Balance a criminal suspect's fair trial rights with the public's right to be informed.

Act Independently

Journalists should be free of obligation to any interest other than the public's right to know.

Journalists should:

- Avoid conflicts of interest, real or perceived.
- Remain free of associations and activities that may compromise integrity or damage credibility.
- Refuse gifts, favors, fees, free travel and special treatment, and shun secondary employment, political involvement, public office and service in community organizations if they compromise journalistic integrity.
- Disclose unavoidable conflicts.
- Be vigilant and courageous about holding those with power accountable.
- Deny favored treatment to advertisers and special interests and resist their pressure to influence news coverage.
- Be wary of sources offering information for favors or money; avoid bidding for news.

Be Accountable

Journalists are accountable to their readers, listeners, viewers and each other.

Journalists should:

- Clarify and explain news coverage and invite dialogue with the public over journalistic conduct.
- Encourage the public to voice grievances against the news media.
- Admit mistakes and correct them promptly.
- Expose unethical practices of journalists and the news media.
- Abide by the same high standards to which they hold others.

Sigma Delta Chi's first Code of Ethics was borrowed from the American Society of Newspaper Editors in 1926. In 1973, Sigma Delta Chi wrote its own code, which was revised in 1984 and 1987. The present version of the Society of Professional Journalists' Code of Ethics was adopted in September 1996.

Figure 7-3
This is the Code of Ethics adopted by the Public Relations Society of America in 2000.

Preamble

This Code applies to PRSA members. The Code is designed to be a useful guide for PRSA members as they carry out their ethical responsibilities. This document is designed to anticipate and accommodate, by precedent, ethical challenges that may arise. The scenarios outlined in the Code provision are actual examples of misconduct. More will be added as experience with the Code occurs.

The Public Relations Society of America (PRSA) is committed to ethical practices. The level of public trust PRSA members seek, as we serve the public good, means we have taken on a special obligation to operate ethically.

The value of member reputation depends upon the ethical conduct of everyone affiliated with the Public Relations Society of America. Each of us sets an example for each other—as well as other professionals—by our pursuit of excellence with powerful standards of performance, professionalism, and ethical conduct.

Emphasis on enforcement of the Code has been eliminated. But, the PRSA Board of Directors retains the right to bar from membership or expel from the Society any individual who has been or is sanctioned by a government agency or convicted in a court of law of an action that is in violation of this Code.

Ethical practice is the most important obligation of a PRSA member. We view the Member Code of Ethics as a model for other professions, organizations, and professionals.

PRSA MEMBER STATEMENT OF PROFESSIONAL VALUES

This statement presents the core values of PRSA members and, more broadly, of the public relations profession. These values provide the foundation for the Member Code of Ethics and set the industry standard for the professional practice of public relations. These values are the fundamental beliefs that guide our behaviors and decision-making process. We believe our professional values are vital to the integrity of the profession as a whole.

Advocacy

- We serve the public interest by acting as responsible advocates for those we represent.
- We provide a voice in the marketplace of ideas, facts, and viewpoints to aid informed public debate.

Honesty

- We adhere to the highest standards of accuracy and truth in advancing the interests of those we represent and in communicating with the public.

Expertise

- We acquire and responsibly use specialized knowledge and experience.
- We advance the profession through continued professional development, research, and education.
- We build mutual understanding, credibility, and relationships among a wide array of institutions and audiences.

Independence

- We provide objective counsel to those we represent.
- We are accountable for our actions.

Loyalty

- We are faithful to those we represent, while honoring our obligation to serve the public interest.

Fairness

- We deal fairly with clients, employers, competitors, peers, vendors, the media, and the general public.
- We respect all opinions and support the right of free expression.

PRSA CODE PROVISIONS

Free Flow of Information

Core Principle

Protecting and advancing the free flow of accurate and truthful information is essential to serving the public interest and contributing to informed decision-making in a democratic society.

Intent

- To maintain the integrity of relationships with the media, government officials, and the public.
- To aid informed decision-making.

Guidelines

A member shall:

- Preserve the integrity of the process of communication.
- Be honest and accurate in all communications.
- Act promptly to correct erroneous communications for which the practitioner is responsible.
- Preserve the free flow of unprejudiced information when giving or receiving gifts by ensuring that gifts are nominal, legal, and infrequent.

Examples of Improper Conduct Under This Provision

- A member representing a ski manufacturer gives a pair of expensive racing skis to a sports magazine columnist, to influence the columnist to write favorable articles about the product.
- A member entertains a government official beyond legal limits and/or in violation of government reporting requirements.

Competition

Core Principle

Promoting healthy and fair competition among professionals preserves an ethical climate while fostering a robust business environment.

Intent

- To promote respect and fair competition among public relations professionals.
- To serve the public interest by providing the widest choice of practitioner options.

Guidelines

A member shall:

- Follow ethical hiring practices designed to respect free and open competition without deliberately undermining a competitor.
- Preserve intellectual property rights in the marketplace.

Examples of Improper Conduct Under This Provision

- A member employed by a "client organization" shares helpful information with a counseling firm that is competing with others for the organization's business.
- A member spreads malicious and unfounded rumors about a competitor in order to alienate the competitor's clients and employees in a ploy to recruit people and business.

(continued)

Figure 7-3 *(continued)*

Disclosure of Information

Core Principle

Open communication fosters informed decision-making in a democratic society.

Intent

- To build trust with the public by revealing all information needed for responsible decision-making.

Guidelines

A member shall:

- Be honest and accurate in all communications.
- Act promptly to correct erroneous communications for which the member is responsible.
- Investigate the truthfulness and accuracy of information released on behalf of those represented.
- Reveal the sponsors for causes and interests represented.
- Disclose financial interest (such as stock ownership) in a client's organization.
- Avoid deceptive practices.

Examples of Improper Conduct Under This Provision

- Front groups: A member implements "grass roots" campaigns or letter-writing campaigns to legislators on behalf of undisclosed interest groups.
- Lying by omission: A practitioner for a corporation knowingly fails to release financial information, giving a misleading impression of the corporation's performance.
- A member discovers inaccurate information disseminated via a Web site or media kit and does not correct the information.
- A member deceives the public by employing people to pose as volunteers to speak at public hearings and participate in "grass roots" campaigns.

Safeguarding Confidences

Core Principle

Client trust requires appropriate protection of confidential and private information.

Intent

- To protect the privacy rights of clients, organizations, and individuals by safeguarding confidential information.

Guidelines

A member shall:

- Safeguard the confidences and privacy rights of present, former, and prospective clients and employees.
- Protect privileged, confidential, or insider information gained from a client or organization.
- Immediately advise an appropriate authority if a member discovers that confidential information is being divulged by an employee of a client company or organization.

Examples of Improper Conduct Under This Provision

- A member changes jobs, takes confidential information, and uses that information in the new position to the detriment of the former employer.
- A member intentionally leaks proprietary information to the detriment of some other party.

Conflicts of Interest

Core Principle

Avoiding real, potential, or perceived conflicts of interest builds the trust of clients, employers, and the public.

Intent

- To earn trust and mutual respect with clients or employers.
- To build trust with the public by avoiding or ending situations that put one's personal or professional interests in conflict with society's interests.

Guidelines

A member shall:

- Act in the best interests of the client or employer, even subordinating the member's personal interests.
- Avoid actions and circumstances that may appear to compromise good business judgment or create a conflict between personal and professional interests.
- Disclose promptly any existing or potential conflict of interest to affected clients or organizations.
- Encourage clients and customers to determine if a conflict exists after notifying all affected parties.

Examples of Improper Conduct Under This Provision

- The member fails to disclose that he or she has a strong financial interest in a client's chief competitor.
- The member represents a "competitor company" or a "conflicting interest" without informing a prospective client.

Enhancing the Profession

Core Principle

Public relations professionals work constantly to strengthen the public's trust in the profession.

Intent

- To build respect and credibility with the public for the profession of public relations.
- To improve, adapt, and expand professional practices.

Guidelines

A member shall:

- Acknowledge that there is an obligation to protect and enhance the profession.
- Keep informed and educated about practices in the profession to ensure ethical conduct.
- Actively pursue personal professional development.
- Decline representation of clients or organizations that urge or require actions contrary to this Code.
- Accurately define what public relations activities can accomplish.
- Counsel subordinates in proper ethical decision-making.
- Require that subordinates adhere to the ethical requirements of the Code.
- Report ethical violations, whether committed by PRSA members or not, to the appropriate authority.

Examples of Improper Conduct Under This Provision

- A PRSA member declares publicly that a product the client sells is safe, without disclosing evidence to the contrary.
- A member initially assigns some questionable client work to a non-member practitioner to avoid the ethical obligation of PRSA membership.

▶ **Gifts**

- We must not allow our coverage to be bought or influenced by favors. We also must avoid the appearance of being bought or influenced. Therefore, we do not accept benefits of more than token value unavailable to the public. That includes but is not limited to travel, lodging, club memberships, loans, merchandise and discounts. Unsolicited gifts should be returned with a note explaining our policy. If this is not possible, the gift should be donated to a charity with a note to the donor explaining the circumstances. Gifts of token value may be accepted. If you are unsure what might be of token value, ask a department head or higher editor. Meals and drinks shared with news sources should be paid for, whenever possible, by The Olympian. [The Olympian (Olympia, Wash.)]

- Gifts of more than nominal value may not be accepted. When practical, gifts of more than nominal value shall be returned to the sender with our thanks and an explanation of our standards. When this is not practical, such gifts shall be donated to a suitable charity. [Danbury (Conn.) News-Times]

▶ **Junkets**

- We pay travel expenses of employees on assignment. We pay the proportional costs of staff members who travel on sports team or political candidate airplanes, trains or buses. Staff members may exercise their own judgment in accepting travel in emergency situations with the understanding payment will be made. [Wisconsin State Journal (Madison, Wis.)]

- Within the bounds of common sense and civil behavior, staffers should not accept free transportation or reduced-rate travel, or free accommodations. When access to a news source is best served by traveling on charters or at the expense of that news source, reimburse that news source later, at a more appropriate time, for the reasonable going rate for the costs incurred. [Los Angeles Times]

- Junkets and reduced travel rates should be refused. The newspaper will pay for transportation, meals and lodging for travel associated with an assigned story or other professional activity required by your job. If a story is worth doing only if someone else pays the expenses, it's not worth doing.

  We should inform travel writers, freelancers and community members contributing travel pieces that we expect them to adhere to strict pay-your-own-way standards for all food, transportation and accommodations.

  In rare situations, the only available transportation to a legitimate news story may be provided by the armed forces, government or other entity. Acceptance of any such transportation must be discussed with and approved by your supervisor. When compromises are made out of such necessity, the paper can help maintain its credibility by full disclosure of the arrangement in the story.

  If you travel on a campaign- or team-chartered plane or are put in team housing, insist that the newspaper be billed. The amount paid should represent the actual cost of travel, not a subsidized rate. [Newport News (Va.) Daily Press]

▶ **Meals**

- Employees may not accept free meals or drinks from potential sources, newsmakers or their agents. Employees of the paper should offer to purchase the meal, split the check or reciprocate at a later date. Employees assigned to attend an event that involves the offer of free food and drink should attempt to find out the per-head cost of the event and pay their own way. When impractical to assess the per-head cost at the time of the event, a reasonable payment should be made at that time or as soon after the event as possible. All payments described in this paragraph will be reimbursed to the staff member by The Denver Post. [The Denver (Colo.) Post]

- The Star prefers to pay for meals that staff members share with news sources. (In instances where insistence on paying would be awkward or otherwise inappropriate, staff members should make it clear that the newspaper will reciprocate in the future.) [Minneapolis Star]

▶ **Connections**

- News employees should not use the newspaper or information gained through their employment to push their personal agendas; solve their personal problems; or benefit their friends, relatives or associates. For example, a news employee should not write a letter of complaint to a merchant on Times-Dispatch stationery. [Richmond (Va.) Times-Dispatch]

- To further avoid conflicts, staffers should not use their position or the name of the newspaper to gain advantage in personal activities. (In applying for a loan for a house, car, business or anything of that nature, you will, of course, be expected to say where you work, what you do and how much you get paid. That is normal, acceptable practice and should not be a conflict. But if you're worried about some aspect of such a transaction, discuss it with your supervisor.) Your Tribune business card or stationery should only be used for company business. Staffers should not refer to their newspaper connections to try to resolve consumer grievances, to get quicker service or to seek discounts or deals. [Chicago Tribune]

▶ **Merchandise**

- Items sent to The Star should be paid for if kept or donated to The Star's designated charities. Only staff members with a valid reason should accept review materials. After the review is completed, those materials should be donated to charity or paid for if kept as reference material. To avoid the appearance of impropriety, no employee should accept materials at home. Freelance writers should follow these guidelines, during any projects they do for The Star. [The Kansas City (Mo.) Star]

- Books and recordings sent to The Inquirer for review purposes are accepted as news releases. They are not for the private use of Inquirer staff members, and they may not be sold for any reason or under any circumstances.

  Individual books and recordings may be kept by the persons assigned to review them. If a distributor requests that a videotape be returned, we will do so.

  A specialist on The Inquirer staff may retain works that might be of particular use as a reference.

  Books and recordings that are not reviewed or that are returned to The Inquirer by the reviewer shall, because of the expense and difficulty of sending them back to the distributor, be made available to a public or charitable institution.

  Books and recordings that are of insignificant value and are not desired by public or charitable institutions may from time to time be made available to anyone on the staff who wants them.

  Computer materials: Staff members should not make unauthorized copies of material for computers, including software and related documentation, that is write-protected, copyrighted or otherwise restricted. [The Philadelphia Inquirer]

▶ **Tickets**

- We pay our own expenses to cover the news. Reporters, photographers and editors assigned to cover sports, other spectator events or political events for spot news or future use of information may use press boxes, review seats, press rooms and other special facilities. However, The Times wants to pay for its share of such accommodations and will wherever possible.

  When possible, staff members should pay for tickets and food and refreshments served at such events.

  It is improper for staff members who are not on assignment to attend events as nonpaying spectators or to accept free meals provided by sports, political or other news source organizations.

  Free tickets or passes to sports events, movies, theatrical productions, fairs, circuses, ice shows and other events for which the public pays shall not be accepted by staff members and their families. When tickets to such events are delivered to a Times editor, the tickets should be returned with a letter courteously declining them and with an explanation of our policy.

  Staff members who attend the events for professional reasons will pay for tickets and will be reimbursed by The Times.

  Nightclub admission or cover charges and costs of meals and other refreshments incurred in professional work will be paid by The Times.

  When it is socially awkward or even impossible to pay for a meal, refreshments or entertainment, a staff member should use good judgment in how far to go in insisting on paying. When someone insists on buying a staff member a meal or a drink, the staff member should try to reciprocate at a later date. [The Seattle (Wash.) Times]

▶**Conflicts of interest**

- Our news staff does not advise or work for politicians or political organizations. We encourage good citizenship by exercising our right to vote in referenda, primaries and general elections, but we do not engage in partisan activity beyond that. [Asbury (Neptune, N.J.) Park Press]

- Avoid membership and involvement in political and governmental groups and activities. Serving on a board or commission is dubious; volunteering for a campaign or running for office is unacceptable. Signing political petitions, making campaign contributions or displaying campaign material is strongly discouraged for all newsroom employees and forbidden for those involved in political coverage. Note: this does not apply to including a party affiliation on your voter registration and voting. [Statesman Journal (Salem, Ore.)]

- Employees shall not write, photograph, illustrate or make news judgments about anyone related to them by blood or marriage, or with whom they have a close personal relationship. This does not apply to first-person stories or stories in which the relationships are clearly spelled out. Nor shall personal relationships within the newsroom affect news judgment.

  For example, it is clearly a conflict to report on a public official with whom one is romantically involved. [San Jose (Calif.) Mercury News]

- Reporters and editors who hold stocks or other investments whose performance might be affected by articles they write or the way stories are played in the newspaper should report the conflict to a supervisor and offer to recuse themselves from any involvement with the story. Buying or selling stocks or other securities with knowledge of a story that might affect their price or while in possession of other nonpublic information also could subject the employee and the company to criminal and civil liability under the federal securities laws.

  By the same token, it would seem apparent that theater critics should not be investing in plays they may be reviewing or restaurant critics in restaurants. Certainly any such conflicts should be reported. But not all potential conflicts are so clear-cut. In all cases, it is wise to avoid any investment or relationship you would not like to read about on Page One of a newspaper, your own or someone else's. [Chicago Tribune]

The Tampa Tribune's Newsroom Ethics Policy finishes with the following:

"The ethical decisions we face can't all be covered here. Even if they were, there's little to keep a crafty journalist from finding ways to benefit between the lines. Consider this code to be a yardstick. See how your own situations measure up to the spirit of these words. If it's not on the list, talk it over among people whose values you trust. Think critically. All we have are our principles."

Editing with good taste and sensitivity

Of all the copy editor's duties, eliminating passages that are in poor taste or harbor stereotypes can be the most challenging. Just as it is important to edit stories for accuracy, style, consistency, conciseness and libel, it is likewise crucial to be alert to issues of sensitivity.

The stylebooks for most publications contain guidelines for handling references to age, dialect, disabilities, race, nationality, religion, gender and sexual orientation. They also outline when it is and is not acceptable to use profanity or graphic detail in a story. In addition, some groups, including the National Center on Disability and Journalism and the National Lesbian & Gay Journalists Association, have developed their own stylebooks for media use. Here are some commonly adopted rules for these issues:

▶**Age.** Ages of individuals should be mentioned in stories and headlines only when relevant or useful in describing the individuals. Avoid terms such as *old, senior, senior citizen, retiree, middle-aged* and *teenager* unless they are specifically relevant to the story.

The legal age for adulthood is 18. People 18 and older are women and men, not girls and boys. Do not refer to young children with obvious or implied adjectives, such as *tiny* or *little.*

▶ **Sexism.** The basic rule is that people of different genders should be treated the same unless their gender is relevant to the news. Physical descriptions of women or men are permissible only if relevant to the story. Generally, avoid terms that specify gender. For example, use *journalist* instead of *newsman* or *newswoman, firefighter* instead of *fireman* or *firewoman.*

Avoid phrases, such as *male nurse* or *woman doctor,* that suggest we think there is something unusual about the gender of the person holding those jobs. When in doubt about sexist word usage, consult Casey Miller and Kate Swift's *The Handbook of Nonsexist Writing* or Rosalie Maggio's *The Nonsexist Word Finder: A Dictionary of Gender-Free Usage.*

▶ **Race and ethnicity.** Do not mention race, ethnicity or national origin unless it is clearly relevant to the story. In stories involving politics, social action or social conditions, race is not automatically relevant. Avoid terms such as *ghetto, barrio, inner city, suburbs.* They are inaccurate and stereotypical. Do not use a person's race when reporting a crime story unless the incident is racial or ethnic in nature. State the country the person is from if race or ethnic origin is relevant, rather than lumping all Africans, Asians or Central and South Americans into continental categories. Be aware of questionable connotations. *Culturally deprived* or *culturally disadvantaged* implies superiority of one culture over another. In fact, people so labeled often are bicultural and bilingual.

▶ **Disabilities.** Avoid degrading and inaccurate references to disabilities. Disabilities should not be mentioned in stories or headlines unless they are pertinent. People who are permanently disabled generally do not like to be described as handicapped.

Use *disabled* or specify the nature of the disability. When a disability requires use of a wheelchair, say *uses a wheelchair,* not *confined to a wheelchair.* The word *handicapped* is acceptable in describing a temporary disability: "The baseball player was handicapped by a sprained wrist."

▶ **Sexual orientation.** Sexual orientation—or identifying places and products as being favored by those of a particular sexual preference—should be mentioned only if demonstrably pertinent. When sexual orientation is mentioned, exercise caution in word usage. *Gay* may be used as an adjective but not as a noun: *gay man. Lesbian* is generally preferred in reference to homosexual women, *gay* in reference to homosexual men. Use *gay-rights activist,* not *gay activist.* Avoid terms such as *admitted* or *avowed.*

▶ **Profanity, obscenity and violence.** Profanities and obscenities should not be used unless something significant about the story would otherwise be lost. The test should be "Why use it?" rather than "Why not use it?" The simple fact that a person used profanity or obscenity is not in itself justification for printing it. However, it may be used if the term was used in public—especially by a public official or celebrity—and it reflects a mood or frame of mind that can be conveyed in no other way or if the words themselves play a role in the story (as in reports about Supreme Court obscenity rulings). Detailed descriptions of a pornographic film or an episode of violence or mayhem should not be used unless the descriptions provide significant information or understanding that would otherwise be lacking in the story.

Stylebooks cannot suggest guidelines for handling every issue of sensitivity. As both our society and our language change, the ways by which we communicate will necessarily change as well. Editors recognize that both writing styles and technical styles must adapt to those changes.

In the late 1980s, a coalition of black leaders, including two-time presidential candidate the Rev. Jesse Jackson, called for use of the term *African-American* in place of any other name for a member of the black community. Jackson argued that "*black* tells you about skin color. . . . *African-American* evokes a discussion of the world." Many newspapers and magazines adopted the new appellation, but linguists, historians, anthropologists and politicians continued to debate its propriety. William O. Beeman, a teacher of linguistic anthropology at Brown University, wrote in the Baltimore Sun:

> In linguistic matters, time is the only arbiter. If enough people begin to use the new label, nothing can stop its introduction into general American parlance. When the style sheets of major publications and news syndicates shift, it is clear that American usage has also shifted. The term *Negro* was dropped in favor of *black* in the early 1970s. When the media begin to refer to black Americans as African-Americans on a routine basis, we will know that this important linguistic change has taken root. We will also know that in a subtle and important sense the way the African-American community is viewed in the United States has changed forever.

Sometimes, campus publications are at the forefront of style changes. Former student editor-in-chief Nora Wallace and her team of editors at the Golden Gater, a twice-weekly newspaper at San Francisco State University, added this entry about AIDS to their stylebook in spring 1989, very early in the news media's awareness of the epidemic:

> Human Immunodeficiency Virus (HIV) is a disease encompassing three levels: a stage with no symptoms, AIDS Related Complex (ARC) and AIDS. HIV disease is an increasingly common way of referring to people with AIDS. In all cases, be precise and ask the source.
>
> People with HIV don't necessarily have AIDS.
>
> Use "people with AIDS" or "persons with AIDS" on first reference.
>
> AIDS is not a gay person's disease, and it never should be implied that gay people are the only population affected by AIDS.
>
> People with AIDS should not be referred to as "victims," unless the term is used as "victims of the AIDS epidemic."

Careful editors should have precision as their goal. Whether handling issues of race and gender, referring to the opposing sides on the abortion debate (pro-choice? anti-abortion? pro-life?) or developing precise terminology in stories about AIDS, remaining alert to issues of sensitivity is a key responsibility of copy editors and one to be taken seriously.

Situational ethics

Editors face many day-to-day ethical decisions beyond remaining alert to issues of good taste and sensitivity. The ethical dilemmas that reporters face are different from those copy editors face, and copy editors face different dilemmas than do managing editors or publishers.

Reporters are likely to be concerned with questions involving the news-gathering process:

■ Should confidential sources be used? Under what circumstances?

■ Should classified information be used? Under what circumstances?

■ Is going undercover to get the story ever justified? When?

■ Is invasion of someone's privacy ever justified? When?

Copy editors are likely to be concerned with decisions involving the writing, editing and production processes:

■ Is the use of profane language or obscene photographs ever justified? When?

■ Are the implicit biases of the editor or the newspaper as a cultural institution evident in the selection of stories and photos? Should they be?

- Do certain people, groups or institutions receive more play than others?

- Conversely, are some people, groups or institutions ignored?

- Are headlines and captions fair and accurate?

- Are stories edited to eliminate bias and opinion? Are subjective words or words suggesting a viewpoint given thoughtful consideration?

Managing editors and other senior editors are likely to be concerned with questions of policy:

- Should victims of crimes be identified? If so, when? In stories about rape? About incest? About battering? In stories involving juveniles?

- Should suspects in crimes be identified? If so, when? At their arrest? When they are charged? At the time of trial?

- Should the cause of death be listed in obituaries involving victims of suicide or AIDS?

- Who in the newsroom should know the identity of confidential sources? Just the reporter? The supervising editor? The managing editor? The publisher? If a reporter pledges confidentiality to a source, are editors bound by the same promise?

- How involved should newsroom employees be in writing and editing special sections that promote consumer products?

- How should corrections and clarifications be handled?

Journalists face these moral and ethical decisions daily and often have little more to guide them than their own sense of justice and fair play.

Public relations practitioners also face ethical challenges in the course of doing their jobs: Should a PR professional representing a sports-shoe company give a pair of expensive shoes to a sports columnist to influence the columnist to write a positive story about the product? Should a company's public information officer keep financial information from the news media, giving a misleading impression of the company's performance? Should a PR practitioner publicly declare that a client's product is safe, without disclosing evidence to the contrary? All of these scenarios are included as examples of improper conduct in the PRSA Code of Ethics (see Figure 7-3).

Press response to criticism

In recent years, journalists have begun to heed the messages delivered by readers and viewers that indicate they want a more responsible and credible press. Many newspapers have created staff positions for reader representatives, or ombudsmen. These journalists answer reader questions and investigate reader criticism, providing a necessary link between the newspaper and the public. Some large, metropolitan newspapers also employ media critics, who write about the good and bad trends in the press as an industry.

In late 1998 a group of about two dozen senior managers from major Web news sites formed the Online News Association, devoted to "tackling thorny issues of ethics, credibility and credentials faced by Web journalists." By early 2006 the association had grown to more than 600 professional members, sponsored an annual conference and began handing out awards for achievements in English-language Web journalism in conjunction with the University of Southern California. The organization explains that its primary goal is to ensure that Web journalists are given the same treatment and access to news events as print or broadcast journalists.

In addition, the print media often provide readers access to their pages through consumer columns, op/ed pages, letters to the editor and online chat rooms to elicit reader response. For many years newspapers and magazines also have encouraged readers to bring errors to the attention of the editors.

The Philadelphia Inquirer stylebook includes this policy about corrections:

> We promptly and forthrightly correct our published errors. An allegation of factual error in our news columns should be treated with the utmost seriousness and should be referred to the appropriate assigning editor immediately. ... A "Clearing the record" notice may also be used to clarify published facts that, while technically not in error, may have been confusing or misleading.

Many newspapers "anchor" their corrections in the same place every day so readers will know where to find them. One newspaper's "Corrections & Clarifications," for example, are found on Page Two of the sections in which the original errors appeared. Exceptions are corrections of TV listings, which appear with the TV logs, and corrections for nondaily sections, such as Food and Travel. Those corrections are published twice, the day after the error was made and the next time the section in which the original error appeared is published.

In addition, editors have begun to listen to others within the organization, such as those in advertising, circulation and marketing. The relationship between the news staff and the revenue-generating departments historically has been strained because of the perceived need for separation between objective news and the subjectivity of advertising.

In recent years, however, because of the need to market publications to remain competitive with other media, the newsroom and the other departments have become less distant from one another. News departments often are involved in writing and editing special advertising sections, such as back-to-school and home-improvement sections. News executives will sometimes participate in marketing promotions and surveys.

These new alliances have their problems, however, and the potential for tripping over ethical land mines is high. For example, a publisher of the Los Angeles Times failed to inform the editor of the newspaper that a percentage of the advertising revenue from a special section about a new downtown sports arena was to be distributed to the owners of the arena. Such potential conflicts also have found their way into the online news world, as discussed in the next section.

Ethics in the 21st century

Computer-based communications, whether in the form of text or graphics, embody a great deal of uncharted legal and ethical territory. But because more and more journalists are using online information in their jobs, the ethical boundaries of such usage are in the process of being established.

As mentioned in Chapter 1, several thousand forms of traditional media worldwide have created online services. As consumers use these services to in turn create their personalized news environments, some ethical questions come into focus:

▶**Question No. 1** Because only about 55 percent of Americans own computers, is the market for online news sources a highly exclusive one? How do editors reconcile exclusive niche audiences with the press's traditional public service role of "comforting the afflicted and afflicting the comfortable"?

▶**Question No. 2.** Studies have indicated that the content of the media changes when it is commercialized. Will online news products continue to be driven by advertisers to the same extent as both print and broadcast news products? If so, what are the ethical implications?

▶**Question No. 3.** If consumers choose *not* to receive information from a wide range of ideological sources online and instead narrow their news choices to information they agree with, what does that mean for the mass media's role as a forum for public opinion?

These broad questions are some that journalists face today. Discussions are going on around the country about how traditional journalistic values might migrate into the new online environment and how such changes might affect the media's concepts about community leadership and the bottom line. But the emerging technologies present many day-to-day ethical questions as well, questions about reporting and editing and photography.

One contentious debate involves the intrusion of e-commerce (advertising) on the editorial content of Web news sites. The debate takes many forms. For example, some people question whether news sites should support the idea of "contextual online transactions," meaning should the news site juxtapose a staff-written review of the latest CD with an advertisement that allows users to order the CD with just one click of their mouse? To make the question even murkier, should the Web news site then earn a commission on each CD sold that way?

Online journalist Steve Outing discussed the quandary in an online "point-counterpoint" with Eric Meyer of Newslink Associates and the University of Illinois journalism school. Meyer feared that such a practice could damage a news organization's credibility. He said online transactions connected to news sites were likely to be "the first uncertain step down a very slippery slope."

"It's not so much a question of whether a sales link tempts your critics to write favorable reviews, although it might," he wrote. "It's more a question of how a sales link influences which performances critics will review."

Outing argued that cyberspace publishing is a very different environment from traditional print media and that the same rules don't apply. "News Web sites should serve the consumer in the best way possible," he wrote. In this case, "the consumer is served with convenience; the retailer is served by having on the news site an effective marketing vehicle; and the news site is served by bringing in additional advertising dollars." Other ethical questions surround the concept of e-commerce on Web news sites. In the struggle to be noticed online, advertisers have tried interstitial ads, which fade in and out on the screen; popouts, which appear in a smaller window on the home page; and banners, which stream across the top of the Web page.

But how far should these intrusions into the news space go? A column in the February 1999 issue of Brill's Content, a now-defunct media-watchdog magazine, reported that advertisers and publishers were moving ads out of these usual online positions and impinging on space reserved for news.

Some publications were experimenting with banners that wrapped around the top of the page as well as streamed across the top of the page. Others featured "extramercials," advertisements that, with one click, actually obscure editorial content on the right-hand part of the page. The column noted that Hot Wired, a very colorful online publication, turned its home page black and white to promote Hewlett-Packard's newest color printers. And USA Today's Web site featured an animated cartoon character (Homer Simpson) running out of an Intel Corp. ad and into the USA Today nameplate.

Current fads include placement of oversize ads in the middle of editorial copy in an effort to persuade Web users to click on the ads; section sponsorships, such as a travel section sponsored by an airline or an auto section sponsored by a car company; and tiered subscriptions that separate premium content from nonpaying subscribers. Each trend has the potential to negatively affect the credibility of the Web site.

The digitization of photography has allowed one common misuse of technology—the computer manipulation of photographs. It is true that editors have always been able to change a photograph, through cropping and sizing or through darkroom techniques such as dodging and burning. But today's technology allows an editor to manipulate any element in the photo in a matter of seconds and to change, in the process, the photo's meaning and substance. In other words, it is quite possible technologically to make the camera lie. Perhaps the most infamous example of computer photo manipulation is the O.J. Simpson arrest picture that appeared on the cover of Time magazine on June 27, 1994.

Time's "photo-illustration" cover of O.J. Simpson raised charges of racism and journalistic irresponsibility. Several magazines and newspapers used the same police photo from Simpson's arrest on murder charges, but Time used a computer to make Simpson appear blurred, darker skinned and more heavily bearded. Magazine representatives said they chose to manipulate the photo electronically to give it an interpretive twist that fit with the somber mood of the story. Former NAACP Director Benjamin Chavis Jr. said of the cover, "The way he's pictured, it's like he's some kind of animal." Dorothy Gilliam, then president of the National Association of Black Journalists, said the alteration made Simpson look more sinister and macabre. Time editors later said they didn't intend to offend anyone or imply Simpson's guilt and that their insensitivity was inexcusable.

As photojournalists continue to debate whether any manipulation of photos is ethical, editors have gone on record as disapproving of such techniques. The Associated Press is adamant in its policy of not allowing any photograph to be manipulated, as is the National Press Photographers Association, which states in its ethics policy: "As journalists we believe the guiding principle of our profession is accuracy. Therefore, we believe it is wrong to alter the contents of a photograph in any way that deceives the public."

In addition to deciding the ethics of photo manipulation, journalists must also grapple with traditional concerns about accuracy, balance and thoroughness, but more frequently they must consider these values as they apply online. For example, good journalists agree that they should identify themselves when they plan to interview someone for a story. The same holds true for use of quotable information from online discussion groups, even though it is possible to view and retrieve information without reporter identification.

Good journalists also agree that they must identify their sources in a story, but in an online world it is very easy for the sender of information to disguise himself or herself or to remain anonymous. Journalists, and particularly copy editors, must be vigilant in checking and double-checking the sources of online information. Two of the best examples of this problem, a phenomenon the Columbia Journalism Review calls a **cyberhoax,** came during the press coverage of the federal-building bombing in Oklahoma City in April 1995. In one, an inflammatory message appeared on an Internet newsgroup viewed as a site used by militia groups the day after the bombing. The posting, widely quoted in the U.S. press, later was discovered to have been a joke perpetrated by a journalism student. In the other incident, Dateline NBC and several reporters for the British media repeated a message that had appeared on America Online, purporting to be from Timothy McVeigh, a suspect in the bombing. The message described its sender as the "mad bomber" and urged readers to "take back the government . . . or die trying. Boom." The only problem was that the real Timothy McVeigh was in police custody when this message was sent.

In a 2004 hoax, the BBC, Reuters and Wired all covered the newest trend in social communication termed "toothing." According to the stories, which were based on information from an online forum, people were using their Bluetooth-enabled electronic devices to initiate communication with strangers, and the contact often resulted in sexual encounters. It turns out that toothing was a hoax made up by Ste Curran, a former editor of a games magazine, covered by the various news agencies and then dramatized by the television show "CSI: Miami."

A related ethical issue is one that involves the appropriation by traditional print publications of "cybergossip" distributed by such nonjournalists as Matt Drudge. In addition to the Monica Lewinsky story, which Drudge reported in his online Drudge Report before it reached publication in the traditional media, he also became known for reporting rumors and gossip without verifying their accuracy. One example was a story about President Clinton's siring of a teenage son of a black prostitute in Arkansas. The story had no validity, but it was picked up by the tabloid press and then as a legitimate news story by several mainstream news organizations.

Online Journalism Review Editor Robert Scheer took the media to task: "The rumor rapidly became a staple for rabid right-wing talk show hosts eager to blast Clinton. Suddenly the airwaves were filled with attacks on him as a 'deadbeat dad' who would not take responsibility for the child he had fathered." The false story "stained the president," Scheer wrote, "and this tawdry tale will be believed and spread by many who have not heard the barely covered retractions or who just don't care what the facts are."

Needless to say, if journalists had used the same rigid techniques for determining the credibility or accuracy of information online as they usually use in the physical world, such hoaxes and fake quotations may not have survived into print or broadcast. The Virginian-Pilot in Norfolk, Va., has established newsroom policies for online issues, including source credibility. Here is the newspaper's policy on Internet activities:

▶ Use of Internet sources

- Verify all facts reported from an online site unless you are confident of its source. For instance, the official Pulitzer Prize Web site can be regarded as a reliable source for names of past winners; a trade association site may not be.

- If using a source via Internet or e-mail, verify the source by phone or in person. Make certain a communication is genuine before using it.

- Generally, credit photos and graphics downloaded from the Internet. Usually, generic mug shots and icons do not need credits.

▶ Researching the Internet

- Internet-derived information should be attributed, just as we would information from any book, magazine or other publication. Our prohibition against plagiarism applies to this information.

▶ Linking to Web sites from a story

- Always review Web sites listed in stories. If you have concerns about including a site in a story because of inappropriate content, check with an editor.

▶ Internet communication

- Use the same standards of representation as you would using the telephone or in person. Using deceptive methods to gain information, including the failure to reveal one's identity as a journalist while using a computer or the use of false identification to obtain access to computer systems, is corrosive to truth telling.

Online journalism promises to unveil a vast new landscape of ethical issues whose boundaries will be debated over time. For now, however, in the physical world in the first decade of the new millennium, discussions of journalistic ethics remain grounded in situations that unfold day by day in newsrooms across the country. Here are some examples:

▶ **The Bakersfield Californian** fired reporter Nada Behziz in October 2005 after it discovered Behziz had fabricated key story elements in more than a third of the stories she wrote for the paper, including misattributing quotes found in other publications to people who did not exist. Executive Editor Mike Jenner wrote this about Behziz's fabrications: "Our findings show a widespread pattern, not an isolated incident. And the problems we discovered are significant, not trivial."

▶ **A short article** in Newsweek magazine's May 9, 2005, issue, which stated that U.S. soldiers had desecrated a copy of the Koran by flushing it down a toilet, led to riots across the Middle East during which at least 15 people were killed. Later reports revealed that the story, originally attributed to a confidential source who was a senior U.S. government official, could not be confirmed. Newsweek later apologized and eventually retracted the story.

▶ **Jayson Blair, a New York Times reporter,** resigned from his position on May 1, 2003, after an inquiry into more than 600 stories he wrote found he frequently fabricated people and situations into existence, plagiarized and "committed frequent acts of journalistic fraud" during his four-year tenure at the paper. Arthur Sulzberger Jr., chairman of The New York Times and publisher of the newspaper, called the situation a "a huge black eye" and added that Blair's behavior was "an abrogation of the trust between the newspaper and its readers."

▶ **A dramatic photo** from the terrorist attacks on the World Trade Center had editors all over the country anguishing over whether to publish it. The photo, of a single jumper from the building, taken by Richard Drew of The Associated Press, was published by many papers, including The New York Times, The Washington Post and the Los Angeles Times, often provoking reader protest.

▶ **The Arizona Daily Star** informed its readers that its editors had "crossed the line of good taste and good journalism" when they allowed two words—"slurs for blacks and homosexuals"—to appear in a story about graffiti in public restrooms. The newspaper said the words "should have been left on the restroom stalls where they were found."

▶ **The New York Times** made an ethical decision and a policy decision of great magnitude when it announced that it would "publish reports of same-sex commitment ceremonies and of some types of formal registration of gay and lesbian partnerships." Howell Raines, executive editor of The Times, said: "In making this change, we acknowledge the newsworthiness of a growing and visible trend in society toward public celebrations of commitment by gay and lesbian couples—celebrations important to many of our readers, their families and their friends."

▶ **CNN and Time magazine** both apologized for and retracted a joint report that claimed the U.S. military used deadly nerve gas to kill American defectors during the Vietnam War. The two organizations are owned by Time-Warner. CNN staffers did the reporting for the TV account of "Operation Tailwind" and two staffers also bylined an article for Time. Both CNN and Time said internal investigations showed the evidence could not support the story. Two CNN producers were fired, and a third resigned.

▶ **Editors at The New Republic** apologized to readers after they learned that associate editor Stephen Glass had invented all or part of most of the articles he had written for the magazine.

Several years ago, a survey by the American Society of Newspaper Editors Ethics Committee indicated that newspaper interns were ambivalent and somewhat skeptical about journalism ethics. One intern had this response:

> Ethics is something that cannot be effectively taught to individuals: that's like teaching morality. Literally, there are no right or wrong answers. Each individual finds a balance between his principles and the established code of the paper, which is, as often as not, an amorphous and ill-defined thing.
>
> Also, situations present varying challenges for different individuals. Frankly, being a plumber is a lot less burdensome.

Professional perspective: Jeanette Chavez

Essential ethics

Q: How are an editor's (assigning editor, copy editor, managing editor) ethical decisions different from those of a reporter or a photographer?

A: The ethical decisions of an editor are similar to those that must be made by a reporter or photographer, but they are broader in scope. For example, many years ago, an intern at The Denver Post was asked to cover a murder-suicide. She did an excellent job of talking to neighbors of the family and the relatives who had taken in the couple's three small children who witnessed the shootings. She also received permission from the adult relatives to interview the children. Although she had done her job well, my job as editor was to determine whether the story served the readers' interest or a gratuitous, sensational interest. I chose not to run the story.

In the case of The Post's coverage of the Columbine High School shootings, we were faced with a litany of ethical dilemmas: They started with whether we should produce an extra edition; we knew our competition would do so. We decided to post our stories online instead because the information was changing so rapidly.

As the daily coverage ran into weeks, we found ourselves facing questions of what photos to run—which ones were too intrusive. The photographer's job is to take the best possible photos. The editor's job is to make sure the photos that run in the newspaper are appropriate for the story and the community's standards. The Post ran photos day after day of funerals, mourners and processions. One day we ran a photo of one of the victims in an open casket.

The newsroom was nervous, but we received no complaints from the public. We almost fell victim to an Internet hoax, but through the dogged work of reporters we determined that the story might be untrue, and we decided not to run anything about it.

Jeanette Chavez graduated with honors from the University of Colorado at Boulder in 1973 with a bachelor's degree in journalism. She has been managing editor of The Denver Post since 1997.

Q: In an age of content and technological convergence, should producers of new content rely on one code of ethics that would apply to print, broadcasting and online journals? How does The Post handle this?

A: It is absolutely essential that all journalists associated with The Denver Post adhere to the same code of ethics. We do not own a television station, but our online operation is part of the newsroom and subject to the same rules as other staff members. Our code of ethics is based on common journalistic principles.

Q: Do strong ethics codes promote credibility? Why or why not?

A: The public has expectations of the media that have nothing to do with whether a publication has a strong code of ethics or not. Those expectations—to get the story right, to be fair, to respect the privacy of those who are not public figures—will be there no matter what the ethics policy says. The purpose of the ethics code is to provide newsroom staff members with a guideline for them to check their actions. In most cases, they would do this instinctively, but if they have questions, the code provides most of the answers.

Some students may lament the need to balance conflicting values when making ethical decisions and may yearn, as this intern does, for a less burdensome way to react to journalistic situations requiring an ethical response. Yet changing professions—becoming a plumber, for example—is not the solution.

Former public television correspondent Hodding Carter suggested that an "ethical vacuum" exists in journalism. It is time for the media to fill that vacuum with a process that encourages careful consideration of today's increasingly sophisticated ethical concerns:

- Terrorism and the media
- The right to privacy
- Gruesome photographs
- Manipulated photographs
- Conceptual photographs
- Anonymous online sources
- Off-the-record information
- Political or advertiser pressure not to publish
- AIDS obituaries
- Deception and going undercover
- Quotations used out of context
- Disclosure of the juvenile crimes of adults in the public eye

Copy editors must be alert to all these potential ethical problems. They must question reporters about their conduct and call perceived ethical problems to the attention of the supervising editors. Copy editors must be especially diligent in editing for accuracy, fairness and completeness and in making news judgments about which stories and photographs will be published.

The industry's codes of ethics and the policy statements drafted by individual publications can be used to help define the ethical situations faced by journalists every day. But only through development, teaching and use of ethical reasoning—based, of course, on subjective cultural values and coupled with an emotional component that often comes into play at the decisive moment—will tomorrow's journalists be prepared to grapple with modern ethical concerns.

Suggestions for additional reading

Alia, Valerie, Brian Brennan, and Barry Hoffmaster (eds.). *Deadlines and Diversity: Journalism Ethics in a Changing World.* Halifax, Nova Scotia: Fernwood Publishing, 1996.

American Journalism Review, http://www.ajr.org.

American Society of Newspaper Editors, http://www.asne.org.

Asian American Journalists Association, http://www.aaja.org.

Bagdikian, Ben H. *The Media Monopoly,* 6th ed. Boston: Beacon Press, 2000.

Benedict, Helen. *Virgin or Vamp: How the Press Covers Sex Crimes.* London: Oxford University Press, 1992.

Bok, Sissela. *Lying: Moral Choices in Public and Private Life.* New York: Pantheon Books, 1978.

———. *Secrets: On the Ethics of Concealment and Revelation.* New York: Pantheon Books, 1982.

Christians, Clifford G., Mark Fackler, Kim B. Rotzoll, and Kathy Brittain McKee. *Media Ethics: Cases and Moral Reasoning,* 5th ed. New York: Longman, 1998.

Cohen, Elliot D., and Deni Elliot, (eds.). *Journalism Ethics: A Reference Handbook.* Santa Barbara, Calif.: ABC-CLIO, 1997.

Columbia Journalism Review, http://www.cjr.org.

Cooper, Thomas W. *A Time Before Deception: Truth in Communication, Culture, and Ethics.* Santa Fe, N.M.: Clear Light Publishers, 1998.

Goldstein, Thomas (ed.). *Killing the Messenger: 100 Years of Media Criticism.* New York: Columbia University Press, 1989.

————. *The News at Any Cost: How Journalists Compromise Their Ethics to Shape the News.* New York: Simon & Schuster, 1985.

Gordon, A. David, John M. Kittross, and Carol Reuss. *Controversies in Media Ethics.* White Plains, N.Y.: Longman, 1998.

Hulteng, John L. *The Messenger's Motives: Ethical Problems of the News Media,* 2nd ed. Englewood Cliffs, N.J.: Prentice Hall, 1985.

Iggers, Jeremy. *Good News, Bad News: Journalism Ethics and the Public Interest.* Boulder, Colo.: Westview Press, 1998.

Limburg, Val E. *Electronic Media Ethics.* Boston: Focal Press, 1994.

McCulloch, Frank. *Drawing the Line: How 31 Editors Solved Their Toughest Ethical Dilemmas.* Washington, D.C.: American Society of Newspaper Editors, 1984.

National Association of Black Journalists, http://www.nabj.org.

National Association of Hispanic Journalists, http://www.nahj.org.

National Center on Disability & Journalism, http://www.ncdj.org.

National Lesbian & Gay Journalists Association, http://www.nlgja.org.

Native American Journalists Association, www.naja.com.

Newspaper Credibility: Building Reader Trust. Research Report. Washington, D.C.: American Society of Newspaper Editors, April 1985.

Online Journalism Review, University of Southern California, http://www.ojr.org.

Poynter Institute, The, http://www.poynter.org.

Public Relations Society of America, http://www.prsa.org.

Radio-Television News Directors Association, http://www.rtnda.org.

Reddick, Randy, and Elliot King. *The Online Journalist: Using the Internet and Other Electronic Resources.* Fort Worth, Texas: Harcourt Brace College Publishers, 1995.

Schmuhl, Robert (ed.). *The Responsibilities of Journalism.* Notre Dame, Ind.: University of Notre Dame Press, 1984.

Schwartz, Marilyn, and the Task Force on Bias-Free Language of the Association of American University Presses. *Guidelines for Bias-Free Writing.* Bloomington, Ind.: Indiana University Press, 1995.

Sieb, Philip, and Kathy Fitzpatrick. *Public Relations Ethics.* New York: Harcourt Brace, 1995.

Society of Professional Journalists, http://www.spj.org.

Typography

THE **personality of most print publications** can be determined from a distance of five feet. Personality is expressed primarily in the kinds of stories that are emphasized and in the quality of the writing. But with relatively few exceptions, story emphasis and writing style have the same flavor as the publication's design. A newspaper or magazine whose splashy design seems to shout at readers is likely to play up highly controversial or sensational stories and to be written saucily, raucously or both. A gray-looking newspaper or newsletter is likely to demonstrate restraint in handling content and to feature quiet, sophisticated prose.

Look at Figure 8-1. The Honolulu Advertiser displays the news with a large, bold banner headline and a dominant graphics package. But it's business as usual for the immutable Wall Street Journal, one of the country's largest dailies. In the Journal's case, even relatively recent typographical changes, such as the use of multicolumn headlines and limited spot color on Page One, are subtle and allow the newspaper to maintain its national market position and million plus circulation. Most American newspapers fall somewhere between these two extremes.

Other publications, including magazines, Web sites and corporate publications, likewise reflect personality through typography. Consider, for example, type display

Figure 8-1

Typography expresses the character of a newspaper. The bold two-line banner and large graphics on Page One of The Honolulu Advertiser contrast with the more subdued typography of The Wall Street Journal. The Advertiser received an Award of Excellence from the Society for News Design for this front page.

in Wired magazine as compared with Reader's Digest or even Sports Illustrated's more restrained approach to type. Or compare the annual reports of media giants Time Warner and Viacom. Or go online to compare the way cnn.com and pbs.org use type and design on their Web sites.

"Type is the foundation for a well-designed publication," said Gabriel Campanario, assistant managing editor for presentation at The Desert Sun in Palm Springs, Calif. "Editors and designers need to have clear guidelines for how information should be presented, should pay attention to consistency, and should respect the basic principles of design."

The earliest known attempts to record thoughts visually—symbols depicting objects, called *pictographs*—date back 20,000 years. Following pictographs was the development of more abstract ideographs, cuneiforms and hieroglyphics. Around 2500 B.C. hieroglyphics were perfected by the Egyptians. Ten centuries later, around 1500 B.C., the Phoenicians developed the first formal alphabet, then made up only of consonants. The Greeks acquired the Phoenician alphabet about 1000 B.C. and refined it over the next six centuries into a 24-letter alphabet that included vowel sounds.

The origins of printing are difficult to trace, but it is known that by the 11th century, the Chinese were using movable type made of metal and clay. In the early 15th century, after the development of papermaking, metal casting and painting with oil (ink), a German goldsmith named Johann Gutenberg saw the connections among these various crafts and developed a process for printing separate characters on paper using a press, ink and individual pieces of metal type. How he did it remains a mystery. By the end of the 15th century, printing presses were operating in all major European cities, publishing hundreds of thousands of books. The common printed typefaces used now are simply imitations of early handwritten letters.

Today, teams of editors and artists design printed and electronic products, often using type styles created centuries ago. Most believe that typographical design should reflect the elements of a product's personality.

Readers who pay attention to their publications find that the design can do the following:

- Attract their attention

- Grade the news for them, expressing the relative importance of items by headline size and placement

- Provide an orderly pattern for the flow of content

A large part of the publication's design depends on typography, which combines with layout to create an integrated, cohesive and sometimes unusual graphic look.

Typography is the art of designing and arranging type to have desired effects on readers. All of us have ideas about typography because some things look better to us than others. But it is the designer's job to ensure that typography and design enable easier and faster reading. To do so, the designer—and the editors who perform page design and layout—must recognize the subtle ways in which type can be differentiated. Typefaces can differ in at least five ways: size, width, slant, weight and family.

Type sizes

Type has its own system of measurement. Feet and inches are the basic units of measurement for most of us, but for printers, the basic units of measurement are picas and points. A *pica* is equal to about ⅙ inch, and a *point* is equal to about ¹⁄₇₂ inch. Therefore, 6 picas or 72 points equal an inch. Within the type measurement system itself, the conversions are easy to make: 1 pica = 12 points. When we measure type-faces, we use points. When we measure larger elements, such as the width of columns or photos, we generally use picas.

Typefaces themselves used to be manufactured in standard sizes. A complete series of type would include at least the sizes shown in Figure 8-2. Today, however, phototypesetting and digital computer systems can produce any size of type simply by electronically manipulating the image.

Figure 8-2
The standard type sizes are still those used most often, although computer typesetting permits the use of nonstandard sizes.

6 point	abcdefghijklmnopqrstuvwxyz
8 point	abcdefghijklmnopqrstuvwxyz
9 point	abcdefghijklmnopqrstuvwxyz
10 point	abcdefghijklmnopqrstuvwxyz
12 point	abcdefghijklmnopqrstuvwxyz
14 point	abcdefghijklmnopqrstuvwxyz
18 point	abcdefghijklmnopqrstuvwxyz
24 point	abcdefghijklmnopqrstuvwxyz
30 point	abcdefghijklmnopqrstuvwxyz
36 point	abcdefghijklmnopqrstuv
42 point	abcdefghijklmnopqrs
48 point	abcdefghijklmnop
60 point	abcdefghijklmn
72 point	abcdefghijkl

Sizes smaller than 14 points are called **text types** or body types, while sizes of 14 points or larger are called **display types.** The text of a newspaper is set in body type—in fact, most newspapers, magazines and newsletters use either 9-point or 10-point body type—and the headlines are set in display type. A 72-point headline is usually reserved for the most urgent news. Larger sizes exist but are rarely used.

In most modern newsrooms, computers can set type in any point size desired, yet most editors continue to use the traditional type sizes, probably because they are easy to use under deadline pressure. Sometimes, however, copy editors may "squeeze" the type size and generate a 33- or 34- or 35-point headline instead of a 36-point headline to get the headline to fit within a particular width. When type was set using molten lead that cooled very quickly into metal characters, squeezing type was unheard of. In fact, many editors recall the days when backshop printers would yell out to the newsroom: "Type isn't made of rubber, you know!" A headline cast in metal wouldn't fit within the column unless it had been written with exact measurement of characters.

On a typical news day, a 48-point or 60-point headline will serve to identify the main story on the front page. On the inside pages, 42-point headlines generally are large enough to identify the most important story on each page.

Type size can be a difficult concept to understand, but for our purposes, it is sufficient to define it as the distance from the top of the ascender (the long upstroke over such letters as *b, d, h* and *l*) to the bottom of the descender (the long downstroke under such letters as *j, p, q* and *y*). Look at Figure 8-3. To measure the type size of the word, first draw a horizontal line across the top of the ascenders *(i, t, i, i* and *t)* and then a horizontal line across the bottom of the descender *(y)*. Next, measure the distance between the two lines, using the point scale on a ruler showing points and picas. Your measurement should tell you that this word is set in 36-point type.

Figure 8-3
Two measures of type are commonly used: type size, from the tops of ascenders to the bottoms of descenders, and x-height, which does not include ascenders and descenders.

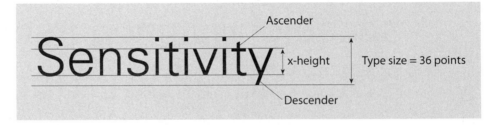

Another way to talk about type is in the x-height of the letters. The **x-height** is simply the height of the lowercase letters without ascenders and descenders (see Figure 8-3). Although not technically a means of measurement, the x-height is important because it helps determine the visual impact of the type. Typefaces of equal point size may appear unequal because of slight variations in the x-height. Look at the following examples of three different typefaces, all set in 10-point type, which appear to be different sizes because of slight variations in the x-height:

To determine the x-height of any typeface, simply use the point scale on your ruler or pica pole to measure the distance between the top and the bottom of any lowercase letter without ascenders or descenders.   (10-point Century Book)

To determine the x-height of any typeface, simply use the point scale on your ruler or pica pole to measure the distance between the top and the bottom of any lowercase letter without ascenders or descenders.   (10-point Times)

To determine the x-height of any typeface, simply use the point scale on your ruler or pica pole to measure the distance between the top and the bottom of any lowercase letter without ascenders or descenders.   (10-point Helvetica)

Type widths

Type is two-dimensional. In addition to its vertical size, editors also need to know its width. In the printing business, the width of a typeface, meaning the width of the lowercase alphabet, is referred to as its *set width.*

This is the lowercase alphabet in 12-point Times; its set width is 12 picas or 144 points

abcdefghijklmnopqrstuvwxyz

The set width of a condensed version of the 12-point Times lowercase alphabet is 10 picas or 120 points

abcdefghijklmnopqrstuvwxyz

In most typefaces, the width of a capital M is equal to the type size. In fact, typesetters in the past referred to the concept of an *em,* which is the square of the type size. The em, therefore, is a variable measure: An 18-point em is 18 points wide and 18 points high; it is bigger than a 14-point em, which is 14 points wide and 14 points high. In body type, "one em space" is a typical paragraph indention.

The em method of measuring type width is gradually being superseded by the more precise *unit system.* The reference point remains the capital M, but instead of being a variable measure, the M is divided into 18 units or a multiple of 18. The width of all other characters, and their letter spacing, is then defined as a certain number of these units. Thin lowercase letters such as i, j and l, for example, are usually 4 units wide.

If we take each character of the alphabet and squeeze it slightly, we reduce the set width of the alphabet; therefore, it is slightly condensed. Both of the following examples are 18-point Helvetica type, but the bottom example is condensed:

Art is life reflected through vision.
(18-point Helvetica)

Art is life reflected through vision.
(18-point Helvetica condensed)

A complete inventory of display types at any publication includes some condensed and some extended typefaces, not only for contrast but also for situations in which the perfect word will not fit the available space. Publications with a predominantly horizontal design, such as magazines (see Chapter 11), use condensed typefaces sparingly and prefer faces of normal width. In a newspaper or other publication with a predominantly vertical design, however, condensed typefaces appear quite normal.

Body types apply the same rules. For example, more news can be packed into a news publication by using condensed body type. But such use of type can make for a gray product, which is difficult to read and tends to draw complaints from readers. To make a publication brighter, designers sometimes use the following techniques:

- Use a larger type size—10-point, for example, rather than 9-point.

- Use a normal, rather than a condensed, typeface.

- Use more paragraph indentions.

- Insert more space between paragraphs.

- Insert more space between lines.

This last technique, inserting more space between lines, is called ***leading*** (pronounced "ledding") or ***leading out.*** The terms come from the practice of inserting strips of lead between lines of type in the days when type was cast from a molten lead alloy. Another term for leading is ***interline spacing.*** Type that has no space between the lines is said to be ***set solid***—and sometimes the descenders of one line touch the ascenders of the line below it.

An 8-point type that has 1 point of leading is said to be set 8 on 9; an 8-point type that has 2 points of leading is said to be set 8 on 10, and so on. Here is an example of 8-point type set solid:

> The quantity and quality of informational graphics in newspapers increased dramatically in the late 1980s, largely because of the use of Macintosh computers and electronic graphics networks.

Here is an example of 8-point type set 8 on 9:

> The quantity and quality of informational graphics in newspapers increased dramatically in the late 1980s, largely because of the use of Macintosh computers and electronic graphics networks.

And here is an example of 8-point type set 8 on 10:

> The quantity and quality of informational graphics in newspapers increased dramatically in the late 1980s, largely because of the use of Macintosh computers and electronic graphics networks.

Leading—spacing between lines—usually makes type easier to read. On the other hand, studies indicate that too much leading may hinder readability because the eye "gets lost" in switching from the end of one line to the beginning of the next line.

For the same reason, type that is set either too wide or too narrow is difficult to read. Research studies differ on the best line length, but a common approach is to use this formula:

> $O = lca \times 1.5$
>
> Optimum line length (O) is equal to the width of the lowercase alphabet (lca) multiplied by one and one-half.

So, for example, if the width of the lowercase alphabet is 112 points, the optimum line length would be 168 points (112×1.5), which equals 14 picas (168 divided by 12).

Type styles

Typefaces can be classified in many ways, none of them precise. The classification system used most frequently in the field of graphic arts puts typefaces in seven main categories, also referred to as races of type: serif, sans serif, square serif, text, italic, script and decorative.

Figure 8-4
The familiar Roman typefaces are characterized by serifs.

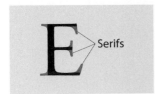

Serifs

▶**Roman typefaces** are familiar to us because most of what we read is set in Roman type. The chief characteristic is the ***serif,*** a small cross stroke at the end of each main stroke of the letter, as shown in Figure 8-4.

Roman type gets its name from the similarity of its capital letters to the alphabetic characters chiseled by stonemasons on the public buildings of the Roman Empire. In 1470 an imaginative Frenchman, Nicholas Jenson, combined these characters with a more ornate set of characters to create the complete uppercase and lowercase English alphabet we know today. (The terms *uppercase* and *lowercase* stem from the early typographers' habit of storing small letters in a case below that of the capital letters.) Jenson's typeface, known today as Cloister Old Style, is a classic example of old-style Roman type, known for its blunt serifs. Other examples of old-style Roman type are Garamond and Caslon.

Bodoni, a Roman typeface, has been a popular headline typeface in American publications. It was introduced in 1789 by Giambattista Bodoni, an Italian printer:

Art is life. (36-point Bodoni)

Times Roman and Century are Roman styles commonly used for body type. Times Roman was designed in 1931 by Stanley Morison for The Times of London:

Art is life. (36-point Times Roman)

Century was designed in 1894 by L. B. Benton and T. L. DeVine for Century magazine, a leading publication of its day:

Art is life. (36-point Century Book)

▶ **Sans serif type,** from the French *sans*, meaning "without," literally means "without serifs." In addition to the absence of serifs, sans serif typefaces—or gothic typefaces, as they sometimes are called—are recognizable by their uniformity of stroke. The following example reveals little or no variation in the widths of strokes used to create the characters:

Art is life. (36-point Futura)

In many news publications, sans serif typefaces play a significant role in headlines, captions and some informational material, such as stock market listings, sports scoreboards and television listings. Futura, Avant Garde and Univers are just a few of the many sans serif typefaces commonly used for headlines.

Art is life. (36-point Avant Garde)

Art is life. (36-point Univers)

Readers often have greater difficulty reading a sans serif typeface than a serif typeface, however, unless the sans serif typeface is either set large or leaded out. Most publications, therefore, have rejected sans serif type as their body type. The gothic typefaces do play important roles, however, in brochures, road signs, billboards, magazine advertisements and consumer product labels—and in Web typography.

▶ **Square serif typefaces** live up to their name. Their serifs are like small, rectangular slabs. Some typographers categorize these typefaces as Roman because they stand vertically and have serifs; others categorize them as decoratives. When treated as an independent group, they have been referred to as the Egyptians.

Examples of square serif, or Egyptian, typefaces include Glypha, Memphis and Lubalin Graph.

Art is life. (36-point Glypha)

Art is life. (36-point Memphis)

Art is life. (36 point Lubalin Graph)

▶ **Italic typefaces,** characterized by slanted letters, were designed to save space:

Art is life. (36-point Italic Goudy Old Style)

Because italic type is difficult to read in large quantities, it is used sparingly in body type—and then only to emphasize words. Italic type is used in headlines, however, and sometimes as a special design element. Serif and sans serif typefaces have italic variations.

▶ **Text typefaces,** which sometimes are called Old English or blackletter typefaces, play only a nominal—albeit curious—role in newspapers and very little role at all in other publications. Many large U.S. newspapers—The New York Times, the Los Angeles Times, The Washington Post, The Oregonian, and the San Francisco Chronicle, among others—use text typefaces in their nameplates, or flags, to display the name of the newspaper on Page One. Despite this apparent allegiance to tradition, the use of text typefaces in this fashion is atypical, according to noted editor Harold Evans:

> The most hideous blackletter titles survive around the world from Victorian days because they are "traditional," but in fact the earliest titles, such as those of the first daily paper, The Daily Courant (1702), and the first evening paper, The Evening Post, and America's New England Courant (1721), were all in good bold Roman lowercase.

With all the breezy, modern sans serif typefaces available today, it is a wonder that the blackletters (the tight, bold types that originated in Germany) have managed to survive. A few famous ones are still in circulation, including Fette Fraktur and Linotext:

Art is life. (36-point Fette Fraktur)

Art is life. (36-point Linotext)

▶**Script typefaces** look like handwriting:

Art is life. (36-point Mistral)

Most of the time, script typefaces should not be used in headlines or in the body of the paper. Occasionally, however, layout editors may use them on feature stories if they are appropriate to the subject matter.

▶**Decorative typefaces** likewise play very little role in news typography but are developed to reflect trends in fashion and advertising. Parisian, for example, usually is associated with art deco and is currently enjoying a revival:

Art is life. (36-point Parisian)

Type weights

Most typefaces are designed and manufactured in lightface and boldface versions. A few also have medium, demibold and extrabold versions. Following are examples of the various weights of 24-point type:

Futura Light

Futura Medium

New Baskerville Bold

Palatino Demi Bold

Cooper Black

Helvetica Black

Futura Extrabold

Research studies on type legibility have indicated that, although boldfaces are more readable than lightfaces, regular weights (medium) are preferred because they contrast more with the background of the page. The extrabolds are the least legible.

Type families

The individual members of type families share similar characteristics, yet they also vary in width, slant and weight. Some families have only a few members; others have quite a few. Here are some of the 30 members of the Helvetica family:

Helvetica Light

Helvetica Medium

Helvetica Medium Italic

Helvetica Medium Condensed

Helvetica Bold

Helvetica Bold Italic

Helvetica Bold Condensed

Helvetica Black

Publication designers generally try to limit the number of typefaces to maintain a consistent appearance. For example, the body type might be Times Roman and the news headline font another serif typeface, such as Century Schoolbook. For captions, section labels and page headers, complementary fonts of a sans serif typeface such as Univers might be preferred.

Legibility

Sophistication about typography means nothing if legibility suffers. Even skillful, experienced designers occasionally engage in typographical experiments that force readers to work too hard to enjoy reading. On the whole, however, type experts guide design choices at newspapers, magazines, newsletters and online publications to enhance legibility, thereby preventing eyestrain and encouraging reading.

Ironically, advanced printing technology in some of its early applications threatened legibility. Computer software for desktop and Web publishing enabled people with little or no knowledge about typography to call themselves editors or publishers, flooding mailboxes and the Internet with difficult-to-read materials. In an article titled "Why Type on the Web Is So Bad," Eric Eaton, former senior designer at Wired Digital, writes that typography is a difficult discipline that "has gone the way of the photograph—into the world of amateur shutterbugs who think being able to select a font from a pull-down menu makes them typesetters." The same idea applies to people who learn to manipulate desktop publishing programs and produce printed materials without knowing the principles of typography.

Professional publications—both print and online—engage professional graphic designers to make dozens of decisions about type and other display elements that will define the overall look of a publication. After management personnel approve the new look, designers meticulously detail type specifications into a stylebook, which becomes a guide for consistently executing the design plan. Although copy editors rarely play a major role in choosing families of type, and the typography stylebook guides many routine decisions, editors still must make multiple typographical decisions every day that influence legibility.

Previous sections of this chapter discussing type size, width, slant and weight include information about how type characteristics hinder or help ease of reading. Those legibility tips, plus a few others, are summarized here:

- Make type decisions according to purpose. Typography appropriate for a billboard, poster, business card or wedding announcement won't work for body copy in a newspaper, magazine, newsletter or Web page.

- For printed publications, use text type (smaller than 14 point) for body type, and use display type (14 point and larger) for headlines.

- Allow appropriate space between lines (leading) for type with a large x-height. Text type with a large x-height appears larger than the same size type with a smaller x-height and corresponding longer ascenders and descenders.

- Avoid body type set solid with no leading between the lines; conversely, too much space between lines hampers legibility.

- Reserve type variations, such as boldface, italics, condensed and expanded, for headlines or other emphasis. Do not use them for long passages or for an entire story. This admonition applies especially to Web sites because italic and condensed body typefaces are particularly difficult to read on a computer screen.

- Save reverse type (white letters on a black background) and type printed over gray or colored screens for special treatment, not for long blocks of copy.

- Use caution when superimposing type on a photograph or other image. Depending on the image, the type may be illegible and may obscure the image.

- Set type in appropriate widths to make it easy for eye movement to track from the end of one line to the beginning of the next line and to avoid excessive hyphenation. Type set too narrow leads to many hyphenated words at the ends of lines and makes reading more difficult. Use the $O = lca \times 1.5$ formula to determine the most legible line width for body type.

- Use a serif typeface for body type rather than sans serif typeface because research shows that the finishing strokes of serifs aid legibility.

- Avoid passages set in all capital letters. A combination of caps and lowercase letters (sentence style) enhances legibility.

- Save script, blackletter and decorative typefaces for emphasis, not body type.

Web typography

Choosing type and designing pages for the World Wide Web can be a complex and highly technical proposition. The mechanics are perhaps best left to computer programmers, although many copy editors and print designers have developed a knack for translating all the x's and o's of computer language into sometimes quite strikingly attractive Web pages.

For people interested in Web typography and design, the Internet can be a helpful teaching tool, guiding users to a multitude of sites. For example, Webmonkey .com (http://www.hotwired.lycos.com/webmonkey), a service of a Web search engine (or portal) known as Lycos, calls itself "the Web developer's resource" and claims to be the "comprehensive source of information for professional and amateur Web enthusiasts, offering daily article and technical updates, as well as an archive of more than 200 features and tutorials."

One recent article posted on Webmonkey.com was a tutorial on Web typography, created by Nadav Savio, who runs Giant Ant Design, "a human-centered interactive design shop." To get a sense of the difference between typography online and typography in the physical world, Savio states, in no uncertain terms: "The Web is a harsh, uninviting environment for the delicateness of fine typography. Along with the usual Web culprit of platform inconsistency, the extreme low resolution of even the best screens means type online can only allude to the geometry of the typefaces you've so carefully chosen and specified."

Joe Gillespie (see Figure 8-5 and the Professional Perspective at the end of this chapter), who created a site called Web Page Design for Designers (http://www .wpdfd.com), admits that the computer screen presents its own set of unique design problems, including line lengths (too long), correct leading (difficult to achieve), headlines (not attractive, especially those in italic), color typography (lack of available fonts and type weights), and the elastic nature of the Web page itself. But he adds that "it is the designer's job to understand these issues and to address them—to maintain some kind of control when everything else is shifting."

David Earls, creator and editor of Typographer.com, a site that "provides a regularly updated news feed, series of articles, interviews and tutorials covering the type industry," voices a similar sentiment about designer control, one expressed by many Web typographers about the current state of the field. The Web revolution, Earls says, "caused millions of people to suddenly think of themselves as designers, when clearly from the quality of work they produced, they were anything but, simply because they don't have the education to back up their usage of the tools." He suggests that the freedom allowed by such design tools as QuarkXPress and Adobe InDesign "must be tempered by education, whether it be in the colleges and universities across the world reinstating proper typographic education and theory into their curriculum or even placing theory into application's online manuals and tutorials."

Figure 8-5
Joe Gillespie's Web Page Design for Designers addresses many typographical problems found in transferring ink-on-paper concepts to the World Wide Web.

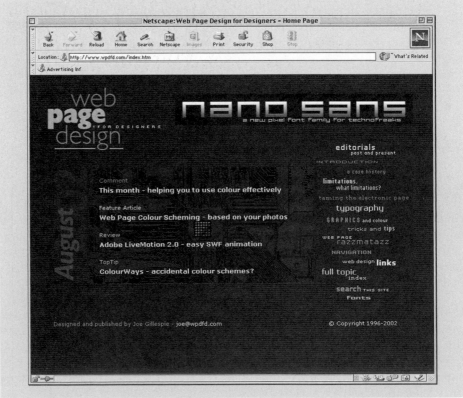

Professional perspective: Joe Gillespie

Typography as performance

Q: What is the most important thing students should know about the state of typographical design?

A: Typographic design is inextricably linked to the media in which it is performed. Whether the letter forms are carved in stone, wood, lead or pixels, the medium dictates what is possible and what is not. We have a wealth of typographic history to draw upon and the technology to emulate and reproduce any facet of it. Today's various media each have their own unique characteristics and requirements and those should be explored and developed. You can learn from the past, but design for the future.

Q: What should students do to prepare themselves to enter the world of digital typography?

A: Virtually all typography is now digital. There are certain basic principles in typography that are as relevant today as ever. Typography is not art, it is design, and that means it has a function to fulfill. Students should first acquaint themselves with the basics of human physiology and how we read before venturing into headier areas. You have to learn the scales before you can write the music.

Joe Gillespie received a master's degree in 1971 in visual communication from The Royal College of Art in London. He is a leading international graphic designer for the Web based in London.

Q: Does digital typography allow for more or less creativity than the traditional typography in print products? Why?

A: Creativity is an attribute of the designer, not the medium. Being creative with typography is all about exploration of the medium. Screen-based typography cannot compete where precision is concerned, but it does have the extra dimension of time. Think of typographic design as a performance. You are delivering words just as would an actress or singer and should be able to express those words in a unique way that complements and enhances them.

In early Web-page development, creating an online page required a knowledge of HTML (HyperText Markup Language), a relatively simple but time-consuming scheme used to code materials for display on the Web. If you compare the appearance of your e-mail messages with the appearance of any Web page, you'll see that some adjustments have to be made to translate the simple text of e-mail into a message ready for display on the Internet. That translation device is known as HTML. It is important to remember that HTML is a markup language, not a typesetting or layout language. Web designers have no way to control, absolutely, the appearance of their pages because different Web browsers and different users set their default font sizes and font colors to their own individual specifications. In the past few years, several companies have developed new kinds of Web-authoring software that serve the same purpose as HTML, but Web designers still encourage beginners to learn the basics of HTML. (See Chapter 11 for more on Web layout and design.)

No matter the medium—whether newspapers, magazines, newsletters or the World Wide Web—the key to outstanding typographical design is an understanding of type itself. Editors and designers who develop an aesthetic appreciation of the differences among type styles, weights and families, as well as a practical knowledge of type sizes and widths, will always be in demand. People who add a basic understanding of computer programming to their tool kits will find a wealth of career opportunities in the coming years.

Suggestions for additional reading

Baird, Russell N., Arthur T. Turnbull, and Duncan McDonald. *The Graphics of Communication,* 5th ed. New York: Holt, Rinehart and Winston, 1987.

Bringhurst, Robert. *The Elements of Typographic Style,* 2nd ed. Vancouver: Hartley & Marks Publishers Inc., 1997.

Carter, Rob, Ben Day, and Philip B. Meggs. *Typographic Design: Form and Communication,* 3rd ed. Hoboken, N.J.: John Wiley & Sons, 2002.

Craig, James. *Designing with Type.* New York: Watson-Guptill, 1981.

Dair, Carl. *Design with Type.* Toronto: University of Toronto Press, 1982.

Design: The Journal of the Society of Newspaper Design, a publication of the Society of Newspaper Design, 11600 Sunrise Valley Drive, Reston, VA 22091.

Eaton, Eric. "Why Type on the Web Is So Bad," *Wired Digital.* Online. http://www.hotwired.com/webmonkey/97/48/index3a.html?tw=graphics_fonts. Dec. 29, 1998.

Kvern, Olay Martin, and David Blatner. *Real World Adobe InDesign2.* Berkeley, Calif.: Peachpit Press, 2002.

Meggs, Philip B. *A History of Graphic Design,* 3rd ed. Hoboken, N.J.: John Wiley & Sons, 1998.

Rehe, Rolf. *Typography and Design for Newspapers.* Carmel, Ind.: Design Research International, 1985.

Siegel, David S. *Secrets of Successful Web Sites: Project Management on the World Wide Web.* San Francisco: Hayden Enlightened Communications, 1997.

Society of News Design, http://www.snd.org.

Solomon, Martin. *The Art of Typography.* New York: Watson-Guptill, 1986.

Spiekermann, Erik, and E.M. Ginger. *Stop Stealing Sheep and Find Out How Type Works,* 2nd ed. San Jose, Calif.: Adobe Press, 2002.

Tschichold, Jan, Ruari McLean, and Robin Kinross. *The New Typography: A Handbook for Modern Designers.* Berkeley, Calif.: University of California Press, 1998.

Typographic Studies. TypoGRAPHIC. Online. http://www.rsub.com/typographic/studies/. Dec. 29, 1998.

Webmonkey: The Web Developer's Resource, http://www.hotwired.lycos.com/webmonkey.

Web Page Design for Designers, http://www.wpdfd.com.

Weinman, Lynda. *Designing Web Graphics.4,* 4th ed. Indianapolis: New Riders Publishing, 2003.

Weinmann, Elaine, and Peter Lourekas. *QuarkXPress 5 for Windows and Macintosh: Visual QuickStart Guide.* Berkeley, Calif.: Peachpit Press, 2002.

Wilson, Adrian. *The Design of Books.* San Francisco: Chronicle Books, 1993.

Writing Headlines

WHETHER **topping press releases or newsletter,** magazine and newspaper stories, headlines are among the most important words in print. A press release without a headline summarizing the key point of the release likely lands in the trash. Brilliant news and feature writing goes unread without headlines to summarize information quickly and to draw readers into the stories. Perhaps no task involved in publishing is both as simple and as demanding as good headline writing, both an art and a skill that can be improved with practice.

Purposes of news headlines

Readers want information quickly. Therefore, the primary purpose of a news headline is to communicate quickly by accurately telling the most important idea in the story.

A second important role of headlines is to attract attention. An inviting headline that signals a story of interest exerts a pull on readers to pause and read the story.

While communicating the main idea of the news story and doing it in a way to attract readers' attention, headline writers must carefully maintain the tone of the story. Just as one wouldn't wear a clown costume to a funeral, don't use an attention-grabbing headline inappropriate to the overall tone or mood of the story. Headlines are important indicators of a publication's general tone and overall approach to the news. Headlines written for a supermarket tabloid would be out of character in The New York Times or in most hometown newspapers.

Headlines are a key element in the design and layout of publications. The skillful layout editor decides the size and placement of headlines to help indicate the importance of the story and to make the page attractive. A single person may edit copy, lay out pages and write headlines for one or more pages of a daily paper, and, typically, one person handles these duties for all pages in a newsletter.

Modern headlines are designed to do the following:

- Summarize the story

- Capture readers' attention

- Maintain the mood of the story

- Help set the overall tone of the publication

- Indicate the relative importance of the story

- Add to the attractiveness of the page

Characteristics of good headlines

The first newspaper in the American colonies in 1690 contained no headlines. Nobody had thought of them yet. Besides, literate colonists were starved for news and needed no headlines as inducements to read every story in the newspaper. The proliferation of media competing for readers' time and attention today boosts the importance of headlines.

Good headlines have these characteristics:

- Accuracy in fact, tone, scope and focus

- Emphasis on the main theme of the story

- Clear, succinct, grammatical, easy to read and understand

- Vitality through strong, active verbs

- Balanced and fair

- Tasteful

- Fresh and immediate

- Legally sound (avoid libel)

How to write headlines

Headlines are written in skeletonlike language. They use present tense to describe past action, and each headline must fit its allotted space. Each letter, punctuation mark and space in a headline is a **unit** or a portion of a unit. (Counting individual units of headlines is explained later in this chapter.)

Copy editors write a headline after editing the story, a process that generally requires three readings of the story. While reading and editing the story, the copy editor makes mental notes about headline ideas. For readers, the process is reversed. They read the headline first. A perfectly crafted headline that lacks meaning until after the story is read is unacceptable. To write a headline that communicates clearly and accurately, the copy editor must first understand the story thoroughly.

Let's say you are writing a headline with a maximum count of 22.5 units to top a story saying that the New York Yankees won the pennant last night in the Eastern Division of the American League. First, frame the most important facts of the story in a skeleton sentence as in this example:

The Yankees won American League Eastern Division pennant

At 53.5 units, this effort is too long to fit the maximum count. It also violates the basic rule that headlines should not be written in the past tense. Present-tense headlines give the news immediacy, and present-tense verbs are often shorter than past-tense verbs. Nonessential words, especially articles *(a, an, the)*, are usually omitted to give the headline a sense of telegraphic speed and enable more ideas to be included in a limited space.

Let's try again:

Yankees win American League East Division pennant

The new headline is better because it eliminates the unnecessary article and is in the present tense. But with 46 units, length is still a problem. Is it possible to shorten the sentence without losing information? How about dropping the word *Division* and abbreviating *American League?* Headline writers in search of a shorter count must resist the urge to use unfamiliar abbreviations, but baseball fans won't have any problem understanding this abbreviation:

Yankees win AL East pennant

At 26 units, the new version is still a bit too long. *Yankees* could become *Yanks,* but we would save only two units on the count. How about *title* in place of *pennant?* That gives us

Yanks win AL East title

Most papers allow headlines to be slightly shorter than the maximum, so this 20.5-unit effort should suffice. But the headline writer willing to think a little longer could come up with a stronger verb and an exact count, 22.5 units:

Yanks clinch AL East title

Professional perspective: Peter Bhatia

Clichés are not my cup of tea

Please, I beg you, avoid clichés. Avoid them like the plague. Avoid them as if there is no tomorrow. Really. That's the long and short of it. No matter how things ebb and flow, or which way the wind is blowing. If you avoid them, it will be a whole new ballgame. The only times clichés are allowed in heads, it seems to me, is when you're making fun of clichés. And you can take that to the bank.

If you do all of that and heed the excellent lessons in this chapter, you can write marvelous headlines such as these:

Peter Bhatia is executive editor of The Oregonian (Portland, Ore.) and was president of the American Society of Newspaper Editors in 2003–2004.

Head for the heels, Imelda Marcos is coming to town

(A reference to Marcos' huge shoe collection, from the Pittsburgh Press)

If you take Amish from famished you get fed

(Toledo Blade)

Hospital workers told to drag their butts outside

(A no-smoking story from the Tampa Tribune)

And can avoid ones such as this:

Chargers may lose Butts for the rest of the year

(Butts in this case was running back Marion Butts . . . although they did lose him for the rest of the season.)

Guidelines for writing news headlines

To satisfy the purposes and characteristics of good news story headlines, a few rules apply, regardless of whether headlines will appear on press releases, in newspapers or on Web sites. Well-edited publications try to conform to principles in this section for *news story* headlines.

▶**Provide a subject for every headline.** Otherwise, the publication becomes sprinkled with commands such as this gem: "Throw child in river." When attribution is essential to avoid editorializing in a headline, copy editors sometimes yield to the temptation to begin a headline with a verb of attribution without any subject: "Says taxes must increase." Resist such temptation.

▶**Use strong action verbs, preferably in the top line of a multiple-line headline.** Avoid *dead heads,* which merely label stories. For example, "Council session" tells readers very little; a better alternative is

Council rejects bids for repaving project

This rule applies to news headlines but not necessarily to feature or news-feature headlines, which often use magazine-style titles. Many editors are flexible about requiring every news headline to have a verb if the final result is an exceptionally good headline.

Do not use forms of the verb *to be* when a strong verb will fit the meaning and the space. They detract from the vigor of a headline.

Lawmakers' pet projects hitch ride on NASA budget

When used, *to be* verbs—*is* and *are*—are often implied rather than stated. But not always, as in this feature headline from The New York Times on a story about quantum physics:

Where uncertainty is king and paradox shares throne

Or this news headline, also from the Times:

Under press curb, bad news is no news

The *to be* verb must not be omitted if it is the principal verb in a clause, unless the clause begins the headline. Generally, a *to be* verb is needed after the verbs *say, deny, assert, warn, allege, maintain, affirm* and *contend,* which would normally be followed by an object. The headline "Mayor says policy fair" sounds awkward, and it is grammatically incorrect. *Policy fair* is a separate clause here, not a direct object of *says.* The word *policy* is used as a subject of the clause *policy is fair.* Assuming that the story isn't about the mayor's ability to enunciate words, the subject of the second clause needs an expressed verb:

Mayor says policy is fair

If the order of the clauses is reversed, then the *to be* verb can be implied without confusing readers:

Policy fair, mayor says

▶Use the present tense to indicate both present and past action; use future tense for future action. Instead of writing "Jones defeated Smith," write

Jones defeats Smith

▶ **Use the active voice, rather than the passive voice.** The active voice gives the headline greater impact. Instead of "Walkout staged by nurses," for example, write

Nurses stage walkout

▶ **Keep thought units on the same line in multiple-line headlines.** That is, don't separate parts of a verb, proper nouns that go together, a preposition from its object or a modifier from the word it modifies. Observe where the lines break in the following examples:

**Teachers seek
pay increase**

**Teachers call
for pay hike**

**New tax revenue
to improve streets**

▶ **Omit the articles *a, an,* and *the,* as a general rule.** This omission saves space and speeds the pace of a headline. Sometimes, however, an article is essential to understanding. The meaning of "King takes little liquor" is different from the meaning of "King takes a little liquor." Sometimes articles are needed for flow and phrasing of a headline, as in this example from The New York Times:

Game trophies: What's good for a goose is bad for a moose

▶ **Avoid "stutter headlines," that is, repeating the wording of the lead so that readers read the same words twice.** For news stories, both the headline and the lead line will convey the same information but should use different wording. Headlines for feature stories written in suspended-interest form should entice readers into the story without stealing the writer's punch line.

▶ **Focus on the most up-to-date information in a continuing story.** Don't put a first-day headline or lead on a second-day story.

First-day headline:
Tornado injures 20

Second-day headline:
'Rebuilding will take years,' mayor says

▶ **Write headlines as specifically as possible within space limitations.** "Killer storm hits" is not as good as

Storm kills four

▶ **Use attribution in headlines that convey opinion and for direct quotations.** Otherwise, the news headline will read like an editorial-page headline. For example, "Budget unfair" is an opinion, which could be taken as the newspaper's unless attributed:

Budget 'unfair,' senator says

▶ **Avoid libelous statements.** (Libel is discussed in Chapter 6.) In many states, a libelous headline is grounds for a successful lawsuit, even if the story contains no libelous statements. Space limitations may not permit qualifying terms that appear in the story, heightening the headline writer's problem.

▶**Respect the rights of criminal defendants.** Don't convict an accused person in a headline. In the U.S. system of law, a suspect is considered innocent unless proved guilty. The burden of proof is on the prosecution, not the defendant. The headline "City manager steals from public treasury" could cause problems; a better alternative is

DA charges city manager with stealing public funds

On acquittal, the correct legal term is *not guilty* rather than *innocent*. Many publications, however, follow AP style and use *innocent* to guard against the word *not* being dropped inadvertently from the phrase *not guilty*.

▶**Avoid headlines with double meanings.** Examples: "2 teenagers indicted for drowning in lake," "FBI ordered to assist Atlanta in child slayings," "Church maintains homosexual bar." More examples of ambiguous headlines are displayed in Figure 9-1. Jay Leno features similar headlines on Monday nights on the "Tonight Show," although many of his laughs come from classified advertising copy or headlines on advertisements.

Figure 9-1
These examples of ambiguous headlines managed to get through the copy desk at various publications.

Ambiguous and confusing headlines

**Drunks Get Nine
Months in Violin Case**

**Include Your Children
When Baking Cookies**

War Dims Hope for Peace

**Panda Mating Fails;
Veterinarian Takes Over**

Teacher Strikes Idle Kids

**Plane Too Close to Ground,
Crash Probe Told**

**Miners Refuse to
Work After Death**

**If Strike Isn't Settled Quickly,
It May Last a While**

**Man Struck by Lightning
Faces Battery Charge**

**New Study of Obesity Looks
for Larger Test Group**

Kids Make Nutritious Snacks

**Typhoon Rips Through
Cemetery; Hundreds Dead**

**Bank Drive-in Window
Blocked by Board**

**Hospitals are Sued
by 7 Foot Doctors**

**Sex Education Delayed;
Teachers Request Training**

Prostitutes Appeal to Pope

**Two Sisters Reunited
After 18 Years in
Checkout Counter**

Eye Drops off Shelf

**Squad Helps
Dog Bite Victim**

**Two Soviet Ships
Collide, One Dies**

**Cold Wave Linked
to Temperatures**

**Red Tape Holds
Up New Bridge**

**Chef Throws His Heart
into Helping Feed Needy**

**New Vaccine May
Contain Rabies**

Air Head Fired

Farmer Bill Dies in House

▶**Don't repeat words in a headline.** Example: "Prosecutor charges city manager with embezzlement of city funds." Occasionally, repetition leads to a good headline. This example from the Lexington (Ky.) Herald-Leader is about an actor who turned his back on Hollywood to become a Benedictine monk:

Hollywood actor trades the footlights for the divine light

▶**Tell what happened rather than what did not happen.** The headline "No one dies in storm," for example, is less informative than a specific statement about storm damage.

Storm topples television tower

Storm rips roofs from homes

▶**Avoid confusing abbreviations and acronyms in headlines.** Except for abbreviations commonly used in writing for a public audience, abbreviations should not appear in headlines. For example, this headline uses abbreviation correctly:

Summitt first female coach to reach win No. 800

The following headline misuses abbreviation in three places: "Floods close Calif., Nev. mtn. passes." *California, Nevada* and *mountain* should all be spelled out, as they are in ordinary writing. State abbreviations are unavoidable in some headlines, but *mountain* used in this sense should never be abbreviated.

Some acronyms—words formed from the initial letters of a name, such as NASA for National Aeronautics and Space Administration—and combinations of initials have become readily understood vocabulary in the United States. *NATO, SWAT* and *AIDS* are acronyms that most readers immediately recognize and understand, as are the abbreviations *U.S., GM, IBM, CIA* and *FBI*. These familiar terms should be used to condense headlines. Acronyms and abbreviations unfamiliar to readers should not be used in headlines. Consult the alphabetical entries in the Associated Press Stylebook for guidance on how to use abbreviations and acronyms.

A practical method for deciding whether to use a particular abbreviation or acronym in a headline is to make a short list of those that are familiar to readers and common in ordinary public writing. Then, when questions arise about using an abbreviation or acronym, check the list; if the term is not on it, spell it out or rephrase the headline.

▶**Punctuate headlines correctly.** In most instances, headlines are punctuated like sentences but without a period at the end. Headline punctuation is discussed later in this chapter.

▶**Communicate specific facts rather than pad the headline to fill space.** For example, in this headline—"Stocks finish ahead, after weak start"—the phrase *after weak start* provides additional information, whereas *in trading today* would have filled the space with obvious information instead of adding more fact. Headline padding is distracting. It is usually obvious and weakens an otherwise good headline.

▶**Use puns sparingly, if at all.** Although sometimes clever, puns often fall flat with readers. Further, pun headlines on news stories rarely communicate the key idea of the story quickly. Some managing editors or copy desk chiefs ban puns in headlines, as happened at the San Antonio Express-News on the day after the April 20, 2006, issue appeared with nine pun headlines. Two examples from that issue: "Old well ends well: River Walk threat wiped out" and "Mumps outbreak swells." Puns can mischaracterize a story's seriousness, as in these examples, also from the San Antonio paper: "Border violence killing tourism," "Bell's name doesn't have a familiar ring for many voters" and "(Pope) Benedict names a flock of new cardinals."

▶**Read the headline aloud.** This will help you spot and avoid clunky "headlinese" and move toward more conversational heads.

▶**Watch for traps.** Does a nearby, unrelated photo create a juxtaposition that could make the headline offensive or ridiculous? Read the headline one line at a time. Does any line, read alone, take on an unintended meaning that detracts from the headline and the story or reflects insensitivity or bad taste? A writer playing off the titles of "for dummies" how-to books used the phrase in a publication welcoming spectators and participants to town for the Special Olympics, an organization dedicated to empowering individuals with intellectual disabilities. Not only insensitive, the usage was also expensive, as the publisher ordered copies destroyed and reprinted.

▶**Check the headline carefully before returning it to the copy desk chief for approval.** Check the facts against the story; double-check the type specifications and ensure that the headline maintains clarity of meaning and appropriateness of tone. One way to check for ambiguity or obscurity is to put the headline back into skeletonized sentence form to see whether it is easily understandable.

The compilation of headlines in Figure 9-2 illustrates the headline-writing guidelines explained in this chapter.

Figure 9-2
These headlines were featured on the American Copy Editors Society Web site. For more examples of good headline writing, see the ACES site at http://www.copydesk.org.

Examples of good headlines

Inmate Flees in Boxers, But Freedom is Brief on a story about an inmate who escaped in his underwear but was soon caught (Mark Misulonas, Chicago Tribune).

Folks flock to be freed from frizz / Stylists straighten tresses at prices that would curl your hair on a story saying that increasing numbers of people are undergoing the pricey process of getting their hair straightened (Karen Sidaway, The Repository, Canton, Ohio)

Headphone / users, listen up! / (if you still can) on audiologists finding hearing loss at earlier ages from use of MP3 players (Jim McNett, The Oregonian).

Six-shooter/6.0 6.0 6.0 6.0 6.0 6.0 6.0 5.9 6.0 / Kwan just misses perfection on a piece about the skater's record-making score (Dan Brown, San Jose Mercury News).

I Sue You, You Sue Me on a story about lawsuits against Barney imitators and others selling the costume without permission (Chuck Ervin, San Jose Mercury News).

CASINO: No dice on a piece about the failure of a casino gambling proposal (Margaret Lord, The Baltimore Sun).

Whole lotta Bacon goin' on for a profile of actor Kevin Bacon (Doug Wagner, the Rocky Mountain News).

A desire named streetcar was a subhead on a story about an artist who paints scenes of bygone Detroit. The piece included a section about the great demand for his paintings of trolley cars in motion (Marty Kohn, the Detroit Free Press).

Professional perspective: Peter Bhatia

The power of headlines

Headline writing is difficult work. It is an art form within the larger art form of journalism. It is an art form that doesn't receive enough attention in newsrooms today. The reasons for that are complex, relating to the necessary emphasis on writing and reporting, the key to any successful newspaper effort. After all, if readers don't read it, why have we bothered? Technology is a factor, too. In an era when how well editors can run a computer is sometimes as important as what they make the computer produce, it is only natural that fine, specific specialties such as headline writing are becoming less and less important in many newsrooms.

But in this contemporary era of new technology, it is very important to not lose sight of the great impact headlines have in our papers. They are our billboard to the news. Write a great head, there's a better chance of getting people to read the story. Write a lousy or inappropriate headline, the opposite occurs. It is really that simple. The headline writer needs to stretch, needs to take risks, needs to push the envelope to make sure the headline is as good and convincing as it can be and sells the story as well as it can. All of that, of course, without overstepping the appropriate bounds of taste and what the market will bear.

And it can't be emphasized too much: The No. 1 rule in headline writing is accuracy, accuracy, accuracy . . . and, of course, you have to do it in five or six words 20 times or more a day if you're working on a copy desk rim. It isn't easy.

Press release headlines

Except at some weekly newspapers, press releases face almost insurmountable competition for space in newspapers, so PR practitioners must make the release match journalistic style. Newspaper Web sites increasingly encourage community announcements and reader input, so press releases with legitimate news value can more likely appear online than in the print newspaper.

Although newspaper or Web site editors may change the headlines to fit their publication's layout, public relations writers should top their releases with strong newspaper-style headlines, following the rules in the previous section. In addition, resist the urge to pitch the client's company, product or service. Obvious sales pitches in news release headlines likely will lead the release to being pitched in the trash. Bill Stoller, who represented Fortune 500 companies during his 20 years as a public relations professional, gives this advice:*

> The reporter isn't interested in helping you make money or driving visitors to your site. He's looking for a story that will be interesting to his readers and pleasing to his editor. He could care less about your great selection, super customer service and commitment to quality. He wants to know only the info that will help him craft a good story. Take your ego out of it. Take your natural inclination to sell, sell, sell out of it. Look at your story (including the headline) with a cold, objective eye.

Stoller advises PR practitioners to emulate newspaper headlines by stating the most exciting news, finding or announcement in as few words as possible. He gives this as an example of a poor press release headline: "New Website that offers herbal weight loss lets teens speak out about weight issues." The following headline is more likely to interest reporters or editors and thus more likely appear in the media:

Teens: Ultra-thin movie, pop stars set bad example

---

*Bill Stoller operates Publicity Insider Web site, http://www.publicityinsider.com/pifaq.asp.

Feature story headlines

Feature stories are often considered "dessert." Copy editors have the same license in composing feature headlines that writers use in feature stories, and a feature headline should strike the same tone as the story. A Lexington (Ky.) Herald-Leader copy editor properly topped a feature story about a convention for match cover collectors in this way:

It's probably not a good idea to smoke around these people

Literary devices such as rhyme, alliteration and even an occasional pun can be particularly effective in feature headlines as long as they reflect the tone of the story. A serious headline tops a feature about a serious topic, while a breezy or funny headline is appropriate for a story written in that spirit. One sure way to anger a feature writer who uses a surprise ending is to give away the punch line in the headline.

Web page headlines

"Never has the art of headline writing been so important" as on the Web, writes Mario Garcia, an internationally renowned designer of print and Web publications.* Garcia compares the role of headlines on the Web to the attention-grabbing headlines of competing tabloid newspapers—all barking to get noticed over the competition. Like traditional print media, Web sites rely heavily on well-written and informative headlines to induce readers to click deeper into the site.

Figure 9-3 illustrates a home page with headlines that draw readers into stories. A second deck accompanies each main headline. Navigation labels at the top of The Harvard Crimson Online Edition lead to the display pages of other sections on the site.

Web page headlines often lack the contextual cues—photographs, headline decks, accompanying article and placement on a page—that add meaning to headlines in printed publications. Editors for online media cannot totally control the appearance of their headlines on computer screens, as varying screen sizes and Internet browsers yield different looks. Even the context in which headlines appear varies. Online readers may view headlines as a long list of search engine hits, bookmarks for a Web browser or multiple home page links to stories.

If a brief summary of the article accompanies the headline, it competes with other headlines and summaries, navigational tools and advertisements in the small space of a computer window. Research shows that people dislike reading large amounts of text online and tend to scan headlines and ignore the summaries. Online readers don't have time to click on each headline and wait for each story to load from its home server and appear on the computer screen. Unlike print media, in which stories and headlines appear together for immediate reading, skimming or skipping, each mouse click to retrieve a single story from a Web site becomes a time investment. The headline alone triggers the decision to invest in retrieval and reading time for a particular article.

Headline writing guidelines described earlier in this chapter—with accuracy leading the list—also apply to online headlines. An online environment suggests these additional guidelines:

▶ **Concentrate on key information for the first word of a headline.** The key first word facilitates reader scanning and gains better positioning in alphabetized lists or from search engine results. Definitely avoid articles *(a, an, the)* as the first word in an online headline.

---

*Mario Garcia, *Redesigning Print for the Web,* Indianapolis: Hayden Books, 1997.

Figure 9-3
The Harvard Crimson Online Edition relies on well-written and informative headlines with second decks to induce readers to click deeper into the site. Shown here is the first screen of the three-screen home page.

USED BY PERMISSION OF THE HARVARD CRIMSON

Eric Ulken, the night managing editor at latimes.com, told a meeting of copy editing teachers that keywords make headlines more search-engine-friendly. Copy editors at the Los Angeles Times now write two versions of each headline—a print version, which must fit the page design and can rely on surrounding art to augment its meaning, as well as a stand-alone, keyword-laden Web version. Los Angeles Times columnist Joel Stein wrote this ultimate keyword-based headline for one of his columns: "Secret Bible Verse Foretells Housing Crash, Spawns New Diet Craze and Scares a Porn Star Straight." Stein's column had little to do with his headline, but it rose to the top of latimes.com's "Most E-mailed" category.

▶**Focus on the central idea of the article rather than using teaser headlines.** This includes avoiding puns or other cryptic heads that leave readers guessing about the nature of the story and unwilling to take time to download. Reserve puns and teaser headlines for newspaper or magazine feature stories.

▶**Avoid words that lead readers to mistake news or feature content for unwanted advertising messages.** Readers are increasingly annoyed by pop-up ads on Web sites and unsolicited commercial messages, known as spam, in their e-mail in-boxes. Readers likely will avoid clicking on headlines that seem to lead to more advertising. Those who wish to shop online will go to sites specializing in sales.

Magazine titles

While magazine and newspaper headlines share similarities, key differences exist. For example, the magazine industry uses the words *title* and *subtitles* instead of *headlines*. Except in news magazines, the primary purpose of magazine titles is to draw readers into the story.

Attracting attention is also one purpose of news story headlines, but their main purpose is to summarize the most important news in stories. Magazine titles lure readers by giving a hint of what the story is about. They generally need subtitles to expand and clarify ideas and further pull readers into the story, as in this example from Popular Science.

ALL EYES ARE ON YOU

Tollbooths, ATMs, doctors' offices, online chat: You leave critical personal data behind wherever you go. Let's follow one American as he scatters his digital DNA.

Magazine pages often integrate the title into the page design by using color type and specialty typefaces, a technique newspapers, particularly Sunday editions, often use for section fronts but less often on front pages. This integration of titles into the page design plus the use of white space on magazine pages provides magazine copy editors greater space leeway for writing titles. In fact, magazine copy editors may write the title and subtitle before the page layout is completed, and then the art designer incorporates the titles into the finished page layout.

Like newspaper headlines, magazine titles and subtitles should do more than merely label the story. The magazine title might not have a verb, but the subtitle will, as shown in these two titles from National Geographic magazine.

THE BIG BLOOM
HOW FLOWERING PLANTS CHANGED THE WORLD

Essential to life—and to romance—flowering plants lure paleobotanists with the sweet mystery of their origin.

THE H. L. HUNLEY
SECRET WEAPON OF THE CONFEDERACY

In 1864 eight sailors slipped out of Charleston Harbor in an ingenious submarine, sank a Union ship, and disappeared—until now.

Notice that, like newspaper headlines, magazine titles do not end with a period. Subtitles written as sentences, however, do end with periods.

Magazine titles in the form of questions can be effective if they are not overdone. Questions can lead readers into the story to learn answers. This example from Time magazine shows questions in both the title and subtitle.

Should We All Be Vegetarians?

Would we be healthier? Would the planet? The risks and benefits of a meat-free life.

Headline punctuation

Headlines are generally punctuated like a sentence without a period at the end.

▶ **Commas** may be used to replace the word *and,* as in these examples:

Wind topples tower, rips roofs from homes

President selects Smith, Jones as envoys

▶**Semicolons** are used in headlines, as in sentences, to separate independent clauses:

Wind topples tower; city streets flood

A semicolon is needed in the previous example because the headline contains two separate clauses, each with its own subject and predicate verb.

▶**Periods** are used in headlines for some abbreviations. They are not used to designate the end of a headline.

U.S. military meets fierce resistance in Iraqi capital

▶**Ampersands** should not be used in headlines except when they are a customary part of a title or phrase, such as *AT&T.*

▶**Hyphens** should not be used at the end of a line in a headline because they interfere with the line-by-line approach that readers use for reading headlines.

Avoid this: **Post goes to write-**
                in candidate, Jones

Better: **Write-in candidate**
            wins mayoral race

▶**Exclamation marks** are almost never needed in a headline. However, in its zeal to emphasize the unusualness of two major league no-hitters in a single day, an Ohio newspaper used seven exclamation marks:

O my! 2 no-hitters!!!!!!!

It was a rare feat. One exclamation mark in a headline is normally one too many.

▶**Question marks** are rarely effective for newspaper stories because headlines should answer questions rather than ask them. Exceptions to the rule are those few stories that pose questions without answering them, such as

Will voters elect a woman president?

or the occasional headline that not only asks a question but immediately answers it, as in this example from The New York Times:

Fake Cheese? No Whey!

▶**Quotation marks** in headlines should be single quotation marks, rather than double quotation marks, to save space:

Senate leader calls tax plan 'a windfall for big business'

▶**Colons and dashes** may be used in headlines to indicate attribution. A verb of attribution, such as *says,* is preferred. But where space does not allow a word, a colon or dash may take its place. Use a colon after the name of the person and *before* the opinion. If the opinion comes first, use a dash.

Sen. Jones: budget 'unfair'

Budget 'unfair'—Sen. Jones

Headline capitalization

In an earlier era, newspapers and magazines commonly set headlines in all capital letters. But legibility research has demonstrated that type set in all capitals is more difficult to read than type set in capitals and lowercase letters. Most publications have now abandoned the all-caps headline style except for rare occasions.

Try reading this paragraph:

> DOWNSTYLE AND UPSTYLE HEADLINE CAPITALIZATION HAS SEVERAL ADVANTAGES OVER USING ONLY CAPITAL LETTERS. MORE CHARACTERS FIT LEGIBLY IN EACH LINE OF A HEADLINE IN DOWNSTYLE THAN UPSTYLE, AND DOWNSTYLE REQUIRES FEWER KEYBOARD FUNCTIONS FOR TYPISTS. MOST IMPORTENT, RESEARCHERS DISCOVERED DURING THE '50S THAT USING ALL CAPITAL LETTERS SLOWS READING.

All-cap type is just as hard to read in headlines as it is in body type. In the previous paragraph, for example, you may have put so much effort into making out words that you didn't spot the spelling error *(importent)* purposefully included in the paragraph.

Some newspapers, such as The New York Times and The Washington Post, capitalize the first word of each line and all other principal words. This practice is called "false capitalization" or **upstyle.** Researchers have discovered that upstyle also slows reading.

Try reading this paragraph in upstyle:

> Downstyle Headline Capitalization Has Several Advantages Over Upstyle. More Characters Fit Legibly in Each Line of a Headline in Downstyle, and Downstyle Requires Fewer Keyboard Functions for Typesetters. Most Important, Researchers Discovered During the '50s That Starting Each Word With a Capital Letter Slows Reading.

The same reading difficulty you experienced as you read this paragraph affects readers of headlines as well.

Most U.S. newspapers now use **downstyle** headlines, meaning that sentence style capitalization is used—the first word of the headline and proper nouns. All other words are set in lowercase letters:

Stocks finish ahead after weak start

Headline counting

Earlier in this chapter we referred to the difficulty of writing a good headline within limited space. Now it's time to face the problem squarely by learning how to count the units—letters, punctuation marks and spaces—that make up a headline.

Until recent years, copy editors wrote their headlines on paper, often on half-size sheets of typing paper, and counted each unit. A single headline usually required counting units many times as words were changed repeatedly in an effort to compose a well-written headline that fit the allotted space.

Although computers can be programmed to "head fit," students should know how to count headlines without the aid of a computer. A young journalist shouldn't risk being rejected for an internship or job for not knowing how to manually count headlines, and many written tests for such positions include headline counting.

Counting manually

Various styles of type vary slightly in width, but the unit value of each letter, punctuation mark and space in a headline can be estimated as follows:

Lowercase letters = 1 unit (except *l, i, f, t* = ½ unit; *m* and *w* = 1½ units)

Uppercase letters = 1½ units (except *M* and *W* = 2 units; *I* = 1 unit)

Numbers and symbols = 1 unit (except the numeral *1* = ½ unit)

Punctuation marks = ½ unit (except a dash and a question mark = 1 unit)

Space between words = ½ unit

At a typical newspaper, the process of headline writing begins when the copy editor is given a story to edit. Usually a headline size and style have already been assigned to the story to conform to the page layout. But sometimes the copy is marked *HTK,* meaning "headline to come" so the copy editor can work on editing the story while the layout is being completed.

Headline size and style are usually specified in code. For example, the headline designation 1-30-3 BB shown in the following illustration means that the editor wants a headline one column wide, in 30-point type, with three lines. *BB* refers to the family of type, in this case Bodoni Bold. (Type styles and sizes are discussed in Chapter 8.) Because 72-point type is an inch tall, each line of a 30-point headline is slightly less than half an inch tall.

After receiving the headline assignment, the copy editor consults a **headline schedule** for the appropriate type font to determine the maximum number of units in a 1-30-3 headline. The schedule illustrated in Figure 9-4 is for Bodoni Bold type. It

Figure 9-4
A headline schedule is used to determine how many units can fit in the space allotted for a headline. The entries in the body of the table are the maximum numbers of units for a given type size and column width. The absence of exact multiples in some columns is due to space between columns.

Typeface: Bodoni Bold (BB)
        Bodoni Bold Italic (BBI)

Type size in points	Number of columns wide					
	1	2	3	4	5	6
14	22	45				
18	18	35	52			
24	13	26.5	40	53		
30	11	21	33	47	55	
36	9	18	27	35	44	53
48	7	13.5	20	27	34	41
60	5	11	17	21.5	27	33
72	4.5	9	13	18	22	26

Figure 9-5
To estimate the length of a headline, some editors use pencil marks. Marks above the line of type count as one unit, those below as half a unit.

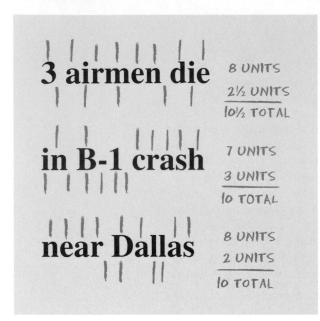

shows that a maximum of 11 units of 30-point Bodoni Bold type will fit on each line set one column wide. The same size of type set two columns wide will accommodate 21 units.

After a few weeks on the copy desk, editors have most of the headline schedule for their publication memorized. The unit counts listed in the headline schedule are the maximum number that will fit for each type size and column width. Most publications allow headlines that are as much as two units short of the maximum count.

Copy editors who count headlines manually develop their own techniques for counting units. One system is to use pencil marks above the line for each whole unit and marks below the line for each half unit. Figure 9-5 shows how to count a headline that will fit the 1-30-3 BB assignment. With practice, you should be able to count quickly without using little marks above and below the line.

Counting with computer software

Computers simplify the job of headline counting. A copy editor working at a computer screen can strike one or more keys to instruct the computer to count a headline. Commands vary slightly according to the computer system and layout software, but all are relatively easy to learn.

With one widely used computer system, the copy editor hits one key to instruct the computer to enter the "head fit" mode. Then the editor inserts a code for the typeface and size, hits the Execute key, moves the cursor to the top of the story and begins composing the headline. A line at the top of the screen provides a running count of the width as each unit is typed. All guesswork is removed from the process. The computer has been programmed with the precise width of each letter, number and punctuation mark for all available typefaces and sizes. Another popular computer system displays a highlighted bar at the top of the story to show exactly how much space the assigned headline can occupy. Any letter typed beyond that highlighted space exceeds the maximum.

Special software isn't essential for headline counting, as word processing software commonly loaded on PC or Mac computers permits writers to set the margins, type font and size for each individual headline. Depending on letter-spacing settings on the particular computer, the count may not be exactly the same as printer's type, but it should be close.

Headline writers in the computer era receive another break in fitting headlines because computers are not bound by the standard point sizes of display type: 14, 18, 24, 30, 36, 42, 48, 60, 72, 84. Let's say that the copy editor has written an excellent headline for a 2-36-2 BB assignment, but one line of the headline counts 18.5 units. As you can see from the headline schedule for Bodoni in Figure 9-4, 18 is the maximum number of units for each line of a 2-36-2 headline. The editor might achieve the desired width by instructing the computer to set the type at 35 points or even 34 points, just a little smaller than 36 points. Although purists object to deviating from standard point sizes in headlines, this slight variation usually goes unnoticed by readers. A note of caution: Check with the copy desk chief before attempting such type changes. It is absolutely forbidden at some publications.

Until recently, copy editors were instructed that the maximum headline count was absolute because "you can't squeeze type." While true in the days of hot type, today type can be "squeezed" slightly through a technique known as *kerning.* Computers can be programmed for *positive kerning,* which means fitting letters together more closely, or *negative kerning,* moving letters farther apart. But many editors frown on kerning because squeezed and stretched type has an unnatural look. Reread the note of caution at the end of the previous paragraph. Kerning is also forbidden at some publications.

Headline writers often face great difficulty because of space limitations. The restrictive unit counts indicated by the headline schedule can so intimidate new copy editors that they feel defeated before they begin. The real difficulty may be a reluctance to discard old ideas and try new ones when writing a headline.

Hanging onto a headline idea that is not working is symptomatic of new and experienced copy editors alike. Many experienced editors become so attached to the first line of a headline that they are reluctant to give it up even when they are unable to find an appropriate second or third line. Editors should see the headline as a whole rather than as a group of separate lines.

Able headline writers keep a good thesaurus close at hand and have many synonyms filed away in their brain. Their headline vocabulary includes many short words, as in Figure 9-6.

Placement of headlines

Typically a headline is placed above the story, as in this example:

Japanese company to build auto plant in Tennessee

A headline should never appear below the story, but it may be placed to the side. A *side head* is almost always placed to the left of the story, although in extremely rare circumstances a side head to the right can be effective. A side head is particularly useful for filling a wide, shallow space at the top of an inside page, like this:

Japanese company to build auto plant in Tennessee

Generally, a headline should cover all columns of a story. That is, if the layout calls for the story to be wrapped across more than one column, then the headline should extend across the top of all the columns. *Raw wraps,* also called *Dutch turns,* are columns of type without a headline above them. Used sparingly, raw wraps can help give good display to a graphic or other artwork. They also prevent the layout problem of side-by-side headlines, which are called *tombstones.* The following example shows raw wraps at the tops of columns 2, 3, 4 and 5.

Crash diets don't work

Chapter 11 explains in greater detail headline placement within a page layout.

Figure 9-6
A vocabulary of short synonyms is a great aid to headline writers.

accident: crash, wreck, collide
accuse, charge: cite
acknowledge: admit, confess
acquire: get
advocate: urge, push, spur
agreement: accord, pledge, pact, harmony, compact
allocate: give, allot, issue, award
alteration: revise, fix, change
answer: reply
appointment: post, job
apprehend: catch, arrest, seize, trap, capture
approve: accept, back, confirm, laud
argument: debate
arrange: set, plan, shape, slate
arrest: seize, hold, net
assemble: meet, gather, rally, unite
attempt: try
beginning: start, opening, initial
bewilderment: puzzle, confusion, mystery
celebrate: mark, stage, perform, fete
celebration: fete, event, party
choose: name, elect, pick
climax: peak
command: lead, rule, direct, reign, sway
commander: leader, guide, chief, ruler
committee, commission: body, panel, board
compete: vie
confess: admit
conspiracy: plan, plot, scheme
construct: build, erect, rise
contract: pact
convene: meet
criticize: score
criticize strongly: blast, flay
damage: hurt, impair, raze, scar, wreck, harm
danger: risk, peril, threat
decision: rule, order, writ, decree
decline, decrease: dip, fall
defeat: loss, fall
defraud: steal, dupe, fleece, rob, swindle, trick, raid
demonstrate: show, display, exhibit, test, try, melee, rebellion, revolt, riot, tumult, turmoil, uprising, uproar, discord, din
destroy: raze
diminish: trim, reduce, lop, cut
discrimination: bias, prejudice
earthquake: quake, jolt, shock, temblor, tremor
encourage: spark, help, aid
examine: scan, study
expose, reveal: bare
former: ex
impede, halt: balk
increase: hike, rise, add, gain, up, add
inform: tell

investigate: probe, study
leader: guide, chief, head, expert, ruler
limit, restrain: curb, relax, save, soften, temper
meeting: session, parley, assembly
murder: kill, slay
nominate: slate, pick, choose, name
nullify: void
opposition: battle, clash, challenge, combat, differ, divide, lash, quarrel, rap, rebuff, upbraid
organization: board, body, band, club, firm, group, unit
organize: join, form, unite, tie, link, merge
overcome: win, beat
perceive: see, understand, envision, foretell
pledge: vow, agree, oath
position: job, post
postpone: delay, defer, put off, shelve
prevent: bar, ban, curb, stop
promise: vow, pledge, agree
pursuit: chase, hunt, seek, track, follow, trail
puzzle: awe, confuse, stun, mystery, surprise, nonplus, perplex
quarrel: tiff, clash, argue
question: quiz, ask, inquire
realignment: revise, alter, change, shake up
reconcile: settle, peace, patch, pacify, heal
relieve: allay, cure, ease, end, free, help
request: ask, beg, bid, exhort, implore, plead, urge, seek, plea
resign: quit
restrain: stop, avert, check, curb, curtail, deter, foil, halt, hinder, impede, limit, quell, repress, slacken, slow, stall, stem, tie up, pause
reveal: tell
revise: alter, change, shift, vary, switch, transfer, modify
ridicule: chide, deride, insult, jeer, mock, taunt, tease, twit
salute: greet, hail
schedule: slate, set, plan, arrange
separation: rift, break, split
settlement: accord, deal, pact, truce, bargain
silent: mum, mute
steal: rob, loot, take
suggestion: plan, idea, offer, design
suspend: stop, end
thwart: foil, stop, limit
transfer: shift, alter, adjust
violence: battle, struggle, fray, fracas, furor, brawl, chaos, clamor, clash, combat
wrangle: argue, debate
wreck: raze
zealous: ardent, fervent, avid

Headline alignment

When newspapers were printed on flatbed presses, mechanical restrictions limited headlines to one column wide. Typographers wedged lead strips, called **column rules,** between each column to hold the metal type in place. These strips prevented type from extending beyond a single column. In addition, although newspaper pages were wider than pages today, they were divided into eight or nine narrow columns, leaving headline writers even less space per column to work with than today's copy editors.

These space restrictions led to multiple-deck headlines that, for a major story, might run most of the length of a page. Lines were centered within a single column. The 15-deck headline shown at right, beneath a top headline label "THE WAR," centers each line and ends each deck with a period.

After reading all those decks, readers found little new information in the body of the story. The New York Times published seven decks topped with the words *AWFUL EVENT* above its story about the assassination of President Abraham Lincoln. The Civil War headlines featured lines centered within one column and a mixture of upstyle and all-capital decks.

Banner headlines extend the width of the page, and in U.S. newspapers usually stand alone. They are sometimes accompanied by a readout head to guide readers into the story or at most one or two decks, generally set flush left. Exceptions to this rule were some of the **extra editions** published on Sept. 11, 2001, to document the terrorist attacks in New York City and Washington, D.C. Extras, extremely rare in this era of 24/7 news coverage, are editions a newspaper publishes in addition to its regular editions. On Sept. 11, within three hours after the attacks, extra editions hit the streets in quite a few cities across the nation. While information in those extras and Sept. 12 editions repeated broadcast and Internet news, the newspapers provided a special permanence beyond fleeting newscasts and Web pages. The Times-Picayune of New Orleans, for example, used a two-line banner plus multiple centered one-column decks with a mixture of serif and sans serif typefaces and upstyle and downstyle headlines on its front page:

TERROR HITS HOME

DARKEST DAY

NEW YORK

HIJACKED JETS BLAST TOWERS INTO FIERY RUBBLE

WASHINGTON

Third plane slices into Pentagon

PENNSYLVANIA

Fourth airliner crashes outside Pittsburgh

THE WAR.

Highly Important News from Baltimore.

The Massachusetts Volunteers Opposed in Their Passage Through the City.

Bloody Fight Between the Soldiers and the Mob.

Two Soldiers and Seven Citizens Killed.

The Volunteers Succeed in Forcing Their Way Through.

TOTAL DESTRUCTION OF THE ARSENAL AT HARPERS FERRY BY THE FEDERAL TROOPS.

Seizure of Northern Vessels in Virginia.

Delaware Assumes the Position of Armed Neutrality.

IMPORTANT FROM WASHINGTON.

PROCLAMATION OF THE PRESIDENT.

BLOCKADE OF THE SOUTHERN PORTS.

Departure of the Rhode Island, Massachusetts and New York Troops for Washington.

The Seventh Regiment, Nearly One Thousand Strong, En Route for the Capital.

Immense Turnout of Ladies and Citizens to See Them Off.

Pathetic Leave Takings at the Railroad Depot.

Figure 9-7
The style of headline alignment used by modern publications varies considerably, although flush-left style is used most frequently.

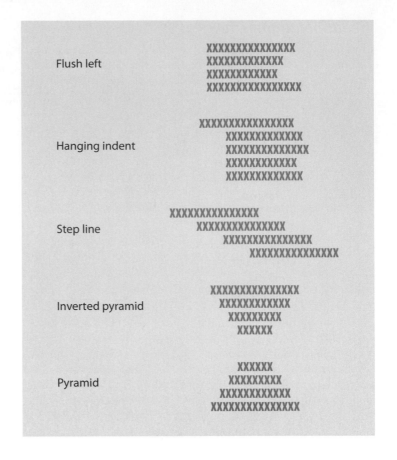

Although flush left headlines dominate in newspapers and news magazines, Figure 9-7 illustrates some other alignment styles.

Headline styles

The main element of a newspaper headline is known as the *top.* A secondary heading under the top is known as a *deck* or *bank.* The top of a headline should contain the main highlights of the story. Decks, if used, should give more information about the story rather than expressing in different words what is already said in the top. Although both the top and the decks should follow the usual headline-writing rules and should be able to stand alone, the decks generally depend on the top for full meaning. Here is an example from The Miami Herald of a headline with a deck below the main headline.

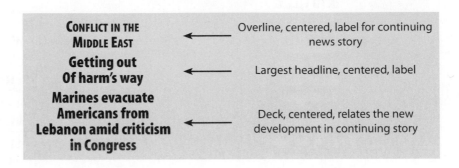

Modern typesetting and printing technology accommodate a wide variety of headline sizes, typefaces, widths and arrangement of type. Following are names and descriptions of various headline styles:

▶**Banner.** A top head that extends across the entire width of a page; sometimes called *screamers* or *streamers.*

▶**Skyline.** A banner head placed above the nameplate.

▶**Promo.** A skyline banner used to promote or call attention to an important story on an inside page of the paper; also referred to as a *teaser.* Promos often appear elsewhere on the front page or section front.

▶**Readout.** A deck under a banner headline to draw the reader into the columns where the body of the story begins; also called a *dropout* or *drophead.* The readout headline should add information and be independent of the main headline. The example in Figure 9-8 shows two readout heads beneath the banner headline. The pictures and text above the banner refer readers to related stories on inside pages.

▶**Underline.** A deck placed under a multicolumn top headline. Type for the underline is about half the size of the main headline and often centered. Each headline should be a complete thought unit underline amplifying the main headline. A page from The Times-Picayune in New Orleans, whose Hurricane Katrina coverage won the 2006 Pulitzer Prize for public service, is shown in Figure 9-9. Notice the skyline above the nameplate and three banners that mix serif and sans serif typefaces. Each related story below the dominant photograph has its own headline.

▶**Overline.** Reverses the positions of the two lines from an underline; the deck in smaller type is set above the larger type. Each headline should be a complete thought unit with the overline amplifying the main headline.

▶**Kicker.** One or two words placed above the main headline in type about half the size of the main headline and in a different type weight. The main headline should not depend on the kicker for its meaning; rather, the kicker depends on the main headline for its meaning. One purpose of the kicker is to introduce white space into the layout. Therefore, the kicker should extend no more than two-thirds the width of the main headline, usually less, and the main headline should be indented by the same number of points as the size in which it is set. Some publications underline kickers, also called an *eyebrow.*

▶**Hammer.** A headline that reverses the ratio of the kicker to the headline's main element, using type twice as large as the main element of the headline. The hammer is set either flush left or centered above the main headline. The main element of a hammer headline should be two lines to create enough optical weight to draw the reader's eye; also called a *reverse kicker* or *barker.* The headline *UNDER WATER* in the New Orleans page in Figure 9-9 is a hammer.

An all-capital hammer head in the Pascagoula, Miss., paper after Hurricane Katrina read:

GONE
'We lost everything'

Figure 9-8
The News & Observer (Raleigh, N.C.) used two readout headlines, centered within one column, under a banner head in the Sept. 12, 2001, edition of the paper. Above the banner are photos and references to related stories on inside pages. As published, the page used color photographs.

▶ **Tripod.** A headline with a single line of large type at the left and two lines of smaller type at the right.

> **U.S. forces uncover Saddam Hussein**
> ## CAPTURED: 'hiding like a rat' near home town

▶ **Wicket.** A variation of the tripod; two lines of smaller type are at the left of the main headline.

> **Saddam**
> **captured** 'WE GOT HIM'

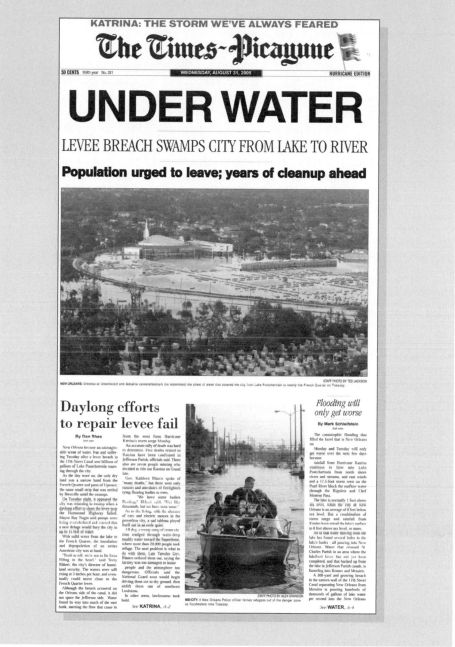

Figure 9-9
This front page from The Times-Picayune of New Orleans includes a skyline above the nameplate and three banners that mix serif and sans serif typefaces.

▶**Slash.** Like the wicket and tripod headlines in type sizes and arrangement, but a 2- to 4-point rule is set at a 45-degree angle between the two parts of the headline.

The top edge of the left module should be as high as the top of the slash, and the bottom edge of the right module should be as low as the bottom end of the slash. For maximum effectiveness the large type in a tripod, wicket or slash headline should be at least twice the size of the smaller type. To avoid confusion, the break between the two modules composing such a headline should occur in the middle of a column of body type.

Two other types of headlines—the *subhead* and the *jump headline*—are named for their purpose rather than for their appearance. Many newspapers, magazines and newsletters use subheads to break up large gray areas of copy, making pages look more inviting for readers. Although subheads run in the body of the story rather than above it, copy editors write them. Subheads may be centered or flush left, in the same size as the body type or slightly larger, in boldface or bold italic. Subheads function as little headlines for the paragraphs immediately below them. They may be only one line long, yet subheads are written just like headlines, but often without verbs.

To break up long columns of type, some publications simply insert 12 or 18 points of white space between occasional paragraphs. Others use *boldface lead-ins,* meaning that the first two or three words of occasional paragraphs—every fifth or sixth paragraph, for example—are set in boldface, either capitals and lowercase or all caps.

Another popular method of breaking long passages of type is to use a *breakout quotation,* or *pullout quotation,* within a story. This is an interesting or important passage in the story, often a direct quotation, that is repeated in larger type and set in a box or sideless box within the story. A very long story, particularly one that jumps to another page, may have more than one breakout quotation. This treatment relieves the grayness of small print on the page and provides another point of entry to lure readers into the story.

Jump heads are used to identify a story that continues from a previous page. Readers often complain about having to turn to another page to read the rest of the story, and they find it particularly irritating to have to search for the continuation of the story on the jump page. How a newspaper or magazine treats its "continued" lines and its jump headlines is part of the publication's overall design and should be consistent from page to page and issue to issue so readers become familiar with the style.

Some newspapers write a separate display headline, often multicolumn, for the part of the story that is jumped. A line placed at the top of the first column of body type under the headline informs the reader that the story is "continued from Page 1." Other editors dislike this style because they think it confuses the reader and wastes valuable space. These editors prefer to use a one-word headline that repeats the main word of the top headline or is the key word of the story. That word is followed by the "continued from Page 1" line or simply "from Page 1."

The next chapter will include information about headlines as used in page layout and design.

Suggestions for additional reading

Bernstein, Theodore M. *Watch Your Language.* New York: Atheneum, 1976.

Boczkowski, Pablo J. *Digitizing the News: Innovation in Online Newspapers.* Cambridge, Mass.: MIT Press, 2004.

Foust, James C. *Online Journalism: Principles and Practices of News for the Web.* Scottsdale, Ariz.: Holcomb Hathaway, 2005.

Garst, Robert F., and Theodore M. Bernstein. *Headlines and Deadlines,* 3rd ed. New York: Columbia University Press, 1961.

"Headlines," American Copy Editors Society. Online. http://www.copydesk .org/words/

Larocque, Paul. *Heads You Win.* Oak Park, Ill.: Marion Street Press Inc., 2003.

"The Lower Case," a regular department in Columbia Journalism Review, published bimonthly by the Columbia University Graduate School of Journalism.

McGuire, Mary, Linda Stilborne, Melinda McAdams, and Laurel Hyatt. *The Internet Handbook for Writers, Researchers, and Journalists.* New York: The Guilford Press, 2002.

Scanlan, Christopher. *Reporting & Writing.* New York: Oxford University Press U.S., 1999.

Sunil Saxena. *Headline Writing.* New Delhi: Sage Publications India, 2006.

Walsh, Bill. *The Slot.* Online. http://www.theslot.com.

Editing Pictures and Infographics

THE term *visual journalist* has assumed increased importance for both print and online publications at the dawn of the 21st century. The concept of repackaging the news to attract new readers has sparked a flurry of newspaper and magazine redesign projects and ongoing discussion about Web page design. Generally, redesigns, like Web pages, call for shorter stories and increased use of visual elements to help produce reader-friendly products. Journalists skillful at communicating information concisely and clearly, including graphic specialists and photojournalists, have gained enhanced status at their publications.

Better visuals through teamwork

Marty Petty, executive vice president for The St. Petersburg Times and former publisher of the Hartford Courant, speaking at an American Press Institute seminar, said the visual journalist of the future will be a hybrid reporter-editor-artist:

> The artists producing news graphics must also strengthen their journalistic skills. Newspapers will shift responsibility for the basic one-column and two-column chart, graph or map to the layout desks, copy editors and maybe reporters and origination editors. We will rely on them to have advanced computer skills, solid reporting and research skills and analytical skills as well as possibly a specialization in illustration. . . .
>
> The graphics editor, art director and photo editor will play much more active roles in planning the news sections, news packages and special sections. Technology will make the execution of their traditional tasks simple and fast, and increase the number of graphics on our pages. Again, solid journalistic skills will be a first priority for them as well as a complete understanding of the production process. They will need to know how to build data for expanded news packages and graphics.

Visual journalists as the hybrid reporters-editors-artists whom Petty envisioned several years ago have arrived, and they work not only at newspapers but at the entire array of publications, including Web sites. As noted earlier in this book, management strategy today increasingly emphasizes a team approach that involves workers at every stage of product development, whether the final products are automobiles, printed materials or Web sites. Now, instead of the old Life magazine procedure in which photographers had absolutely no control over their pictures after shooting them, photographers today often work closely with reporters, writers, editors and page designers throughout the process: generating story ideas, planning the most effective methods for gathering information and combining text and visuals to package information clearly and concisely.

Professional perspective: Steve Dorsey

On design

I'm Steve Dorsey. As design and graphics director at the Detroit Free Press, I work with more than 20 artists, news designers and features designers on the establishment of the overall look of the newspaper.

Steve Dorsey is the assistant managing editor for presentation at the Detroit Free Press.

The reason that graphics and design have grown in importance, or at least been recognized, finally, is that we package the paper; we are responsible for the presentation of the product. It's a daily product that's remade every single day. That makes it very, very important to be able to tell readers what's there each day.

Technology has been changing extremely quickly, and keeping up with that has been hard. What we do now is drastically different than what we did 10 years ago, and a night-and-day difference from 20 years ago. What we need to do for tomorrow is to just keep abreast of that and to try to grow and develop with it. We need to maintain training, which we have done, and we need to continue to look for the next big thing before it happens.

For design to be considered "good design" and not just "layout," it helps to have good tools. (But remember, ultimately, they are just tools.) What keeps me here, and what keeps me wanting to be here, is the abundance of news and the urgency with which we have to tell it. But also the people with whom we work; a lot of great, talented people work here. The key to getting a good newspaper out of that is letting them do their job and letting them be who they are.

Selecting pictures

When selecting pictures for publication, copy editors should follow the advice that Rob Heller, a design consultant and photography teacher, suggests for photographers. He tells them to give special attention to these elements:

▶**Point of view.** Always look for a more interesting angle from which to take the photograph. High or low angles can present the world in a unique way.

▶**Subject contrast.** Make sure that the subject stands out from the background. Dark against light or light against dark allows the viewer to distinguish the important parts of the photograph.

▶**Framing.** Examine all parts of the frame very carefully as you look through the viewfinder. This is the time to look for distracting elements such as a telephone pole coming out of a subject's head.

▶**Lighting.** The lighting should enhance the photograph, not detract from it. Stay away from flat, frontal lighting. Look for more interesting light from the side or back of the subject.

▶**Camera-to-subject distance.** An overall or long shot establishes the location of an event. A medium shot describes the action. A close-up examines the details of a situation. Shoot all three to give coverage as complete as possible.

▶**Decisive moments.** Make sure to always tell the story of an event or news situation. Try to capture the decisive moment, the instant when all the aforementioned elements come together to form a powerful photograph.

The procedures for showing photographs to editors vary from publication to publication. Newspapers and Web sites now use digital photography, so editors view pictures on computer screens. Magazine editors, especially at publications that print high-quality color on glossy paper, often prefer contact prints or hard-copy photographs. Some photographers make **contact prints,** proofs of the negatives that are the same size as the negatives themselves (see Figure 10-1). Although small, they are easily inspected with a **_linen tester_** or **_loupe,_** a small 8- or 10-power magnifying glass. Editors work from contact prints to select the photographs to be printed. The prints are usually enlarged to 8-by-10- or 5-by-7-inch prints. At other publications, the photographer may skip the contact prints and make 8-by-10 or 5-by-7 prints of the best photographs. Increasingly, digital photography is replacing film and photographic prints on paper. In a digital environment, editors display multiple small pictures on their computer screens, select those to be published and then electronically crop and size them (see Figure 10-2).

Editors and photographers use the primary goals of photojournalism in making picture selections:

- To communicate effectively, as either stand-alone art or accompaniment to a story

- To attract readers' attention and provide a point of entry to the page

- To enhance the overall appearance of the page

Figure 10-1
A contact print is a photo proof printed directly from film negatives laid out in contact with an 8-by-10 sheet of light-sensitive paper. From the contacts, editors select pictures to be enlarged for publication.

PHOTOS BY ROB HELLER.

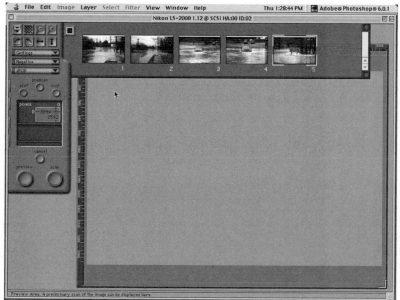

PHOTO BY MICHAEL ANDERSON

Figure 10-2
Digital shots are displayed on a computer screen. After editors choose which ones to publish, image-editing software, such as Adobe Photoshop®, is used to crop, scale and size the pictures. Then they are moved into pagination software for the final page layout and design.

Space is a valuable commodity, so editors must choose wisely in allocating that space. Will a photograph best accomplish the goals within limited space, or should an informational graphic be used? Or perhaps a sidebar to accompany the main story?

Criteria that make a story newsworthy also apply to picture selection:

▶**Impact.** Pictures that illustrate events and situations with an impact on many people are more likely to be published than pictures with limited scope.

▶**Unusualness.** Shots of an unusual happening or pictures taken from unusual angles or that use different approaches to routine events win favor with editors.

▶**Prominence.** Readers like to see photographs of famous and infamous people.

▶**Action.** Modern cameras, with fast shutter speeds and high-speed film, allow photographers to freeze action. Editors may be compelled to use an occasional "grip and grin" or lineup photo, especially in small-town papers, but such trite pictures are largely a relic.

▶**Proximity.** People want to see pictures of their friends and neighbors, of people in their own community. Other factors being equal, editors give the nod to local photographs over wire photos.

▶**Conflict.** Just as conflict makes an event or situation worth writing about, it also adds to the value of photographs. But editors must guard against selecting a conflict-filled photo that distorts an event. It would be poor news judgment, for example, to publish a photo of a minor fight that was an isolated incident at an otherwise peaceful event.

▶**Timeliness.** In judging the timeliness of photographic coverage, editors must consider whether readers are still interested in something that happened last week or even just this morning. Television also influences newspaper photo selection because editors seek to publish pictures different from those seen on television.

▶**Technical quality.** A blurry, out-of-focus print rarely attracts a second look from photo editors—unless its news value vastly outweighs its poor quality. Pictures of the first moon landing and the assassination of President John F. Kennedy are among the rare examples of news value overcoming poor technical quality.

Preparing photographs for publication

Once the responsible editor has selected photos and other illustrations, the art must be cropped, sized and scaled for the production department. Depending on the size and staff organization of a publication, the copy desk or a separate layout department may perform these tasks.

Handling photographs

When working with prints rather than digital images, everyone who handles photographs and other artwork should do so with care. Fingerprints and smudge marks may show up when the art is published, so keep it clean. Never cut a picture to eliminate unwanted parts. Instead, use a wax or soft-lead pencil to mark along both the horizontal and vertical dimensions, the part of the photograph to be reproduced. These pencil *crop marks,* as they are called, can be erased and changed if necessary.

Never write on the face of a photograph. Place crop marks in the margins of the photo, and write instructions to the production department on the back of the picture or on an instruction tag attached to the picture. To write on the back of a picture, use a grease pencil or soft-lead pencil. A ballpoint pen or hard-lead pencil may crack the glossy face of the photograph or show through.

Cropping

To *crop* a picture is to decide how much or what part of a print should be published. Editors crop to eliminate busy backgrounds of people who are superfluous to the photo's theme and of other elements that distract from the picture's center of interest.

If cropping from a print, begin by covering parts of the photo that contain no information or irrelevant information. What remains will have greater impact if reproduced at an adequate size. To help decide how the picture should be cropped, editors often frame the picture with a rectangle formed between extended thumbs and forefingers, with strips of paper or with "cropping angles" designed for this purpose.

If working with a digital photograph and cropping with computer software, drag the cropping tool across the portion of the photograph to be published. That portion will be outlined with a dotted line. "Handles" at the corners and middle of each dimension allow the crop to be adjusted. When you are satisfied with placement of the dotted line, a double click within the part to be published or selection from a drag-down menu will execute the cropping.

Regardless of the form of the original photograph—print or digital—keep in mind the following guidelines for cropping:

- Avoid cropping pictures in fancy or irregular shapes unless there is an unusual and compelling reason.

- For head shots, leave some space on the side that the subject is facing. At a few newspapers and magazines, however, all head shots—also called mug shots—are cropped extremely tightly so that part of the ears and sometimes the top of the subject's head are trimmed.

- For an action picture—for example, a racing boat or a runner—leave space in front of the thrust of the action.

- Body parts can be cropped but avoid amputating at joints such as ankles, knees, wrists or elbows.

- Remain sensitive to the mood or atmosphere captured in the photograph.

- Avoid tight cropping if background elements help tell the story.

- Consider that extreme enlargements will reduce picture quality. If the layout calls for a large photo, avoid enlarging just a small portion of the original. Select a different picture for that particular layout.

- Keep pictures small for Web pages. Large photos mean long waits for readers without broadband connections.

Figure 10-3 shows how to place crop marks in the margins of photos and how cropping affects an image's impact. A photo is cropped with image-editing software in Figure 10-4.

Figure 10-3
Crop marks are placed in the margins of the photograph, along both the horizontal and the vertical dimensions. Cropping a photograph gives it greater impact.

Original photo with crop marks

Anxious moments during championship game

Cropped and enlarged photo as it appears in print

Scaling

After a photo is cropped for its greatest impact, the next step is to *scale* it to fit the desired page layout. Other terms for scaling are **proportioning** and **sizing.** Few publications print photographs or draw artwork "to size," meaning the exact size that they will appear in the finished publication. Deadline considerations preclude a return to the darkroom to print photographs to size after page layouts are completed; in fact, layouts for the latest news and sports pages often are finished only minutes before press time. Thus, publications that still work with film and hard-copy prints rather than digital images generally use 8-by-10 or 5-by-7 glossy prints and scale them for enlargement or reduction, which is called the **reproduction size.**

Proportion is the key concept in enlarging or reducing photographs. A vertical picture cannot fit a horizontal space on the layout, unless, of course, the picture can be cropped to make it horizontal. In an ideal world, the person who does the page layout has a variety of excellent photographs to select from and, knowing that the desired shape is available, can design an attractive page.

But this isn't an ideal world. Often the layout editor has no choice about the shape of the photographs and must plan the layout accordingly. The layout editor can choose, however, to enlarge or reduce the photos.

Figure 10-4
This version of Photoshop darkens the area outside the selection marquee, making it easier to visualize the finished crop.

Editors can figure the reproduction size while maintaining proportionality in one of four ways:

- ■ Compute it with a mathematical formula

- ■ Use a mechanical scaling device, such as a proportioning wheel or slide ruler

- ■ Apply the diagonal-line method

- ■ Work from digital images with image-editing software

A ruler, preferably one calibrated in picas, is needed for the first three methods.

Regardless of the method used, remember to work with the dimensions of the photograph or other artwork *as cropped*. If part of an 8-by-10 photo has been cropped, then the part of the picture that has been eliminated is not used in figuring the new size. After cropping, when we speak of the *original* or *present* size, we mean the cropped size, the size within the crop marks.

Figure 10-5 explains how to use the formula method or a proportioning wheel to scale a photograph. Figure 10-6 illustrates the cropping process for the same photograph, using image-editing software.

Digital images

Proportioning wheels and the formula method soon may become as obsolete as Linotypes—huge, noisy, smelly machines once used to set type from molten lead. This edition of "Creative Editing" continues to explain manual cropping and scaling because some editors and PR personnel crop and size photos manually as they draw page layouts on paper to pass along to people who execute those layouts with computer software for image editing and pagination. Figure 10-7 pictures an editor working with a proportioning wheel and a layout sheet.

Few copy editors are expected to become expert at computer graphics software; many more will exercise news judgment to determine story and art page placement and lay out pages. Those who know how to crop and scale without computers loaded with special software can perform well in any work environment, especially at deadline time.

Cameras that use film, darkroom chemicals and light-sensitive paper may also be relegated to museums, replaced by digital cameras and electronic darkrooms and picture desks—all widely used today. Digital image-editing software, such as the popular Photoshop® and Corel Paint Shop® programs, enables editors to crop, size and even manipulate images, all with the touch of a mouse. Instead of using grease pencil marks in the margins of a photograph, an editor simply drags a "marquee" around the desired area to crop and then gives a command to enlarge or reduce the picture while keeping both dimensions in proportion, as shown in Figure 10-6.

Scanning images. While low-resolution digital cameras have become common, digital cameras capable of producing maximum quality printing remain too expensive for some small newspapers and public relations agencies. Photographic prints or negatives can be converted to digital images by scanning the print or negative.

Scanning photographs or other art is relatively simple. Using a scanner linked to a computer, open the scanner and place the image on the glass bed. To view the image on a computer, activate the image-editing software program that accompanies the scanner. The image should appear on the computer screen, ready for you to crop and size.

Click on the "scan" icon, and the scanner lights up and electronically converts the hard copy image into *pixels* (picture elements). The more pixels a scanner can capture, the greater the image quality, referred to as *resolution,* or *pixels per inch,*

Figure 10-5
This illustration explains how to use a proportioning wheel or a mathematical formula to compute the reproduction size and percentage of a photograph.

Original photograph

12 picas (2 inches)

8 picas (1.33 inches)

If this picture is cropped and enlarged from 8 picas wide to 12 picas wide, what will be the new depth?

Reproduction photograph

New depth?

12 picas (2 inches)

Using the proportioning wheel :

1. Align original cropped width (8 picas) on the inside wheel with the desired reproduction width (12 picas) on the outside wheel.

2. Without moving the wheel, look for the original depth (12 picas) on the inner wheel and note that it lines up with 18. The reproduction depth, then, will be 18 picas (3 inches).

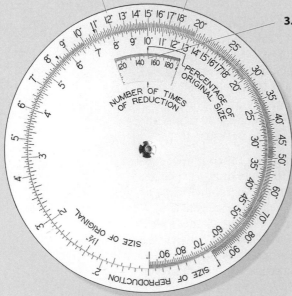

3. Look in the window to see that the reproduction photo will be 150% larger than the original photo within crop marks.

Using the formula method:

$$\frac{Repro\ width}{Original\ width} = \frac{Repro\ depth}{Original\ depth}$$

$$\frac{12}{8} = \frac{?}{12}$$ Plug in the known numbers and solve for unknown dimension:

$$\frac{12}{8} \times \frac{?}{12} \rightarrow 8 \times ? = 8?\quad 144 \div 8 = \mathbf{18}$$
$$12 \times 12 = 144$$

To find percentage of enlargement or reduction:

Repro depth ÷ Original depth = Percentage
18 ÷ 12 = 1.50 (150%)

or

Repro width ÷ Original width = Percentage
12 ÷ 8 = 1.50 (150%)

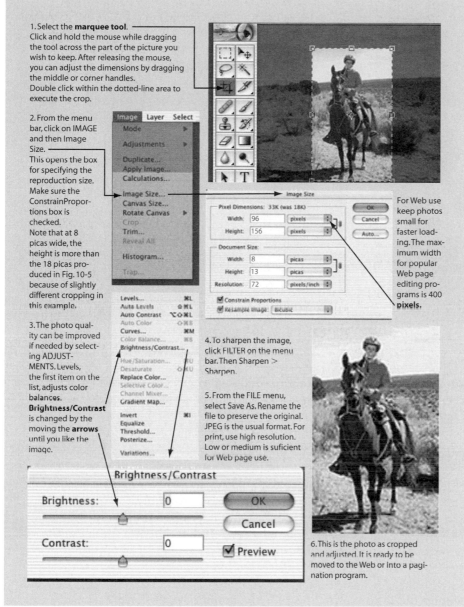

Figure 10-6
Using image-editing software to crop and size a digital photograph, an editor drags the marquee tool around the desired area and then enlarges or reduces the cropped picture while keeping both dimensions in proportion.

1. Select the **marquee tool**.
Click and hold the mouse while dragging the tool across the part of the picture you wish to keep. After releasing the mouse, you can adjust the dimensions by dragging the middle or corner handles.
Double click within the dotted-line area to execute the crop.

2. From the menu bar, click on IMAGE and then Image Size.
This opens the box for specifying the reproduction size. Make sure the ConstrainPropor- tions box is checked.
Note that at 8 picas wide, the height is more than the 18 picas pro- duced in Fig. 10-5 because of slightly different cropping in this example.

3. The photo qual- ity can be improved if needed by select- ing ADJUST- MENTS. Levels, the first item on the list, adjusts color balances.
Brightness/Contrast is changed by the moving the **arrows** until you like the image.

For Web use keep photos small for faster load- ing. The max- imum width for popular Web page editing pro- grams is 400 **pixels.**

4. To sharpen the image, click FILTER on the menu bar. Then Sharpen > Sharpen.

5. From the FILE menu, select Save As. Rename the file to preserve the original. JPEG is the usual format. For print, use high resolution. Low or medium is suficient for Web page use.

6. This is the photo as cropped and adjusted. It is ready to be moved to the Web or into a pagi- nation program.

referred to as *ppi.* A negative scanner works similarly. A strip of negatives is fed into a negative scanner and the accompanying software permits the editor to select and then scan the desired negative.

When the scan is complete, the software program prompts the user to name and save the electronic file to a disk or computer hard drive. Common file formats are *TIFF* (Tagged Image File Format), *EPS* (Encapsulated PostScript), *GIF* (Graphics Interchange Format) and *JPEG* or *JPG* (Joint Photographic Experts Group). Typi- cally, the next step involves importing the image into image-editing software for crop- ping and sizing and then into pagination software such as QuarkXPress or InDesign or loading the finished image to an HTML editor for a Web page. The dog photo in Figure 10-8 was electronically scanned, cropped and sized.

It is beyond the scope of this textbook to provide instruction in image-editing, pagination or Web-authoring software. In addition to instruction manuals com- piled by software companies, books and even online free tutorials are available for explaining various programs. The about.com Web site contains multiple packages of

Figure 10-7
This editor uses a
proportioning wheel to
size a photograph for
publication.

PHOTOGRAPH BY TOM FARRINGTON, SAN DIEGO STATE UNIVERSITY. COURTESY OF THE SAN DIEGO UNION-TRIBUNE

tutorials for several popular image-editing and pagination software packages, as well as tutorials on Web design and HTML editors. See the many resources available in the Computing and Technology section of the site at http://about.com/compute/.

Editing informational graphics

Those ubiquitous charts, graphs, diagrams and maps on printed materials and Web sites are called *informational graphics.* They serve at least two important purposes: to convey information in a visual, easy-to-understand form and to add color and variety to a page. Graphics skills, like copy editing expertise, are in high demand throughout the publishing industry today because of the increased value placed on good informational graphics—also called *infographics.*

Among the factors accounting for the graphics explosion in all media are the following:

▶**Need to attract larger audiences.** Advertising and circulation revenues are based on audience size, so print and broadcast media, as well as the print-broadcast hybrid medium of the Internet, compete with each other and with expanded leisure-time activities for public attention.

▶**Changes in reading habits.** Many people have become scanners, moving quickly through a print or online publication, glancing at headlines and art, stopping less frequently to read articles. Moving numbers from a story to an effective graphic communicates faster, often with less effort from readers. Too, they provide eye-catching *points of entry* to encourage readers to linger on a page.

▶**New technology.** What high-speed cameras and film and offset printing were to photojournalism in the 1960s, developments in color reproduction, computers, computer software and laser printers were to graphics through the 1990s. Relatively

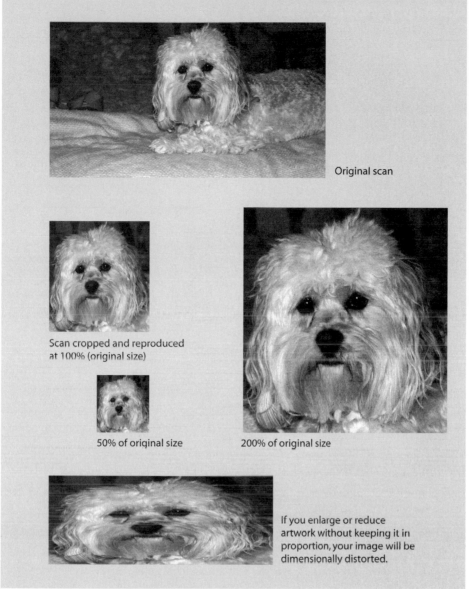

Original scan

Scan cropped and reproduced
at 100% (original size)

50% of original size

200% of original size

If you enlarge or reduce
artwork without keeping it in
proportion, your image will be
dimensionally distorted.

PHOTO BY MICHAEL ANDERSON

Figure 10-8
A photographer took this
picture with a film camera,
scanned the print to convert
it into digital format, and
then, using image-editing
computer software, enlarged
and reduced the original.
The shot at the bottom
shows what happens when
scaling—whether manual
or with computer—is not
proportional.

inexpensive scanners, more-affordable digital cameras, increasingly complex imaging software and the growth of the Internet in the 2000s further broadened the appeal of dazzling graphics, even adding movement to the mix. Satellite technology and computer networks permit fast transmission of computer graphics from news services to individual publications. Desktop publishing is the norm for newsletters and brochures created by public relations firms, and small newspapers without in-house artists can brighten their pages with computer graphics created by nonartist staff members. Digital cameras, too expensive for most news organizations during the 1990s, are now widespread for almost all publications.

▶**Example of USA Today.** USA Today entered the market in 1982 with extensive color and graphics, a formula layout and uncommonly short news stories. The newspaper did not win universal critical acclaim, but it did attract attention. Other newspapers copied its graphics techniques, especially the color weather map.

Advice for graphic artists

Ron Brackett, graphic artist and executive news editor of The St. Petersburg Times, emphasizes the importance of fact-checking graphics. Following are tips that Brackett gave to artists in a Society for News Design infographics quick course at the Poynter Institute. Many of the same tips apply to copy editors for graphics fact checking.

- Be clear on what your graphic is trying to show. Have a discussion with the assigning editor or reporter before you begin.

- Meet all the goals set out in the assignment.

- Use only trusted sources. Ask the research department (or your local library) for help.

- Don't blindly accept even what a trusted source (e.g., MapStudio) spits out.

- Don't look at the piece as a whole—break it down to its most simple elements. Fact-check each element.

- Fact-check on a hard copy, not on a computer screen.

- Double-check the finished graphic with the source material to make sure facts match.

- Is everything in its proper column?

- Are all the names spelled correctly?

- Is the pointer box or the dot in the right location?

- Is it millions or billions?

- If it's a map, compare it with maps on the walls or in atlases. Look at the surrounding states and countries too, not just the one you're focused on.

- Are all the roads labeled correctly? Is it a U.S. highway or a county road? Is it an alternate highway?

- If you don't understand something, neither will the reader. Get an explanation.

- Use your colleagues. In addition to you, another graphic journalist, and then the reporter, his editor, a copy editor and a copy chief should check every graphic.

- If you are creating original text, type it in the editing system (not FreeHand or Illustrator) so the text can be edited by the desk before it reaches the graphic.

- Bring in a copy editor on a complicated graphic. Make arrangements to get editing help earlier in the process.

- Read the big type backward.

Role of the copy editor

As the director of graphics at a major magazine noted, editors don't just want little bar charts anymore. Now, it's "can you anchor the whole page with statistics? 3D?" More complex graphics increase the time and attention needed from copy editors.

Ideally, as Ron Brackett recommends, copy editors are involved in the early stages to check the accuracy of information used to create graphics. After the artist delivers the camera-ready art, the copy editor again is called into service to check every aspect of the graphic. Copy editors should edit informational graphics with the same care they give to stories. In addition to the graphics fact-checking tips just listed, here are some other matters for copy editors to check:

- Make sure the numbers add up.

- Ensure typefaces are consistent sizes and styles for parallel items.

- Scale the graphic to fit the layout size.

- Make sure the type of graphic is correct for the data being illustrated.

- Avoid overdressed graphics, those with distracting extraneous artwork.

- Check for consistent information in related text and graphics.

- Check for a zero point on the graph or a clearly delineated break if the numbers are too large to allow the scale to begin at zero.

- Ensure that all five essential elements of a graphic are present. As shown in Figure 10-9, these are the five essential elements:

  - Headline

  - Explainer

  - Data or body

  - Source of the data

  - Credit line for artist or others

Infographics should be able to stand alone—understandable to people who do not read the accompanying story. Be sure that the infographic format matches the data. Charts relate numbers to facts, but not all charts effectively illustrate all types of numerical data. Figure 10-10 shows the basic graphic styles most appropriate for various kinds of data.

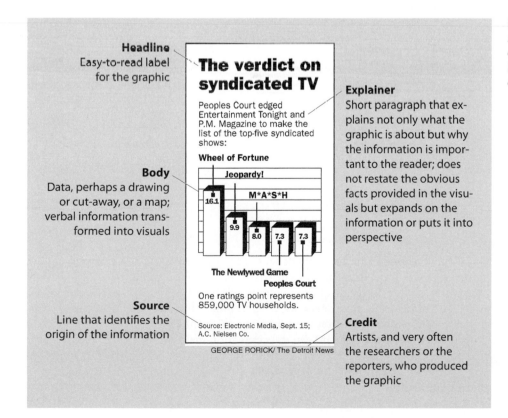

Figure 10-9
An infographic has five essential elements: headline, body, source, explainer and credit.

Headline
Easy-to-read label for the graphic

The verdict on syndicated TV

Peoples Court edged Entertainment Tonight and P.M. Magazine to make the list of the top-five syndicated shows:

Wheel of Fortune

Jeopardy!

16.1　M*A*S*H

9.9　8.0　7.3　7.3

The Newlywed Game

Peoples Court

One ratings point represents 859,000 TV households.

Source: Electronic Media, Sept. 15; A.C. Nielsen Co.

GEORGE RORICK/ The Detroit News

Explainer
Short paragraph that explains not only what the graphic is about but why the information is important to the reader; does not restate the obvious facts provided in the visuals but expands on the information or puts it into perspective

Body
Data, perhaps a drawing or cut-away, or a map; verbal information transformed into visuals

Source
Line that identifies the origin of the information

Credit
Artists, and very often the researchers or the reporters, who produced the graphic

Figure 10-10
Different types of data
require different styles of
informational graphics.

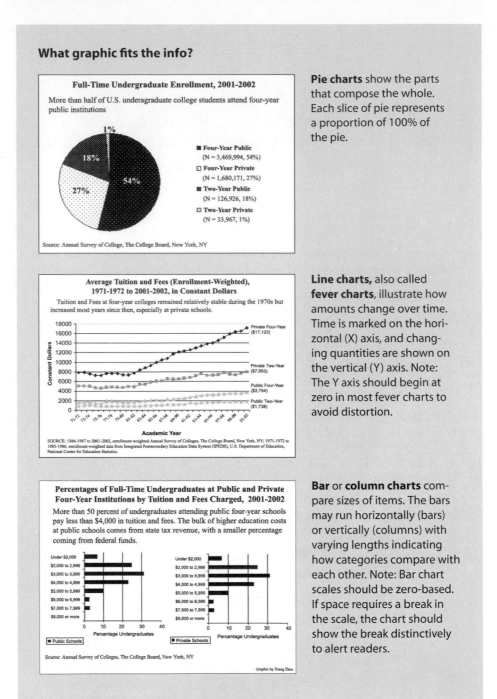

Easy-to-use computer spreadsheet software—Excel, for example—enables almost anyone to produce simple informational graphics suitable for publication, but artists' skills and techniques make even simple graphics more appealing and are essential for the complex artwork used to illustrate multifaceted stories. Artists, rather than editors, typically create informational graphics for corporate public relations materials, newspapers and general circulation magazines. Those artists may use computer software to produce the basic graphic and then "dress" the graphic with artwork, taking care not to clutter or distract from the data. Here are two examples of dressed graphics.

Data for the graphs shown in Figures 10-10 and 10-11 were entered into a spreadsheet software program (Excel in this example), and the program was then instructed to display that data in the desired graphic format.

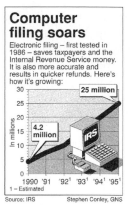

Line chart

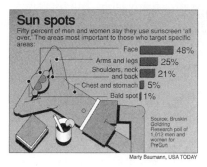

Bar chart

In addition to using correct formats for illustrating different kinds of data, copy editors need to examine the typefaces for consistency in size and style. Attention should be given to the use of white space within and around the graphic. Compare the presentation of identical data in Figure 10-11.

Figure 10-11

The poorly executed graphic at the top uses a pie chart, which is inappropriate for the type of data. The same data is presented in an improved format in the lower graphic.

Poor graphic

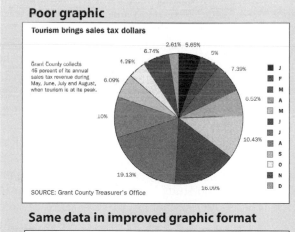

Problems:

- Pie chart is not best format to show changes over time.
- Legend is difficult to decipher with 12 slices in the pie. Various shades of black are confusing.
- Headline and body type are too small in comparison with type size of source line.
- Border is too close to the type.
- Credit line is missing.
- Numbers in explainer graph are inconsistent with pie chart figures.

Same data in improved graphic format

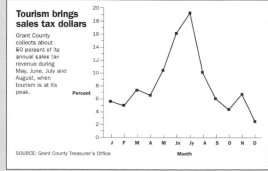

Improvements:

- Line graph better illustrates changes over time.
- Headline larger.
- Body type size in better proportion to source line.
- Border spaced better to allow graphic to breathe.

In addition to pie charts, line charts and column graphs, other graphic formats may more effectively communicate certain kinds of data.

Justices of the Supreme Court of the United States
2006—2007 Term

Name	Born	Appointed
John G. Roberts	1955	2005 by G.W.Bush
John Paul Stevens	1920	1975 by Ford
Antonin Scalia	1936	1986 by Reagan
Anthony M. Kennedy	1936	1988 by Reagan
David H. Souter	1939	1990 by Bush
Clarence Thomas	1946	1991 by Bush
Ruth Bader Ginsburg	1933	1993 by Clinton
Steven G. Breyer	1938	1994 by Clinton
Samuel A. Alito	1950	2006 by G.W.Bush

▶**Tables and lists** provide another way of visually depicting facts and figures for fast, easy reading. Newspapers publish many tables and lists every day for sports scores and statistics, stock market quotations, and even recipes. Public relations agencies use them for items such as financial statements in corporate annual reports. Rules or alternate shading are typically used to separate lines of type in a table, especially if the type is set across multiple columns.

▶**Maps** help readers understand the *where* of the story—where it will be warm or cool today, where the accident happened, where the president is traveling. Maps showing weather patterns across the United States are a daily staple of U.S. newspapers. Also common are locator maps used to pinpoint specific geographical areas where an event took place. Locator maps typically combine two graphics: one map to detail the specific area where the action took place—such as a neighborhood—and another to relate that location to the overall area—such as the city or state containing the neighborhood.

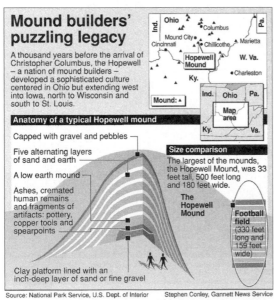

Mound builders' puzzling legacy

A thousand years before the arrival of Christopher Columbus, the Hopewell – a nation of mound builders – developed a sophisticated culture centered in Ohio but extending west into Iowa, north to Wisconsin and south to St. Louis.

Anatomy of a typical Hopewell mound

Capped with gravel and pebbles

Five alternating layers of sand and earth

A low earth mound

Ashes, cremated human remains and fragments of artifacts: pottery, copper tools and spearpoints

Clay platform lined with an inch-deep layer of sand or fine gravel

Size comparison
The largest of the mounds, the Hopewell Mound, was 33 feet tall, 500 feet long and 180 feet wide.

The Hopewell Mound

Football field (330 feet long and 159 feet wide)

Source: National Park Service, U.S. Dept. of Interior   Stephen Conley, Gannett News Service

▶**Diagrams** are drawings that help readers understand *what* something is, *how* it works or the sequence of events. Unlike simple charts that people without art training can produce with computer tools, diagrams are best left to the talents of skilled artists. Diagrams often require careful study on the part of readers, but, if well executed, they can communicate more information faster than paragraph after paragraph of narrative.

A complex diagram may include dozens of type clusters and a headline and body type. In addition to spelling and grammar accuracy, copy editors need to check type for font and size consistency and study every detail of a diagram to ensure that labels—often in balloon format—are clear and concise.

Informational graphics sometimes contain multiple visual techniques and occupy entire pages, as shown in Figure 10-12.

Editing cutlines or captions

What term is correct: cutline or caption? *Cutline* is more often heard at newspapers, although newspaper copy editors often differentiate by using *caption* to describe the copy with a picture that stands alone or a package of photographs and *cutline* to refer to the words explaining a photograph that accompanies a related story. Magazine editors use the term *caption*.

Figure 10-12
Informational graphics can occupy entire newspaper or magazine pages and incorporate photos, illustrations and several charting techniques. These award-winning pages were designed by Dean DiMarzo, Poughkeepsie (N.Y.) Journal (top left), and Paulina Reid, The Ithaca (N.Y.) Journal (lower right). Used with permission.

Professional perspective: Lynne Perri

Communicating visually

To develop a visual strategy for most stories, start with what you know—good journalism: then decide what you want to show in a graphic. Whether the display is with photographs, graphics or a combination of both, use the same guidelines as if you were writing a story: accuracy, clarity and simplicity.

Good visuals illuminate a story and create a partnership with the prose that invites the reader to linger a little longer. Good visuals also allow reporters to write stories differently, sometimes by reducing the need for number-intense paragraphs or complex descriptions of how something works.

Lynne Perri is deputy managing editor/graphics and photography editor at USA Today.

First steps. The best graphics start the way the best stories do—with good reporting.

Over-report statistics. Ask for 10, 20 or 30 years' worth of data rather than only the three years' worth distributed at a press conference. The additional numbers might add depth to the story or result in a better graphic.

Look for surprises. If poll results aren't new or surprising, they probably won't work as graphics.

Sketch out ideas first. If the results show that the content is worth the space, redo the sketches.

Aim for depth. Try to move beyond pie charts. This is more difficult, but the results are more rewarding for the creator and the reader.

Write, edit and rewrite. Rework art and text so that the two don't repeat the same information or message. Tight writing and editing do not mean fragmenting sentences.

Find visual resources. Copies of maps, sketches made at a scene, handout art or videos can be useful. Some sources can draw (ask them); others can provide copies of schematics, blueprints or diagrams.

The word *cutline* comes from the era when newspaper illustrations were carved or cut into blocks of wood for printing. These were called wood cuts, so the lines of type that went with the wood cuts became cutlines. Like printer measurements discussed in a previous chapter, pre-electronic technology supplies much of today's terminology.

Picture *captions* are among the most important elements of newspaper, magazine or Web pages. Captions provide a "point of entry" (explained in the next chapter) to a page. Often readers skim headlines and captions, glance at the photograph and then decide whether to delve further into the page. A picture captures a moment, but few pictures stand alone. They are enhanced by basic information that will help readers understand the particular moment caught by the image.

Copy editors often have sole responsibility for writing picture captions at many publications. Photographers should supply key information like names of people shown, location, date and occasion for the picture, and this information may come to the copy desk written in the form of a caption. Editors should consider this as information for a caption. Rarely should the photographer's words become the final version of a caption.

The key to fusing words and pictures is to write *to*, not merely *about*, a picture or series of pictures. Many editors write successfully to a picture by imagining that the photograph is the lead of the story and that the caption is a continuation that explains and amplifies the lead.

Guidelines for writing picture captions follow:

▶ **Look at the picture as it will be cropped.** Unless it is seconds before deadline and the photograph is still being processed (rare today with digital photography), it is imperative to view the photograph and resist the urge to write a caption without studying the photograph and knowing how it will be cropped. Look at the crop marks to ensure that those identified in the caption have not been cropped out of the photo. Count the number of names in the caption and make sure that number corresponds with the number of people in the picture.

▶ **Don't repeat what is shown in the photo.** This insults readers' intelligence. They can see that someone is waving, shooting a basketball, looking on or gesturing. The caption shouldn't repeat the obvious. Even worse is to state something in the caption that the picture shows is not accurate. Tell who is waving, why, when, where—items not obvious in the photo. Captions should identify anyone whose face is clearly recognizable and who appears to be part of the main action.

▶ **Don't repeat verbatim from the accompanying story.** Write something fresh. Busy readers feel cheated when the headline, cutline and lead use identical phrasing.

▶ **Pretend it's happening now.** A caption for an action picture generally starts with a sentence in the present tense. The photographer has captured a moment in time, and words that enhance the moment should be in the present tense to heighten the effect. Example:

```
Knoxville Police Department K-9 officer John Jones works
with his dog Bunky--who is trained to detect explosives--
for a group of children ages 6 to 12 taking part in the
Kids and Police Day.
```

Sentences that are more indirectly related to the picture—references, for example, to the subject's actions at another time—are usually written in the past tense. A cardinal rule is that verb tense should never be changed within a sentence. Editors and reporters should distinguish between action pictures and posed pictures. Action is in the present; posed is from the past.

▶ **Avoid ambiguity.** Sometimes the principle immediately above may not apply if the photograph is ambiguous. For example, is the pope laughing or crying? Explain unusual objects; don't leave the reader wondering what the main actor is holding or viewing.

▶ **Explain fully.** Few individual pictures exist without the framework of an event. Freezing a particular moment in time freezes only that moment. It tells nothing of the moments and events that preceded that image or what followed. This is the kind of information that the photographer should supply unless the information is available in an accompanying story. A good caption includes the outcomes of events such as sporting contests and elections.

▶ **Give complete facts for stand-alones.** Consider the caption for a stand-alone picture or photo package to be a news story. Include the important five W's and an H.

▶ **Make it interesting.** Tell it with punch, with sound descriptive words. The same standards used for writing stories should be used in writing captions. Use the active voice. The key details should come near the beginning of the caption. Make captions short, but do not write them like telegrams.

▶**Give readers credit.** Avoid using phrases like *is shown, is pictured* and *pictured above.* Identifying a row of people *from left* is sufficient without writing *from left to right.* If one person is shown standing in front of a microphone speaking, readers don't need to be told that Governor Brown, *center,* ... In pictures showing several people, a description might work well as identification (*wearing jersey No. 10; dark suit; wearing a hat*).

▶**Avoid editorializing.** Don't describe a picture as *beautiful, dramatic* or *grisly* or use other colorful adjectives. Let the viewer decide. Don't use facial expression to try to interpret what the photographic subject was feeling or thinking.

▶**Avoid libel.** People can be libeled in a photo caption just as in text and headline copy.

▶**Achieve a compatible tone between photo and caption.** It is just as jarring to read a tragic story and see a smiling face in an accompanying photo as it is to read a caption that is out of tone with the photo. Don't try to be light and bright in the caption unless the photo warrants. Again, look at the photo while writing the caption.

▶**Be honest with readers.** Point out anything unusual about the way the picture was made, particularly if perspective has been altered, magnification is extreme, a wide-angle lens was used, or the photo was taken under unusual lighting conditions. If file pictures are used and the time lag is relevant, let readers know.

▶**Remember: accuracy, accuracy, accuracy.** Check spellings of names. Fact-check as rigorously as for a story. Sometimes a copy editor who writes the cutline differs from the copy editor who handled the story about an event. If unfamiliar with the subject matter or with circumstances of the event, check the facts with reference sources or ask an expert on the subject rather than risk getting it wrong.

▶**Communicate with photographers.** Copy editors can't write what they don't know. It is essential that photographers ask questions and take adequate notes in the field to supply the copy desk with information to translate into lively, interesting and accurate cutlines. Cultivating good relationships with the graphics/photography director and individual photographers can motivate photographers to supply details about the pictures they take. See Figure 10-13 for a list of items that senior editor Anne Glover seeks from photographers.

Picture stories

Good picture stories, like picture essays, must be planned carefully. Great picture stories require a theme or central idea before the photographer starts work. Happy accidents sometimes result from haphazard shooting, but experience teaches that a good picture story is developed rather than stumbled upon. In addition to careful writing for the captions, good layout principles add effectiveness to a picture story.

A good picture story is created by the following:

- Choosing a dominant picture
- Avoiding the cluttered look that results from crowding too many pictures into the available space
- Facing pictures toward the related text
- Writing strong captions for all pictures and a headline to tie pictures together
- Arranging similar captions to have the same width, type and number of lines

> **Give copy editors these things: they'll be happy**
>
> 1. CQ odd names.
> 2. Describe the action in the photo before you give the background on what is happening. This is how copy editors naturally write cutlines, and it throws off their balance to have to search through a lot of information to learn what is happening in the picture.
> 3. Get the dog's name. And the cat's too.
> 4. If you're at a restaurant or any place else that has printed material relevant to the shoot, snag a copy and give it sent to the editor who'll be using the pictures. We can check spellings with that.
> 5. If you can, get a quote. We will be happy to use that.
> 6. If possible, try to give a time element that puts the photo in context: Just after paramedics arrived, before the meeting started, right when she found out she had been crowned Miss Citrus County.
> 7. If something seems unusual, or not quite right in the setting, please try to get more information. Example: a bandage on an old man's head, people on bikes (kids) who aren't wearing bike helmets, etc.
> 8. Don't assume that the people you are photographing will be in the story. Try to get as much information from them as you can. Then check in with the writer. They might want to add some of your stuff to the story, or they might want that information to be used in the cutlines.
> 9. On stand-alone feature photographs, conduct an interview with your subjects. The more information we have to use, the better the caption will be. Stretching is not a pretty sight.
> 10. Be as specific as you can about locations. Example: *On Starkey Road* needs a cross street or some kind of landmark or specific address since it is such a long road.

Figure 10-13
Anne Glover, senior editor at The St. Petersburg (Fla.) Times, says that copy editors will write good cutlines and captions if photographers supply good information.

- Avoiding "rivers of gray" caused by captions meeting irregularly near the same level
- Focusing simultaneously on a subject or personality as well as a theme or mood

Writing to a picture story differs from writing to a single picture. The writer must focus on both individual pictures and continuity from photograph to photograph. Continuity can be achieved with a central block of copy that relates to all the pictures and echoes the spirit of the pictures as a group.

Ruthlessly limit captions to a maximum length. Readers like to leap from picture to picture, so each caption should be short. Captions can be related to pictures by proximity, keyed letters or numbers, or arrows—preferably by proximity. Don't put a caption too far from the photo because reader eye movement goes from photo to caption and back to photo, perhaps several times.

A headline for a photo layout of two or more pictures on the same subject ties the package together.

Caption styles

In addition to giving careful attention to the content of photo captions, editors are concerned about the style of presentation. Captions are an important element of the publication's overall design, and editors should maintain graphic consistency. (This idea is discussed in the following chapter.) The photo caption style for any publication—newspaper, Web site, magazine or newsletter—should include the following components:

▶ **Type size and style.** Publications generally set captions in a typeface that contrasts with the typeface in the body to allow the captions to stand out. For example, captions may be set in a sans serif typeface (such as Helvetica or Gothic), in boldface or in a slightly larger type size, such as 10- or 11-point type alongside 9-point body type. (Type is discussed in greater detail in Chapter 8.)

Some publications introduce captions with a brief ***lead-in,*** also called a ***tagline*** or ***legend.*** The lead-in typically is set in boldface or in capital letters (see Figure 10-14). The first several words of the caption can become the lead-in.

▶ **Width of type block.** The captions that go under one- and two-column photos usually are set the width of the photo. Some publications set captions one or two picas less than the width of the picture on each side so that the resulting white space helps captions stand out.

For photos wider than two columns, captions with only one or two lines of type can run the full width of the photo without hindering readability. When two lines are used, the second line of type should fill most of the space, avoiding a ***widow,*** a line of type containing only a word or two so that the line is mostly white space (see Figure 10-15). If the second line cannot be filled without obvious padding, the caption should be edited to one line.

For placement under photos wider than three columns, captions longer than one or two lines should be set in two columns (see Figure 10-16).

▶ **Placement in relation to photo.** Standard placement for a caption is directly under the photograph, but captions may be placed to the side of photos. Captions rarely are set above photographs except when one caption accompanies two or more related photos.

▶ **Overlines.** An ***overline*** is a word, phrase or clause set in headline type, placed above a photo or between a photo and its caption (see Figure 10-17). Some publications

Figure 10-14
Captions often begin with a lead-in. Notice the variations in the capitalization, type style and punctuation of these lead-ins.

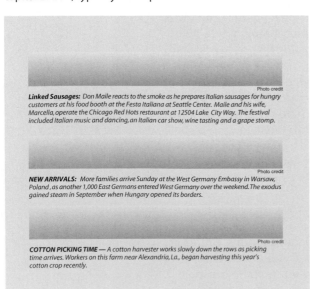

Photo credit

Linked Sausages: *Don Maile reacts to the smoke as he prepares Italian sausages for hungry customers at his food booth at the Festa Italiana at Seattle Center. Maile and his wife, Marcella, operate the Chicago Red Hots restaurant at 12504 Lake City Way. The festival included Italian music and dancing, an Italian car show, wine tasting and a grape stomp.*

Photo credit

NEW ARRIVALS: *More families arrive Sunday at the West Germany Embassy in Warsaw, Poland, as another 1,000 East Germans entered West Germany over the weekend. The exodus gained steam in September when Hungary opened its borders.*

Photo credit

COTTON PICKING TIME—*A cotton harvester works slowly down the rows as picking time arrives. Workers on this farm near Alexandria, La., began harvesting this year's cotton crop recently.*

Figure 10-15
The top caption has a one-word widow, which should be avoided. The lower caption reflects more careful editing.

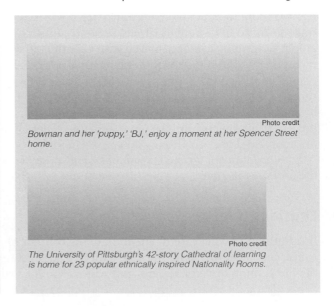

Photo credit

Bowman and her 'puppy,' 'BJ,' enjoy a moment at her Spencer Street home.

Photo credit

The University of Pittsburgh's 42-story Cathedral of learning is home for 23 popular ethnically inspired Nationality Rooms.

Figure 10-16
Multiple lines under a photo three columns or wider should be set in two columns rather than running the width of the photo. Note in this example the unequal number of lines in each column. An even number of lines is preferable.

Photo credit

***WHY'D THE FISH CROSS THE ROAD?* —** *Two fishermen stand in the middle of the road into McFarland Park in Florence, Ala., trying for those fish that might have been brought into the flooded park by recent high waters. The park is closed every now and then when rains are heavy and the dam upstream opens its flood gates and swamps the park, which lies on a bank of the Tennessee River.*

Figure 10-17
Overlines to captions can be treated in various ways. Note the type styles and sizes and the placement of these examples.

Photo credit

An eye for art
Chicago students look over a sculpture called "Song of Spring," which is part of the East Side Sculpture Walk on the banks of the Chicago River east of Michigan Avenue.

Radiant City

TURN ON THE LIGHTS — Many downtown Chattanooga buildings, such as American National, had all their lights on Thursday night to allow local photographers a chance to participate in the Chattanooga at Twilight photography contest. A booklet of the entries will be compiled by Creative Yard Concepts and the Chattanooga Area Convention and Visitors Bureau. Also participating in the project is Downtown Alliance. (Photo credit)

Photo credit

CUBS JEROME WALTON LEAPS INTO IVY
Spearing Long Drive By Giants' Robby Thompson

Photo credit

A gathering of legends
London was the site of a gathering of three of boxing's greats Tuesday when Joe Frazier, left, George Foreman, center, and Mohammad Ali appeared in a ring at the London Areana. The three former champions were promoting the release of Champions Forever, a videotaped tribute to their careers.

Photo credit

Airport protest in Japan
Leftist students and workers on Sunday protest the expansion of the Tokyo International Airport.

consistently use overlines, also referred to as *catch lines* or *taglines,* for stand-alone photos that do not accompany a story. Overlines are effective devices to attract readers' attention, add information about the photo and allow open space into the layout.

▶ **Credit lines.** The source of the photo, usually the name of a photographer or news service, should always be indicated. The photo credit line may come at the end of the caption, set off by parentheses. More commonly, it is set in type smaller than the caption type and placed under the lower right corner of the photograph.

▶ **Other tips:**

- ■ Stay within the same family of typefaces, point sizes and the newspaper's color palette to provide consistency.

- ■ Share visual style guides with all departments. That helps those not closely working with graphics and photo staffs to understand the philosophy behind the packaging and the guidelines to make it happen.

In the next chapter, you will learn how to pull together everything you've learned about graphics, photographs, display type, cutlines and headlines into page designs for newspapers, magazines, newsletters and Web pages.

Suggestions for additional reading

American Press Institute. *Design 2020: Visions of the Newspaper of the Future.* Reston, Va.: American Press Institute, 1999.

American Society of Newspaper Editors. *The Editors' Guide to Newspaper Design.* Reston Va.: American Society of Newspaper Editors, 2000.

American Society of Newspaper Editors Readership Issues Committee. *ASNE Innovative Ideas: Sections, Sites and New Approaches That Are Creating Buzz.* Reston Va.: American Society of Newspaper Editors, 2006.

Ang, Tom. *Picture Editing,* 2nd ed. Oxford, England: Focal Press, 2000.

Baron, Cynthia L., and Daniel Peck. *The Little Digital Camera Book.* Berkeley, Calif.: Peachpit Press, 2002.

Black, Roger, and Sean Elder. *Web Sites That Work.* Indianapolis: Adobe Press/ Macmillan Computer Publishing, 1998.

Bounford, Trevor, and Alastair Campbell. *Digital Diagrams: How to Design and Present Statistical Information Effectively.* New York: Watson-Guptill, 2000.

Design: The Journal of the Society of Newspaper Design, a publication of the Society of Newspaper Design, P.O. Box 17290, Dulles International Airport, Washington, D.C. 20041.

Eccher, Clint, Eric Hunley, and Erik Simmons. *Professional Web Design: Techniques and Templates,* 2nd ed. Boston: Charles River Media, 2004.

Garcia, Mario. *Redesigning Print for the Web.* Indianapolis: Hayden Books, 1998.

Green, Chuck. *Design It Yourself: Graphic Workshop.* Gloucester, Mass.: Rockport Publishers, 2004.

Harris, Christopher R., and Paul Martin Lester. *Visual Journalism: A Guide for New Media Professionals.* Boston: Allyn & Bacon, 2002.

Harris, Robert L. *Information Graphics.* New York: Oxford University Press, 2000.

Harrower, Tim. *The Newspaper Designer's Handbook,* 5th ed. Boston: McGraw-Hill, 2002.

Heller, Steven. *Becoming a Graphic Designer.* New York: John Wiley & Sons, 2002.

Heller, Steven. *The Education of a Graphic Designer,* 2nd ed. New York: Allworth Press, 2005.

Horton, Brian. *Associated Press Guide to Photojournalism.* New York: McGraw-Hill Text, 2000.

Kovarik, William. *Web Design for the Mass Media.* Reading, Mass.: Addison-Wesley, 2001.

Long, Ben. *Complete Digital Photography.* Boston: Charles River Media, 2005.

Romano, Frank (ed.). *Pocket Pal: A Graphic Arts Production Handbook,* 19th ed. New York: International Paper, 2003.

Smith, Bill. *Designing a Photograph.* New York: Amphoto Books, 2001.

Society for News Design. *World's Best-Designed Pages,* 27th ed. (Compact Disc). North Kingstown, R.I.: Society for News Design, 2005.

Weinmann, Elaine, and Peter Lourekas. *Photoshop CS2 for Windows and Macintosh: Visual QuickStart Guide.* Berkeley, Calif.: Peachpit Press, 2005.

Wheeler, Tom. *Phototruth or Photofiction?: Ethics and Media Imagery in the Digital Age.* Mahwah, N.J.: Lawrence Erlbaum Associates, 2002.

Web Production for Writers and Journalists (updated periodically with Web site). Oxford, England: Routledge, 2002.

Wilbur, Peter, and Michael Burke. *Information Graphics: Innovative Solutions in Contemporary Design.* New York: Thames and Hudson, 1999.

Williams, Robin. *The Non-Designer's Design Book,* 2nd ed. Berkeley, Calif.: Peachpit Press, 2000.

Williams, Robin, John Tollett, Dave Rohr, and David Rohr. *Robin Williams Web Design Workshop.* Berkeley, Calif.: Peachpit Press, 2001.

Zeldman, Jeffrey. *Taking Your Talent to the Web: Making the Transition From Graphic Design to Web Design.* Indianapolis: New Riders Publishing, 2001.

Design and Layout

As **you drive to work or to school,** you are likely to spot along the way several billboards and signs advertising all kinds of goods and services. The designers of those signs and billboards know that to capture your attention for just a split second, they must make you look; they must make you see. The same is true for those who design other forms of visual communication—books, magazines, newspapers, newsletters and the World Wide Web. How editors and designers entice readers into the text is the subject of this chapter.

The main purpose of publication design is to communicate, to help move readers easily and efficiently through the page. Editors who design pages are responsible for telling readers which stories are most important and for helping readers find the stories they want to read.

In addition to having a knowledge of news values, copy editing and typography, the layout editor must understand principles of design, the basic structures or forms of layout and the language of design.

Design principles

All designers call on the basic principles of design to help them create. Beginning layout editors should follow these principles as they become experienced. The standard design principles are balance, contrast, proportion and unity. Some designers argue that the same principles apply to both print publications and the Web.

Balance

Many early designers believed that page balance was achieved by matching identical elements (copy, headlines, photos, borders, colors) on the page. This *formal balance* had only one requirement: The right half of the page (at the time, four columns on an eight-column page) had to be matched on the left side with the same elements (see Figure 11-1). Not only were editors required to match the lower right corner with the lower left corner exactly, they also had to match headline weights across the page. For example, a two-column, 24-point, two-line headline in columns seven and eight called for exactly the same size of headline in columns one and two. A one-column, 36-point, three-line headline in column six called for the same size of headline in column three. Even the headlines and photographs at the bottom of the page were balanced symmetrically.

Formal balance, however, tended to sweep the news into a form with no consideration for its importance. In other words, the news of the day didn't seem to matter as much as design—form dictated content. Because formal balance required that the page be divided down the middle, the resulting balance was from side to side. And because headline schedules universally required that important stories be billed with large headlines and placed high on the page, top-to-bottom balance was not feasible. Big, bold headlines and large photos dominated the top of the page, and the bottom trailed off into grayness, like a news story written in inverted pyramid style.

Figure 11-1
The Los Angeles Times of 1979 used formal balance, with elements on the right side of the page balanced by similar elements on the left.

Balance is not achieved by merely matching identical elements on the page. Other factors, such as the apparent weights of the elements on the page, come into play. *Informal,* or asymmetrical, balance can be achieved with little specialized knowledge.

To balance the right against the left and the top against the bottom (remember that formal balance matches only the right against the left), beginning layout editors should section the page into four **modules** or quadrants, splitting the page down the middle vertically and then horizontally across the fold (see Figure 11-2). Each module should contain some graphic mass or weight—a headline, a photograph, a piece of artwork, white space—to help balance the page, but the weighted elements can extend beyond the boundaries of the modules.

Experienced layout editors make little effort to attain line-by-line balance. Neither must the page remain in equal quadrants; an arrangement of several rectangular modules may flow from the basic page division.

The sequence of the design also becomes important in achieving balance. The layout editor should attempt to place the major display element—a photograph, a story or both—just to the left of the **optical center** of the page, which is a point just above the measured center. Such placement serves as a focal point for balancing the rest of the page (see Figure 11-3).

Edmund Arnold, author of several classic books on newspaper design, has written about the way readers visualize and use a piece of printed information. He notes that the first place a reader looks—called the **primary optical area,** or POA—is the upper left corner of the page (see Figure 11-4). The lower right corner—called the **terminal area,** or TA—also has strong visual attraction because readers know they have finished when they reach that area. The two remaining corners of the page, upper right and lower left, are called **fallow corners.** They require special design attention because the reader's eye doesn't travel there automatically.

Figure 11-2
The layout editor should consider left-to-right, diagonal and top-to-bottom balance.

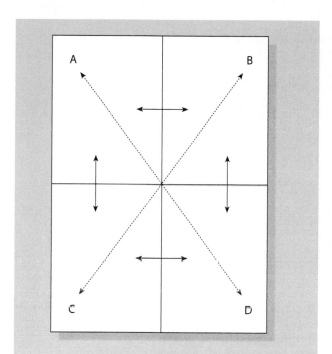

Figure 11-3
This page is laid out in modules. The major visual element—the dominant element—is placed just to the left of the optical center of the page.

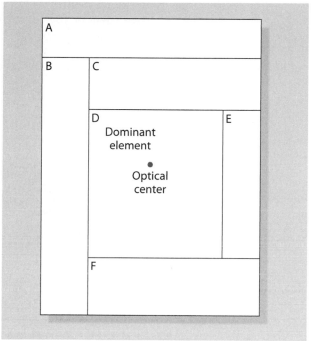

Figure 11-4
The reader's eye progresses diagonally through the page from the primary optical area (POA) in the upper left corner to the terminal area (TA) in the lower right corner. The remaining two quadrants on the page are fallow corners. A strong design will attract the reader's eye to the fallow corners so that it follows a Z pattern across the page.

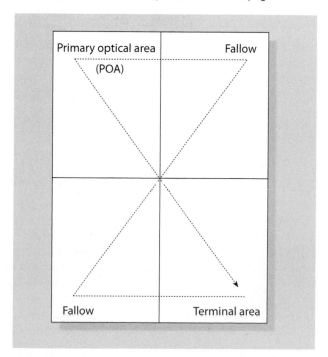

Arnold suggests that the basic movement of the eye follows a diagonal line from upper left to lower right, in a pattern that resembles a *Z*. The reader stops along the way, lured by "optical magnets," such as photographs and headlines (see Figure 11-5). Twenty-five years ago, the designers of USA Today, for example, determined that the lower left fallow corner would be anchored by an infographic (see Chapter 10) and that the terminal area, which USA Today editors called the

Figure 11-5
The dominant story-photo package about campus protests over the Israel-Lebanon conflict is the dominant element near the center of Page One from The Daily Texan of the University of Texas at Austin. The centerpiece package serves as one of several points of entry, or optical magnets, for the reader.

"hot corner," always would contain a bright, interesting story to grab the reader's attention.

Noted designer Mario Garcia makes a case for a somewhat different concept, one he calls the ***center of visual impact*** (CVI). He suggests that the two points on the page traditionally associated with the point of entry (the primary optical area) and the point of exit (the terminal area) need not be located in the corners of the page. He suggests that the CVI, which should attract the reader's visual attention at a glance, may be located anywhere on the page. The CVI then becomes the reader's point of entry into the page (see Figure 11-6).

Garcia recommends using only one CVI on a page because including other strong elements weakens the total effect. Photographs, typography and packaging all can be used as dominant elements on the page, leading the reader's eye to the point of greatest visual interest.

Figure 11-6
Note the large photo at the center of visual impact (CVI) on Page One of the City Times of San Diego City College in California, as well as the modular layout and the graphic element at the bottom of the page, giving the page balance.

Contrast

A broadsheet or tabloid newspaper page, a magazine page, a Web page, a newsletter page or an advertisement should have a focal point or center of visual interest surrounded by smaller, contrasting elements. The point of focus reveals the publication's priorities and shows readers what the editor believes is important. The layout editor may emphasize a particular element—a story or a photograph—simply by making it larger than other elements. This concept of contrast, similar to Garcia's center of visual impact, is called the **dominant element.** On a standard, open (no ads) page, a dominant horizontal element should extend across more than half the page.

In addition, printed materials often rely on color to bring contrast to a page. Some designers use color borders around photographs or color screens behind stories to spotlight such elements for the reader. A current popular design format known as "retro metro" utilizes thin lines (known as rules) between story and graphic elements, eliminating borders and shading, allowing color photos and graphics to stand out on their own.

The layout editor also may use contrasting typefaces and shapes to focus and balance a page. Many modern publications use lightface dropheads, also called **underlines,** and breakout quotations to contrast with boldface main headlines. Designers often choose sans serif type for captions, standing headlines and drop-in logos to accent the serif type used in body type and headlines. For consistency, a publication's design team will establish specific typefaces for text elements as part of a design style guide.

Layout editors also use contrasting shapes to lend visual interest to a page. Items placed horizontally contrast with items placed vertically—for example, a thin, horizontal story contrasts with a strong vertical photograph. The use of differing shapes of elements adds visual impact to the layout. The key is simply to remember to work in modules.

Proportion

The ratio between elements on a page is called **proportion.** Artists have discovered that the most aesthetically pleasing ratio is 3 to 5. Whenever possible, the shapes of elements should be rectangular, similar to a 3-by-5 note card. In design, rectangles are more pleasing to the eye than squares.

Not all elements on the page have to follow this proportion rule, of course. But if many elements do, the one unusual shape will become the focal point.

Unity

To achieve unity, also called structure, a publication carries its design themes throughout all pages as well as within individual layouts. In a unified publication, all elements of the design are related. The section headings, headlines, captions and column logos are stylistically consistent, and the sections and columns appear in the same place in each issue.

Unity also refers to the idea that individual stories or related elements packaged together can have greater visual impact if they are designed in modules. That is, laying out stories or packages of related elements as if they were bounded by an imaginary rectangle helps create a sense of unity and cohesion for the reader. Most contemporary newspapers and magazines use a modular format, and layout editors who imagine each element of the page as a module—a long, vertical photograph or a rectangular, horizontal copy block—are able to create simple, uncluttered designs that aid in readability.

Most publications, including Web sites, have detailed stylebooks that attempt to ensure such consistency in design. Without these stylebooks, clutter and chaos result, and the reader can be left dazed and confused. Most modern design, beautiful in its simplicity, puts a premium on unity because a unified approach communicates the message more effectively to readers.

Several years ago, noted technology expert and newspaper designer Roger Fidler published the checklist for unified design shown in Figure 11-7. It continues to be a good tool to help assess layout.

Figure 11-7
Roger Fidler's checklist can help layout editors evaluate their own work.

A checklist for functionally integrated design

Functionally integrated layouts are not created with magic words or rigid rules. They require organized and creative thinking developed through experience. And even with experience, not everyone has the visual sensitivity and judgment to become a good layout editor.

The following checklist is by no means all-inclusive. It is merely a tool for assessing layouts and should not be regarded as a newspaper design dogma.

If you can answer yes to all questions designated with an open box and no to all those designated with a filled box, the page layout is probably well designed.

Organization

- Are readers guided smoothly and naturally through the page?
- Do all elements have a reason for being?
- Are all intended relationships between elements readily apparent?
- Are packages clearly defined?
- Does the design call attention to itself instead of the content?
- Does the page appear cluttered?
- Do any type or art elements appear to be floating on the page?
- Do any elements appear lost?
- Are any editorial elements easily confused with advertising?

Readability

- Are the starting points for all stories easily determined?
- Do any elements interrupt reading or cause confusion?
- Are any legs of type perceptually truncated by art or sell lines (i.e., quotes, liftouts, etc.)?
- Is the line width of any text too narrow or too wide for easy reading?
- If text is set to follow the shape of adjacent art, is the story difficult to read?

- Do any headlines or sell lines compete with headlines or sell lines in adjacent columns?

Accuracy and clarity

- Does the layout accurately communicate the relative importance of the stories contained on the page?
- Do the art elements accurately convey the tone and message of the stories?
- Are logos consistent and differentiated from headlines?
- Are the devices used in a layout appropriate for the content of the page?

Proportioning and sizing

- Are all elements sized relative to their importance?
- Are the shapes and sizes of elements appropriate for the content of the elements?
- Do the shapes of elements add contrast and interest?
- Does the page have a dominant element or package of elements?
- Does the shape of an element appear contrived or forced?
- Do any logos or headlines seem out of proportion with the size of the story or column?
- Are several elements similar in proportion and size?

Efficiency and consistency

- Do all areas of white space appear as if they were planned? (When it appears as if something fell off the page, the white space is not functional.)
- Is spacing between elements controlled and consistent?
- Are areas of white space balanced on the page?
- Is all type, especially agate material, set at the most efficient measure for the information contained?
- Is the size of column gutters constant?
- Does the number of elements or devices used in a package seem excessive?

REPRINTED FROM NEWSPAPER DESIGN NOTEBOOK, VOL. 2, NO. 1, BY PERMISSION OF ROGER FIDLER.

Design elements

Modern editors combine at least six basic elements to lay out pages:

- Type for body copy
- Display type (headlines)
- Borders or rules
- Open space
- Art, which includes photographs, illustrations and informational graphics, such as maps, graphs and charts
- Color, as a design element

Editors for Web sites add video and sound to this mix of layout elements.

Body type

In most publications, body copy is set in 9- or 10-point type with 1 point of leading, or space, between lines. Magazine formats are very fluid, and column widths are not standardized. Despite the continuing conversion to narrower page widths, most newspaper pages remain set in a six-column format, forced by the standardization of advertising units in the 1980s. Given the narrower page widths, however, front pages and open inside pages are now often set at five columns. Some papers have converted entirely to five-column formats. Most columns are set on a 12- to 14-pica measure, allowing optimum readability. For publications that have converted to a narrower page width, the Newspaper Association of America has recommended a column width of 1.833 inches, or about 11 picas.

Most newspapers continue to *justify* their body type, meaning that the copy is set both flush left and flush right. A few newspapers and magazines, however, set their body copy *ragged right,* meaning that the copy lines up evenly on the left but has irregular space at the end of the lines on the right. Some newspapers use the ragged-right format when setting editorials.

When laying out a page, particularly in a horizontal format, editors often place body copy in several adjacent columns. Such columns of type are called *legs.* A story that is laid out over four columns, for example, has four legs of type.

Display type

Some of newspapering's most colorful jargon is related to headlines. As noted in Chapter 9, headlines serve two major functions: They summarize the news for busy readers, and they grade the relative newsworthiness of each story. As a typographic device, headlines introduce large areas of black and white to give the page visual interest.

Headlines usually range from 14-point type to 72-point type, although some newspapers magnify headline type even larger when an extraordinary story occurs (see Figure 11-8).

As we saw in Chapter 9, layout editors designate headlines according to size and space. A 2-36-3 headline, for example, is a two-column, 36-point, three-line headline. Typically, the most noticeable display type on Page One is the *nameplate,* or *flag,* which tells the name of the publication and usually the date, the price and the city of publication. Some nameplates also include *ears,* information set on either side of the name itself, such as the weather, a daily quotation or a small index.

A *banner* is a headline that extends horizontally across all the columns of the page. Usually the banner is the lead headline, and it is set larger than all the other

Figure 11-8
The Daily Reveille, the campus newspaper at Louisiana State University in Baton Rouge, La., published this front page after Hurricane Katrina ravaged New Orleans and the Gulf Coast. Notice the extra-large (about 100-point) headline and the dominant photo. The page was published in color.

headlines on the page. Many newspapers reserve the use of banners for highly significant stories and use smaller lead headlines, extending perhaps across only three columns, on a day-to-day basis. Other forms of banners are known as **streamers** or **ribbons.** These headlines usually are smaller than Page One banners and are frequently used on inside pages.

A **deck** is a smaller headline just under the main headline that gives the reader more information about the story. Early U.S. newspapers often used one-column decks that numbered scores of lines and extended halfway down the page.

A **kicker** is a small headline above the main headline, used most often by layout editors when white space is desired. They also can be helpful in identifying several related stories in a package. The kicker is set half the point size of the main headline (an 18-point kicker above a 36-point headline, for example). Sometimes it is flush left over an indented main headline, and it may be underlined. Kickers generally extend no more than a third of the width of the main headline.

A **jumphead** appears above a story as it continues from one page to another. The jumphead usually is smaller than the main headline and may contain typographic devices known as **dingbats**—ornamentation such as dashes, stars, **ballot** *boxes* (small squares) or *bullets* (circles or dots). Jumpheads usually repeat a key word or phrase from the main headline to help guide readers to the continuing story. Careful copy editors also make sure that the story's *jumpline,* the last line of type before the jump that refers readers to the correct page number, contains the same keyword or phrase as the jumphead.

Upstyle headlines are those in which the first letter of all the words except prepositions is capitalized; *downstyle* headlines are those in which only the first word and proper nouns are capitalized. Most modern newspapers use a downstyle format. Some traditional newspapers, however, such as The New York Times, retain upstyle headlines.

Examples of these headlines and many others are displayed in Chapter 9.

Borders

Publications use a variety of borders to separate one page element from another. Most advertisements are boxed, some with ornamental borders; some stories are also boxed, but usually with simple, plain lines called *rules*. Because the rules are placed along the edge of the column, elements within the box—body type and art—must be narrower.

For publications that aren't designed on computer, rules and borders are often produced by applying tape manufactured with lines in varying widths and styles. Most commonly used in editorial paste-up are 1-point and 2-point rules. Some publications are designed to use heavy 6-point or even 12-point rules.

Rules are used to box stories and to border photographs and other artwork or to underline kickers. They are also used as design elements in standing headlines, page headers (such as Sports) and column logos, and as cutoffs to separate unrelated elements.

Open space

The use of *open space,* sometimes called *white space,* helps achieve unity of design. Well-designed publications use consistent amounts of open space between columns of type, between photographs and their captions, above and below headlines, between the flag and the rest of the page, between the headline and the byline, and between the byline and the first paragraph of the story.

Open space can also be used to relieve large quantities of gray type. The use of liberal amounts of open space on pages that tend to be type-heavy, such as editorial pages, is a good design technique.

Open space should be thought of as a frame around the page. Layout editors should try to push it to the perimeter of the page, never letting open space become trapped on the interior of the page. Trapped open space is particularly unattractive on photo-page layouts.

Some publications use more open space between elements in certain sections than in others. Liberal use of open space in the arts and entertainment sections, for example, provides them with a personality distinct from that of the news sections.

Art

For most layout editors, art is the starting point for laying out a page. In some cases, the shape of the art actually determines the layout.

Most art requires reduction or enlargement before it is published (see Chapter 10), and the layout editor determines the size.

Simple black-and-white illustrations (sometimes called line art) need only be the correct reproduction size before they can be pasted onto the page. Otherwise, they are scanned, scaled to size and placed on a page in a computer design program.

A good number of publications now use digital photography in some form or another. Digital photos require sizing and color/contrast adjustment through the use of a computer program such as Adobe Photoshop. If photos are in print form, they are scanned into the computer and digitally adjusted in the program.

For publications that are not using digital technology, different processes are required. Black-and-white photographs, for example, require one additional step before they can be printed on a press; they need to be *screened,* or converted into halftones by breaking the continuous image into dots. Other names for a halftone are *PMT* (photomechanical transfer), *velox* or *screened print.* They all mean a photo print whose image is in a dot pattern rather than in continuous tones.

In a digital environment, this halftone screen is applied in photography or graphic design software. The number of dots per inch (the smaller the number, the more detail) can be adjusted in these programs to fit the capabilities of a press.

In a nondigital environment, color illustrations or photographs require several other, more complex production steps before they are ready for printing (see the following section).

The art of layout is to know not only how to size and crop but also how to judge the value of photos and illustrations on a page. In most circumstances, the art is the dominant element on a page; as a result, its quality and use require special attention.

Color

With ever improving digital technology, it is increasingly commonplace for print editors to use color in photographs and artwork to add meaning to the content. Color is quickly and easily processed by the brain, and a person's response to color is both learned and inherited. The response depends on factors such as age, gender, intelligence, education, temperature, climate, socioeconomic background and regional attitudes.

Basically, color consists of various wavelengths of light. A ray of sunlight reflected through a prism is diverted into visible bands of color. Red is the least diverted, violet the most diverted. Red has the longest waves, violet the shortest. This phenomenon, known as the color spectrum, was first recorded by Sir Isaac Newton in the early 18th century.

The main purpose of using color as a design element is to draw attention to the content. Most studies indicate that color is better than black and white for grabbing readers' attention. However, black-and-white images are better for a response requiring more thought. For publications with small budgets, black-and-white production can still be effectively used to convey meaning through the use of contrast and size, among other considerations.

Most of the time, color is available either as *spot color,* which is an extra shade of ink used along with black, or as full color, which is a combination of four color inks: cyan (blue), magenta (red), yellow and black. Full color is also called *process color.* Designers and production personnel refer to process color as CMYK.

Digital technology has revolutionized the way color photos are handled, making their use more affordable and less cumbersome for most newspapers. At many publications and printing houses, all the steps needed to create full-color pages are done with the use of scanners and computer programs. At some larger daily newspapers and printing houses, the completed pages go straight to the plate, ready for the press, never even requiring the process of creating CMYK separations on film beforehand.

For new designers and layout editors, the best rule to follow when adding color to a page is not to use too much. Resist the temptation to splash color everywhere. Instead, color should be used as an accent that connects related elements and enhances the meaning of the content.

Robert Bohle, in his book "Publication Design for Editors," suggests that spot color be used sparingly. He recommends a few of the ways to do so:

▶ **Use color as a content connector, or as a "people mover."** To do so, use color as a background for an entire spread, thus tying everything into a neat package, or use it to link similar items, such as small boxes in an informational graphic so that the reader can see the layout as a whole and not just as a bunch of parts.

▶ **Use color as a background for color photographs.** Sometimes a complementary color can be used to help a photograph pop out from the page. The key is contrast. Selecting a dominant color from the photograph is a weak choice because of the lack of contrast. A light gray is a good choice; the colors look brighter compared with the gray.

As in all good design, the key to using color is to keep it simple. More is not necessarily better.

Forms of layout

Vertical layout, most notably displayed in The New York Times and The Wall Street Journal, is characterized by columns of type that run vertically down the page. Vertical newspapers tend to publish few headlines or photographs more than two columns wide. Most headlines are a single column wide, and stories often run the full length of the column. A striking vertical effect was achieved by early newspapers using eight- or nine-column formats. Today's standard six-column formats generally mean wider columns than in the long-ago past, but a vertical look is still possible, and with great impact (see Figure 11-9).

Newspapers that use a vertical layout generally have a high story count on the front page. They are relatively easy to produce, both in the newsroom and in the composing room.

Horizontal layout is characterized by columns of type that flow across the page. Wide photographs—sometimes spread across the full six columns—contribute to this effect, and the many multicolumn headlines form wide blocks that give the pages their horizontal appearance. These large graphics and headlines attract the reader's attention and add contrast to the page (see Figure 11-10).

Today's modern layouts often are not readily identifiable as either vertical or horizontal. However, almost all are modular. Many layout editors use both vertical and horizontal forms to create balance, focus and contrast on the page (see Figure 11-11).

Newspaper layout

Pagination, the process of designing pages using computer software such as QuarkXPress or Adobe InDesign, is increasingly the norm in newsrooms large and small. Whether a publication utilizes pagination or paste-up, the process of *dummying* a page can be helpful in establishing where key elements can fit best.

The dummy, as a mock-up of a page is called, is used as a map by paste-up personnel for placement of stories, headlines, photographs and captions. The dummy is completed by layout editors in the newsroom and sent to the composing room, where compositors view the map as an exact guide for the placement of page elements. Figure 11-12 is a list of terms used in layout and printing.

Figure 11-9

The Indiana Daily Student at Indiana University in Bloomington, Ind., effectively uses a six-column format on its Sports page to create a vibrant vertical feature package. The page was published in color.

Figure 11-10

The Auburn Plainsman, the campus newspaper at Auburn University in Alabama and a 2002 Associated Collegiate Press Pacemaker winner, is laid out on a horizontal format. One large graphic and its corresponding story run across the full six columns. The small color photos in the promo boxes above the nameplate also provide a point of entry to the page.

Figure 11-11
The Advocate at Contra Costa College in San Pablo, Calif., was a 2004 Associated Collegiate Press Newspaper Pacemaker winner. This page, covering the election of California Gov. Arnold Schwarzenegger and recall of Gray Davis, combines horizontal and vertical elements, as well as color photos and graphics, to attract reader attention.

As more newspapers and magazines have invested in pagination technology, dummies have become relics in many newsrooms. While dummying is rare in many publications using pagination, dummies still have their uses. Advertising departments often produce dummies showing where advertising will be placed on inside pages, helping editors and designers determine what stories will fit best where. Depending on deadline pressures, designers can use dummies for section fronts as a brainstorming process.

Most newspapers are printed in one of two forms: broadsheet or tabloid. The vast majority of daily newspapers in the United States publish broadsheet pages, usually about 13 inches wide by 21 inches deep, although increasing numbers of papers are converting to a narrower width to save newsprint costs. These pages usually are laid out in a six-column format, particularly on inside pages where the advertising department sells standard advertising units (SAUs) to fit in a six-column format.

Figure 11-12
Layout editors and paste-up artists use the following terms as they lay out a newspaper's pages. After the editor sends a page dummy (a kind of map or blueprint) to the production department, the "backshop" staff trims and pastes up type, headlines and other page elements onto a flat. The editor then receives a full-page proof and makes any final changes. The page will be photographed and the resulting negative used to make a plate, which is then mounted on an offset printing press. Computer pagination is replacing the paste-up process.

Agate line: Standard of measurement for the depth of advertisements; roughly, 14 to the inch.

Bleed: Extending the printed image to the trim edge of the page; used more often in magazines than in newspapers.

Crop marks: Indication to eliminate unwanted areas in a photograph or other piece of art.

Double truck: Two pages at the center of a section designed as a single unit.

Dummy: Diagram outlining the layout of a page, as it will appear in its printed form; blueprint for paste-up.

Flat: Layout sheets, also called grid sheets, onto which the publication's copy and artwork are pasted. For offset printing, a photograph is taken of the finished flat, and the negative is used to make a printing plate, which is then placed on the press for printing.

Folio: Page number, date and name of publication on each page.

Galley: Shallow tray used to hold metal type; almost non-existent in today's modern production facilities.

Gutter: Margin between facing pages or between columns on the page.

Legs: Columns of type placed adjacent to each other.

Logo: Specially designed signature in an advertisement or design element used consistently with certain features, such as editorial columns.

Moiré (pronounced muare-ay): Undesirable pattern caused by incorrect screen angles when overprinting halftones.

Register: To fit two or more printing images on the same paper in exact alignment. A color photograph is said to be in registration if all the color layers are aligned and the resulting picture has clarity.

Tombstone: Bumping headlines of the same size, so that one headline reads into the other; to be avoided.

Widow: A line of type with only one or two words appearing at the end of a paragraph, usually at the top of a column of type; to be avoided.

PHOTOGRAPHS BY TOM FARRINGTON, SAN DIEGO STATE UNIVERSITY. COURTESY OF THE SAN DIEGO UNION-TRIBUNE.

Each column is about 11 picas, or a little less than two inches, wide, with a pica of gutter space between columns.

Many broadsheet newspapers use a variety of layout formats on Page One and section fronts, however, adopting a more creative approach for these cover pages. Many are experimenting with seven-column formats. Much of the college press publishes tabloid pages, usually about 11 inches wide by 14 inches deep. These pages are usually laid out on either a four-column or a five-column format (see Figure 11-13).

Tabloid-size newspapers use one of two sizes—one approximately 11 inches wide by 17 inches deep and the other about half the size of a broadsheet.

Figure 11-13
The Daily Aztec, the campus newspaper at San Diego State University, published this dramatic Page One the day after the United States invaded Iraq in March 2003. Many collegiate newspapers are tabloids, usually laid out on either a four- or a five-column format. All of the photos on this page are in color, and the main headline is set in all caps, 144-point demi-bold type.

A good dummy is proportional in size to the actual printed page. For a broadsheet page, a proportionate dummy page would be 6½ inches wide by 10½ inches deep, roughly half the actual size of the page. Or the dummy could be 8½ inches wide by 13½ inches deep, roughly 65 percent of the actual size. The point is that the layout dummy sheet should be proportional to the printed page (see Figure 11-14).

The first and most important rule of dummying the page is to keep the dummy neat and legible. The more precise and detailed the dummy, the better the chances of precise and accurate paste-up.

Basic guidelines

Sometimes, beginning editors peer at the blank computer screen or dummy sheet resting on the desk in front of them—what will eventually become their first page layout—and freeze, wondering how to begin. Following are some suggestions that may help.

▶**Choose the stories.** Before designing begins, the layout editor must assess the day's news. At small newspapers, news judgments may be made by the editor who also does

Figure 11-14
The broadsheet dummy (a) is scaled to the new narrower dimensions recommended by the Newspaper Association of America. This dummy sheet is for a six-column page and has inches marked along the left and right borders, columns marked across the top, and pica column widths across the bottom. The tabloid dummy (b) is scaled to a tabloid page, which is usually about 11 inches wide by 14 inches deep. This dummy sheet is for a five-column page and has inches marked along the left border.

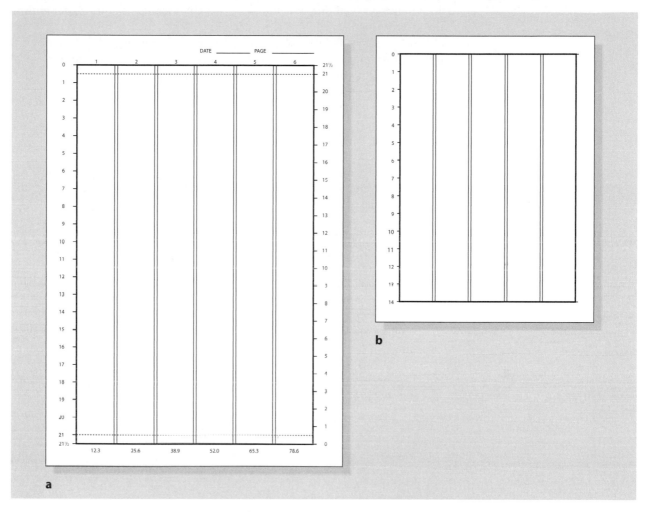

the layout. At midsize and large newspapers, however, the judgments about what stories are placed on which pages are made by news editors in consultation with other department editors at meetings called *story conferences* or *news meetings.* Section editors (sports, business, local news, wire news, lifestyle and so on) at morning newspapers usually bring the budgets, or summaries of each section's stories for that day, to the late-afternoon news meeting. Editors of evening newspapers have the same kind of meeting, but often very early in the morning because the newspaper "goes to bed," or gets put on the press, at midday. Regardless of the time of day, the editors bring all the major stories together and begin the process of assessing what stories, photos and art will be published in the next edition.

Most newspapers rely on the traditional news values discussed in Chapter 1 when judging the significance of stories:

- Timeliness

- Proximity

- Prominence

- Relevance

■ Unusualness

■ Conflict

■ Human interest

Judgments vary about which stories are significant, of course, depending both on the newspaper's philosophy and mission and on the individual editor's (or publisher's) interests or biases. Some newspapers emphasize local news; others emphasize national or international news. Some (especially morning papers) might put a premium on timeliness and consider last night's city council meeting important enough for Page One. Others (especially evening papers) might emphasize another news value, such as unusualness, and play up a story about a bizarre occurrence.

In addition to the traditional news values, editors also make judgments about what to publish based on a very pragmatic consideration—space. For each day of the week, and for each section of the paper, space for news is generally determined by the amount of advertising sold. Some publishers allow editors to allot a minimum number of columns of space each day. Others base the entire daily "news hole" on the amount of advertising sold and determine a news/advertising ratio. Often, publishers determine that 40 percent of the day's space will be devoted to news and 60 percent will be devoted to advertising. The more space advertisers buy, therefore, the more columns of news hole that can be allotted to the various sections (news, sports, features, business and so on).

The news services help local editors make news judgments by providing summaries of the major wire stories of the day. Often the news budgets, also called news digests, lead with the stories considered most important by the news-service editors. The Associated Press also transmits a separate list of stories that AP recommends editors consider for Page One.

▶**Dummy the standing items.** After decisions have been made about what stories to use on the page, the layout editor is ready to begin dummying. The first step is to dummy all the standing items, those elements that appear every day. For Page One, standing items include the nameplate (or flag), the index, promotional boxes (sometimes called refer boxes), the weather and so on. Usually, the nameplate appears at the top of the page, just under promotional boxes, if they are used. The index and weather often appear at the bottom of the page. In a paginated system, these items are already on the day's blank master page. Depending on the publication, these standard items will already have been updated for the edition or the layout editor (also called a designer) will have to update them.

▶**Choose and position the dominant element.** Next the layout editor selects and dummies the dominant visual element for the page. Often the dominant element is a piece of art—a photograph, illustration or infographic, such as a map. Sometimes the dominant element is a combination of several related elements, such as a story, a sidebar and a photograph all packaged in one modular unit. The page's dominant element is not necessarily the most significant or important story of the day; it simply is the most visually attractive and represents a point of entry for the reader's eye.

Placement of the dominant visual element automatically creates positions for the other elements on the page. The lead story, if it is not the dominant element, can be dummied above or adjacent to the dominant element. Secondary stories and packages can be placed below the dominant element. Special care should be taken, however, to make certain that the bottom of the page also contains interesting visual elements.

Actual markings on the dummy generally include the following:

- The areas allocated for all pieces of art—photographs, illustrations and infographics—are marked with a large *X* to distinguish them from stories.

- Stories that will be boxed are drawn as boxes on the dummy and are labeled with the story slug and the word *box*. Usually the size of the border rule to be used is noted as well (1-point, 2-point, and so on).

- Stories that will jump to an inside page are indicated by writing on the dummy the word *jump* and the page number to which the story will be continued.

- A small *x* usually signals the start of the story; a number sign (#) signals the end. Both symbols are circled on the dummy.

Pagination programs have adopted elements similar to what is drawn on a dummy. For example, drawing a graphics box in the program will create a box with an *X* in it. When a photo or graphic is ready for placement, the layout editor enters a command to place the photo or graphic in that box. Text, on the other hand, can be a different story. Some publications will create "dummy text" in their pagination systems as a placeholder until the real stories are ready. Either way, the layout editor is placing text of some kind, not a symbolic representation, making it doubly important to make sure dummy text doesn't actually run in print.

One difficult problem facing layout beginners is choosing headline sizes. Traditionally, headlines at the top of the page are larger than those at the bottom. Horizontal formats have changed that tradition, however, and today the length of the headline often is more of a determinant of size than is placement on the page.

Another factor is the design philosophy of the publication. Some newspapers are designed to use smaller headlines than other newspapers.

Here are some general rules for choosing headline sizes:

▶**One-column headlines.** Usually one-column heads range between 18- and 36-point type. The larger type size is generally used at the top of the page. A larger headline requires greater writing skill than a smaller one because of its short count (see Chapter 9). Most one-column headlines run two or three lines, although some contemporary newspapers allow five or six lines.

▶**Two-column headlines.** Generally two-column heads range between 24- and 42-point type; larger sizes appear near the top of the page. Most two-column headlines run two lines, although some newspapers allow three lines on larger-size headlines, such as those used on lead stories.

▶**Three-column headlines.** Generally three-column heads range between 36- and 48-point type. Most three-column headlines run two lines, although some newspapers allow one line with a kicker.

▶**Four-column headlines.** Generally four-column heads range between 36- and 60-point type, depending on placement on the page. Most four-column headlines are one line.

▶**Five- and six-column headlines.** These large heads range between 48- and 72-point type, depending on placement on the page. Some newspapers allow 36-point headlines on five- and six-column stories at the bottom of the page. Most five- and six-column headlines run one line.

Headline sizes and the number of lines are clearly marked on the dummy, as is the headline slug (first two words).

Pagination programs and digital editing systems make headline writing a much less arduous process than in eras past. At publications utilizing separate editing and design programs, headline writers can create a headline and use a "fit" command to test whether it will fit in a layout editor's design. The layout editor will then flow the headline in the spot set for it in the design program. More often, the layout editor will write the headline directly on the page, using keyboard or mouse commands to size it properly and rewriting as needed.

Good layout editors are careful to mark any special instructions on the dummy sheet. Such instructions might designate colors, screens, "refers" to related stories, special typesetting instructions or art sizes and the like. As a final check, the layout editor makes sure the dummy reflects the following do's and don'ts:

- Think about balance, contrast, proportion and unity as you dummy the page.

- Remember to work in modular units.

- Avoid tombstones (bumping headlines) unless your newspaper's design allows them.

- Avoid raw wraps (when a story wraps into an adjacent column without a covering headline).

- Avoid juxtaposing similar elements; don't dummy unrelated photographs next to each other, for example.

- On inside pages, avoid placing art adjacent to advertising.

- Avoid "paneling," allowing the gutter between columns to run the full length of the page.

Dummying Page One

Beginning layout editors can learn to dummy Page One by following the step-by-step procedures listed next, using as the model Figure 11-15, Page One of the Chronicle at Richland College in Dallas, Texas, and its paper dummy. Remember that in many newsrooms this page would be designed directly in the program with no dummy. Using a dummy can be helpful in "previsualizing" a page before committing it to pagination, however.

▶**1.** The first order of business when dummying a page is to make proper news judgments about the content; the form of the page will follow. In this case, the Chronicle's layout editor, probably in consultation with other senior editors on the staff, has decided to use these stories: *MADD*, lead story about a student killed by a drunk driver; *TB*, a story "localizing" the announcement about tuberculosis exposure in Dallas; *Mail*, about an unknown substance found in the campus mail; and *Briefs*, a series of short items about campus life.

▶**2.** The first six-column horizontal line on the dummy shows how deep the nameplate (or flag) is: about 2½ inches from the top of the page. The size of the nameplate is constant from day to day. The layout editor should designate on the dummy the ears within the nameplate.

▶**3.** Immediately under the nameplate, about 3½ inches from the top of the printed page, are two headlines, one for the anchored "News Briefs" column and another for the lead headline. The "Briefs" column is anchored in the same place for every issue. Because it is set in one long galley, the dummy does not require separate headline

Figure 11-15

The Chronicle at Richland College in Dallas, Texas, won second place for Page One design for two-year schools in the 2001 Associated Collegiate Press/Adobe Designs of the Year competition. Notice that the dummy for this Page One is neat and legible and that all elements are marked for easy identification. The Chronicle is paginated on QuarkXPress, but many campus editors are encouraged to create paper dummies as well.

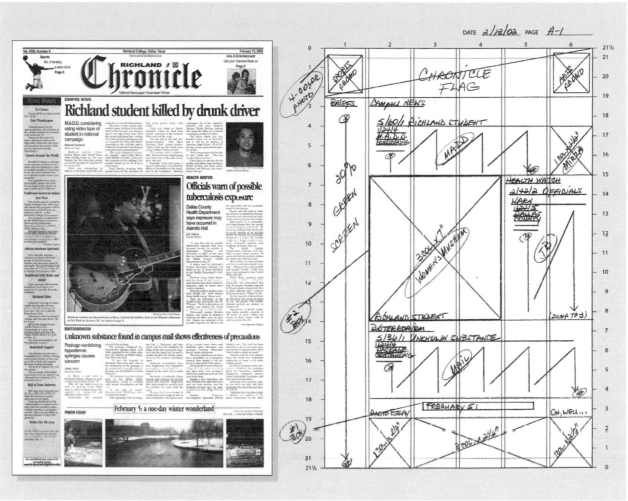

designations for each brief, although the layout editor may do so if he or she chooses. The lead headline is placed below a standard kicker, "Campus News," and is a five-column, one-line head, set in 60-point type. It is slugged on the dummy with the first two words of the headline, "Richland student." Both the kicker and the headline must be marked on the dummy. In addition, the lead headline has a drop headline, set in 24-point type, four lines deep and slugged "M.A.D.D. considering." The next headline down the page also is placed below a standard kicker, "Health Watch," and is two columns wide, set in 42-point type and two lines deep, with a drophead in 24-point type, five lines deep. The main headline is slugged "Officials warn," and the drophead is slugged "Dallas County." Note that lines are drawn on the dummy for each line of the headline; six lines are drawn and centered above the *MADD* story, one for the standard kicker, one for the five-column headline and four for the drophead. Eight lines are drawn and centered above the *TB* story, one for the standard kicker, two for the two-column headline and five for the drophead. Also note that the slugs of the stories, which may be different from the headline slugs, are written on the dummy as well.

▶ **4.** Adjacent to the *TB* story is a stand-alone photograph. Photographs and artwork are designated by an *X*. Each piece of art requires the marking of its size, a slug and the first couple of words of the cutline. The *Women's Museum* photo is three columns wide by seven inches deep and is marked 3 col × 7″ on the dummy. The cutline begins, "Richland student."

▶ **5.** The vertical lines drawn down the center of the columns show where the body copy is to be placed. Some layout editors mark a small *x* (circled) at the beginning of each story to help compositors paste up quickly. If a story extends across several columns, diagonal lines should be drawn to connect the legs of type. The vertical lines end in an arrow. An end mark (# circled) is also required if the story ends on the page. If the story jumps to another page, that fact should also be marked on the dummy (see "Jump to 3" on the *TB* story, for example).

▶ **6.** Borders or other unusual typographical treatments are marked in the margins of the dummy. Note the markings for colorizing the promos in the nameplate, for using a 20 percent green screen behind the News Briefs, and for using a No. 2 rule around the *Women's Museum* photograph.

▶ **7.** Type or artwork requiring special treatment should also be noted on the dummy. The three-photo layout across the bottom of the page, for example, is displayed with a boxed headline, a kicker below the headline and an unusually placed cutline above the far-right photo.

▶ **8.** The dummy is now ready to send to the composing room for paste-up or to a paginator. If the dummy is neat and accurate, the page will be produced just as the layout editor envisioned.

Dummying inside pages

Laying out pages inside the newspaper is at once easier and more difficult than laying out Page One or section covers. Although most of the same rules apply—such as maintaining a modular design—inside-page layout differs because inside pages contain advertisements.

Usually, layout editors for daily newspapers receive the inside-page dummies from the "product makeup" person in the advertising department the day before publication. Updated dummies may be delivered the day of publication as well. The product makeup person dummies ads on pages based on a variety of factors, including their size (only one five-column-by-17-inch ad will fit on a page, for example), their content (tire ads usually go in Sports, movie ads usually go in Entertainment), their use of color (only a few color positions are available), and their competition (competitors are not usually placed adjacent to each other).

Most modern newspapers and magazines are laid out using one of two advertising configurations: pyramid construction or modular construction (see Figure 11-16). In a pyramid format, ads are stacked either to the left or to the right on the page. News content touches each ad, as desired by the advertising department. In a modular format, ads are "squared off" across the bottom of the page. Some ads may be stacked atop others to accomplish this modular design.

Most editors like to work with a modular ad format because it is easier to design and it often improves the look of a newspaper or magazine. But for editors who must lay out stories and art around ads in a pyramid format, attractive design is still possible. Professor Daryl R. Moen, in his book "Newspaper Layout and Design," suggests that editors can create modular units with the nonadvertising space on a page by working off the corners of the ads. By that he means that editors may

Figure 11-16

In this pyramid ad layout, ads are dummied to the right of the page. In the modular layout, ads are squared off across the bottom of the page, giving editors greater flexibility in dummying stories and pictures.

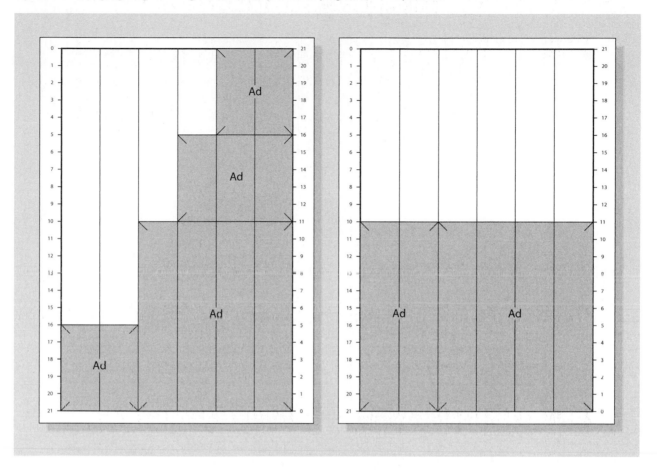

draw imaginary dotted lines from the corners of the ads to the margins of the page to create modular layout units (see Figure 11-17). Such modules may then be used for editorial copy and artwork.

Pagination

Pagination poses a special set of challenges for editing staffs that are responsible for both copy editing and page design. Most often known as **universal** copy desks, editors are charged with the task of effectively and accurately editing stories while designing several pages a shift, perhaps including the front page or B-section front.

Newspaper industry analysts predicted years ago that pagination would sweep through newsrooms in the 1980s and 1990s and that most U.S. newspapers would be fully paginated by the turn of the century. While pagination might have been slow to catch on for a variety of reasons, it is commonplace in the industry today in at least some form.

Bob Sims, writing in TechNews, a magazine about newspaper operations published by the Newspaper Association of America, wrote in mid-1999 that research indicated that about 70 percent of U.S. papers achieved some level of pagination, but only 26 percent were completely paginated and 3 percent were not paginating at all.

Figure 11-17

Designing modular units for editorial content is a matter of drawing imaginary dotted lines from the corners of the ads to the edge of the page. The letters designate the modular units created; each module may be divided into more modules.

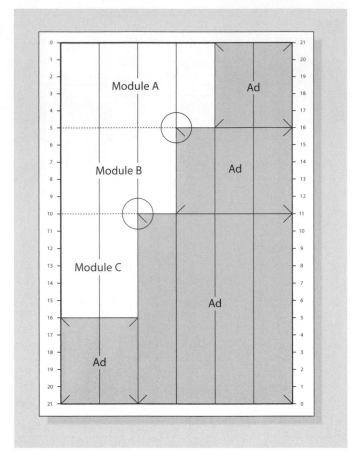

Figure 11-18

Pagination software, such as this QuarkXPress interactive design program, is expanding for Web use as more and more publications extend their franchises online.

The use of pagination has grown considerably since the 1990s. By 2006, in the estimation of David M. Cole, a newspaper consultant based in San Francisco who publishes a Web site about news technology (www.colegroup.com), only a handful of metropolitan newspapers were not paginating at least 90 percent of their design work.

According to Sims, a key turning point in the technology came in 1987, when QuarkXPress, "a desktop software that gave editors and designers the ability to shape pages as never before," was introduced (Figure 11-18).

In the meantime, other software manufacturers have appeared on the scene, in particular, Adobe, whose Illustrator and Photoshop software became the industry standard. In 1999 Adobe also released InDesign, a challenger to QuarkXPress. According to Sims, InDesign's design allows developers to tailor the program to specific customer needs. More recent updates of the software have allowed for greater integration between InDesign, Photoshop and Illustrator. Still, newspaper executives can spend years deciding which software brand fits their company best.

Sims noted, however, that the question of which software to choose may be less significant

Balancing copy editing and design

The North County Times, a merger of The North County Blade-Citizen and Times Advocate in north San Diego County, was one of the first daily newspapers in the country to introduce pagination to news and production. The Blade-Citizen began paginating at the start of the 1990s, successfully introducing a fully paginated newsroom to the merged Times by late 1995.

Q: At a newspaper where design and copy editing are combined, are there particular challenges to the job?

A: I think of them as opportunities more than challenges, but yes, there are different ways that you must budget your time on a universal desk. Paginators and designers often find themselves with free time while waiting for stories to arrive. Likewise, copy editors are in similar situations waiting for stories. In a universal situation, that free time can often be utilized designing when there's no copy to read and reading copy when there's nothing available to design. The challenge lies where there's a lot of both at the same time and how to prioritize your time to get the most accomplished.

Q: What are some advantages to having a combined copy/design desk?

A: Headlines. We've found the more paginators work with the copy and the more familiar they are with the stories, the better the headlines become. This is a particular advantage in a zoning situation like our own (different editions geared to specific communities) where the same story may have a one-column, four-deck headline in one zone and a six-column, one-deck in another.

Q: What usually comes first, copy editing or design?

A: Copy editing. The early stories are read and moved before much else is done in the day. Some paginators produce "shells" of their section front early in the day, especially when something unique is involved, but largely each day starts with copy reading.

Q: What might be some basic procedures to get the work done during a shift?

Michael Donnelly has been the night editor for the daily North County Times in Escondido, Calif., since March 2005. He has been with the North County Times since November 1999, when he was hired as the sports editor of the The Californian, the Times' sister paper in Temecula, Calif. Donnelly eventually went on to lead the copy desk there, moving to the Times as assistant night editor in May 2003. Before working for the Times and Californian, Donnelly worked at The Daily Star in Hammond, La., as a sports reporter.

A: Again, the trick lies in time management and making the most of downtime in the copy process and downtime in the design process. Proper ETAs on stories help give the paginator an opportunity to chart their day, and work around late and potential problem stories. Generally, we'll lock in our designs as best we can about three hours prior to deadline, and often get an incomplete proof done when one or more stories is estimated to be close to our deadline. This also frees up time later in the evening for the zoning process.

Q: Do you have any tips on how an editor/designer can handle their duties, especially in a deadline crunch?

A: There's a certain art to knowing what to do when in order to avoid downtime and the inevitable crunch at the end. But if all processes still conspire to provide the dreaded deadline adrenaline at the end of night, my advice would be this: Work big to small. Concentrate on the big things (headlines, cutlines, proper jump words, jump ends, etc.) and push the small things aside (body copy, design candy and aesthetics). Big will always get noticed ahead of small in these circumstances.

to the future of pagination than whether the system used to produce content can at the same time manage the workflow of all these activities. At many news companies, he said, Web-browser-powered intranets are already being used to train and inform workers. These intranets (databases) can handle archives, graphics and editorial systems. The advantage, he said, is that "by doing these things with a standard Internet

Figure 11-19
A designer uses a computer to plan a page layout. Pagination, the process of using a computer to place elements on a page, has become widespread in newsrooms, eliminating the paste-up stage of print production.

PHOTOGRAPH BY TOM FARRINGTON, SAN DIEGO STATE UNIVERSITY. COURTESY OF THE SAN DIEGO UNION-TRIBUNE.

browser and protocols, everyone can share information despite all the varied software and platforms found in a typical media company."

Full pagination means that editors can put together entire pages—including copy, ads, photos and graphics—on a computer terminal. Manipulating this much computer data requires sophisticated technology. The resulting material is then printed as a complete page, bypassing the paste-up function formerly served by compositors. Then the page is photographed, producing a negative from which a printing plate is made. Some systems use laser platemakers or direct-to-film output, eliminating the manual steps of both page paste-up and negative/plate production.

Publications using pagination systems have on-screen layout grids corresponding to the former paper dummies (see Figure 11-19). Editors may electronically position, move or remove from a page such elements as stories, captions, headlines, photographs and graphics. Type for stories is electronically wrapped from column to column, and the editor may watch this phenomenon on the video screen.

Editors who responded to a technology survey, cosponsored by the American Society of Newspaper Editors and the Society of Newspaper Design in 1996, indicated that no perfect model to integrate pagination into a newsroom's production process exists. What works for an editor in Maine might not work for an editor in Colorado. This remains true today.

Publishers and owners invest in pagination because it can result in substantial labor savings. However, many editors believe that at least one downside to pagination is that editing suffers as copy editors devote a disproportionate amount of their time to layout. "What do you lose?" asked one small-newspaper editor. "Stories that aren't read or are read only once. You lose overall thinking. Pagination has hurt our ability to edit." At the same time, editors believe that pagination helps put ultimate control of the content of the newspaper in the hands of newsroom personnel, resulting in the improvement of overall quality.

Newsletter layout

Most newsletters are designed to inform and to create a sense of unity among readers. Some newsletters emphasize factual information, whereas others are primarily opinion pieces. Many newsletters are published for an organization's members or a company's employees, whereas other newsletters are published and distributed for profit to subscribers, such as stock market investors. Still other newsletters serve audiences with a special interest, such as bird-watchers, college alumni or journalists.

Newsletters may be published in a small, letter-size format constructed from an 11-by-17-inch sheet of paper folded in half to create four pages. Others are tabloid-size publications that use a vertical format and are laid out similarly to tabloid newspapers (see Figure 11-20).

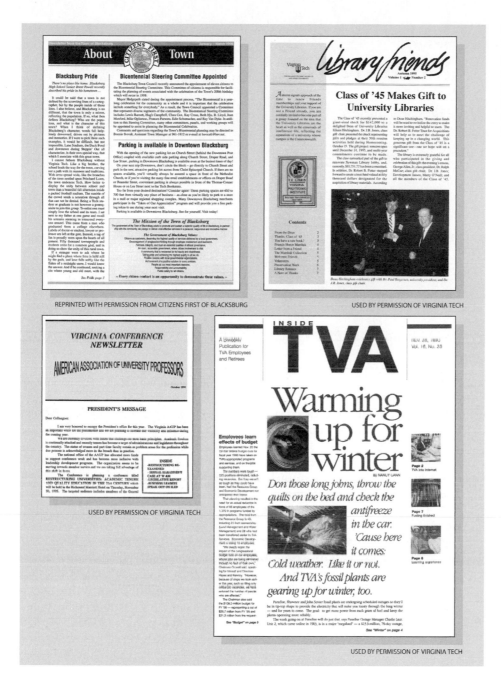

Figure 11-20
Newsletters come in all shapes and sizes. The format reflects the newsletter's purpose, distribution method and frequency, organizational culture, resources, and audience.

The basic principles of newspaper design, discussed earlier in this chapter, apply to newsletter design as well. There are, however, some special newsletter considerations.

Paul Swift, editor of The Newsletter on Newsletters (www.newsletterbiz.com) in Rhinebeck, N.Y., says simplicity is the key.

"The soul of newsletters—in both design and editorial content—is simplicity," he explains. "There's no need for an elaborate layout—as in glossy magazines—because you're not competing with fancy ads."

All four design principles—balance, proportion, contrast and unity—should be applied with a specific audience in mind. For example, a newsletter for stockholders of a conservative company might have a traditional formal design while a newsletter for Internet users might have a more contemporary look.

Figure 11-21
All design elements on a
page have weight and are
used to achieve a balanced
layout.

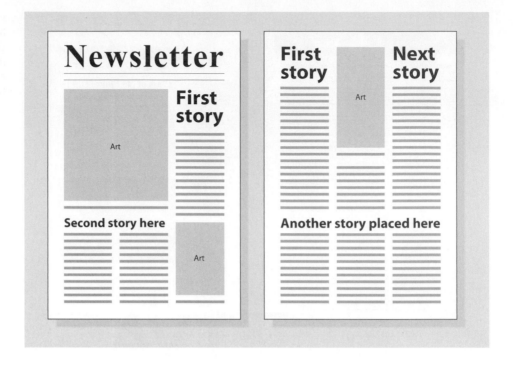

Newsletter format also determines how design elements are applied. A large, tabloid-size newsletter can support larger graphics and headlines than a standard-size, four-page newsletter.

Some beginning designers find it easier to use a symmetrical, formally balanced design rather than the asymmetrical design used by many newspapers. Recall, however, that balance does not mean you must have equal amounts of text to text or art to art. All elements of design have weight, including open space and color (see Figure 11-21).

It is helpful to think of proportion, a ratio or relationship measure, in terms of larger and smaller elements on a page. For example, in an article with accompanying art, if the copy and headline consume two-thirds of the space assigned to the story, the art and cutline, if in proportion, would take one-third of the space. Conversely, if a large photograph takes two-thirds of the assigned space, the proportional amount of body copy, including headline, would take the remaining one-third of the space.

With the overall look of the newsletter in mind, editors develop specifications for design elements such as type size and family for body copy and headlines, borders, art, typographical devices and use of open space and color. "Stick to only two typefaces, maybe three if you count sidebars and captions," Swift notes.

Of the many considerations, one of the most important is the basic grid for the newsletter: the number of columns and the widths of external and gutter margins.

Most newsletters have three columns because of the flexibility the design affords. The three-column format allows editors to give primary emphasis to a story by using a one-, two- or three-column headline. With a two-column format, article emphasis can be more difficult because the headline and story widths are limited to either one or two columns (see Figure 11-22). A one-column format with a wide margin is another functional newsletter layout (see Figure 11-23). Four columns are rarely used for an 8½-by-11-inch page size because the narrow column width causes excessive end-of-line hyphenation. A five-column format is typically reserved for tabloid-size newsletters.

Avoid jumping articles, Swift suggests. If a story needs to jump, send it to the next page as opposed to several pages in.

Figure 11-22
Two- and three-column grids are the most common in newsletters.

Figure 11-23
Another functional newsletter design has a single column and a wide margin, which can be left blank or used for graphics, headlines, pull quotes or other content. This is the format used for the pages of this textbook.

Once the name for the newsletter is decided, the next task is to design a nameplate to showcase it. Typically, a newsletter nameplate has a unique design. Achieving the simplicity of an attractive, attention-getting design is extremely difficult, a job best left to a graphic designer. Although perfectly acceptable nameplates have been designed by editors, the extra expense of hiring a graphic artist to create a nameplate is money well spent.

A newsletter's distribution method also influences its design and layout. When newsletters are designed as self-mailers and not distributed within companies and organizations or inserted in an envelope, editors face the additional restrictions of folding, address and postal requirements. For example, without an envelope you will need to decide where to place the address on your newsletter. As a general rule, select an area that meets postal regulations but consumes as little space as possible. Rather than leaving half a page of a folded, 8½-by-11-inch newsletter for an address, consider two folds, which reduces the address space to a third of a page.

Once determined, design specifications should remain constant from issue to issue. A consistent corporate or organizational image allows readers to more quickly identify with the organization or company. Readers take pleasure in the ability to recognize their newsletter from all others and to find their favorite features or opinion columns quickly in each issue.

Production considerations

Type of paper, use of color, and frequency and method of distribution all affect the cost of a newsletter. To reduce expenses, you should consider the following questions:

- Can your newsletters go third-class mail, not first class? Although third class is slower and special postal restrictions apply, postage is cheaper.

- Can the newsletter qualify for bulk mailing or presorting discounts? Check with the Postal Service and consider these options.

- Can you use a cheaper, lightweight paper, or does the overall newsletter appearance and organizational image require a more expensive, heavier-weight paper? Paper weight affects mailing costs.

- Can your newsletter be a self-mailer? Envelopes add to the cost.

- Can the newsletter be distributed through interoffice mail or left at predetermined drop-off points? Does it have to be mailed?

- Can you achieve the desired effect with colored paper stock or a dark ink other than black? An added color necessitates an additional press run, increasing printing costs.

- Can your newsletter be a two-fold rather than a three-fold? Every fold requires additional time and money.

- Can you publish once a month instead of every two or three weeks? How timely does the newsletter need to be?

Magazine layout

The basic principles of design—balance, contrast, proportion and unity—as well as the six design elements described in this chapter apply to both newspapers and magazines. Likewise, newspaper and magazine editors follow similar guidelines to design pages.

Formats

Magazine formats, meaning the shape, size and style of the publication, vary more than the typical broadsheet or tabloid format of newspapers. During their careers, magazine editors might lay out small, pocket-size magazines (Reader's Digest, TV Guide), or 8½-by-11-inch pages (Time, Newsweek) or even large-format 10½-by-13-inch pages (Life magazine). Printing press mechanical limitations influence publishers' format decisions. In addition, magazine editors must consider using only standard paper stock sizes to avoid waste when multiple pages are placed together on one large sheet of paper to go through the printing press.

A magazine's primary purpose also plays a major role in format choices because content, ranging from primarily text, primarily art or an equal mix of the two, flows from purpose. If the purpose is to convey information—from television listings to scholarly research results—then text, not photographs, will dominate pages. This makes the additional paper and postage costs of a large-format publication unwarranted. If, however, photography best suits the purpose of a fashion magazine, for example, then the larger the page, the more impact good photographs and drawings will have.

A magazine's subject matter also helps set its style or tone, another aspect of its format. Serious subject matter needs a more conservative approach to layout and design than less serious subjects.

Most magazines today, unlike Life and Look magazines of two generations ago, serve special-interest audiences, not broad cross-sections of the population. This niche approach enables magazines to attract advertising targeted at special audiences. By the same token, special-interest audiences vary widely in their enjoyment or appreciation of wild, splashy graphic designs as contrasted with low-key, traditional design elements. Magazine editors, like successful newspaper editors, must know their audiences and tailor layout and design accordingly.

Basic guidelines for magazine layout

After identifying the subject matter, target audience and purpose and taking into account available printing facilities, graphic designers create an overall format for a magazine. With the magazine's basic design and "look" in place, editors and designers, working in tandem, plan page layouts to display content most effectively and imaginatively.

▶ **Use a layout grid.** A *grid* is a layout sheet with page margins drawn to show the printed area of the page, plus vertical and horizontal lines dividing the printing area into multiple rectangles, referred to as modules. The grid shows columns, like a typical newspaper layout sheet, plus horizontal lines. In fact, some newspapers use layout sheets with both vertical and horizontal lines. For magazines, double-page grids rather than single pages are the norm. Here are three samples of magazine grids: a two-column, a three-column, and a grid with two equal columns plus a narrower column on the outer side of each page.

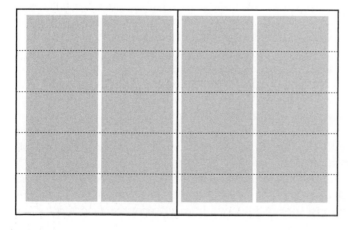

Two-column grid

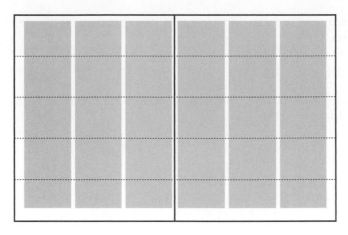

Three-column grid

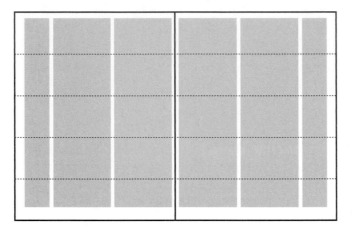

Varied column widths

Some editors prefer to use paper grid sheets, either the same size as their magazine pages or a miniature, proportional size. Others use layout and graphic design software to create computer templates.

Grids help layout editors align text and art elements to maintain a unified, orderly look to pages throughout the magazine. This does not mean that every page or double-page spread looks exactly alike, which would be boring. But when editors adhere to a basic grid from spread to spread, it gives readers a foundation. Readers want variety, but they also want enough consistency to recognize that all spreads are part of the same magazine.

▶**Use consistent and progressive margins.** As with newspapers, the open space surrounding the page acts as a frame for the elements on that page. Margins should be the same throughout the magazine, and no type should extend beyond the margins.

Most magazines use progressive margins, meaning that the smallest width is the gutter margin, the side where facing pages come together. Margin widths increase progressively around the page, counterclockwise for left-hand pages and clockwise for right-hand pages. This places the widest margin at the bottom of pages, in keeping with the principle that a page's optical center is slightly higher than its geometric center. The gutter margin is typically half as wide as the bottom margin. If gutter margins are too wide, the alley of open space between two facing pages visually separates instead of unifying the spread.

Some magazine designers insist that at least one layout element—art, display or body type—touch every margin on each double-page spread. Certainly this should be the practice on most spreads to maintain margin consistency through the magazine.

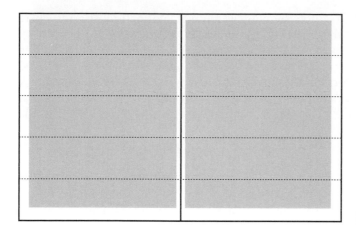

Progressive margins

For special effect, editors occasionally allow photographs to extend beyond margins and **bleed** off the edge of the paper, giving the art greater impact. Depending on its content and composition, the photo can give the illusion of extending indefinitely instead of stopping at the edge of the page. Bleeding beyond margins also provides editors with several picas of space for more layout. Two cautions about bleeds:

- Never bleed type because letters can be cut away when printed pages go through the folding and trimming process.

- Either bleed artwork off the edge of the page or stop at the established margin; bleeds aren't a halfway proposition.

▶ **Work in double-page spreads.** Magazine layout editors must work in double-page spreads because readers see facing pages when they open a magazine. If advertising occupies part of the spread or if a one-page article is on the left-hand page and a new article begins on the right, the layout editor must design for best effect. Some techniques:

- Use a two-column layout for one page and a three-column for the other.

- Don't let photographs or other art compete for attention. Art for a new article starting on the right can be placed later in the article on the next spread.

- Box one page or use a tint block to set the articles apart.

- Use different display type on each page.

Ideally, the layout editor works with two facing pages for the start of a new article. To link the two pages into one unit, design elements must cross the gutter without disappearing into it. Never let type fall into the gutter. Keep body type within the margins and make sure that the gutter space falls between words if display type crosses from one page to the other. If you bleed photographs across the gutter, make sure that faces, or the center of action, in the photograph aren't lost.

To understand the concept of facing pages requires a little knowledge about magazine printing and binding and the **imposition** of pages on a printing press. Magazine pages are grouped together (imposed) and printed on both sides of large sheets of paper that are called **press sheets.** Each side of the sheet is called a **printing flat.** After the sheets are printed, they are folded and trimmed, producing a four-page, eight-page, 16-page or 32-page **signature.** A **natural spread** is a pair of facing pages within a printing signature that falls on the same side of the printing flat.

If the two facing pages are not a natural spread, alignment problems can result, causing two sides of a photograph or a continuing border to look slightly out of kilter.

By the same token, layout editors should take advantage of natural spreads where photos or rules can cross the gutter with alignment assured.

Imposition varies from printer to printer, based on several factors, including how sheets are turned over and gripped on the press after one side has been printed ("work-and-turn" or "work-and-tumble" methods). Magazine editors should ask their printer for a printer's dummy, which shows placement of pages on the press sheet and how that sheet will be folded and trimmed so that pages will be in the proper order.

Editors seeking to get the most color into their magazines for the least cost must know which pages fall on the same side of a printing flat. As explained earlier in this chapter, a page must go through the printing press four times for process (full) color. If all process color within one printing signature is placed on pages imposed on the same side of the printing flat, printing costs are less than if color photos are placed on both sides of the flat.

The number of pages determines the number of printing signatures needed for a magazine, which in turn influences how magazine pages are bound for delivery. The large size of broadsheet newspaper pages makes binding unnecessary, but magazine pages must be stapled or glued to keep them from falling apart.

Two types of magazine binding are saddle-stitched and perfect. For **saddle-stitched** binding, signatures of folded and trimmed pages fit into each other on a V-shaped saddle, and stitches, usually wire staples, go into the back and fold at the center spread. Newsweek and Sports Illustrated are examples of saddle-stitched bindings. In a 64-page saddle-stitched magazine printed in two 32-page signatures, for example, page 1 and page 64 will be imposed on the printing press in the same signature and on the same side of the flat.

Saddle stitching is insufficient to hold together thick magazines. The number of pages at which a magazine outgrows saddle stitching depends largely on the paper stock it uses. In **perfect** binding, signatures are stacked on top of each other and glued together within a four-page cover (front, back, inside front and inside back pages). For example, a 128-page perfect-bound magazine printed in four 32-page signatures would have page 1 and page 32 in the first signature, page 33 and page 64 in the second signature, page 65 and page 96 in the third, page 97 and page 128 in the fourth signature. All four signatures would be glued inside a four-page cover signature.

▶ **Start with a dominant center of interest.** Once the layout editor establishes a grid pattern, the first decision about page content is to select an element to give the double-page spread a center of visual impact. To immediately attract readers' attention, a large, dramatic photo, strong informational graphic or perhaps a typographical special effect like an oversized initial letter or tint block provides a starting point for looking at the spread. Without such a dominant center, layout elements compete for readers' attention and make the spread seem confusing and disorderly (see Figure 11-24).

▶ **Align elements with the grid pattern.** Once the dominant element is in place, other artwork, display type, body type or borders are placed in alignment on the layout grid. Alignment can be vertical, horizontal or both, as shown in Figure 11-25. Dominant and secondary elements can be placed in relation to each other to achieve perfect balance or informal balance.

Careful alignment demands absolute accuracy in copyfitting and photo cropping and sizing. Layout shouldn't dictate content of copy blocks, but creative editing can often trim a line or two to bring a copy block into perfect alignment with another page element. Editors must copyfit more precisely for magazine layouts than for newspaper pages.

Figure 11-24
These double-page spreads from The Razorback at the University of Arkansas feature strong photographs as the center of visual impact. Creative use of headline type, large caption lead-ins and ragged right copy blocks also add visual interest.

USED WITH PERMISSION OF THE RAZORBACK AT THE UNIVERSITY OF ARKANSAS

▶**Plan open space.** News magazines, academic journals and many other magazines whose primary purpose is to impart information fill most of the space on each page, much like typical newspaper pages. Other magazines go for an open, airy look with ample amounts of open space on facing pages. Editors must plan the effective use of open space carefully. The amount of space between design elements—called ***internal margins***—should be a consistent width, often one pica. Larger blocks of open space should be placed to the outer edges of double-page spreads, never trapped doughnut-fashion in the center, giving the visual effect of elements pushed apart rather than unified.

Figure 11-25
The headline is the dominant center of interest in this spread from the Columbia Journalism Review. In the original, the word *lust* was printed in red. The photograph on the right page aligns with the top of the subhead, and the small photo in the lower left corner aligns with the byline. Under the byline, the first paragraph of the story exactly fills the space to touch the bottom margin, illustrating careful copyfitting.

▶**Control eye direction.** The dominant center of the spread alerts readers to the starting point, but from there the layout editor must place elements to create visual motion to guide readers' eyes in the intended direction. English speakers are accustomed to reading from left to right, so a logical starting point for headlines and body copy is the upper left of a double-page spread. The dominant center of interest may be elsewhere on the spread, but a secondarily strong element, such as a graphic or large headline, must draw attention to the upper left. Alternately, the dominant visual center may occupy the upper left spot, with display type immediately below or to the right.

Other elements that influence the direction of eye movement are borders and rules or photographs depicting action or faces. The action within a picture or the eyes of photo subjects should face into the double-page spread, not off the page toward the right, which visually invites readers to turn the page.

▶**Work for contrast.** Variety in sizes, shapes and textures gives page spreads life and makes them more visually exciting. Art should be rectangular—rarely, if ever, any hearts, star shapes or weird cutouts—but the size and shape of the rectangles should vary. Variations among widths of borders and rules and percentages for screens or tint blocks can also create contrast.

While using contrast for best effect, editors want to reflect a sense of harmony in the overall look of the magazine. This can be achieved with some standardization on each spread—perhaps the body type or something as simple as the folio lines—but the subject matter and tone of each article should guide its layout and design. An article predicting future technological developments, for example, would dictate different type and layout treatment than an article depicting pioneer life in the 1800s.

Once the mood is set on the opening spread of an article, it should remain consistent on subsequent pages of that article. Figure 11-26 from two university yearbooks illustrates effective use of open space and contrast.

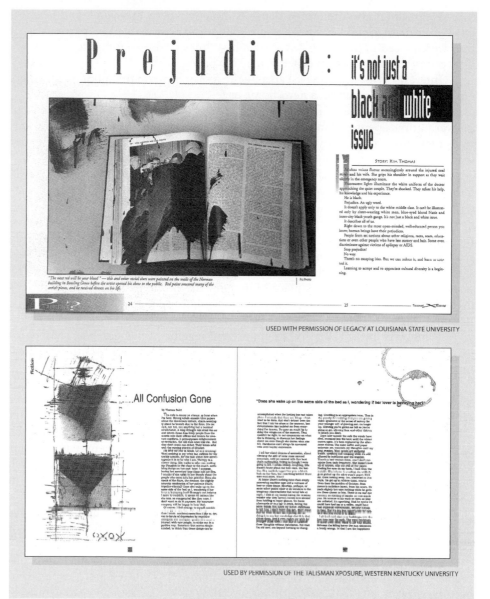

Figure 11-26
Each spread illustrates effective use of open space and contrast. The top example is from the Legacy at Louisiana State University, and the example below it was published in Talisman Xposure at Western Kentucky University.

Web layout and design

As noted throughout this book, professionals who design pages for both traditional print media and the Web agree that most rules of classic design also apply on the Web. Designing for the Web simply opens up a new range of possibilities.

Considering those possibilities, it's important to understand how viewers perceive Web pages. Research done in 2004 offers some insight as to how a Web user physically navigates a news home page with his or her eyes.

The project, called Eyetrack III, found a general pattern in the viewers who participated in the research. Eyetrack III was a collaboration of The Poynter Institute, the Estlow Center for Journalism & New Media, and Eyetools.

"The eyes most often fixated first in the upper left of the page, then hovered in that area before going left to right," the researchers stated in their report. "Only after perusing the top portion of the page for some time did their eyes explore further down the page."

Eyetrack III also discovered that—as in newspapers, magazines and newsletters—dominant headlines drew the eye's attention first on a page, particularly if they were placed in the upper-left corner. Headlines were also found to be effective if placed in the upper-right corner of the Web page.

Interestingly—unlike newspapers—the research found that photographs were not a typical entry point on a news home page.

"Text rules on the PC screen," the researchers noted, "both in order viewed and in overall time spent looking at it." Eyetrack III also found that smaller text seems to attract closer reading by viewers, while larger type tends to encourage lighter scanning.

In newspaper design, focus is often on what grabs a reader "above the fold," followed by items below the fold of the paper that could also grab a reader's attention once they pick it up and unfold it. The same could be said about news home pages, based on Eyetrack III research. Among the test subjects, items below the initial screen where the viewer would have to scroll down were not as deeply read as the first impression, so to speak. What happens after that first impression is that viewers scroll down actively looking for something to grab them. The researchers referred to items placed lower on the home page to grab a viewer's eye as **hot spots**—headlines or blurbs about something particularly interesting or newsworthy.

While Web design concepts might present specific challenges, Web technology imposes its own set of design limitations. Editors must understand the technical limitations of their medium and work within them.

Two limitations of current Web technology influencing designers are bandwidth constraints and lack of total control over how pages will appear on computer screens. Limited bandwidth adds to the time it takes pages to appear on computer screens, discouraging designers from taking advantage of exciting Web features such as animated graphics, and video and sound clips. Once loaded to individual computer screens, pages vary in appearance according to the brand and version of Web browser used and readers' personalized default font selections (see discussion in Chapter 8).

The quality of the user's monitor also influences how pages appear. Whereas designers can control type and color selection for printed pages, the same level of control is not possible with current Web technology.

Just as their counterparts at newspapers, newsletters and magazines don't operate printing presses or analyze computer systems, Web editors aren't expected to become wizards at HTML, JavaScript or cascading style sheets, or at creating mouse-over tricks, snapping buttons, crackling menus, pop-up windows or whatever Web innovation emerges next. Staff members or contract personnel hired for their computer skills perform those tasks, and develop templates for writers and editors to insert copy and images to build Web pages. Experts in the computer intricacies of creating and maintaining Web sites are referred to as **webmasters.**

Still, editors should know enough about the fundamentals of good Web site design and page layout so that they, rather than computer technicians, dictate a Web site's overall appearance, usability and content. Effective communication is the site's primary goal, not to show off the multimedia potential of the Web.

Content, not technical gimmickry, is key to the Web. Recall the five Web site purposes described in Chapter 4—personal, advocacy, informational, marketing and news. Good ideas for content executed in good writing and editing will enhance any site, regardless of its purpose. The Web's full complement of visual and sound effects, on the other hand, is not uniformly appropriate for all types of Web sites.

Clean, simple design is essential for Web sites, noted designer Roger Black explains in his book, "Web Sites That Work." Accessible design includes minimal, consistent choices in typefaces and graphics, straightforward color schemes and useful content.

"A reader should never have to plow through forests of buttons to get simple news," Black says in the book, explaining that content, not decoration, should guide a Web page's design.

It is relatively easy to create Web sites today, either by learning HyperText Markup Language (HTML) or with the aid of readily available Web-authoring software. At this writing, serious Web site builders prefer the greater flexibility and creativity they achieve by writing their own HTML instead of relying on off-the-shelf software. Several programs are on the market, however, that allow varying degrees of sophistication in designing Web pages—software such as Dreamweaver (an industry standard recently acquired by Adobe) and even QuarkXPress, print design software that now incorporates Web page design capabilities. With diligence and patience, anyone who may not have sophisticated computer knowledge can incorporate the Web's sophisticated multimedia features.

Books exist to lead newcomers through the process, but usually the most up-to-date information about the ever-changing Internet world resides on the Web itself. Online references for HTML tags and Web-building information are among the resources listed in Chapters 4 and 8 of this textbook. Internet search engines, also described in Chapter 4, can uncover even more online help.

The purpose of this Web layout and design section is to teach editors how to evaluate sites and communicate with Web designers and computer technicians so that the informational purposes of sites receive top priority and aren't overwhelmed by the bells and whistles of Web technology.

Mapping a Web site

Editors find paper and pencil dummies useful in determining the overall look of individual Web pages, much as newspaper and magazine page designers use dummies or layout sheets. However, Web designers must give additional consideration to planning an entire Web site and determining how individual Web pages work within that site. This is not to underestimate the attention editors give to ordering newspaper and magazine pages, but designers for traditional print media generally can assume that readers see the cover or front page of the publication and that readers know what publication they are reading. Web surfers, however, can enter a page from anywhere in the virtual world, not necessarily through the front door. People often arrive at a site by using search engines, URLs they receive from friends and colleagues and links from other pages.

Editors and Web designers must structure their site carefully so that users know exactly where they are within it, what else the site contains and how to get to selected pages quickly. In Web terminology, planning the site's individual sections and pages is referred to as mapping, architecting or storyboarding the site.

Hierarchical arrangements work well for Web sites. A *hierarchy* is a treelike structure that begins with a single point, or *node,* which describes the most general aspect of a topic. This node, often referred to as the root, is then divided into branches that contain increasingly specific information. For example, a Web site about basketball might include branches for professional, college, high school and youth leagues. Offshoots for each playing level could be separate segments of the site for men's and women's teams with secondary branches for each individual professional team, each NCAA division, subdivided further by conferences, followed by each college team, and so on. This tree structure could comprise thousands of individual pages. Web designers recommend building deep sites with short pages because testing shows that users tend to prefer short pages with clear navigational tools.

Helping readers navigate a site

Like its namesake spider web, a site on the World Wide Web is a complex structure of intricately woven threadlike filaments. Editors and site designers must work together to craft navigational devices that help readers move through the site efficiently, avoiding entanglements in the spider web of pages.

The front door or first page of a Web site is called the ***home page.*** A home page, at a minimum, should show the name of the site, identification of its sponsor, a list of major subject categories it covers and navigational tools for moving from page to page within the site. In his book "Redesigning Print for the Web," Mario Garcia, a print media and Web site designer, refers to subject categories as "baskets." A news site's home page might have four or five well-defined baskets—news, business, sports, community, entertainment—identified on the home page, with sub-baskets of content on inside pages. Even though the trend seems to call for more elements on a news medium's home page, including advertising, page designs should not be overly complex or busy; otherwise, site visitors can't get a quick read of what's available.

The opening page of xpress.sfsu.edu, shown in Figure 11-27, uses a design that, in addition to the latest news, has links to promote particular features, such as job listings blogs, podcasts and a photo gallery. Other navigational tools on the opening screen offer calendar listings and a search engine. Unlike most news Web sites, The Golden Gate [X]Press does not have advertising on its home page, although other pages on the site do.

Buttons, icons, labels, headlines, words within sentences and toolbars at the top, bottom or along the side of a page serve as typical navigational tools. Black, an award-winning print and Web designer who has worked for The New York Times and Rolling Stone magazine, argues that icons make better hypertext links than simple text because they are more intuitive, but not all designers agree.

Also, images take longer to download. In fact, users may turn off their browser's image capabilities to save download time. For that reason, editors should insist that images be accompanied in HTML scripts by ***ALT tags***—text that identifies content and provides a link for users to select if they aren't viewing images. The alternate text and accompanying images will not appear simultaneously on the screen, so they aren't redundant.

Whether in the form of images or text, all pages need pointers or highlighted labels so that users always know where they are within a site and what they can expect if they click to a different page within the site. As shown in Figure 11-28, a pointer in the sfgate.com index panel along the upper left of the screen shows that "Today's

Figure 11-27
The Web site of The Golden Gate [X]Press uses a series of lists and tabs to help readers find their way to the news and information they are seeking. The site also includes interactive features such as a photo gallery (a central focal point of the page), podcasts and blogs.

USED BY PERMISSION OF THE GOLDEN GATE [X]PRESS

Figure 11-28
The San Francisco Chronicle Web site was designed a couple of years ago to resemble the print version of Page One, with promo boxes above the nameplate and no advertising, at least at first glance (advertising does appear as the reader scrolls down the page). Links to the site's various sections appear at the left of the page as well as directly under the nameplate. "Pink" is a pseudonym for a popular Sunday entertainment section called Datebook, which used to be printed on pink newsprint. Today's Chronicle Web site has done away with promos and has lots of ads.

Chronicle," which is highlighted in a different color than all the other index items, is now loaded.

Current Web bandwidth constraints increase the importance of designing sites so that pages load to the user's computer as quickly as possible. For that reason, page logos, if used, should be simple but distinctive. Web sites and individual Web pages should be uncluttered so that users don't waste time loading or deciphering content. Experts recommend stripping from sites all doodads that add nothing to the information or navigation.

In consideration of variations in browsers, Web editors should avoid reference to particular browsers because it is impossible to know which browsers individual readers are using. For the same reason, editors shouldn't instruct users to "select a number" from a list. Just link a keyword or number because not all browsers accommodate number selection. Web users will understand how their particular browser works to connect to a link, so it isn't necessary to tell them to "click here" or "select this link." Editors should check for logic and ease of navigation within a single page, especially one that requires readers to scroll through several screens. A listing like a table of contents at the top or side of the document with each item linked to its place within the document will enable readers to jump to specific portions.

Consider whether the end of each section of the document needs a link to take readers back to the table of contents at the top of the page. Links can be an integral part of screen displays to emphasize text and make it easier for readers to skim. Like boldfaced words in a copy block, however, links can be overdone and will disrupt the flow of reading. Choose links that support sentence and concept structure, and try to match the link text users click on with the title of the resulting page.

Test all links frequently, especially links to sites owned by others. Web pages and even entire sites are transient. A great list of links to additional information about a subject covered on a company's site is useless if the linked pages no longer exist. If people hit dead ends, they get frustrated and doubt the accuracy of information contained on the referring site, figuring if the links aren't reliable, neither is the other information.

Editing pages within a site

Editors handling layout and design for Web sites—whether the sponsor is a news organization, a company, an association or a nonprofit organization—should follow the design principles discussed earlier in this chapter. Once editors ensure that the site's hierarchical structure and navigational tools are sound, they can turn their attention to the layout and design of individual pages within the site. Items to consider are discussed in this section.

▶**Tables.** Bandwidth constraints, browser variations and computer screen resolution problems were described earlier in this chapter. Other Web technology limitations for editors are the inability to control spacing (leading) between lines of type and difficulty in placing elements precisely on pages (see discussion in Chapter 8). Tables come in handy for addressing the latter problem.

HTML tags can be inserted to create tables that break text or images into columns, much like columns in printed publications. Web editors must take into account, however, that newspaper-style columns running the entire length of a page won't work for placing long articles on Web pages. Such an arrangement would force readers to scroll up and down, perhaps for several screens, from the bottom of a column to the top of the next column. Typically, editors and webmasters use tables to design multicolumn pages. A common layout features a narrow column containing a table of contents and navigational tools on the left side of the page with the remaining page width divided into two or more columns. The Los Angeles Times has developed an unusual five-column format, which places the contents and navigational tools on the left side of the page; runs advertising down the right side of the page; and sandwiches news content in between. The Web site is shown in Figure 11-29, as is that of the Public Relations Society of America, which includes a horizontal scrolling news ticker.

▶**Frames.** The Web technique of framing divides a page into two or more mini-pages, each separately scrollable. Although some attractive, effective sites employ this Web technique, most news media sites do not. Frames are in disfavor with designers and users because they exacerbate the load-speed problem and cause headaches if users try to save the page electronically or print it.

▶**Page length.** To scroll or not to scroll? Research of users in the earliest years of the Web indicated that only 10 percent scrolled beyond the information visible on the screen when a page appeared. Thus, designers worked to place all critical content and navigation options on the top part of the page and to avoid pages that filled more than one screen. More recent studies show, however, that users are more willing to scroll now for interesting content than they were earlier because it is faster to scroll to subsequent computer screens than wait for a new page to load. This may change in the future if increased bandwidth permits pages to load significantly faster.

Still, editors and designers should take advantage of the nonlinear features of the Web and devise ways to break long stories into multiple angles, each with a separate page. Readers can decide for themselves whether to follow all links or to select particular ones. This will automatically result in brief stories and minimize scrolling. To facilitate printing or saving to personal computers, editors can instruct webmasters to provide a separate page combining all segments of multiple-page documents.

In mid-1998, for example, boston.com, a pioneer in today's ubiquitous city sites, redesigned its home page, moving away from a compact design with navigational buttons that steered visitors to the extensive content of The Boston Globe and its Web partners. The redesigned opening page was lengthy, requiring extensive

a

Figure 11-29
The Los Angeles Times site
(a) was designed on a five-
column format, including
one for advertising, one for
navigational labels and the
other three for news. The
Public Relations Society
of America home page
(b) features navigational
buttons across the top of
the page with a horizontal
scrolling news ticker to the
center-right. Reproduced
here in black and white,
both sites use color
effectively.

b

Figure 11-30

The home page for boston.com, a city site sponsored by The Boston Globe, switched from a compact design to one with more content that requires scrolling. The screens are combined here.

scrolling to see all the headlines and story summaries with links to full stories and photographs (see Figure 11-30). The site has since been refined to include clearer section headings, more graphics and advertising.

This same trend soon became apparent worldwide as Web sites, particularly those sponsored by news organizations, reverted to a more traditional newspaper look with greater emphasis on news or other textual content.

▶ **Page backgrounds.** Anything that can be produced as a digital image can be incorporated into a page background, referred to as "wallpaper." The key rule is to avoid backgrounds that interfere with legibility. Generally, avoid patterns or photographs because they increase download time and decrease legibility of type. White backgrounds enhance legibility over the gray used by default in many browsers.

▶ **Color.** If you use background colors other than white, be careful about text color. Black type on a dark blue background, for example, is difficult to read and vice versa. Text set in light hues isn't as easy to read as brighter hues. Black and red are the most legible colors with a white or appropriately colored background.

Avoid the temptation to use too many colors on a page, causing the page to lack unity and giving it an overly busy appearance. Color works well to emphasize items on a page, as well as provide readers a sense of their place on the Web. Color can also improve the perceived resolution of images (see Figure 11-31).

Editors used to insist that the default colors for hypertext links be maintained because readers expected them to be blue then change to purple or red after a link had been visited. This particular color scheme is no longer viewed as necessary, although most news Web sites continue to use blue as the hypertext link color. At some sites, the blue changes to gray or a gray-blue after a user visits the link, but at many others the original hypertext link color, whether black, blue or red, remains the same even after a user has visited the link. This practice may confuse some readers and cause them to get lost within the site or leave without exploring it fully. Changing the color of the original link after it has been visited allows readers to retrace their steps or prevents them from selecting links that already have been followed. It also alerts readers to the new territory that remains to be explored within the site.

▶ **Graphics.** A good rule is to minimize the use of graphics files and to use ALT tags so pages make sense with graphics switched off. Likewise, use Java scripts and constantly running animations sparingly except perhaps for personal Web pages. Even though more phone and cable companies are offering high-speed Internet

Figure 11-31
A Web promotion for the "Weekend Best" (a) pops up on the screen when a reader accesses the Sunday Dallas Morning News. The promotion embraces the design concept of simplicity and uses an elegant color combination of red (page background), white (text background), gray (screen on "Best of News") and black (type). The Web site of the Eugene (Ore.) Register-Guard (b) is one of the few in the United States to offer readers the opportunity to download a PDF file of Page One of its print version. Both the Web version and the print version use color extremely well.

a   REPRINTED WITH PERMISSION OF BELO INTERACTIVE, INC.   b   REPRINTED COURTESY OF THE REGISTER-GUARD, EUGENE, ORE.

access, many Internet users still own relatively slow modems. Friends and family may not resent waiting minutes for an animation or sound or video clip to load, but busy users in search of specific information or news don't want to be bothered.

The same idea applies to blinking words or images. Human physiology has us wired to treat motion as a "blink" feature. People notice change or motion more readily than color or size. Blinking text on a page will draw a reader's eye away from all other text or image content. Good designers have found these devices to be largely ineffective.

Some Web designers recommend never using a graphic where HTML text will do, cautioning editors that designers sometimes design more for their own pleasure than for their users. They will put text labels within graphics as a way to ensure that users see a particular font. (Remember that text can be controlled by users' browser settings, whereas an image will appear as the designer intended—unless, of course, the user has images turned off to save loading time.) Don't label icons. They are a graphic way of conveying meaning, so if a label is necessary, the icon isn't doing its job.

Designers shouldn't ignore the multimedia features of the Web. Obviously, sound and video can convey additional information about a news event, a feature story or advertising. The best plan is to incorporate these features, but make them optional for Web users. Don't force users to listen to excerpts from a speech or a song, much less a sales pitch. Include enough information about the accompanying sound or video clip to let users decide whether to select them and wait for them to load. Let users know also whether special plug-ins are required to hear or see the clip. If they are, make the programs easy for users to download.

▶**Page titles.** The ideal length is 64 characters or less to accommodate screen width, search engines and index services, some of which truncate longer titles. Every page should have a title or headline that indicates the content of the page.

▶**Orphaned pages.** Because readers can enter a page from anywhere in cyberspace, editors should include a logo or text to identify the site and the place of this page

Professional Perspective: Chris Barber

Design and content

Q: Does design spring from content, or does design determine the content?

A: In newspapers the design should be determined by the content. Design should enhance the story being told and not detract or distract from the idea of the story.

Q: How can designers use layout to help convey the theme and tone of a story?

A: Arrangement of the basic elements of a story package (headline, photo and text) in the most legible way in a given space is the main goal of newspaper design, but we can enhance how a story is received by where the package is placed on a page (top of the page usually conveys priority) and the size of the headline we allow it. Also, depending on the fonts a paper has to work with, a bold headline or lightface can imply a story's news value. We can also use photography and illustrations to visually tell the story and there are numerous ways to use them to help readers better understand a story.

Q: Are basic design principles still important in today's print media, or have publications embraced new ones?

A: There are certainly trends that pop up occasionally, such as the L-shape refer package used by papers like The Baltimore Sun (Figure 11-32) and Bakersfield Californian, but the fundamentals are still key to a well-designed publication. Tricks and trends cannot work in every situation and people still read top to bottom left to right, so basic design principles are still important.

Q: Has the Web affected print design, or vice versa? How?

Chris Barber has been a designer at The San Diego Union-Tribune since 2000, starting as a news designer and eventually moving to features. He graduated with a B.S. in journalism from Ball State University in Muncie, Ind., which offers a specific program for design and graphics. He did his first internship, as a news artist, at The Times-Picayune in New Orleans, La. Barber went on to The Gazette in Colorado Springs, Colo., where he worked as a page designer and graphic artist.

A: I think a lot of what we see on the Web is related designwise to print publications. It seems many newspaper Web sites haven't really embraced what is possible online, as most are just digital versions of the print product. So yes, I think print does affect some things we see online. I also think the Web has affected many facets of the newspaper as well. At the U-T, we've tried to implement things like blogs into the paper and have many short-form, quick-read types of stories taking the place of the more narrative types of stories in certain sections. As for design, there are a lot of ideas everywhere, and the Web is certainly another area to draw inspiration from.

Q: When you're given a design job, what are the first things you consider?

A: I generally collect all the elements I'll be working with and evaluate what is most important based on

Figure 11-32

The Baltimore Sun uses a reverse L shape for its "Inside" teaser items, beginning in the middle column below the fold and extending into the first three columns at the bottom of the page.

the story. In features we have a lot more room for creativity in a design. We occasionally use typography as a dominant element; often we'll have an illustration, either created by the designer or an artist, that goes with a story; and other times we have documentary photography to work with. After evaluating all the content I have an idea where I can go with the page.

Q: Is the design process ever collaborative (with other editors, photographers, designers, writers)?

A: In features, the process is often collaborative. I have weekly meetings with each section editor, a photo editor and anyone else involved with a particular upcoming story. We generally are presented with a story idea and make decisions on how that story will be visually displayed. If the story is something conceptual and cannot be photographed, we discuss illustration ideas and decide on a style and how the page might come together. I generally get input from other designers and my design editor while I'm working on a page. You can never have too many eyes on something because everyone will look at it differently.

Q: Are there times when collaboration is not necessary?

A: Many times there are pages that are very straightforward. Generally in news design, everything has been gathered and it's up to the designer to assemble a final page from the elements. In this case there isn't much more to do than put it together. Of course, collaboration is still going on since someone knew to assign a story and assign photos to be shot or a graphic to be made. But as a designer, especially on a deadline news section, collaboration is just a step in the process of completing the page. They may need to work with the copy desk to make a headline fit or to trim the story to fit the space, but collaboration isn't always necessary.

within the hierarchy of the Web site. Blind-alley pages confuse users, so avoid them. Every page should have a link to the site's home page and navigational devices to give readers a sense of where to go next within the site.

▶ **Sign it.** Even personal Web sites should include identifying information about the author because it helps users judge the credibility of material found on the site. A separate link can take users to another page with information about the sponsoring company or individual, or names and titles can be included somewhere on the page. Clickable e-mail addresses will encourage feedback, which commercial sponsors generally desire.

▶**Date it.** Remember, content is king on the Web, but up-to-date content is the most royal of all. News sites must be perceived as timely, and all Web pages should include information to tell users how current the information is.

▶**Accessibility.** Depending on the intended audience for the site, editors should be alert to special requirements of some Web users. For example, colorblind people can't distinguish red from green, so it is best to design pages where distinguishing between these two colors won't matter. People with other visual impairments may use machines to read Web pages aloud, so avoid spot art or navigational images unrecognized by such machines.

Suggestions for additional reading

Bohle, Robert H. *Publications Design for Editors.* Englewood Cliffs, N.J.: Prentice Hall, 1990.

Campbell, Alastair. *The Graphic Designer's Handbook.* Philadelphia: Running Press Book Publishers, 1983.

Editors of the Harvard Post. *How to Produce a Small Newspaper: A Guide for Independent Journalists,* 2nd ed. Harvard and Boston: The Harvard Common Press, 1987.

Garcia, Mario. *Contemporary Newspaper Design: A Structural Approach,* 2nd ed. Englewood Cliffs, N.J.: Prentice Hall, 1987.

Garcia, Mario. *Redesigning Print for the Web.* Indianapolis: Hayden Books, 1997.

Guide to Quality Newspaper Reproduction. New York and Washington, D.C.: American Newspaper Publishers Association and National Advertising Bureau, 1986.

Harrower, Tim. *The Newspaper Designer's Handbook,* 4th ed. New York: McGraw-Hill College, 1997.

Kvern, Olay Martin, and David Blatner. *Real World Adobe InDesign2.* Berkeley, Calif.: Peachpit Press, 2002.

Lichty, Tom. *Design Principles for Desktop Publishers,* 2nd ed. Belmont, Calif.: Wadsworth, 1994.

Meggs, Philip B. *A History of Graphic Design,* 3rd ed. Hoboken, N.J.: John Wiley & Sons, 1998.

Moen, Daryl. *Newspaper Layout and Design: A Team Approach,* 4th ed. Ames, Iowa: The Iowa State University Press, 2000.

Morrison, Sean. *A Guide to Type Design.* Englewood Cliffs, N.J.: Prentice Hall, 1986.

Newspaper Links, http://www.newspaperlinks.com.

The Next Newspapers. Future of Newspapers Report. Washington, D.C.: American Society of Newspaper Editors, 1988.

Pocket Pal: A Graphic Arts Production Handbook, 18th ed. New York: International Paper, 2000.

Rehe, Rolf. *Typography and Design for Newspapers.* Carmel, Ind.: Design Research International, 1985.

Siegel, David S. *Secrets of Successful Web Sites: Project Management on the World Wide Web.* San Francisco: Hayden Enlightened Communications, 1997.

Society for News Design, http://www.snd.org.

Webmonkey: The Web Developer's Resource, http://hotwired.lycos.com/ webmonkey.

Web Page Design for Designers, http://www.wpdfd.com.

Weinman, Lynda. *Designing Web Graphics.4,* 4th ed. Indianapolis: New Riders Publishing, 2003.

Weinmann, Elaine, and Peter Lourekas. *QuarkXPress 5 for Windows and Macintosh: Visual QuickStart Guide.* Berkeley, Calif.: Peachpit Press, 2002.

STUDENT WORKBOOK

Paragraph this

No ¶ (written in margin)

Or run it in,
    with connecting line

Join words: week end

Insert a word or phrase _single_

Insert mising letter

Take out onne letter

Transpose elements two

Transpose wfo letters

Make this lower case

Capitalize houston

CAPITALIZE ALL COPY

Indicate boldface

Indicate italics

Abbreviate (street)

Spell out (abbrev.)

Spell out symbol (£)

Put number (twelve) in figures

Separate twowords

Join let ters in word

Write in period (x)

Bracket sluglines like this

Show story length: (75 wo)

Use end marks (#) (30)

18   (typesetting instructions
8/9reg. written opposite copy block)

(Set 8-pt. solid)

    (type specifications

    circled)

Hyphen (=)

Dash ⊢⊣

P1—Cutline—Hearing

With #1—Many demands

   ] Mark centering like this [

Do not obliterate copy;

  mark it out ~~with a thin line~~ so

  it can be compared with editing

Insert comma �

Take out ~~some~~ word

Don't make ~~this~~ correction _stet_

There's more of this on the next

  page

              (more)

These are traditional copy editing symbols to use when editing copy with paper and pencil rather than with a computer.

Chapter 1 Exercises

1. Conduct an online search for World Wide Web sites created by different types of news media. Locate a newspaper Web site, a magazine Web site and a broadcast network Web site. Compare the news selections, the layout and design, the amount of advertising, and the way headlines are written. Then search for a corporation's Web site and compare it with the others.

2. Observe the copy editors at your campus newspaper, or interview a staff member in your university's marketing and communications department. How does their work compare with the work of professional copy editors, as described in this chapter? Make notes on the differences so you can discuss them in class.

3. Define the following:

   a. HTK

   b. Slot editor

   c. Rim editor

   d. Assigning editor

4. Try to get an interview with a copy editor at your local newspaper and ask about his or her role and responsibilities in the newsroom. From your discussion, develop your own list of the virtues of a good copy editor.

5. Try to line up an interview with a newsletter editor or an editorial assistant at a local public relations agency and ask about his or her role and responsibilities within the organization. Do the editing functions differ from those at a print publication? If so, how?

6. On weekends, large metropolitan dailies contain inserts that are not produced locally but are transported in and inserted in the mailrooms as newspapers come off the presses. Find a Sunday edition of the largest daily in your region and identify inserts that were not produced by the newspaper's regular staff. What characteristics suggest these were produced out of town? Does this Sunday edition also contain inserts that were produced by the newspaper's regular staff? How can you tell?

7. Review the news values listed in this chapter on page 00. Applying those news values, plus others that your instructor may add to the list, consider whether each of the following items is suitable for publication in the **news** section of your hometown newspaper. Tell which news values apply for each item.

   a. Meteor showers will crackle across the night sky through the weekend, streaking to their fiery demise. The meteors—some the size of a grain of sand, others the size of a baseball—will crash into the Earth's atmosphere as fast as 165,000 miles per hour. (story from science beat)

   b. An effort to contain a 62,000-acre fire pays off, but a second blaze ignites just miles away and forces even more evacuations of weary residents. The fires are 60 miles away from your town. (wire story)

   c. The local professional football team is playing its first exhibition game of the season tomorrow, and the quarterback position is still up for grabs.

   d. For the second time since the economic downturn began, mortgage rates have dipped to historic lows. Rates for 30-year fixed-rate mortgages fell to 5.5 percent this week. (wire story)

   e. Tiny blankets and booties knitted by a legion of volunteers keep premature babies and their parents comforted.

8. Review the news values listed in this chapter. Applying those news values, plus others that your instructor may add to the list, consider whether each of the following items is suitable for publication in the **news** section of your hometown newspaper. Tell which news values apply for each item.

   a. After a successful run on Broadway, the cast of an award-winning musical is beginning a tour of the United States. The nearest performance to your hometown will be in a city 200 miles away. (wire story) *no — no names, town far away, entertainment*

   b. Scientists working in Washington, D.C., think they may have made a breakthrough in cancer research. The National Science Foundation awarded them a $2.5 million grant this week. (National Science Foundation press release) *Timeliness / relevance / human interest*

   c. This is the right time for gardeners in your area to get their tulips and other bulbs into the ground. (material from local agricultural agent) *Timeliness / proximity / relevance*

   d. Business analysts expect a bullish market for mining stocks in the next few months. (business wire story) *timeliness / relevance*

   e. "Tiger," a German shepherd owned by a local woman, won "best in show" yesterday at the annual dog show in Madison Square Garden. (wire story) *timeliness / proximity / human interest*

9. Review the news values listed in this chapter. Applying those news values, plus others that your instructor may add to the list, consider whether each of the following items is suitable for publication in the **news** section of your hometown newspaper. Tell which news values apply for each item.

   a. A student from the local junior high school placed second in the national spelling bee, conducted yesterday in Washington, D.C. (story from education beat) *timeliness / proximity*

   b. A train derailed 30 miles away. Emergency rooms at local hospitals were crowded with injured passengers. (story from police beat) *proximity / relevance / conflict*

   c. Fashion designers say that unisex clothes will be in vogue next year. (wire story) *no*

   d. The local school board decided last night to build a new high school in town. (story from education beat) *timeliness / proximity / relevance / human interest*

   e. A city official says that property taxes will increase dramatically to pay for the costs of building a new high school in town. (story from city government beat) *proximity / relevance / conflict / human interest*

10. Review the news values listed in this chapter. Applying those news values, plus others that your instructor may add to the list, consider whether each of the following items is suitable for publication in the **news** section of your hometown newspaper. Tell which news values apply for each item.

   a. A 75-year-old man was the first customer at a new bungee-jumping attraction that opened yesterday on the outskirts of town. (story from business beat) *Timeliness / proximity / unusualness*

   b. To mark its 100th anniversary, the Metropolitan Opera in New York City performed the classic "Madame Butterfly," and thousands of opera fans attended. *no — entertainment*

   c. The local museum announced it would receive a traveling exhibit of ancient Chinese stone warriors from the Denver Museum of Natural History next month. *Timeliness / proximity*

   d. Environmentalists warned owners of new beach homes along the North Carolina coast that the structures were built too close to the sea and would not withstand another hurricane season. *conflict / relevance*

   e. The local chapter of the League of Women Voters announced yesterday that it would sponsor the first senatorial debate between Republican candidate Elizabeth Dole and her Democratic challenger. *timeliness / proximity / prominence / conflict / relevance*

Chapter 2 Exercises

1. Label each word in the following sentences according to its part of speech.

   a. President Dwight D. Eisenhower promoted the idea of the interstate highway system.

   b. Congress passed a law authorizing the road system.

   c. That was in 1956.

   d. During World War II, Eisenhower observed the efficiency of the German autobahns built in 1935.

   e. Stop! That is an exit ramp.

2. Identify the subject, verb, direct object or complement in each clause in the following sentences. Draw one line under the subject, two lines under the verb, and three lines under the direct object or complement. Mark whether the verb is completed by a direct object, predicate nominative or predicate adjective.

   a. The FBI conducted raids across the country yesterday to break up movie piracy rings.

   b. Agents arrested 13 people in raids across the country.

   c. Using computer file-sharing networks, the suspects distribute counterfeit films to countries around the world, an official for the Motion Picture Association of America said.

   d. If they are convicted of copyright infringement, suspects could face five years in prison.

   e. A young woman wanted to tell the invading soldiers that they were unwelcome in her city.

   f. Thinking they wouldn't shoot a woman, she walked fearlessly toward their lines.

   g. They fired. She fell. A bullet wound turned her white shirt scarlet.

   h. Although some people buy three or four pairs of sunglasses at a clip, the average number of sunglasses purchased per person is 1.3 pairs, according to Ray-Ban research.

   i. Thomas Edison had 400 species of plants in the garden of his winter home on the Caloosahatchee River in Fort Myers, Fla.

   j. With intentions of revising his travel book annually, Arthur Frommer tells of travels that are politically oriented, vacations on campuses and digs with archeologists.

3. Label each sentence in Exercise 2 according to sentence type: simple, compound, complex, compound-complex.

4. Circle the correct verb in these sentences. To show that you understand the rules of subject-verb agreement and are not relying only on what sounds right, write the number of the rule (as numbered in Chapter 2) that applies to each choice.

   a. Five passengers on the plane and a farmer working in the field [was, were] killed.

   b. Like other produce wholesalers on the three-block-long market, she [know, knows] the ultimate follower of seasons [is, are] the farmer. 2/4

   c. Each of the children [is, are] enrolled in music lessons. 6

   d. Neither John nor his brothers [know, knows] what to expect when election day [come, comes]. 3

   e. The final hours of the legislative session [was, were] chaotic. 4

   f. Two-thirds of the protesters [was, were] arrested before noon. 5

   g. Club members [was, were] scheduled to vote for new officers.

   h. The committee, composed of three members of the board of directors, [is, are] going to plan the annual convention. 4

   i. A number of animals [was, were] trapped in the burning barn. 8

   j. The majority [is, are] in favor of the legislation limiting immigration, which [is, are] to be voted on today. 8

   k. Politics [was, were] interesting when I studied it in college, but the courses [has, had] little effect on my personal politics, which [was, were] firmly fixed.

   l. Good manners [is, are] best learned when young.

   m. The mayor's delegation, as well as several Chamber of Commerce members, [was, were] scheduled to meet with the executives visiting from Japan.

   n. Everyone [hope, hopes] that the contract will be awarded to this company. 6

   o. The National Council of Churches [is, are] planning a convention in Washington, D.C., this year.

   p. The company's earnings [was, were] greater this year than last year because new products [was, were] popular.

   q. The total sold [was, were] 450, but a total of 10 [was, were] returned because of faulty construction.

5. Mark each pronoun in the following sentences, and tell whether it is in the nominative, objective or possessive case.

   a. The message of "Charlotte's Web" has softened the heart of a farmer who has decided a piggy who posed as Wilbur won't be going to market after all. *nominative*

   b. The celebrity asked him not to take photographs of her children. *pos*

   c. The searchers said they would resume the hunt after it became dry enough to use vehicles. *objective nominative nom.*

   d. After thanking his doctors, whom he credits for his remarkable recovery, the injured auto racer said it would be a long time before he races again, if at all. *possessive obj nominative pos. nom. nom.*

   e. Who do you think will become the next superstar? *nom. nom.*

6. Indicate correct noun and pronoun agreement by marking through the incorrect pronoun choices in these sentences.

   a. Jeff Mayer bills [hisself, himself, themselves] as the most expensive maid in the nation. Business executives pay [his, him] $1,000 so [he, him] will tell [they, them, it] how to clean off [they, them, their, there, its] cluttered desks.

   b. Some financially strapped cities can't make across-the-board purchases of semiautomatic pistols, [that, which] cost from $350 to $550. But police departments frequently permit officers to buy [they, them, there, their] own sidearms.

   c. Each male officer was required to buy [his, him, its, their, them] own uniforms.

   d. Uniforms were expensive, but [they, them, it] lasted for several years if [they, them, their, its] owners kept [their, its] weight constant so the uniforms fit properly.

   e. Listen carefully to those [who, whom, whose] you have reason to believe know how to express [theirselves, themselves] well.

   f. I will exchange letters with [whoever, whomever] writes.

   g. [Who, Whom] shall you choose as captain?

   h. The company needs to know [who, whom] it is insuring.

   i. I thought [she, her] to be my friend.

   j. [Who, Whom] do you suppose [he, him] to be?

k. Between you and [I, me], I think [she, her] previous boyfriend was friendlier.

l. None but [I, me] was able to complete the work.

m. Some of [we, us] editors think students need to know much more about grammar.

n. The editors decided to hire the student [who, whom] scored highest on the English usage test.

o. The newly married couple went to a resort in the Smoky Mountains on [their, its] honeymoon. [They, It] will return home next week.

p. The women's basketball team is in [their, its, it's] first season of competition.

7. Circle the correct pronoun choices in the following sentences. Add commas where needed to set off non-essential clauses.

a. Three victims were members of a Delaware Army National Guard unit [that, which, who] had just completed [their, its] first week of training.

b. Officer Glenda Jones [who, whom] has been coordinating police patrols in housing developments plagued by drugs, gangs and gambling, said most of the problems stem from nonresidents.

c. Widely publicized safety breakdowns at the government's nuclear weapons plants are rooted in a perverse devotion to secrecy and poor management, congressional investigators said in a report issued Sunday. The safety problems [that, which] came to light during the past two years were aggravated by a lack of outside scrutiny and effective oversight from the Energy Department [that, which] pays private companies to run the facilities, the report said.

d. He criticized the students [who, whom, that, which] led the demonstrations [that, which] were crushed by army assaults.

e. Eight-year-old Chad Brenner said he would have liked to use the $39,541.55 tax refund check [that, which] was mistakenly mailed to him to buy a new bicycle.

8. Complete this list of nouns and pronouns to show the plurals and possessives:

	Singular	Singular possessive	Plural	Plural possessive
a.	Smith			
b.	girl			
c.	man			

	Singular	Singular possessive	Plural	Plural possessive
d. attorney general				
e. church				
f. Jones				
g. army				
h. monkey				
i. mouse				
j. piano				
k. oasis				

9. Use the correct verb and verb tense in each of the following sentences.

Lie or lay

a. The gun ~~laid~~ lay in the street. (past tense)

b. The gun had ~~lied~~ lain in the street for several hours before police recovered it.

c. The police officer laid the gun on the table.

d. The officer thought that he had laid the gun on the table, but his supervisor could not find it.

e. The woman ~~lied~~ lay on the beach to get a suntan. (past tense)

f. She had ~~laid~~ lain there for several hours before she noticed that she was getting sunburned.

g. lay the soft drinks on top of the ice in the cooler.

h. Ten bottles were ~~laid~~ lying in the ice cooler. (meaning the bottles were reclining)

i. Laying her books aside, she spoke to him.

j. He laid his baby daughter on the floor to change her wet diaper.

Sit or set

k. They had sat in the car for two hours.

l. She set the silverware on the table.

m. The fat man sat on the chair and broke it.

n. She had set the alarm clock for 6 a.m.

o. The sun was _____setting_____ as we began our run.

Rise or raise

p. Please _____raise_____ the flag.

q. He _____arose_____ from the water and surprised me.

r. The dough has _____risen_____ sufficiently.

s. The student _____raised_____ her hand.

t. He had _____raised_____ his hand several times, but the teacher did not call on him to respond.

u. The stage was designed to allow the orchestra to _____rise_____ from the orchestra pit.

Your teacher may instruct you to use the electronic version of workbook exercises, available at the Web site for this textbook. Otherwise, use correct copy editing symbols to correct the remaining exercises in this chapter and throughout the workbook. The symbols are on the inside cover of this workbook section.

Before personal computers became widespread, copy for mass media was typed double- or triple-spaced. Copy editors used standard symbols to indicate changes in the copy, and typesetters then retyped each story into "printers' type." Other instructions:

- Use pencil instead of ink to make changes so erasures can be made if needed.

- Write changes parallel to and above the line that is being changed.

- Punctuation marks are written above or below the line, according to normal placement of the punctuation mark (above for apostrophes and quotation marks; below for commas and periods, for example).

- Draw attention to the punctuation mark by using a caret (^) or an inverted caret (∨). Circle periods.

- Draw a heavy line through words to be eliminated, but do not make the original unreadable in case the material needs to be restored to the story or is needed for checking purposes.

10. Edit the following sentences to correct misplaced or dangling modifiers and double negatives.

a. Running the fastest time in Kentucky Derby history, more than $1 million was awarded to the owner of the winning horse.

b. Originally snapped up by Warner Independent Pictures after it played at last year's Sundance Film Festival, the distributors canceled its fall release date and eventually discarded it.

c. A Manchester woman, on the pretense of searching for someone, allowed a man to enter her home and was assaulted.

d. After training the tiger cub to walk on a leash, it could be used in the zoo director's presentations to schoolchildren.

e. Still searching for an incinerator site, a previously rejected location is getting a second look by the city council.

f. The baby kitten doesn't have scarcely any hair.

g. The zoo doesn't have but one gorilla, but the director says another one will be added next year.

h. The jail is the first in the state to be operated by a private management firm that accommodates 100 inmates.

i. Police described the suspect as a burly, white, middle-aged male with brown hair and a beard, more than 6 feet tall.

j. Accused of making errors on telephone bills for the past four months, students living in residence halls will receive a refund from the phone company for long-distance calls.

k. The miners discovered that the place they excavated did not have none of the minerals they wanted.

11. Change the following sentences from passive voice to active voice. Be alert also for errors in the sentences.

a. The building was found to be energy inefficient by inspectors. _____

_____

_____

b. Hemlock trees in the Great Smoky Mountains are being infested by woolly adelgid. _____

_____

_____

c. The hemlock wooly adelgid infestation was discovered by park rangers last year. _____

_____

_____

d. A link between between students' academic achievement and their socioeconomic status is often cited by education researchers. _____

_____

_____

e. Labels on food at the grocery store are checked carefully by a majority of shoppers. _____

_____

_____

f. He called the most unique quarterback to come into the NFL in a long time by Sports Illustrated that featured him on its cover last week.

_____

_____

_____

12. Punctuate the following sentences. Do not rewrite or revise sentences. Use correct copy editing symbols.

a. In one area where officials ordered 200000 people to evacuate in and around Wilkes Barre, Pa. a system of levees appears to have succeeded in holding back the surging Susquehanna River.

b. In Conklin N.Y. on the banks of the Susquehanna near Binghamton John Jones 41 surveyed his house and his auto sales lot behind it where all that could be seen in brown oil-streaked water were the tops of the vehicles that the flood had not carried away.

c. Honda also sells hybrid versions of its Civic and Accord and its developing a new lower cost hybrid vehicle that will go on sale later this decade.

d. Nonetheless Ford was the first American auto company to sell a hybrid vehicle the small Escape sport utility vehicle.

e. The law offered legal status to aliens who had lived in the United States continuously since before Jan. 1 1982 and imposed penalties on employers who knowingly hired illegals.

f. Meanwhile the Immigration and Naturalization Service has proclaimed the law a clear success but the current administration has yet to put it's own stamp on immigration policy.

g. He said that he had but one thing on his mind sleeping.

h. Gardeners who wear broad brimmed hats, coveralls, and heavy duty gloves while using an electric hedge clipper to trim bushes are displaying common sense but not enough of it says the American Optometric Association.

i. Down's syndrome has been linked to a defect on a tiny slice of one of the human chromosomes an important step toward prevention and treatment of the disorder researchers said Saturday.

j. "By mapping a gene you can find it isolate it and develop new means of therapy" said the scientist from Yale University one of the sponsor's of the conference.

13. Punctuate the following sentences correctly. Use correct copy editing symbols.

a. She announced that newly developed tests would be used during the upcoming tournament to detect drug using athletes.

b. A 4 foot boa constrictor a scary tarantula and a baby Bengal tiger gave Joey Black a front line education about zoos.

c. Every state has reported influenza activity except New Hampshire and Rhode Island with three states New York Connecticut and New Mexico listing widespread outbreaks.

d. Gosh It will be a 15 to 20 minute procedure and I don't think I can lie still that long.

e. It was identified as a Russian plane but US planes were in the area also Maj Gen Larry Jones said.

f. The inmate said to the parole board "Jones should not be released from prison. He is a dangerous man. He has told me several times, I will kill again if I get a chance.

g. Davis who is usually soft spoken talked in loud tones yesterday.

h. The 25 member board held a five day conference.

i. The 1000 word feature story had a pro American tone and a definite anti Arab slant.

j. Durham shot his father in law with a 12 gauge shotgun and received a 15 year sentence when the 12 man jury recommended mercy.

14. Read pages from your hometown newspaper until you find something that should have been changed at the proofreading, as opposed to copy editing, stage of production. Mark the errors and be prepared to justify your improvements in class. If you can't find such errors in the newspaper, consider writing the editor or publisher a letter of congratulations.

Chapter 3 Exercises

1. Now that you have studied this chapter on style and correct word usage, you should recognize that the press release leads used toward the beginning of Chapter 3 did not follow AP style, although they were posted online for national distribution. Correct style and word use errors in the following press release leads. If you are editing with pencil rather than the electronic version of these exercises available online, use correct copy editing symbols and don't forget to indent paragraphs. Unless your teacher instructs you otherwise, do not rewrite these leads.

   a. Lexus announced today that the RX 350, the top-selling luxury SUV, is now available with a savings of $900 on its most popular option packages. The new RX 350, available as both front-wheel drive (FWD) and all-wheel drive (AWD) models, features a powerful 3.5-liter V6 engine that improves both performance and fuel efficiency.

   b. July is heating up and so is Mega Millions. Friday's Mega Millions drawing produced more than 345,000 winning tickets from coast to coast. That includes five tickets that came within a heartbeat of hitting the jackpot. Since no ticket matched all six numbers to win the $12 million jackpot, the jackpot for the drawing next Tuesday grows to an estimated $15 million.

   c. Over 120 Hooters Girls from Taiwan to New York are heading to Las Vegas to compete for $150,000 in cash and prizes at the 10th Annual Hooters International Swimsuit Pageant.

   d. America's favorite talent show, American Idol, is heading to the New Jersey Meadowlands to hold auditions for its upcoming 6th season. The Meadowlands, home to some of the most prominent sports franchises in the region and a major tourism destination, is expected to swell with thousands of people during the days leading up to the August 14th audition.

   e. NEW YORK, N.Y. -- Electric Fuel Corporation, the world's leading zinc-air fuel cell company, today announced it will be launching a new line of INSTANT POWER(TM) Mini Chargers for cell phones, aimed at competing with lower performance alkaline based emergency chargers. The new Mini Charger will be launched this quarter, initially in the UK and later on in the US markets. With Electric Fuel's superior zinc air fuel cell technology and featuring a new and sleek design, the $9.95 (MSRP) Mini Charger will outperform any other disposable charger currently on the market.

   f. LOS ANGELES, CA. -- The median price of existing homes in California in June rose 21.3% and sales increased 1.4% compared to the same period a year ago, the California Association of REALTORS(R) and Real Estate Solutions, a real estate information service, reported today.

   g. *(for business section)*
   Landry's Restaurants, Inc. (NYSE: LNY), one of the nation's largest casual dining, hospitality, and entertainment companies, announced it will retain

Wachovia Securities and Northpoint Advisors to assist in evaluating strategic alternatives for the Joe's Crab Shack chain and enhancing shareholder value through the Saltgrass Steak House chain which has experienced positive same store sales for eleven consecutive quarters and attained an average unit volume in excess of 4.3 million dollars.

h. *(for business section)*

West Coast Bank (Nasdaq: WCBO) has awarded 5 one-thousand-dollar scholarships to children of it's employees. Executive Vice President of Human Resources Cynthia Sparacio said, "West Coast Bank's dependent scholarship benefit is much anticipated and appreciated each year by a highly competitive group of high school and college students. It's another way the company increases value to our employees and ensures that we are an employer of choice," she said.

i. *(for business section)*

RadioShack Corporation (NYSE: RSH) today announced a net loss of three million dollars or ($0.02) per diluted share for the quarter ended June 30th, 2006 versus net income of 52 million dollars or $0.33 per diluted share for the quarter ended June 30th, 2005. Earnings results were adversely affected by lower sales of wireless, particularly post-paid products, in RadioShack company operated stores.

j. Slingo, Inc., a leader in the casual games industry is treading new ground today by launching the first on-line social-networking community geared towards women. Slingo.com is further tapping into the consistently growing casual games market by focusing the attention of their community towards giving women a place to congregate. Slingo Inc.'s Director of Online Operations Peter Czech said, "Slingo.com has a population of almost 80% women and has had a consistently growing community for the past four years. We want to give women a place where they can connect with each other, make new friends and have fun," he said.

2. Use the Associated Press style rules given in this chapter and in the AP stylebook to circle the correct style in each of the following sets. The Associated Press revises its stylebook annually; resolve inconsistencies between this textbook chapter and the stylebook in favor of the most recent stylebook. All are first reference unless otherwise noted.

a. 4th and Iowa streets
4th & Iowa
Fourth and Iowa streets
Fourth and Iowa Streets

b. 5 cents
five cents
5¢
$.05

c. The Supreme Court ruled eight to one.
The Supreme Court ruled 8–1.
The Supreme Court ruled 8 to 1.
The Supreme Court ruled 8/1.

d. *(news story)*
She is 5 feet 8 inches.
She is 5-8.
She is five feet eight.
She is 5 feet 8.

e. 12 noon
noon
12 a.m. noon
12:00 p.m.
12:00 noon

f. 8 p.m. tonight
8 P.M. tonight
8 tonight
8:00 tonight

g. 1999 A.D.
1999 AD
A.D. 1999
AD 1999

h. Number One choice
Number 1 choice
No. 1 choice
No. one choice

i. Joe Jones, 7
Joe Jones, seven
seven-year-old Joe Jones

j. the '60s
the '60's
the 60s
the 60's

k. The odds were 5-4.
The odds were five to four.
The odds were 5 to 4.
The odds were five-four.

l. The baby weighed 8 pounds,
   13 ounces.
The baby weighed 8#13.
The baby weighed 8 lbs., 13 oz.
The baby weighed eight pounds,
   13 ounces.
The baby weighed eight lbs.,
   13 oz.

m. The boy is nineteen.
The boy is 19.
The man is 19.
The man is nineteen.

n. The girl is nineteen.
The girl is 19.
The woman is 19.
The woman is nineteen.

o. I owe you three dollars.
I owe you $3.
I owe you $3.00.
I owe you 3 dollars.

p. She represents the 8th
   Congressional District.
She represents the Eighth
   Congressional District.
She represents the 8th
   congressional district.
She represents the eighth
   congressional district.

q. the 9-by-12 rug
the nine-by-12 rug
the 9 by 12 rug
the nine by 12 rug

r. Queen Elizabeth 2nd
Queen Elizabeth Two
Queen Elizabeth the Second
Queen Elizabeth II

s. $1,200,000
1.2 million dollars
1,200,000 million dollars
$1.2 million

t. Fifth Armored Division
5th Armored Division
Fifth Armored Div.
5th Armored Div.

3. Circle the correct Associated Press style in each of the following sets. All are first reference unless otherwise noted.

a. from $6 to $7 million
from $6-$7 million
~~from $6 million to $7 million~~
from six to seven million dollars

b. 10 knots
10 knots per hour
ten knots
ten kph

c. Her sons are 15, 12, and seven.
Her sons are 15, 12 and 7.
Her sons are 15, 12, and 7.

d. They have 12 chairs, five tables
and four lamps.
They have 12 chairs, 5 tables
and 4 lamps.

e. Act 1, Scene 3
act 1, scene 3
Act One, Scene Three
Act I, Scene 3
Act I, Scene III

f. The incumbent beat King
11,101 to 9,706.
The incumbent beat King
11,101-9,706.
The incumbent beat King
11.1 thousand to 9.7 thousand.

g. Go to Cumberland Avenue
Go to Cumberland Ave.
Go to Cumberland avenue
Go to Cumberland ave.

h. 123 9th St.
123 Ninth St.
123 9th Street
123 Ninth Street

i. Captain Mary Brown
Capt. Mary Brown
Mary Brown, Captain

j. Chancellor Marvin Smith
Dr. Marvin Smith, Chancellor
Chancellor Dr. Marvin Smith
Chanc. Marvin Smith

k. *(second reference)*
Chancellor Smith
Chan. Smith
Smith
Dr. Smith

l. Carol Bass, Vice-Chancellor of
Student Affairs,
Vice Chancellor for Student
Affairs Carol Bass
Carol Bass, vice chancellor for
student affairs,
Carol Bass, vice-chancellor of
student affairs,

m. *(second reference)*
Vice Chancellor Bass
Bass
V-C of student affairs Bass

n. *(second reference)*
Attorney General Herman
Att. Gen. Herman
A.G. Herman
Herman

o. *(second reference)*
Dr. Smith
Mary Smith
Ms. Smith
Smith
Mary

p. from Jan. 22-25
     from January 22 to 25
     from Jan. 22 to Jan. 25
     from Jan. 22 to 25

q. Marilyn Jones, dean of law
     Law School Dean Marilyn Jones
     Marilyn Jones, dean of the
          School of Law

r. the English Department
     the Department of English
     the English department

s. the History Department
     the History department
     the history department
     the Department of history
     the Department of History

t. Grade Point Average
     GPA
     grade point average
     g.p.a.

4. Circle the correct Associated Press style in each of the following sets. All are first reference unless otherwise noted.

a. National Organization for Women
     National Organization of Women

b. His birthday is in Feb.
     His birthday is in February.

c. His birthday is Feb. 8.
     His birthday is February 8.
     His birthday is 8 February.
     His birthday is the eighth of
          February.

d. It is a large Corp.
     It is a large corporation.
     It is a large corp.
     It is a large Corporation.

e. She is an executive at the
          Hanover Corp.
     She is an executive at the
          Hanover Corporation.
     She is an executive at the
          Hanover corp.
     She is an executive at the
          Hanover corporation.

f. 35 m.p.h.
     35 mph

g. Mount Everest
     Mt. Everest

h. *(in a sports story)*
     first base
     First Base
     1st base
     1st Base

i. the television show "Jeopardy"
     the television show Jeopardy

j. The New York Times
     the New York Times
     the "New York Times"

k. Dorothy Bowles, professor of
          journalism
     Prof. Dorothy Bowles, journalism
     Professor of Journalism Dorothy Bowles
     Dorothy Bowles, prof. of journ.
     Prof. Dr. Dorothy Bowles

l. *(second reference)*
     Prof. Bowles
     Professor Bowles
     Bowles
     Dr. Bowles

m. Carmen Jones, asst. prof. of
history,
Asst. Prof. Carmen Jones
Carmen Jones, assistant professor
of history
Carmen Jones, assistant professor
in history,

n. 7 a.m.
7 A.M.
7:00 a.m.
7:00 A.M.

o. the Tennessee River
the Tennessee river
the Tenn. River
the Tenn. River

p. 17th Century
Seventeenth Century
17th century
seventeenth century

q. *(second reference, midsentence)*
Coach Hufford
coach Hufford
Coach Bonnie Hufford

r. They traveled through the West
Coast states.
They traveled through the west
coast states.

s. The oil spill was along the East
Coast.
The oil spill was along the east
coast.

t. Knox County District Court
Knox County district court
district court of Knox county

5. Circle the correct Associated Press style in each of the following sets. All are first reference unless otherwise noted.

a. the Mississippi and Ohio Rivers
the Mississippi and Ohio rivers
the Miss. and Ohio rivers

b. He drove northwest.
He drove Northwest.
He drove north west.

c. Philippine islands
Aleutian islands
Pacific islands
Mediterranean Islands

d. Department of Defense
defense department
department of defense
Defense department

e. Western Texas
western Texas
W. Texas
West Texas

f. Knox County jail
Knox County Jail
Knox Co. jail

g. Knoxville Fire Department
Knoxville fire department
Knoxville Fire Dept.

h. The town has no Fire Department.
The town has no fire department.

i. U.S. House of Representatives
United States House of Representatives
US House
U.S. House of Reps.

j. Gen. William Smith
General William Smith
general William Smith
William Smith, General

k. National Anthem
     National anthem
     national anthem

l. National guard
     national guard
     National Guard

m. Pacific Ocean
     Pacific ocean
     pacific ocean

n. He is the Pope.
     He is the pope.
     He is the Pontiff.

o. the State of Texas
     the state of Texas
     The State of Texas

p. Detroit, Mich.
     Detroit
     Detroit, MI
     Detroit, Michigan

five-ninth place

q. Tuesday at 7 p.m. in 127
     University Center
     In 127 University Center Tuesday
     at 7 p.m.
     7 p.m. Tuesday in 127 University
     Center
     7 p.m. Tuesday night in University
     Center room 127

r. Liverpool, Great Britain
     Liverpool, England
     Liverpool, United Kingdom
     Liverpool

s. El Paso, Texas
     El Paso
     El Paso, Tex.
     El Paso, TX

t. Paris, France
     Paris, Fr.
     Paris

6. Circle the correct Associated Press style in each of the following sets. All are first reference unless otherwise noted.

a. San Juan, Puerto Rico
     San Juan, P.R.
     San Juan

b. Temperatures fell 5 degrees.
     Temperatures fell five degrees.
     Temperatures fell 5°.

c. *(standing alone in sentence; not a title)*
     Chief Justice of the Supreme Court
     Chief Justice of the United States
     chief justice of the United States
     chief justice of the Supreme Court

d. pom-pom squad
     pom pom squad
     pompom squad
     pom-pon squad

e. We will play this coming Saturday.
     We will play Saturday.
     We will play next Saturday.

f. U.S. Congress
     U.S. congress
     United States Congress
     United States' Congress
     United States congress

g. daylight-saving time
     daylight savings time
     DST
     daylight-savings time

h. 62 degrees Fahrenheit
     62F.
     62 Fahr.
     Fahrenheit 62 F
     62

12. Entries T–Z

   a. What does the Talmud consist of?

   b. Where is the Tennessee Valley Authority headquartered?

   c. TriMotor is the proper name for what?

   d. Why did Harry S Truman not use a period after the S in his name?

   e. What is a U-boat?

   f. When should you use the term *user friendly*?

   g. What does the U.S. Customs Court do?

   h. What does Veterans Day commemorate?

   i. Is Virginia legally a state?

   j. What is vernacular?

   k. What is the preferred, nonsexist term for weatherman?

   l. As defined by the U.S. Census Bureau, the West is considered to include how many states?

   m. Wilson's disease is characterized by the abnormal accumulation of what metal in the brain, liver and other organs?

   n. What is a generic term for Xerox?

   o. Are yams botanically related to sweet potatoes?

   p. Is it acceptable to begin a sentence with a figure that indicates a year?

   q. What is yellow journalism?

   r. To what age range is the term *youth* applicable?

   s. What is Zionism?

   t. Is yo-yo currently a registered trademark?

13. This exercise is based on the "correct word usage" section of this chapter and words beginning with an *A* in the "frequently misused words" list in this chapter. Mark through the incorrect choices in the following sentences.

   a. [A while, awhile] before he came to the party, refreshments were served.

   b. As mayor, she hoped to [affect, effect] change.

   c. Because of the [adverse, averse] weather conditions, we must [altar, alter] our plans.

   d. Her status as a celebrity was an [allusion, illusion].

   e. It is [alright, all right] for you to paint it green.

   f. My dream of becoming a film star was an [allusion, illusion].

   g. She [alluded, eluded] to her past glory as an actress.

   h. The fall [aggravated, irritated] his knee injury.

   i. The new drug has a powerful [affect, effect], but it may not be [affective, effective] for treating cancer.

   j. Has he been [appraised, apprised] of the situation?

   k. The teacher's [advice, advise] to her was to study harder.

   l. We mailed 150 invitations [all together, altogether].

   m. Were you able to get her to [ascent, assent] to our proposal?

   n. He didn't seem to understand the [affect, effect] of his actions.

14. This exercise is based on the "correct word usage" section of this chapter and words beginning with a *B* in the "frequently misused words" list in this chapter. Mark through the incorrect choices in the following sentences.

a. A [burro, burrow] has sure footing on mountain trails.

b. After all the monthly bills were paid, the family had a [balance, remainder] of [fewer, less] than $50.

c. After careful consideration, I [believe, feel, think] I should accept the job offer.

d. Beef [bouillon, bullion] was used in the recipe.

e. She retired to her [birth, berth] on the train.

f. He enjoys going to the horse races, and he is a big [better, bettor].

g. She seemed reluctant to [broach, brooch] the subject with her boss.

h. His explanation sounded like [baloney, bologna] to me.

i. I don't like [baloney, bologna] sandwiches.

j. It was a [bazaar, bizarre] situation.

k. Members of labor unions voted as a [bloc, block] in the spring election.

l. Please [boar, boor, bore] holes in this piece of lumber.

m. She could hardly catch her [breath, breathe].

n. He froze the [balance, remainder] of the meat.

o. He gave his mother a beautiful [broach, brooch] for Christmas.

p. She placed the ball [beside, besides] the tennis racket.

q. The [biannual, biennial] event is in April and October.

r. The game was canceled [because of, due to] rain.

s. The judge set his [bail, bale] at $10,000.

t. The papers must be in a [bail, bale] or the recycling plant will not accept them.

u. The room was filled with smoke, making it difficult to [breath, breathe].

v. The tennis player was a [boar, boor, bore] with his frequent complaints about the referee's calls.

w. To raise money, the church sponsored a [bazaar, bizarre].

x. We used the bucket to [bail, bale] water from the leaking boat.

y. While they were on vacation, a [burglar, robber] broke in and stole a television set.

15. This exercise is based on the "correct word usage" section of this chapter and words beginning with a *C* in the "frequently misused words" list in Chapter 3. Mark through the incorrect choices in the following sentences.

a. Although she was in her mid-30s, her [childish, childlike] mannerisms made her a popular elementary-school teacher.

b. He was [censored, censured, censered] for his unethical behavior.

c. The [climactic, climatic] moment was when Jim met his birth mother for the first time.

d. Some NFL players receive salaries that are not [commensurate, commiserate] with their playing abilities.

e. How do NFL salaries [compare to, compare with] those of the NBA?

f. His behavior at the party shows that he is a [callous, callus] person.

g. It was a [cement, concrete] driveway.

h. The tent was made of [canvas, canvass].

i. The truck [collided with, hit] a fence.

j. To [censor, censure, censer] in that manner was a violation of the First Amendment, the court ruled.

k. We admired the murals on the walls of the [capital, capitol].

l. When editing copy without a computer, use a [carat, caret] to show insertions.

m. I think he is too [complacent, complaisant] to be the team leader.

n. How many sources did you [cite, sight, site] in your term paper?

o. While in the army, he was assigned to [calvary, cavalry] duty.

p. We received [complementary, complimentary] tickets to the play.

q. This policy provides [comprehensible, comprehensive] coverage.

r. Although the foreign student had an excellent grasp of formal English, she sometimes did not understand the [connotation, denotation] of words.

s. Mammals, reptiles and birds [compose, comprise] the zoo.

t. The local city [council, counsel] meets every week.

u. The red tie is a good [complement, compliment] to your new suit.

v. Ask the treasurer to [disburse, dispense, disperse] payment for these bills.

w. Was she [conscience, conscious] after the accident?

x. A synonym for intermittent is [continual, continuous].

y. His story did not seem [creditable, credible, credulous] to me.

z. This was the [cite, site] of a World War II [interment, internment] camp.

16. This exercise is based on the "correct word usage" section of this chapter and words beginning with *D* and *E* in the "frequently misused words" list in Chapter 3. Mark through the incorrect choices in the following sentences.

a. Because the judge seemed biased, I thought that she would not give a(n) [disinterested, uninterested] decision.

b. Don't talk; it might [detract, distract] the golfer.

c. I asked the real estate agent whether she [felt, thought] the property would [deprecate, depreciate] during the next two years.

d. In the movie two men fought a [dual, duel].

e. The scientist spent much of his career trying to [disapprove, disprove] Einstein's theory.

f. The room has a [distinctive, distinguished] odor.

g. The [desert, dessert] was a perfect [complement, compliment] to the meal.

h. The car has [dual, duel] mufflers.

i. He hurled [epithets, epitaphs] at his opponent.

j. The new law makes a jail term mandatory for [drunk, drunken] drivers.

k. She always feels [eager, anxious] on the night before a big test.

l. The scene [evoked, invoked] memories of his boyhood home.

17. This exercise is based on the "correct word usage" section of this chapter and words beginning with *F* and *G* in the "frequently misused words" list in Chapter 3. Mark through the incorrect choices in the following sentences.

a. [Fliers, Flyers] were placed throughout the campus to announce the meeting.

b. After many years as a successful newspaper reporter, he became a [flack, flak] for a politician.

c. In his dealings with children in the neighborhood, he was an [erasable, irascible] old man.

d. The mother told her child to be careful at summer camp, [especially, specially] when swimming.

e. They chose this hotel [especially, specially] for the wedding reception.

f. Did you [elicit, illicit] a promise from the child?

g. The family [emigrated, immigrated] to the United States in 1945.

h. As part of her physical training program, she walked at least a mile [farther, further] each week.

i. He [figuratively, literally] hit the ceiling when he heard about the ruling.

j. He [flaunted, flouted] his wealth.

k. It was a [flagrant, fragrant] foul, but the referee did not see it.

l. Please cook some [flounder, founder].

m. Please study the matter [farther, further] before deciding what to do.

n. Two [fewer, less] candidates filed for office this year.

o. His colleagues did not think his [factious, factitious, facetious] remarks were amusing.

p. His presence seemed to [ferment, foment] trouble.

q. Jim is her [fiancé, fiancée].

r. The 400-pound wrestler was a [forbidding, foreboding] opponent.

s. To accomplish the task on time, workers had to [forego, forgo] vacations.

t. He was a [gorilla, guerrilla] in Nicaragua.

u. Jury members flinched when the prosecutor showed pictures of the [grisly, gristly, grizzly] crime scene.

18. This exercise is based on the "correct word usage" section of this chapter and words beginning with *H* through *L* in the "frequently misused words" list in Chapter 3. Mark through the incorrect choices in the following sentences.

a. [Hopefully, I hope] it will not rain on July 4.

b. If your mother marries my father, we will become [half sisters, stepsisters].

c. He was an [inapt, inept] carpenter.

d. The Bible is a [holey, holy] book.

e. The city wanted to erect a [historic, historical] marker at the site.

f. The commander ordered that all flags on the [naval, navel] fleet should fly at [half-mast, half-staff].

g. The temperature today will be [lower, cooler] than yesterday.

h. After the discussion, the marriage [counselor, councilor] had a better [incite, insight] into the couple's problems.

i. Grease is [insoluble, insolvable, insolvent] in water.

j. Have you decided [if, whether] you will attend this university?

k. He was [impassable, impassible] during the funeral.

l. She was [incredible, incredulous] at the sales representative's claims for the product.

m. You should be polite to John, [irregardless, irrespective] of your dislike for him.

n. It was an [ingenious, ingenuous] solution to the problem, and she wondered why no one had tried it earlier.

o. The [eminent, imminent] scientist was born in Germany but [emigrated, immigrated] to the United States.

p. The teachers did everything they could to [insure, ensure] the students' safety.

q. The doctors had no explanation for the higher [incidence, incidents] of cancer in that county.

r. The County Commission has the power to [levee, levy] property taxes.

s. The paint had the [affect, effect] of [lightening, lightning] the wood.

t. He was [judicial, judicious] in his handling of money.

u. I am [loath, loathe] to go to the dentist.

v. The convicted drug lord told authorities that he simply was involved in (interstate, intrastate) commerce along the Canadian border.

w. When you talked to him, did you mean to [imply, infer] that you were unhappy?

x. The sky is dark; it looks [like, as though] it will rain.

y. Newspaper advertising [linage, lineage] has increased 10 percent this year.

z. He [lay, lain, layed] in the sun too long.

19. This exercise is based on the "correct word usage" section of this chapter and words beginning with *M* through *P* in the "frequently misused words" list in this chapter. Mark through the incorrect choices in the following sentences.

a. He was selected parade [marshal, marshall].

b. The challenger was able to [marshal, marshall] his strength to defeat the reigning champion.

c. The car [motor, engine] overheated.

d. The commander asked that someone volunteer for the [odious, odorous] duty.

e. The experienced driver won the race with a [masterful, masterly] display of racing ability.

f. After taxes, her salary increase was [negligent, negligible].

g. He became [nauseated, nauseous] on the plane.

h. The parents were [negligent, negligible] in their treatment of the child.

i. [More than, Over] 2,000 attended the performance.

j. He could not get the company to honor the [oral, verbal] promises made by the sales clerk. Only written warranties were valid.

k. The reporter became [nauseated, nauseous] when he saw the mangled bodies.

l. An artist uses a [palate, palette, pallet].

m. He bit into the pizza, burning his [palate, palette, pallet].

n. She hoped to [parlay, parley] his fame into fortune.

o. The district attorney will [persecute, prosecute] the murder suspect.

p. The [councilor, counselor] was able to [persuade, convince] the students that a college education is important.

q. The senior class will [proceed, precede] the junior class.

r. He sent his son into town to [pedal, petal, peddle] the wooden toys.

s. She wanted to uphold the [principal, principle] of equality although it would cost her company more money.

t. I was flattered when the boss asked for my [perspective, prospective] of the situation.

u. Students who engage in [prescribed, proscribed] behavior will be expelled from this university.

v. The [principal, principle] shareholder spoke at the annual meeting.

w. The company announced its [perspective, prospective] earnings at the annual meeting today.

x. The fancy car was a [perquisite, prerequisite] that came with his new position at the company.

y. The guest speaker climbed the stairs to the [podium, lectern] and placed her notes on the [podium, lectern].

z. The [burglar, robber] gained entry to her home on the [pretense, pretext] of going there to repair the telephone.

20. This exercise is based on the "correct word usage" section of this chapter and words beginning with *Q* through *Z* in the "frequently misused words" list in this chapter. Mark through the incorrect choices in the following sentences.

a. The doctor [prescribed, proscribed] medicine for my illness, but she seemed [quiet, quite] [reluctant, reticent] to do so.

b. The politician was [reluctant, reticent] during the interview.

c. We will finish the project [irregardless, regardless] of our financial situation.

d. You have made some serious errors, but I think that the situation is [remediable, remedial].

e. He is a [reckless, wreckless] driver.

f. Although the pay was good, the work was [seasonable, seasonal], and he wanted to work throughout the year.

g. The baker wanted the dough to [raise, rise].

h. In his eagerness to please everyone, he is [reluctant, reticent] to make decisions.

i. The veterinarian suggested that the dog be [spade, spayed].

j. The barber used a [strap, strop] to sharpen the razor.

k. Magicians engage in [sleight, slight] of hand.

l. Police erected a [stationary, stationery] barrier.

m. It was a [tenant, tenet] that guided him in his business dealings.

n. It was a [tort, torte] that could have been avoided with careful copy editing.

o. Stained-glass windows are [transparent, translucent].

p. She wore a [shear, sheer] blouse.

q. She hoped to join the state highway patrol as a [trooper, trouper].

r. Here is the book [which, that] she ordered.

s. This version of the computer program will [supercede, supersede] the one issued two years ago.

t. Unexpected expenses will [wreak, wreck] havoc on my budget.

u. Her argument was [tortuous, torturous].

v. He said it was a [venal, venial] sin.

w. It is a [viral, virile] disease.

x. Having gone without food for two days, the hunters had [veracious, voracious] appetites.

y. He said he would [wangle, wrangle] an invitation.

z. The recipe called for three egg [yokes, yolks].

Chapter 4 Exercises

1. Go to the source indicated in the chapter and select a communications-related discussion group. Subscribe to the group, and then print the welcoming message that you receive. After monitoring the discussion group for several days, write a brief summary of the topics covered by members during those days. If there's no discussion in the group after a couple of days of monitoring, subscribe to a different group.

2. Use The World Almanac and Book of Facts or a similar printed or online reference source to answer these questions. Indicate the name of your print or online source and specific page number or URL for each answer.

   a.   Who was the architect for the General Motors Building in Detroit: Albert Kahn or Louis Kahn?

   b.   When did Pakistan become a republic?

   c.   What is the name of the highest point in Australia?

   d.   Is it Southwestern or Southwest Baptist Theological Seminary? Is it in Dallas or Fort Worth?

   e.   In what year was Hillary Rodham Clinton born?

   f.   How many stars does the flag of Honduras have?

   g.   What were the top five U.S. companies in terms of advertising expenditures in 2005?

3. Answer the following questions in complete sentences. Cite your source for each answer. For printed sources, give the name of the reference work, page number and date published. For Web sites, give the complete title of the Web site, name of sponsor and URL. Follow AP style.

   a.   During what years did the "cultural revolution" during Mao Zedong's leadership happen in China? When did Deng Xiaoping re-emerge as the de facto ruler of the People's Republic of China, and when did his leadership period end?

   b.   You are editing a press release about the opening of a new museum exhibit about first ladies of the White House. In one or two sentences, give Martha Washington's full name, age and marital status at the time she married George Washington. Include the date of their marriage.

   c.   One paragraph in the press release reads: "The Atlantic cable was completed in 1858 to carry instantaneous communications across the ocean for the first time. Although the laying of this first cable was seen as a landmark event in society, it was a technical failure because it remained in service only a few days. Subsequent cables laid a few years later were successful and compare in importance to events like the moon landing of a century later." You need to check the accuracy of the 1858 date and to add a date for the successful cable completion to be more specific than "a few years later."

   d.   How many people have immigrated to the United States since 1880?

   e.   Give the full names of the U.S. senators from your home state and the names of the Senate committees they serve on in the current session of Congress.

4. Answer the following questions in complete sentences as though the information were part of a story you are editing. Give a complete citation for your source for each answer. Follow AP style.

   a.   Who won the Pulitzer Prize for fiction in 2006?

   b.   Use information from Who's Who in America or a similar biographical source to write several sentences about the winner of the Pulitzer Prize for fiction in 2006.

   c.   Who won the Pulitzer Prize for criticism in 2006? What was the usual topic of criticism for this journalist?

c. A woman, who asked that her name not be revealed, said in an interview that John Politician, local mayor, raped her last year after the Christmas party for city employees. She said that she did not report the rape to police because she was afraid that she would lose her job at city hall.

☑ Plaintiff has no case because _____"actual malice"_____ (element of libel) is not present.

☐ All elements are present; the common-law defense is:

_____

d. In passing sentence on John E. Smith yesterday, Judge James Hangman said, "You are a sorry excuse for a man. The lowest animal known to mankind deserves more mercy than you gave your victim. I wish this state gave me the authority to pronounce the death penalty on such dregs of humanity like you."

☐ Plaintiff has no case because _____ (element of libel) is not present.

☑ All elements are present; the common-law defense is:
_____actual malice_____

e. Unless you're in the mood for a middle-of-the-night visit to the hospital emergency room, don't eat at the Country Style Delights restaurant. The desserts are pretty good, but the rest of the food isn't fit for a dog to eat.

☐ Plaintiff has no case because _____ (element of libel) is not present.

☐ All elements are present; the common-law defense is:

_____

f. John X. Doe, 2468 Kingston Ave., was drunk when he raced his car through the red light at Green and Main streets and struck the pedestrian, police on the scene said.

☑ Plaintiff has no case because _____actual malice"_____ (element of libel) is not present.

☐ All elements are present; the common-law defense is:

_____

g. John X. Doe, 2468 Kingston Ave., was arrested and charged with driving under the influence of alcohol after an accident at Green and Main streets last night.

☑ Plaintiff has no case because _____ (element of libel) is not present.

☐ All elements are present; the common-law defense is:

_____

h. "You are a murderer!" Sarah Bitter screamed from the witness stand as she pointed at the defendant, John E. Smith.

☐ Plaintiff has no case because _____ (element of libel) is not present.

☐ All elements are present; the common-law defense is:

_____

i. "All sorority girls are whores," the evangelist told a campus crowd yesterday. "State universities shouldn't condone the sinful activities of sororities and fraternities."

☐ Plaintiff has no case because _____ (element of libel) is not present.

☑ All elements are present; the common-law defense is:
_____actual malice_____

j. At a meeting of the city council yesterday, a social worker told council members that Mayor John Politician was "charging big money to poor people who rent his rat-infested hovels."

☐ Plaintiff has no case because _____ (element of libel) is not present.

☐ All elements are present; the common-law defense is:

_____

k. The Coffee Cup Cafe was ordered closed yesterday by the county health department. Records indicate that the cafe has scored below the "acceptable" rating on each of the last three sanitary inspections by health officials.

☒ Plaintiff has no case because ____actual malice____ (element of libel) is not present.

☐ All elements are present; the common-law defense is:

_____

3. Describe a situation in which the president of your college or university would be considered a private person in a libel suit. *If he/she has not "thrust" themselves into public controversy*

4. Show that you understand the legal distinction between a limited public figure and a private person by naming two people in your town and the contexts in which each would be considered a limited public figure. *limited — woman vocal about schools* *private — Mary — older woman everyone knows*

5. Consider each of the following situations in terms of privacy. Tell which privacy tort the plaintiff would best claim. Then tell what defense, if any, would apply. Based on information given in this chapter, which side is likely to win if a privacy suit is filed?

a. Suzy Goodtan, movie celebrity, was sunbathing nude in her backyard, which is surrounded by an 8-foot privacy fence. A freelance photographer stands on a 10-foot ladder to look over the fence and take Suzy's picture. The picture is never published.

Privacy tort that best applies here ____intrusion upon physical solitude____

Best defense against that particular privacy tort ____in public view?____

Likely winner of this privacy case: ☒ Plaintiff ☐ Defendant

b. Mark Jones was shopping at the Super Save Supermarket yesterday when a big display of tomato soup cans fell on his head. He is now in the hospital, suffering from a head injury. A videographer who happened to be in the supermarket at the time of the accident took some footage of Mark lying on the floor awaiting the ambulance. In its evening newscast, a local TV station included the footage with a tagline reading "Freak Accident" and the anchorperson gave Jones' name and address. Jones files an invasion of privacy lawsuit.

Privacy tort that best applies here ____publication of private info.____

Best defense against that particular privacy tort ____—not offensive____

Likely winner of this privacy case: ☐ Plaintiff ☒ Defendant

c. If the newscast mentioned in Exercise 5b included the name and address of the Super Save Supermarket, would the owner of the market have a good chance to win either a libel or privacy suit?

Privacy tort that best applies here _____ *none* _____

Best defense against that particular privacy tort _____ *it's a public place* _____

_____

Likely winner of this privacy case: ☐ Plaintiff ☒ Defendant

Would Super Save have a better chance of winning a libel suit than a privacy suit? Explain.

d. Mark Jones was surprised a few days later when he saw a television commercial showing his cute 4-year-old daughter standing in a Super Save aisle. It seems that the public relations/advertising agency that represents Super Save obtained outtakes from the TV newscast to create a television commercial. The voice-over for the commercial said: "Four-year-old Heather enjoys tagging along with her parents to shop at Super Save where the family can purchase all its grocery needs at the lowest prices in town."

Privacy tort that best applies here _____ *appropriation* _____

Best defense against that particular privacy tort _____

_____

Likely winner of this privacy case: ☒ Plaintiff ☐ Defendant

e. A famous actress is in town to appear in a play. The local newspaper publishes a picture of a prominent local executive, who is married, embracing the actress in a hotel lobby. The picture caption identifies both the man and the actress.

Privacy tort that best applies here _____ *false light* _____

Best defense against that particular privacy tort _____ *they didn't depict*
them as lovers _____

Likely winner of this privacy case: ☐ Plaintiff ☒ Defendant

f. The caption for the picture of a famous actress and prominent local executive embracing in a hotel lobby implies that a romantic relationship exists between the two.

Privacy tort that best applies here _____ *false light* _____

Best defense against that particular privacy tort _____

_____

Likely winner of this privacy case: ☒ Plaintiff ☐ Defendant

g. A magazine reveals that 25 years ago Sam Goodman was released from prison after serving a 10-year term on a conviction of molesting children. During the past 25 years, Goodman has been an outstanding citizen in town and has been honored for his volunteer work with children. Goodman's family, friends and business associates were unaware of his past criminal conviction.

Privacy tort that best applies here _____ *publication of private info.* _____

Best defense against that particular privacy tort _____ *public records* _____

_____

Likely winner of this privacy case: ☐ Plaintiff ☐ Defendant

h. A magazine reveals that 25 years ago Sam Goodman (Exercise 5g) was arrested and charged with molesting children, but the magazine does not include the information that Goodman was acquitted of the charges after a trial.

Privacy tort that best applies here _____ *false light* _____

Best defense against that particular privacy tort _____

_____

Likely winner of this privacy case: ☒ Plaintiff ☐ Defendant

i. To attract subscribers, the local newspaper uses direct mail advertising to all nonsubscribers in town. The ad includes a page reprinted from the newspaper, showing a color picture of a former star quarterback at your university in a game photo that ran previously on the sports page. The quarterback now stars in the NFL and commands large endorsement fees.

Privacy tort that best applies here _____ *appropriation* _____

Best defense against that particular privacy tort _____

_____

Likely winner of this privacy case: ☒ Plaintiff ☐ Defendant

j. A magazine publishes a story revealing intimate, graphic details about the sex life of a famous Hollywood actor. The story is based on interviews with two longtime employees at the actor's home.

Privacy tort that best applies here _____ *publication of private info* _____

Best defense against that particular privacy tort _____

_____

Likely winner of this privacy case: ☒ Plaintiff ☐ Defendant

6. You are a magazine staff photographer. A nationally circulated sports magazine contacts you about buying some of your pictures that have appeared in the magazine.

    a. Discuss this situation in terms of copyright.

    b. Would copyright considerations differ for a public relations professional employed by a PR firm that edits a newsletter for one of its corporate clients? Explain your answer.

7. A public relations firm hired by an author to promote her first novel is considering the idea of trying to place a condensed, serialized version of the book in a magazine or a newspaper, along with a feature story about the author. Explain whether such a series is likely to qualify as fair use. Your discussion should illustrate that you understand the meaning and application of fair use.

8. A public high school prohibits students from wearing T-shirts that convey commercial messages, including names and logos of popular musical groups. If this ban is challenged in court, explain the legal rationale that the court is likely to use. (Assume that this school does not require students to wear uniforms.)

9. If students at a private high school challenge the same T-shirt ban, would the same legal rationale apply? Explain your answer.

10. Might your answer to Exercise 9 vary from state to state? Explain.

11. A high school newspaper staff working in a journalism class plans to publish an article about safe sex. The principal prohibits the article, arguing that safe sex is an inappropriate subject for immature high school students.

    a. If this censorship were challenged in court, which legal test would be used: the "substantial disruption" test or the rationale from the 1988 Supreme Court case? Explain your answer.

    b. What will be the outcome of the case? Explain your answer.

12. If the student publications department at a public college wished to publish an article about safe sex on its Web site or newspaper, might it encounter problems from school administrators? Explain your answer.

13. A reporter wrote a straight news lead for the complaint shown in the following illustration, but the supervising editor wanted a short human-interest feature instead of a straight news story. It is nearly deadline and all reporters are busy, so it's your job to rewrite the lead to make it a "bright" for your hometown paper. Read the following complaint carefully and write a two-paragraph lead to put on top of the story the reporter submitted.

IN THE CIRCUIT COURT FOR PINELLAS COUNTY FLORIDA
CASE NO. _98-4224-CI-020_

PAUL SHIMKONIS,
        Plaintiff

vs

DIAMOND DOLL'S LIMITED,
PANIC BROTHERS, INC. d/b/a
BLOOPERS, individually,
jointly and severally,
        Defendant
_____/

COMPLAINT

Plaintiff, PAUL SHIMKONIS, by and through his undersigned attorney, hereby sues Defendant, DIAMOND DOLL'S LIMITED, PANIC BROTHERS, INC. d/b/a BLOOPERS, individually, jointly and severally, and alleges:

1. This is an action for damages in excess of FIFTEEN THOUSAND DOLLARS ($15,000.00) exclusive of costs, interest and attorney fees.

2. Plaintiff resides in Pinellas County, Florida.

3. Defendant is doing business in Pinellas County, Florida.

4. On or about September 27, 1996, at approximately 10:00 p.m., Plaintiff, PAUL SHIMKONIS was attending his bachelor party at BLOOPERS, commonly known as DIAMOND DOLL'S, located at 16361 U.S. Highway 19 North, Clearwater, Pinellas Park, Florida.

5. Since this was Plaintiff's bachelor party, he was with a group of friends, out for an evening of entertainment.

6. During the course of the evening, while at DIAMOND DOLL'S, the Plaintiff, PAUL SHIMKONIS, being the guest of honor, was requested, by the star dancer, to sit low in a chair, resting

1

his neck on the back of the chair with his eyes closed, to be specially entertained by the star dancer. The Plaintiff, PAUL SHIMKONIS, complied with her request.

7.   The DIAMOND DOLLS' star dancer proceeded to dance in front of the Plaintiff, PAUL SHIMKONIS and then suddenly, without warning and without Plaintiff's consent, jumped on the Plaintiff forcing her very large breasts into his face causing his head to jerk backwards.

8.   That as a direct and proximate result of the conduct of the Defendant, DIAMOND DOLLS entertainer, as alleged above, Plaintiff, PAUL SHIMKONIS, was injured in and about his head, neck, body and limbs; and the Plaintiff has sustained the following past and future damages:

> (a) Bodily injury.
>
> (b) Disability.
>
> (c) Pain and suffering.
>
> (d) Disfigurement.
>
> (e) Mental anguish.
>
> (f) Loss of capacity for the enjoyment of life.
>
> (g) Medical and related expenses in seeking a cure for

his injuries.

> (h) Loss or diminution of earnings or earning capacity.
>
> (i) Aggravation of pre-existing conditions or diseases.

WHEREFORE, the Plaintiff, PAUL SHIMKONIS, demands a trial by jury and judgment against Defendant, DIAMOND DOLL'S LIMITED, PANIC BROTHERS, INC. d/b/a BLOOPERS, for a sum within the

2

13. Explain what is meant by "set width."

14. As layout editor for a company newsletter, you want to determine how wide to set a block of copy for best legibility. Explain how you would go about determining this.

15. The screens of your favorite Web site will look different depending on the Web browser used to open the page. Use Internet Explorer to open your favorite Web site. Print out a copy of the page. Now use Mozilla Firefox to open the Web site, and print out another copy of the page. What differences do you notice? Do Web designers have absolute control over the appearance of their pages? Why or why not?

Chapter 9 Exercises

1. For each of the following words, list at least three synonyms that would take less space:

   a. suggestion   *advice, proposal, pointer*

   b. organization   *agency, group, union*

   c. contributor   *donor, giver, sponsor*

   d. falsehood   *fiction, falsity, untruth, lie, fib*

2. Shorten each of the following phrases:

   a. capital city   *capital*

   b. on the order of   *___ ordered by, like*

   c. at that time   *when, then*

   d. due to the fact   *due to*

   e. a softly blowing wind   *a wind, breeze*

   f. attain victory   *win, won*

   g. during the time   *when*

3. The two headlines that follow have "bad breaks," or awkward line splits. Rewrite each one to keep verb phrases together on one line and to keep modifiers and the words they modify on the same line. Don't worry about the count, but try to keep all lines about the same length.

   a. **Provost will**
      resign today   *Provost resigns today*

   b. **Russia may**
      ratify new
      treaty today   *Ratify needs to be on top line*

4. Rewrite these headlines to remove unproven accusations:

   a. **Child murderer goes on trial**   *~~Accused~~ Child-murder suspect ~~goes~~ on trial*

   b. **Cops nab 40 hoods in gambling raid**   *Cops arrest 40 in gambling raid*

5. Rewrite this headline to correct unattributed opinion:

Regents hit students with stiff tuition

The Board of Regents today set tuition for next year at $2,000, an increase of 12 percent more than the current level.

Regents raise tuition for students

Regents raise tuition by 12%

6. Correct the punctuation in these headlines:

   a. **Mayor opposes tax cut;**
      prepares new budget.   *Mayor opposes tax cut, prepares new budget*

no period

The five were captured, one by a worker at the daily Arab Times and the others by police after a car chase, an Interior Ministry statement said.

No one was injured. The U.S. comic strip, about a boorish but lovable Viking and his eccentric family, showed Hagar on a hill saying: "I pray and pray, but you never answer me." A voice from the clouds answers: "Sorry if you don't get through right away, keep trying. These days everyone wants to talk to me." Many Muslims saw the cartoon as sacrilegious. A magazine published by a group of fundamentalist Sunni Muslims said the comic strip was "mocking God and communication between humans and their God." The Al-Mujtama magazine accused the newspaper's non-Muslim employees of poking fun at Kuwait's laws and religion.

The newspaper ran an apology Thursday, 11 days after the cartoon appeared. It said the "inclusion of the cartoon was inappropriate but unintentional and done without malice."

"They took the mistake and turned it into a conspiracy," said the paper's American managing editor, Tadeusz Karwecki. "Everyone makes mistakes, but you don't go out and shoot people for them."

18. Refer to the headline schedule in Figure 9-4 (page 193) to write a headline for this story. Practice writing your heads on scrap paper, then transcribe the completed version to the appropriate place at the top of each story. Or, if writing headlines on a computer, follow your instructor's directions.

2-24-3:

Jacques Bailly, a 14-year-old eighth-grade student from Denver, yesterday won the National Spelling Bee by correctly spelling "elucubrate."

Jacques got his chance when Paige Pipkin, a 12-year-old seventh grader from El Paso, Texas, missed on "glitch." She spelled it "glitsch." After Jacques properly spelled "glitch," he breezed through "elucubrate" before pronouncer Richard Baker could provide the definition.

Jacques is no stranger to elucubration—laborious work, especially at night or by candlelight.

"Well, you read a lot and you work a lot," he said, explaining his secret of success.

Jacques and Paige were the top of 112 finalists who came to Washington for the 53rd annual competition sponsored by Scripps Howard Newspapers.

Jacques spelled "auburn," "finesse," "maladroit," "nimiety," "juratory," "davit," "abecedarian," "frijoles," "blatherskite," "wassail" and "halcyon" to reach the final face-off.

Jacques won $1,000 and a loving cup. Paige won $500.

19. Refer to the headline schedule in Figure 9-4 (page 193) to write a headline for this story. Practice writing your heads on scrap paper, then transcribe the completed version to the appropriate place at the top of each story. Or, if writing headlines on a computer, follow your instructor's directions.

`4-48-1 with 4-30-1 underline:`

WASHINGTON—More than two-thirds of Americans believe television contributes to violence, erodes family values and fosters a distrust of government, according to a new poll released Saturday.

The public also is troubled by increasingly graphic portrayals of sex during prime time, said the poll, which will appear in the U.S. News & World Report issue on newsstands Monday.

Nearly 80 percent of Hollywood executives questioned by mail in a separate survey agreed there was a link between TV violence and violence in real life, but they were not nearly as concerned about TV's role in other social problems.

Fifty-three percent of the executives said TV contributed to distrust of government, and 46 percent thought it contributed to the decline of family values. Thirty-four percent believe TV played some role in America's divorce rate.

One thousand adults were interviewed for the poll, which had a margin of error of plus or minus 3 percent. U.S. News said 570 of the 6,500 Hollywood executives who received the mail surveys responded to them.

"It is not a scientific survey, but the total number of responses was significant and suggests that many Hollywood leaders are concerned about trends in the television business," the magazine said.

Eighty-four percent of the general public said they were concerned about the relationship of extramarital sex on TV and real-life problems.

In contrast, 43 percent of the Hollywood executives said they were concerned.

Seventy-five percent of the public said they were concerned about the portrayal of passionate encounters and heavy kissing on TV, compared to 28 percent of Hollywood leaders.

When asked about the solutions they would favor, 95 percent of both groups agreed that parental supervision was the most important step, the magazine said.

20. Write a news brief headline (1-14-2) for this press release.

ORLANDO, Fla., July 27 /PRNewswire/—Ozzy Osbourne has conquered it all. This rock 'n' roll rebel pioneered the heavy metal revolution, became a reality TV star (of the Emmy-winning "The Osbournes") and has even been invited to the White House—turning a passion for music into a rock empire.

Now, the "Godfather of Heavy Metal" is taking on Hard Rock International to become the hardest rocker yet in the company's Signature Series. Hard Rock today unveiled its latest Signature Series T-shirt, designed by the "Ironman" himself, Ozzy Osbourne.

Proceeds from the new Ozzy Osbourne T-shirt benefit the Sharon Osbourne Colon Cancer Program at Cedars-Sinai Medical Center, established by Ozzy's wife Sharon following her own battle with colon cancer.

Ozzy Osbourne, the 22nd rocker to become part of Hard Rock's Signature Series T-shirt program, joins music icons and legends, such as Elton John, Eric Clapton and Bruce Springsteen, helping to raise millions of dollars for a number of charitable causes worldwide.

21. Write news brief headlines (1-14-2) for each of the press release leads you edited in Exercise 1 of Chapter 3.

22. Write headlines for the stories in the exercise section of Chapter 5. Use head specifications assigned by your instructor.

23. For more headline and editing practice, select press releases from PR Newswire at http://www.prnewswire.com/ and follow your instructor's directions.

24. Clip some stories and headlines from today's edition of a printed newspaper without looking at the online version. Write headlines suitable for the online version. Then compare your headlines with those for the same stories on the newspaper's Web site.

Chapter 10 Exercises

Photographs in these exercises are available on the textbook Web site if your instructor directs you to use Photoshop or other digital editing software.

1. Define or describe each of the following:

   a. contact print

   b. linen tester

   c. crop marks

   d. scale a photograph

   e. pixel

2. Define or describe each of the following:

   a. Lead-in (also called a tagline or legend) picture caption style

   b. At least three different variations for lead-in captions

3. Refer to the following photo:

a. Size this picture to be reproduced four columns wide for a newspaper that uses columns 12 picas (2 inches) wide with 1 pica (1.6 inch) of white space between columns. Show crop marks, even if you decide not to crop anything out of the photo. Indicate the size of the original as cropped, the size of the photo as it will be published and the percentage of reproduction.

b. Write a caption with an overline to accompany this stand-alone photo. Here is information for the caption:

Who: estimated 300 marchers, sponsored by ProChoice of your state

What: parade by pro-choice group, with anti-abortion adherents watching from along parade route

Where: around state Capitol building in your state

When: yesterday at noon

Why: pro-choice and anti-abortion proponents seeking to persuade state legislators to pass legislation supporting their respective points of view; state legislature expected to vote this session on legislation concerning abortion

Photo credit: Miles Cary, Knoxville (Tenn.) News-Sentinel

4. Refer to the following photo:

a. Crop this photo to run one column (12 picas or 2 inches) wide. Show your crop marks, the size of the original as cropped, the reproduction size and the percentage of reproduction.

b. Write a caption that can be used in a layout combining this photo and the photo in Exercise 3 (see the information in Exercise 3).

Who: Molly Yard, former president of the National Organization for Women

What: rally of pro-choice supporters

Where: on steps of state Capitol building in your state capital

When: yesterday at noon, immediately after pro-choice parade

Why: (see information in Exercise 3)

Other: size of crowd at rally, which included supporters of both pro-choice and anti-abortion positions and curious onlookers, estimated by Capitol security officers at 3,000

Photo credit: Miles Cary, Knoxville (Tenn.) News-Sentinel

5. Refer to the following photographs:

PHOTOS BY HEATHER McCOY.

a. To illustrate a newsletter story about ROTC at your school, size and crop one of these photographs for two columns (25 picas wide) and the other for one column (12 picas wide). Be prepared to justify the decision you make regarding which photo will be one column wide and which will be two columns. Show your crop marks, the size of the original as cropped, the reproduction size and the percentage of reproduction for each photo.

b. Write one caption to accompany both photographs, drawing from these notes supplied by Heather McCoy, a photographer who spent much of a day with the ROTC cadets.

Reserve Officer Training Course (ROTC) cadets demonstrate dedication and commitment during their on-campus training. The group I accompanied started their day with a physical training class at 6 a.m. in the ROTC facility. Then they ran several miles through the campus. Then they hurried back to the ROTC building to shower and attend their other university classes. Late that afternoon they all gathered at the ROTC building again and went by truck to go through the obstacle course at the Marine base near campus. This year there are only about seven women enrolled in ROTC. The officer in command of the group I observed said that the females keep up with their male counterparts on the obstacle course. Heather McCoy, staff photographer

6. Refer to the following photograph:

a. Crop and proportion this photo to fit a layout space 38 picas wide by 19 picas deep in the zoo news-letter. Specify the reproduction size of the original as cropped and the percentage of reproduction. Don't forget to show your crop marks.

b. Write a caption with an overline, using this information:

Who: an employee at the Knoxville Zoo

What: unloading a truckload of straw

Where: Knoxville Zoological Gardens

When: 6 a.m. yesterday

Why: straw used as bedding for many of the hundreds of animals at the zoo

7. Refer to the following photograph:

a. Crop and size to fit a layout space 25 picas wide by 31 picas deep in the zoo newsletter. Specify the reproduction size of the original as cropped and the percentage of reproduction. Don't forget to show your crop marks.

b. Write a caption with a tagline from this information:

Who: an employee at the Knoxville Zoo

What: preparing individual bowls of food

Where: Knoxville Zoological Gardens

When: 6 a.m. yesterday

Why: to feed animals at the zoo

8. Refer to the following photograph:

a. Crop and size for a two-column newspaper layout (25 picas wide) to accompany a news story. Specify the reproduction size of the original as cropped and the percentage of reproduction. Don't forget to show your crop marks.

b. Write a caption from this information:

What: Jeep stranded

Where: in 1100 block of Eighth St.

When: yesterday at 7 p.m.

Why: rain storm; 4 inches of rain fell in less than an hour, according to local weather bureau. Police issue warning to motorists to avoid driving into standing water because it is impossible to know how deep the water is.

9. Refer to the following photograph:

a. Size this photo to run three columns (38 picas or 6⅓ inches) wide. Specify the reproduction size of the original as cropped and the percentage of reproduction. Don't forget to show your crop marks.

b. Write a caption from the following information. Use an all-capital, boldface lead-in.

Who: John Smith (No. 41 in white uniform) from Central High, Bryan Langford (No. 3 in dark uniform) from Halls High School

What: Smith's touchdown run during fourth quarter; 30 seconds left to play

Where: Central High Stadium

When: last night

Other: Central High had ball on Halls' 45-yard line; Smith took handoff from quarterback, went around right end and scored; Bryan Langford had hold of Smith's jersey as Smith turned corner, but Langford lost his grip; no other Halls defender could catch Smith; this was winning score; Central won 14–7.

10. Refer to the following photograph:

a. Crop and proportion this photo to fill a space four columns (51 picas or 8½ inches) wide by 28 picas (4⅔ inches) deep. You may crop one or more of the young dancers from the photo if necessary. Show crop marks, the size of the original as cropped, the reproduction size and the percentage of reproduction.

b. Write a caption for the picture. Unfortunately, the list of names of the children has been misplaced, and it is close to deadline time, so you will have to write the caption without naming the children.

Who: five girls waiting their turn to audition

What: audition for "The Nutcracker"; 28 girls auditioned

Where: at Monroe Auditorium

When: auditions last night; "The Nutcracker" to be presented at the Monroe Auditorium December 1 through December 6

11. Crop and size the following photo two different ways:

a. Without cropping anything, size the photo so it can be reproduced two columns (25 picas) wide. Specify the depth and the percentage of reproduction.

b. Crop and size the photo so the piece of sculpture alone will be published in a space two columns wide by 46 picas deep. Don't forget to mark the margins for cropping. Specify the size of the original as cropped and the percentage of reproduction.

12. The public relations department of an insurance company is preparing a brochure to promote life insurance sales. A selling point will be the cost of raising a child from birth to age 17. Decide which type of informational graphic is most appropriate for this information and use the following figures to create a graphic.

> A middle-income family raising a child born in 1995 can expect to spend $7,610 on the child in 1995; $8,020 in 1996; $8,450 in 1997; $9,140 in 1998; $9,640 in 1999; $10,160 in 2000; $10,790 in 2001; $11,370 in 2002; $11,990 in 2003; $12,620 in 2004; $13,300 in 2005; $14,020 in 2006; $16,130 in 2007; $17,000 in 2008; $17,920 in 2009; $19,170 in 2010; $20,210 in 2011; $21,300 in 2012 when the child is 17 years old and ready for college. These figures come from the U.S. Department of Agriculture, Center for Nutrition Policy and Promotion, and assume an average annual inflation rate of 5.4 percent.

13. A newspaper reporter has included the following information in a story. Decide which type of graphic is most appropriate for the information in each paragraph and use the figures to create two graphics.

a. According to a survey at the local shopping mall yesterday, a 7-year-old child here in Centerville receives an average of $2 a week from his or her parents as an allowance. A typical 8-year-old gets $2.50 a week allowance. By the time the child is 10, he or she typically receives $3.50. On average, an 11-year-old will get $4.25 for a weekly allowance; at age 12 that increases to $4.50; $5 by age 13; $10 at age 15; and $15 at age 16.

b. What do children spend their allowances on? Our survey indicates that this varies from age to age, but here is the breakdown for the average 16-year-old respondent: 20 percent on food; 15 percent on tapes and CDs; 23 percent on clothes; 10 percent on gifts, including church contributions; 6 percent savings toward a specific purchase; 1 percent on school supplies; 25 percent on tickets for movies, concerts, athletic or special events.

14. Create an informational graphic that shows gains that women have made in winning elected offices. The graph should compare the number of women in office in 1992 and 2006. The information comes from The White House Project.

> The U.S. Senate was composed of 97 percent men and 3 percent women in 1992. By 2006, women composed 14 percent of the senators. In the House of Representatives in 1992, 7.7 percent were women and 92.3 percent were men. By 2006, women held 66 seats in the House of Representatives. In total, 80 of the 535 members of Congress (both houses) are women (15 percent overall). The number of women governors has changed from 8 percent in 1992 to 16 percent in 2006. Women members in state legislatures were 18.4 percent in 1992 and 22.5 percent in 2006. The United States ranks 69th in the world in terms of women's representation in national legislatures or parliaments out of 187 countries, as of March 2006. In April 2005, the United States ranked 49th in the world, but our standing declined between 2005 and 2006.

15. Create an informational graphic from the following information. Find a suitable piece of artwork to incorporate into your graphic.

> The percentage of adults in the United States who surf the Internet increased significantly between 1998 and 2006. According to a Harris Poll, 35 percent of Americans said they used the Internet in 1998. That number had increased to 56 percent the following year. By 2000, 57 percent reported using the Internet. In 2001, that figure has increased to 64 percent. By 2002, a total of 66 percent of Americans said that they surfed the Internet. Seventy-four percent of all U.S. adults went online in 2004, and 77 percent went online in 2006.

Chapter 11 Exercises

1. Describe the purposes of publication design. Do they change depending on the medium (newspaper, magazine, newsletter, Web)? If so, explain how.

2. Go online to find three examples of news Web sites. Keeping the principles of design in mind, how do the three sites differ from each other? Which do you prefer? Why?

3. Pin up on the wall three different newspaper front pages. Judging from the display type and layouts, guess from five feet away which papers feature highly controversial stories. Then read the three front pages and report on your findings at the next class meeting.

4. Compare the layout of Page One of The New York Times to the layout of the first page of the Times' business section. What differences do you notice, and why do you suppose such differences exist?

5. Review the Sports cover in three daily newspapers for one week. Choose the page that, in your view, is the best-designed Sports page. Write a one-page explanation of why you think so, using as criteria what you have learned in this chapter about layout and design and what you have discussed in class. Include with your explanation a tear sheet of the page you have chosen.

6. Using the Sports page you selected in Exercise 5, copy the layout of the page on the dummy sheet provided on the following page.

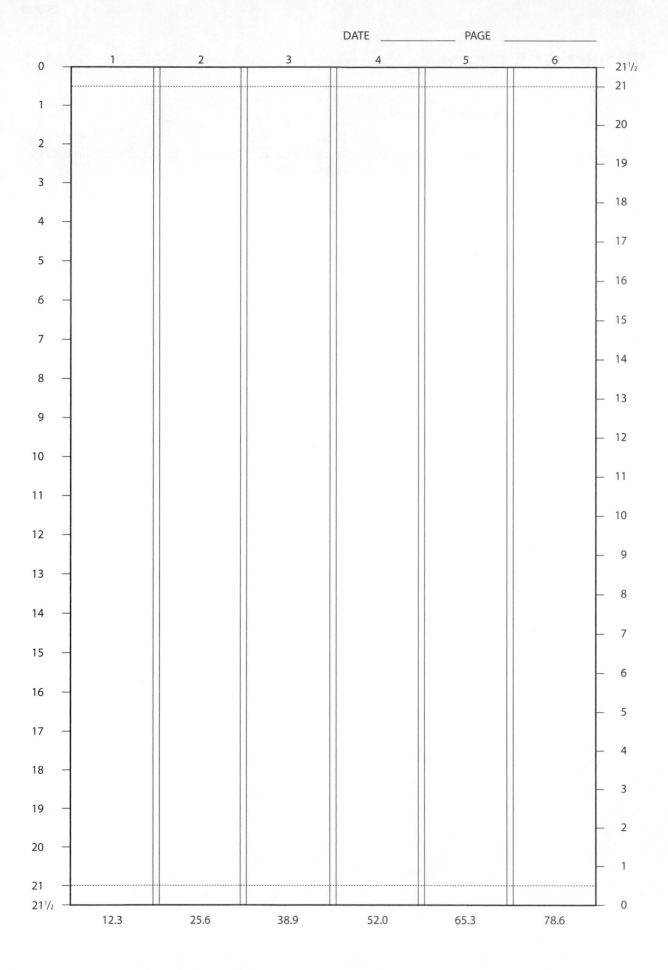

7. Find a magazine double-page spread that you consider to be poorly designed. Then rework the page, using the same elements, on the dummy sheet provided.

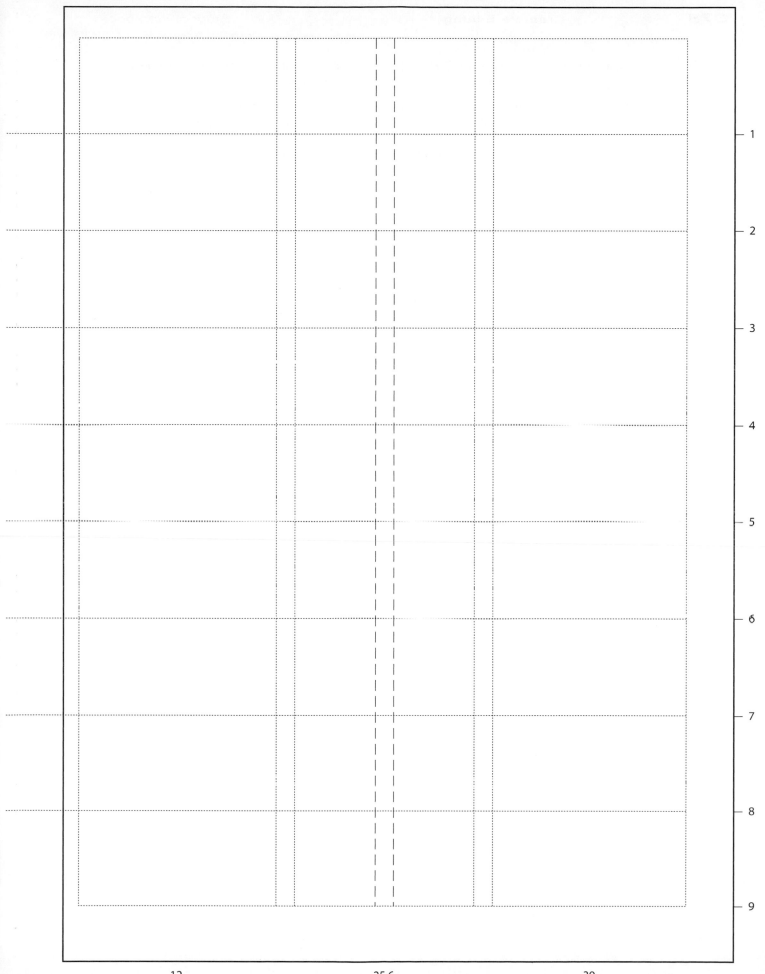

8. You are the news editor of the Daily News. Your newspaper has a six-column format, and the nameplate is six columns across and 2 inches deep. The headline type runs from 14 points to 72 points.

You have 10 stories and six pictures available for Page One (see the following table). You cannot place all of them on Page One, so use your editorial judgment to select the most important stories while providing variety on the page. Keep in mind that you can jump stories. A 30-inch story, for example, need not be finished on Page One. How much of the story will appear on the front page is up to you.

A dummy sheet is provided on the following page.

Story slug	Col. inches	Description
Ahearn	21	Local story. Karen Ahearn, president of the local university, announces her resignation after losing a bitter fight to get a better budget.
Streakers	15	Wire story. Roundup showing a nationwide revival of the streaker craze.
Demos	30	Wire story. Ben McClinton wins the party's nomination for the presidency at the Democratic National Convention.
Demo clash	18	Wire story. Demonstrators and police clash outside the Democratic convention hall in Miami.
Hurricane	12	Local story. The U.S. Weather Bureau warns that Hurricane Adam may come close enough to do damage.
Mayor	10	Local story. Mayor Joyce Durham holds a press conference and says she supports salary increases for firefighters.
China—space	20	Wire story. China announces that it has put its first spaceship into orbit.
Ransome	25	Local story. William Ransome, local author and recent winner of the Pulitzer Prize, is interviewed by the Daily News.
Burglary	8	Wire story. Burglars break into the Museum of Modern Art in New York and steal a valuable Picasso.
Diet	15	Wire story. Physician in Atlanta, Ga., devises a new diet. The dieter eats nothing and drinks a gallon of sarsaparilla every day.

Picture slug	Size	Description
McClinton	2 col. × 5"	Wire photo. Presidential nominee speaking to convention delegates.
Ransome	1 col. × 3"	Local photo. Mug shot of the interviewed author.
Clash	3 col. × 5"	Wire photo. Action shot of the fight at the Democratic convention.
Streakers	4 col. × 4"	Wire photo. Streakers disrupt a viola recital; one of the incidents mentioned in the roundup story.
Ahearn	1 col. × 3"	Local photo. Mug shot of the university president.
Kids	4 col. × 7"	Local photo. Three boys, each 4 years old, try to boost a large dog into a bathtub; good stand-alone feature picture.

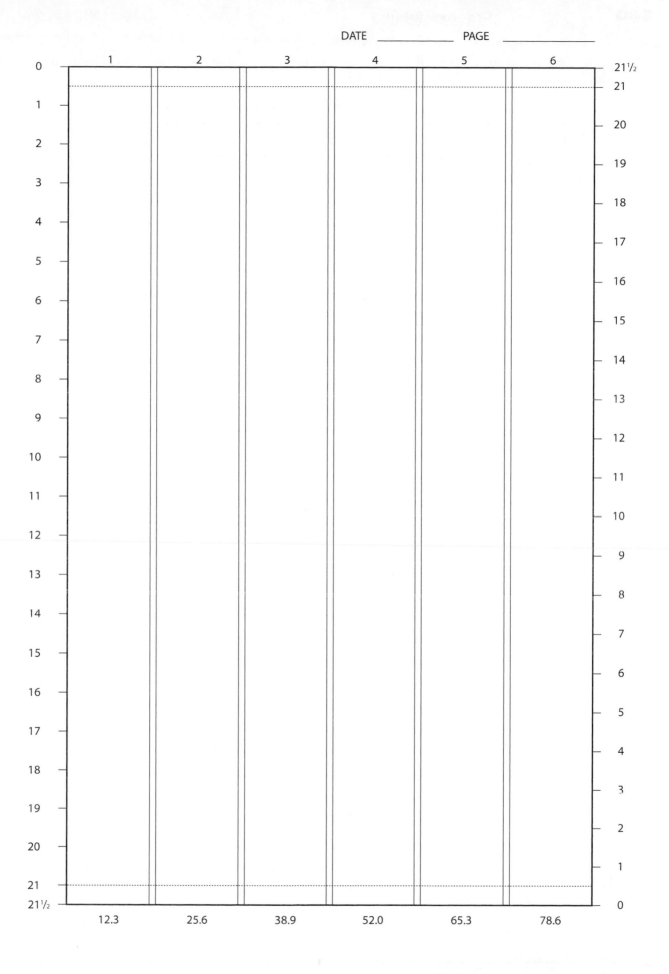

9. Use the copy and pictures left over from your Page One layout in Exercise 8 to fill the news holes on the following two inside pages. Use a modular format.

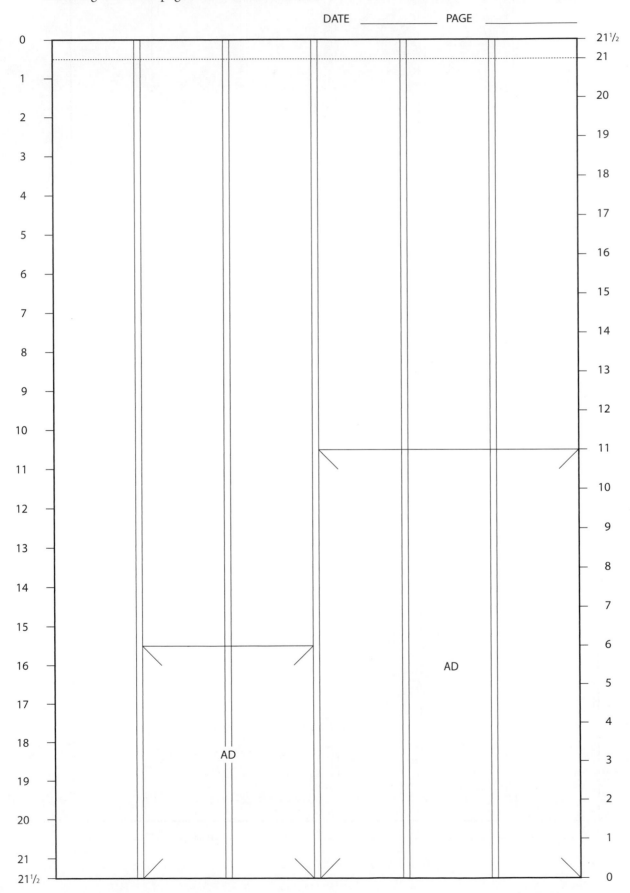

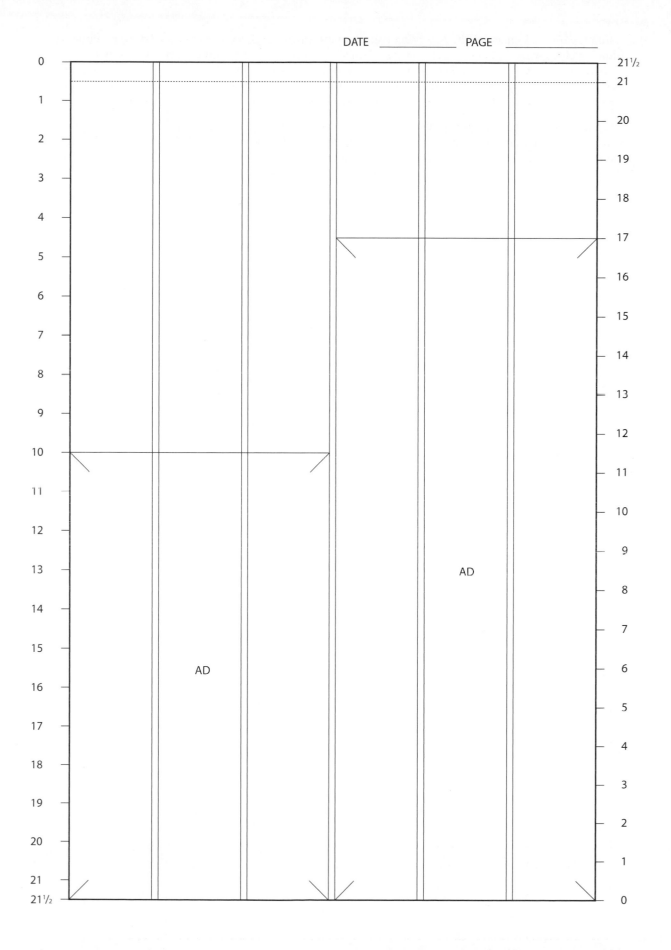

10. Using the dummy sheet on the following page, prepare a front page for tomorrow's Trumpet, Philadelphia's lively new newspaper. Select no more than six important or interesting stories and illustrations for display on Page A-1. The stories and art are listed in the following table. Design the page, making certain that you identify all elements on the dummy with the appropriate slug. That includes stories, headlines, art and cutlines. Reread the information in this chapter to determine the appropriate headline size.

Keep in mind that you can jump stories to an inside page. You may make the art any size you choose, and you may assume that you have mugshots to illustrate any of the stories, in addition to the art that accompanies some of the stories. If you dummy a mugshot, however, you must dummy it in one of only two sizes: ½ column by 1½ inches (this is called a half-column mug), or 1 column by 3 inches.

National/International

Story slug	Col. inches	Description
Crash	15	The pilots of a corporate jet and a small plane that collided in New Jersey knew they were near each other minutes before the crash.
Budget	30	Congressional leaders prepared an escape hatch to prevent an unprecedented financial default by the government. **With art**.
Justice	21	In Raton, N.M., a group has formed to deal with terrorists. They call themselves Bounty on Terrorist Inc., and they're for real.
Rapist	5	In New York City, a prosecutor turned in her own brother as a serial rape suspect after seeing his face on a wanted poster.
Death	15	The House has amended a crime bill that would allow condemned state and federal convicts to escape the death penalty if they can show a pattern of racial bias.
Japan	20	Tsutomu Hata is expected to be named Japan's prime minister after a government dispute over economic issues is settled. **With art.**

State/Local

Story slug	Col. inches	Description
Garbage	15	Philadelphia garbage could fill a Christmas list that would bring tears to any shopper's eyes.
Weather	12	Area to receive a dose of winter after a brief fling with spring. **With art.**
Port	15	A consultant has found that two port sites in Philadelphia meet the requirements for handling new, super-fast ships.
Provost	25	Judith Rodin, the new president of the University of Pennsylvania, has chosen a San Diego professor for her second in command. **With art.**
Sclerosis	30	As a result of AIDS research, scientists at Thomas Jefferson University Hospital have found what could be a treatment for multiple sclerosis.
Chase	8	The Philadelphia police commissioner has banned high-speed traffic chases by city police officers because of injuries and lawsuits.

DATE _____ PAGE _____

	1	2	3	4	5	6	
0							21½
							21
1							20
2							19
3							18
4							17
5							16
6							15
7							14
8							13
9							12
10							11
11							10
12							9
13							8
14							7
15							6
16							5
17							4
18							3
19							2
20							1
21							0
21½	12.3	25.6	38.9	52.0	65.3	78.6	

11. Use the copy and pictures left over from your Page One layout in Exercise 10 to fill in the news holes on the following two inside pages. Use a modular format.

DATE _____ PAGE _____

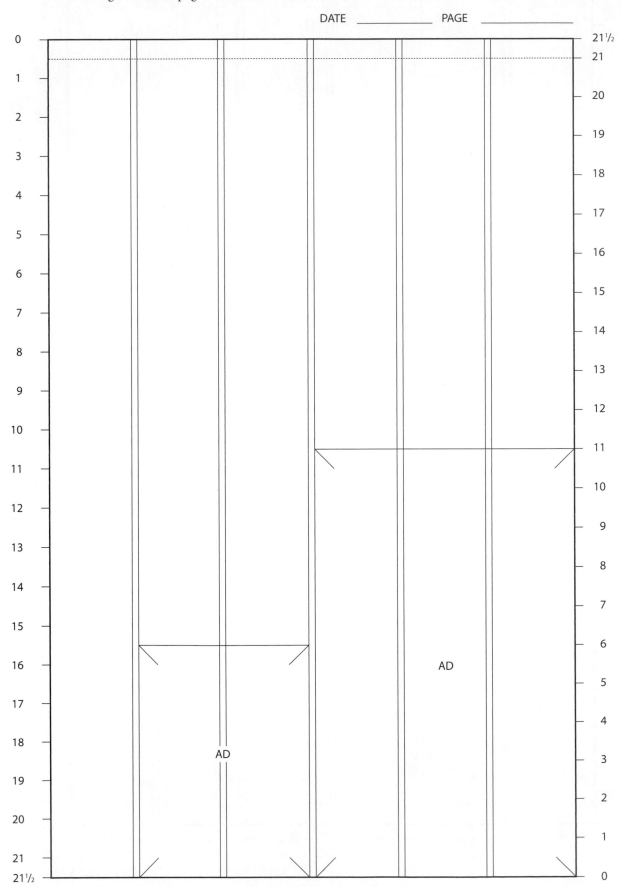

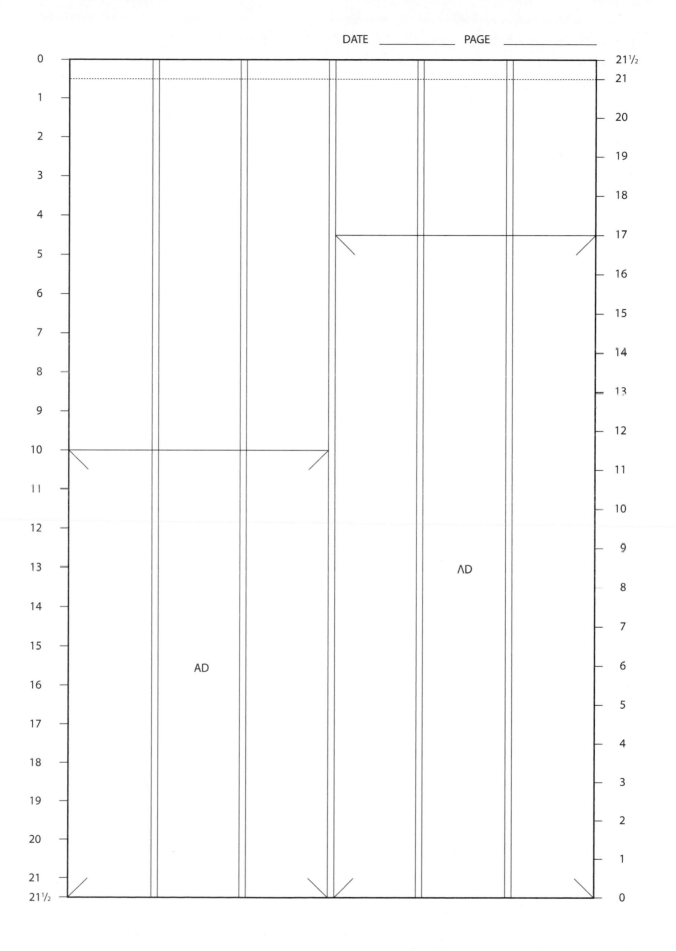

12. Now, try dummying a tabloid page. The elements include:

- The newspaper's nameplate (The Trumpet), which is five columns wide by 2 inches deep.

- A standing feature of campus briefs, which is boxed in the far-left column each week and runs down the whole page.

- A lead story about a campus drug bust, about 12 inches long, but trimmable. The story is accompanied by a strong, vertical photo of the police leading suspects away.

- A second story about a hike in tuition costs, about 12 inches long, but trimmable. The story is accompanied by a mugshot of the school president.

- A very short, humorous story about a dog and a Frisbee, about 5 inches long, with no art.

Use the tabloid dummy on the following page.

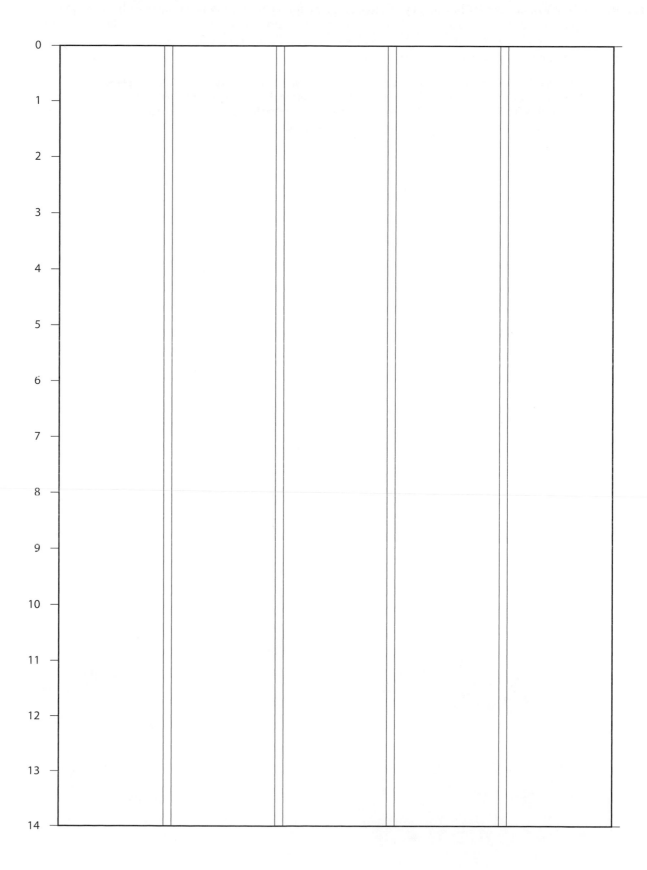

13. Peewee baseball newspaper layout. Lay out a photo page for a community newspaper with a tabloid page size 60 picas wide and 14 inches deep. Select from these six photos and write captions for those you use. In addition to the photos and captions, you have a story that is 8 column inches long for the page. A dummy sheet is on the following page.

> **Caption information:** This is a summer peewee baseball league. The Rocky Hill Rangers are playing the Bearden Bobcats. In this league, adults serve as pitchers and try to pitch so that every batter has a good chance of hitting the ball. Both boys and girls play on the teams. In this particular game, the Rocky Hill Rangers beat the Bearden Bobcats by a score of 12 to 8.
>
> *Photo #1:* Parents of the players cheering on the sidelines.
>
> *Photo #2:* Joel Cantrell is returning to his second-base position. He has just hit a home run that put his team, the Rocky Hill Rangers, ahead by one run. This is the last time at bat for the opposing team.
>
> *Photo #3:* Sammy Sowell bats for the Bearden Bobcats during the final inning. The Rocky Hill catcher is Jimmy Sweet. The pitcher is James Sweet, Sr., Jimmy's father.
>
> *Photo #4:* Sarah Leaverton standing in centerfield.
>
> *Photo #5:* Tiffany Smyth is on first base during the third inning of the game. She has just hit a ground ball and beaten the shortstop's throw to first base.
>
> *Photo #6:* This is the Rocky Hill Rangers' coach, Mr. Robert Sowell. He is standing at first base while his team bats.
>
> All photos were taken by Rob Heller

Photo 1

Photo 4

Photo 2

Photo 5

Photo 6

Photo 3

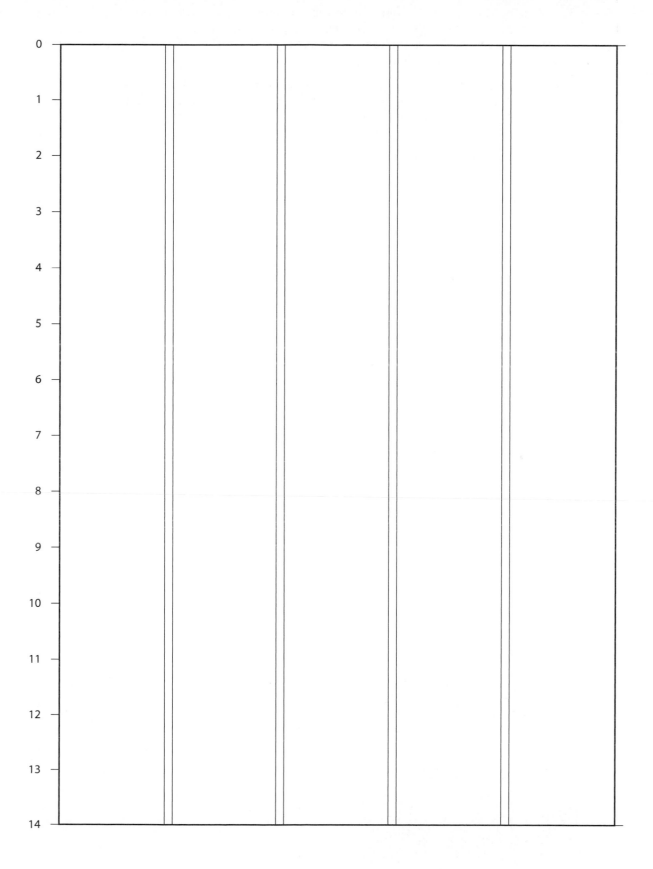

14. Peewee baseball magazine layout. Use the same pictures, caption information and copy length to lay out a double-page spread for a magazine published by the city recreation department. The printed page is 6½ × 9 inches. Use the grid sheet furnished here or one that your instructor provides. The story is 8 column inches long when set in a column 12 picas wide. The grid sheet is divided into 3 columns, each 12 picas wide with a 1½-pica (1 pica, 6 points) gutter. Or you may use a 2-column format with each column 18.9 (18 picas, 9 points) wide with a 1½-pica gutter.

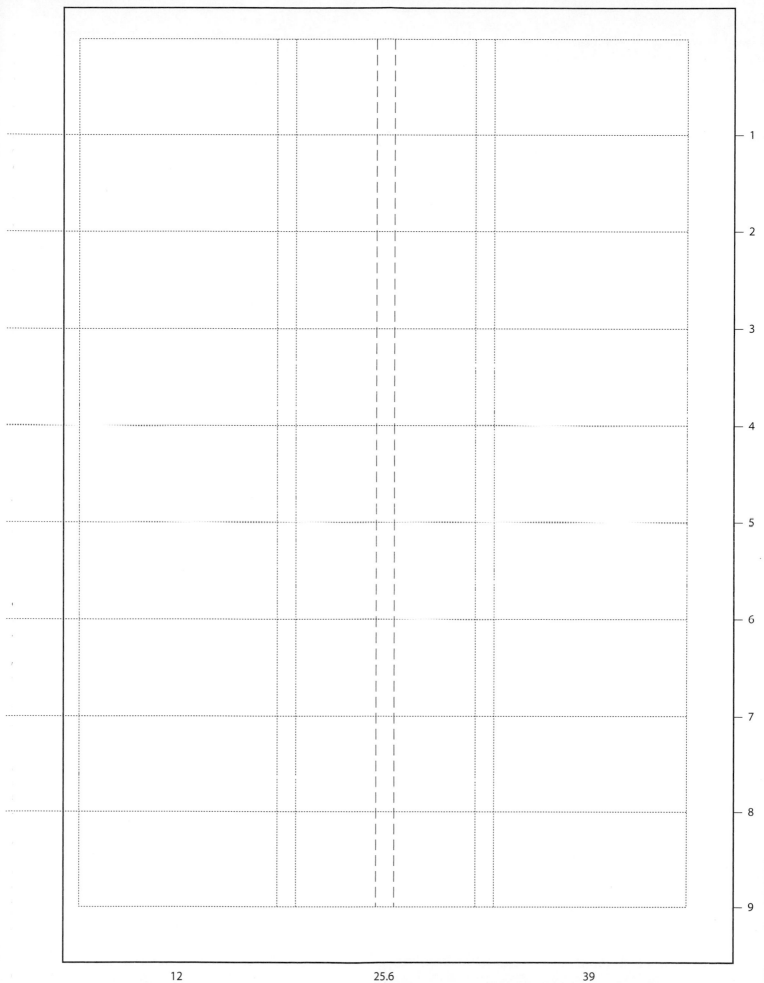

15. Outlaw Historical Endurance Ride. This package is about an endurance ride in which equestrians race over rugged terrain for five days, covering 250 miles. Such races are strictly supervised by veterinarians. This particular race—the Outlaw Historical Endurance Ride—is in Utah and is described as the "Ultimate Endurance Adventure."

The story for this package was written by a woman who rode her horse, Salazar, in the race. It is written in first person like a diary with a day-by-day description of the experience.

Using the same elements for each, lay out both a newspaper page and three magazine pages (6½ × 9 printed format with this package beginning on a double-page spread and continuing on a third page).

Material to select from for this package:

■ Four photographs shown on next page

■ A map of Utah, showing the route of the 250-mile ride

■ Story 30 column inches long when set in 12-pica width (you must use the story in both the newspaper layout and the magazine layouts)

■ Sidebar story (can be a separate story or you may use this information to create an informational graphic for your package). Here is the information for the sidebar or graphic:

How do you pack for a 12-hour day on a horse in the wilderness when the day may be in the 80s or may bring snow? Most riders pack carefully and with the worst-case scenario in mind.

Water: Four water bottles: two on the saddle and two in the wither bags that hang on either side of the horse's shoulders.

Rider food and supplies: In the right wither bag are homemade trail mix with raisins, M&Ms and peanuts, sesame sticks, homemade beef jerky, a small camera, a Powerbar, Advil.

Horse food and supplies: In the left wither bag are grain, carrots, electrolytes and a hoof pick.

Essentials: In a mini-waist pack are personal hygiene items, knife, map, lip balm, sunscreen, emergency space blanket, waterproof matches, mini-flashlight.

Extra items for rider and horse: A "rump run" under the saddle that can be unrolled to keep the horse's hindquarters from cramping in the cold, a Gore-Tex jacket for the rider, a sponge tied to the saddle to use if horse overheats.

Rider clothes: Polartec fleece tights and T-shirt, flannel shirt, jacket, gloves, helmet, boots good for both riding and walking.

Horse tack: Custom-made endurance model, breast collar to help keep saddle in place and provide space to tie items to, a hackamore that allows horse to eat and drink more freely than a bit.

Caption information:

Photo #1: A "hoodoo" or pinnacle formed by centuries of erosion at Bryce Canyon, Utah. The word comes from "voodoo."

Photo #2: A rider from Washington grabs her horse's tail for help up a steep ascent.

Photo #3: Wynne Brown and Salazar at a veterinary checkpoint.

Photo #4: Wynne Brown, Knoxville, Tenn., and her horse, Salazar, pose for a picture at the finish line.

Story written by Wynne Brown

Photographs by Wynne Brown and Hedley Bond

Photo 2

Photo 1

Photo 3

Photo 4

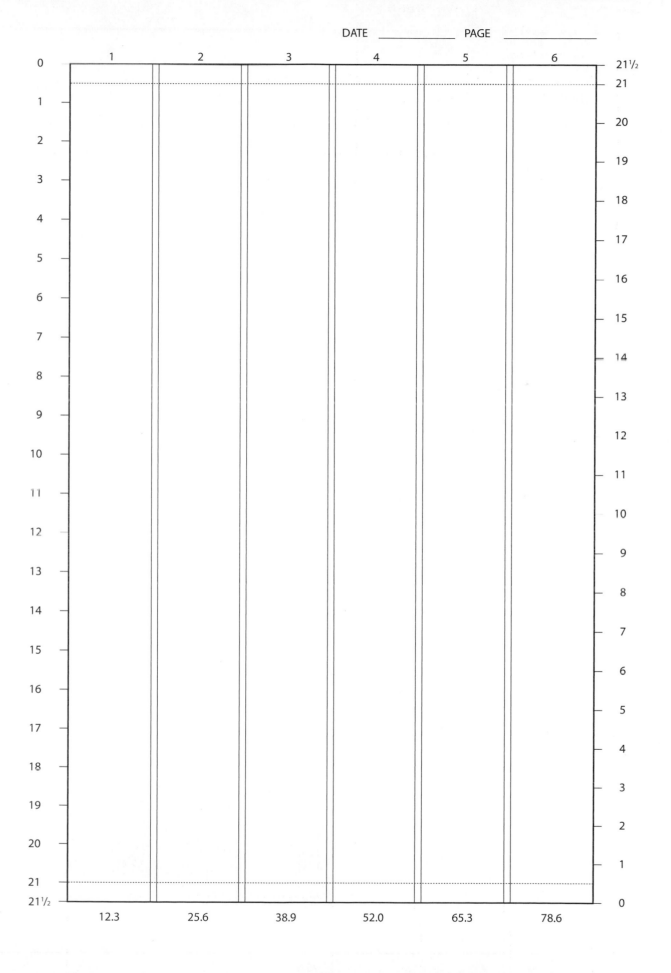

16. The communication department at your university would like you to prepare a design, including all design specifications, for an alumni newsletter. (If one exists at your school, assume you have been asked to redesign the publication.) It is up to you to prepare a mockup of the newsletter's exterior and interior pages. In addition to the design specifications, prepare a typewritten statement about the newsletter's purpose, content and method and frequency of distribution. Your statement should also include your justification for content selection and for the method and frequency of distribution.

17. Use the following photos to create two photo layouts:

    a. Lay out a double-page spread in a newsletter for the Knoxville Zoo. The newsletter format is 8½ by 11 inches. The photo spread is accompanied by approximately 3 column inches of copy.

    b. Lay out a newspaper feature photo page, using the same photographs and 6 column inches of copy.

    Photo #1: Zoo entrance; ticket booth.

    Photos #2–#4: Zoo employees preparing food for animals.

    Photos #5–#7: Lion is anesthetized, loaded into mobile facility for medical attention.

    Photo #8: Veterinarian inspects Al, an Aldabran tortoise, the largest species of tortoise in the world.

    Photos #9–#12: Some of the hundreds of animals on display at the zoo: giraffes, rhinoceros, red panda.

    Photos by Michael Anderson

Photo 1

Photo 2

Photo 3

Photo 4

Photo 5

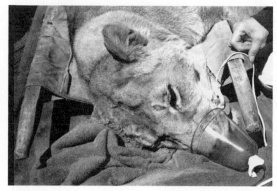
Photo 6

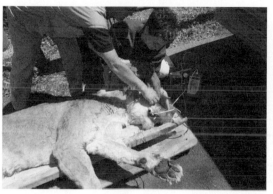
Photo 7

Photo 8

Photo 9

Photo 10

Photo 11

Photo 12

	1	2	3	4	5	6	

0 — 21½
— 21
1 — 20
2 — 19
3 — 18
4 — 17
5 — 16
6 — 15
7 — 14
8 — 13
9 — 12
10 — 11
11 — 10
12 — 9
13 — 8
14 — 7
15 — 6
16 — 5
17 — 4
18 — 3
19 — 2
20 — 1
21 — 0
21½

12.3   25.6   38.9   52.0   65.3   78.6

Index